The Sacred Meadows

Genealogical Chart of the Lamu Sharifs

LEGEND

→ Indicates that the light was directly transmitted to them

┈→ Indicates that the light was not transmitted directly to them

(1) Numbers indicate the order of naming in the recitation of the sacred genealogy

(A) * Letter or asterisk indicates that the person is mentioned in the text

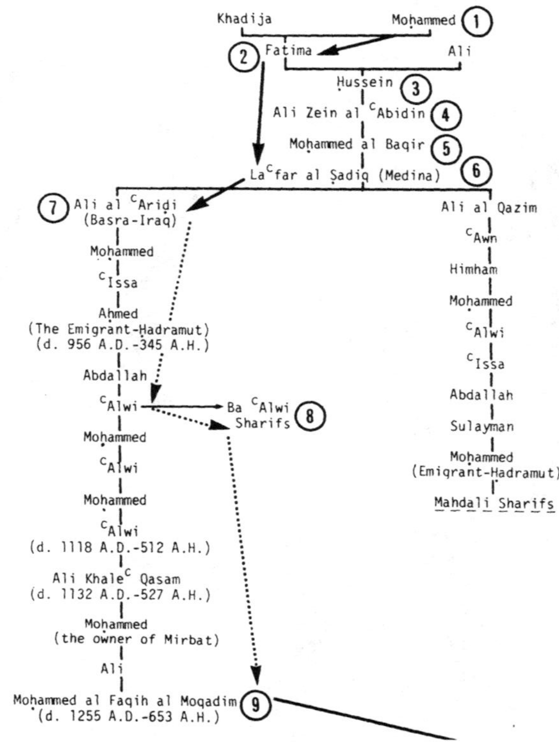

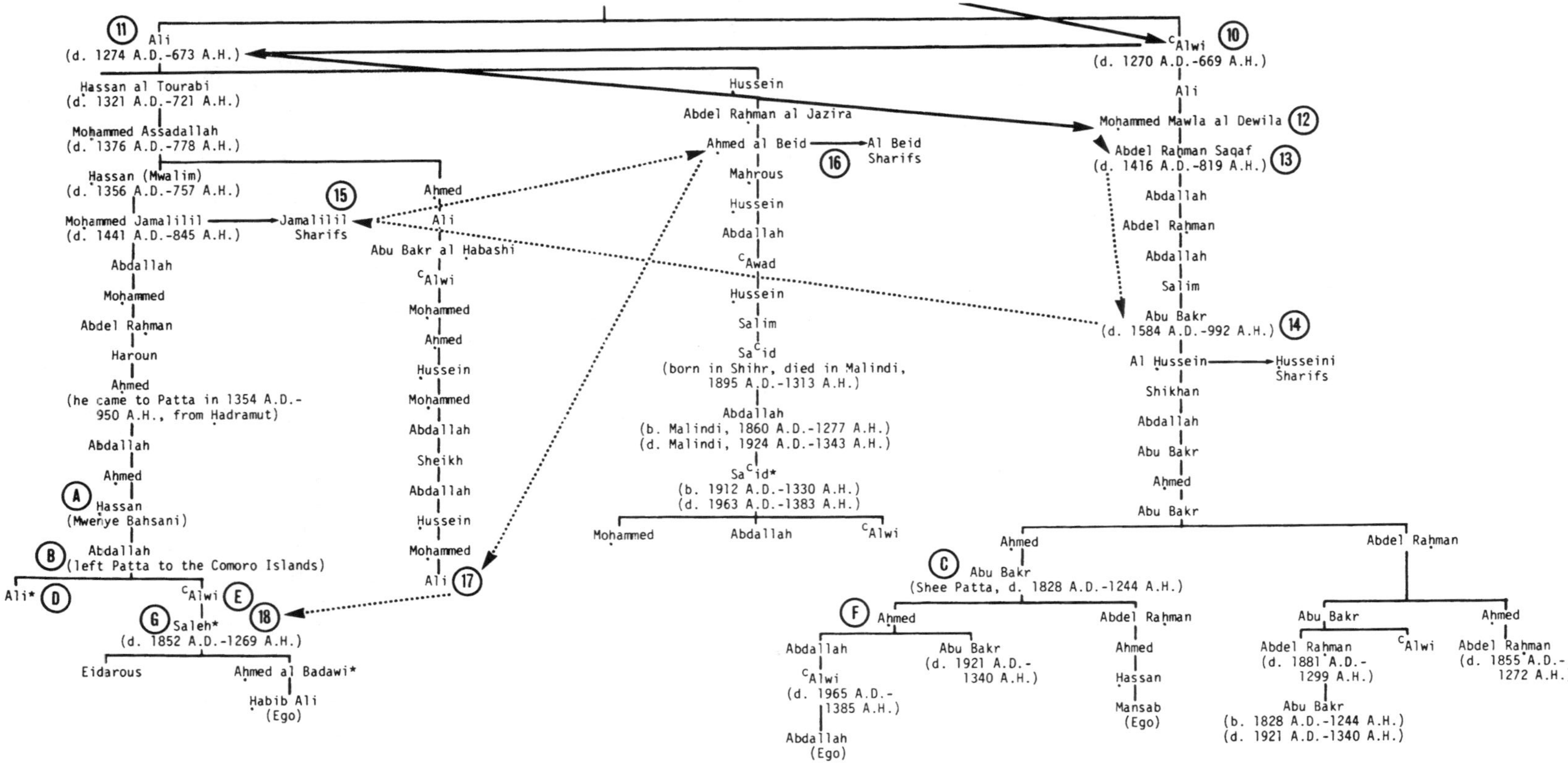

11
Ali
(d. 1274 A.D.-673 A.H.)
Hassan al Tourabi
(d. 1321 A.D.-721 A.H.)
Mohammed Assadallah
(d. 1376 A.D.-778 A.H.)
Hassan (Mwalim)
(d. 1356 A.D.-757 A.H.)
Mohammed Jamalilil
(d. 1441 A.D.-845 A.H.)
15
Jamalilil
Sharifs
Abdallah
Mohammed
Abdel Rahman
Haroun
Ahmed
(he came to Patta in 1354 A.D.-
950 A.H., from Hadramut)
Abdallah
Ahmed
A
Hassan
(Mwenye Bahsani)
Abdallah
B
(left Patta to the Comoro Islands)
Ali*
D
cAlwi
E
G
Saleh*
18
(d. 1852 A.D.-1269 A.H.)
Eidarous
Ahmed al Badawi*
Habib Ali
(Ego)
Ahmed
Ali
Abu Bakr al Habashi
cAlwi
Mohammed
Ahmed
Hussein
Mohammed
Abdallah
Sheikh
Abdallah
Hussein
Mohammed
Ali
17
Hussein
Abdel Rahman al Jazira
Ahmed al Beid
Al Beid
Sharifs
16
Mahrous
Hussein
Abdallah
cAwad
Hussein
Salim
Sacid
(born in Shihr, died in Malindi,
1895 A.D.-1313 A.H.)
Abdallah
(b. Malindi, 1860 A.D.-1277 A.H.)
(d. Malindi, 1924 A.D.-1343 A.H.)
Sacid*
(b. 1912 A.D.-1330 A.H.)
(d. 1963 A.D.-1383 A.H.)
Mohammed
Abdallah
cAlwi
cAlwi
10
(d. 1270 A.D.-669 A.H.)
Ali
Mohammed Mawla al Dewila
12
Abdel Rahman Saqaf
(d. 1416 A.D.-819 A.H.)
13
Abdallah
Abdel Rahman
Abdallah
Salim
Abu Bakr
(d. 1584 A.D.-992 A.H.)
14
Al Hussein
Husseini
Sharifs
Shikhan
Abdallah
Abu Bakr
Ahmed
Abu Bakr
Ahmed
Abdel Rahman
C
Abu Bakr
(Shee Patta, d. 1828 A.D.-1244 A.H.)
F
Ahmed
Abdel Rahman
Abdallah
cAlwi
(d. 1965 A.D.-
1385 A.H.)
Abdallah
(Ego)
Abu Bakr
(d. 1921 A.D.-
1340 A.H.)
Ahmed
Hassan
Mansab
(Ego)
Abu Bakr
Ahmed
Abdel Rahman
(d. 1881 A.D.-
1299 A.H.)
cAlwi
Abu Bakr
(b. 1828 A.D.-1244 A.H.)
(d. 1921 A.D.-1340 A.H.)
Abdel Rahman
(d. 1855 A.D.-
1272 A.H.)

The Sacred Meadows

A Structural Analysis
of Religious Symbolism
in an East African Town

by

Abdul Hamid M. el Zein
عبد الحميد محمد الزين

Northwestern
University
Press

1974

Open access edition funded by the National Endowment for the Humanities/Andrew W. Mellon Foundation Humanities Open Book Program.

Abdul Hamid M. el Zein. The Sacred Meadows: A Structural Analysis of Religious Symbolism in an East African Town. Evanston, Ill.: Northwestern University Press, 1986.

ISBN 978-0-8101-0443-3 (cloth)
ISBN 978-0-8101-3947-3 (paper)
ISBN 978-0-8101-3948-0 (ebook)

Printed in the United States of America

Original edition LCCN 73-91310

To my father, who loved and appreciated education, and to Lloyd A. Fallers, my teacher, who showed me the dedication of the scholar, the knowledge of the wise man, and the humility of the mystic, I dedicate *The Sacred Meadows*

Contents

List of Figures

List of Maps

List of Tables

Foreword

It is indeed an honor to be asked to write a brief foreword to Abdul Hamid M. el Zein's analytic account of Islam in the East African island community of Lamu, for the book, is, I believe, certain to become a classic in the field of religious studies and in the social-anthropological study of culture generally.

The "historic" or "world" religions are extremely complex sociocultural systems, highly differentiated in time and space and yet possessing centers or cores consisting of common tradition, concretized in scripture and commentary, and of shared faith in the ultimate unity of believers. Standing outside the faith community, we can see that Islam has held quite different meanings for Arabs, Persians, Southeast Asians, and Africans, and, within these regional groups, for various segments of society. It has meant different things to particular Muslim communities at different points in their histories. Through time, we can trace as well the intricate, ever-changing network of communication among regional Muslim communities from Morocco to Indonesia, from eastern Europe to the borderlands of China, and between the religiously learned and charismatic and their followers—a network, with its focal point at Mecca, which has sustained the sense of common faith and tradition through centuries of rivalry, and even warfare, both secular and religious, within and among Muslim communities.

The meaning-world of Islam is thus an exceedingly large and difficult subject for investigation, inviting a wide variety of approaches, among which social anthropology has only begun to establish a place of its own. This has not been easy. The social anthropologist is trained in the special skills and perspectives of field work—the participant-observational study of meaning and social action in the microcosms of everyday life, most often in the context of a local community. Thus, his perspective on Islam would be Islam in its local reception; he observes, records, and interprets the role of faith and tradition in the lives of people in one small corner of the Islamic world. And yet, because the wider Muslim world is in some degree an ideal and experiential reality for people within the local microcosm—certainly this is the case for the people of Lamu—and because the tradition has an internal logic of its own, a working knowledge of the history and literature of the Islamic tradition is an essential tool for the social anthropologist working in this field. He must, ideally, be something of an Islamic scholar as well as a fieldworker and a student of sociocultural theory. Since this is the work of a lifetime and more, it is hardly surprising that we have so few really good studies of what might be called "local Islams."

Zein's study is certainly one of the very best, and it is perhaps worth noting that he came to it with a well-educated Egyptian Muslim's command of the Arabic language and of Islamic literature. This background was very useful to him, since Lamu, like other communities of the East African coast, has been in interaction with Muslims of the Middle East and the Indian Ocean throughout its history. Although it is African, it has been fully within the Islamic network. Its everyday language is Swahili, but Arabic is also spoken and read, particularly in religious contexts. But Zein did not make the easy assumption that his Arabic-Islamic background and his earlier field studies in Nubia automatically gave him a quick and easy understanding of Islam in Lamu. Rather, taking nothing for granted, he combined these with the skills of an exceedingly meticulous fieldworker to penetrate the meaning-world of religion in Lamu in all its peculiar individuality. Zein's Lamu represents a quite unique recombination—or series of recombinations, for this community of 6,000 persons is intricately differentiated—of Islamic themes and symbols.

Field work is always a taxing business, and Zein has been too modest to mention the difficulties he and his family faced and overcame in gathering the materials for this book; for if their background gave them an initial intellectual advantage, it also imposed burdens which non-Muslims would not have faced. Like members of local Muslim communities elsewhere, the Lamuans naturally assume that their reception of Islam is the correct one, and so they at first regarded the Zeins as ignorant, if not positively heretical. The demands made upon them to correct their errant ways were sometimes quite uncomfortable. It will be apparent to the reader, however, how conscientiously and sensitively they must have dealt with this problem, for they clearly achieved the confidence and affection of the people with whom they worked.

All this has enabled Zein to assemble a splendid ethnography of Lamu religion, but he has gone beyond that to a convincing analytic explication of his data, drawing judiciously upon some of the most sophisticated current conceptions of language and culture. He calls his analysis "structural," and he draws upon the insights of "structuralism" without, however, allowing himself to be constricted by its rigidities. He finds inspiration in Chomsky's notion of "deep structure," in Turner's treatment of symbols, and in Ricoeur's conception of hermeneutics, but his interpretation of the dialectical relation between myth, ritual, and symbol on the one hand and everyday social action on the other is, finally, very much his own.

To say more about this book's content would be, at best, to gild a lily and, at worst, to risk distortion of the author's own design. I can only recommend it to the reader as a first-rate intellectual achievement which will do much to give a firmer footing to the social-anthropological study of historic religions.

L. A. FALLERS

Preface

> Many know the surface of
> this ocean, but understand
> nothing of the depths.
> —Farid Ud-Din Attar

The field study for this work (which took altogether eighteen months during 1968–69) was done on Lamu, an island belonging to Kenya, lying below the Somali border in what is known as the Lamu Archipelago. The largest town in the area is on that island and is also known as Lamu. The population of the town of Lamu, according to the 1962 census, is about 6,000 persons; and approximately 5,600 of that number are Muslims. Islam has long played a role among the people of Lamu; indeed, according to their oral tradition, they have never been isolated from the larger Islamic world.

My analysis is concerned with exploring the structure of a religious system and the relations between its constituent parts and everyday life. All ethnographic and historical detail, therefore, rests on a broad theoretical base which, though not always explicit, is nevertheless important. I think that it is because man uses symbols to cope with everyday life that religion must be viewed as an integral and very real part of his world. Religion is that system of symbols which makes the world more meaningful and desirable. Above all, I view it not as a conservative force but rather as a dynamic symbolic system engaged in a dialectic with social reality.

Symbols, in my view, are neither entities nor fixed essences. They are rather clusters of relations which are structured and restructured. This process of continuous structuring contributes to their being multivocal and polysemic. The different levels and shades of meaning depend on the structural arrangements of the relations constituting the symbols. Referring now to the religious system, we find that a dialectical tension exists between the possible meaningful interpretations of religious symbols and the possibilities for meaningful action within any given society at any given period of time. In this work, the lived world is treated as the outcome of this dialectical relationship. One advantage of this point of view is that it clearly assumes that society is never a finished and stable construction but is always in the process of becoming. It is the multivocal and polysemic character of symbols which allows for the articulation of social and cultural ambiguities, and so keeps the world always in the process of being defined. By studying the lived world as an outcome of a continuous dialectic, and by paying careful attention to the ambiguities that arise within it, the anthropologist is able to uncover the existing relations of a symbol's meanings to the social reality of and for a particular group at a given point in time.

In Lamu, myth, ritual, the Qur'ān, and Mohammed are not in themselves integrative forces. They are the cast of an ongoing play, continually awaiting script and direction—their precise characters changing from scene to scene. The sociological and ideological differences attending the various social categories of Lamuans are the themes: their relationship to each other, the plot. The main characters—condensed symbols—are the perfect vehicles for the expression and articulation of changing values in varying contexts.

It is extremely interesting that, in Lamu, masters and slaves have used the same Swahili myth to support quite divergent positions. I have argued here that the same written version of the myth has different meanings for those belonging to different social categories. Because the slaves lived in a different world from that of the masters, for example, they had different experiences and a different way of looking at life. For example, Mohammed is described in the myth as "Light." The masters took that to mean: "Mohammed is Light, and we are part of Mohammed's tribe, and we are his relatives; therefore we are pure like him and we are saved." On the other hand, the slaves say that "Mohammed is eternal Light, who is alive and we love him; and he reciprocates that love and therefore we are saved." The symbol of light has never been questioned by either, yet while the masters interpreted it according to their concept of descent, the slaves interpreted it according to their existential experience and never mentioned descent.

In this study, I have paid particular attention to the concepts of purity and impurity; they are crucial, and Lamu's religious life cannot be understood without them. The masters valued purity, unity, and culture, and viewed themselves as the sole possessors of these attributes. When they spoke of the slaves they spoke of their impurity, their multiplicity, and of the fact that they still live in a state of nature, as opposed to culture. The slaves accepted the idea that purity and culture are related, yet they insisted that neither is achievable through inheritance alone. Both can be earned and both can be lost.

My intention throughout this analysis has been to uncover the "deep" or "unconscious" structure of the religious ideology. In order to do that, I have focused on the different contexts in which the symbols are used and on the different definitions which the people themselves give the symbols in each con context. In all, my aim has been to expose the richness of Lamu's culture, without seeming to reduce it to simple formulas.

In my treatment of the material from Lamu, I have deviated from the traditional modes of studying religion. Usually anthropologists have stressed religion's functional role in maintaining social equilibrium and perpetuating social cohesion. Durkheim, for example, defined religion as a "unified system of beliefs and practices relative to the sacred things . . . which unite into one single moral community . . . all those who adhere to them."[1] Religion is, from this point of view, a force that "unites" society. The mechanism through which society achieves its unity is the ritual or the "practices relative to the sacred things." These practices enforce the belief system and transform the various groups into a moral community with a high degree of cohesion and integration. But I would argue that there is a problem with this assertion, since it seems obvious that there must be a high degree of unity within a society prior to the performance of any ritual. How else could the people come together in such highly structured activity? It seems to me that, rather than being a unifying device of a primary sort, ritual is a language through which certain structural tensions or contradictions are unconsciously expressed and communicated.

Taken together, the various components of religion (and here I mean the network of myth, ritual, and magic) form a complex system of communication which expresses, in a highly condensed form, the theoretical and existential problems confronting the society of which it is part. The symbols within the system acquire their significance from the structural positions they occupy relative to each other and to the secular world. They are elevated from the secular realm to the sacred, and it remains for the anthropologist to discover the structural rules of transformation through which this semantic elevation is effected. In ritual, for example, where ordinary acts and items are "sacralized," their meaning as symbols is most intense, and the grammar of the collectivity constitutes a substantial part of their religious etymology. The minutest differences in the positional arrangement of ritual items constitute the distinctive features of the ritual language, and therefore are key elements in the structural analysis of this aspect of religion.

1. Emile Durkheim, *The Elementary Forms of Religious Life* (New York: Free Press, 1965), p. 62.

PREFACE

As part of a communication system, ritual presents some interesting characteristics. The ritual field is delimited and separated from everyday life at the direction of a "ritual expert"—whether this be a real individual or a collective functionary—wherein the amount of noise or interference is reduced to the minimum. Yet ritual contains a maximum amount of redundancy; essentially the same message is repeated at different levels through various media. For example, singing to musical accompaniment, singing unaccompanied, body movements, seating positions, the ritual items themselves, etc., all operate in particular ways to convey the ritual message. Each medium is used to clarify the transmission of the message and to ensure its proper decoding. The messages are sent continuously, allowing the receiver to become progressively more sensitive to the meaning. The complexity and polysemy of the ritual symbols demand redundant articulation, even in the relative absence of noise: the reception of the ritual message is crucial. The ritual message is a statement of theoretical and existential contradictions, which it does not resolve but only articulates. It is these contradictions and their ritual expression, along with the mythic background, which are the chief heuristics of this study of Lamu, in which I hope to show the structural foundations of a religious system.

I would like to acknowledge my debt and express my gratitude to those whose influence has shaped the following pages. It is to Professor Lloyd Fallers that I owe the most. Though never sparing his interest and assistance, he gave me the time and freedom to develop my own ideas. I also am deeply grateful to Professors R. T. Smith and Nur Yalman for their helpful criticism. To the University of Chicago, which helped me intellectually and financially, and to my colleagues and students at Temple University, who gave me the chance to test and communicate some of my ideas, I am greatly indebted. Special thanks are due to my colleagues Melvin Mednick and Elmer Miller, and to Karen Brown, R. W. Fredericks, C. R. Myers, and M. A. Myers, who have worked hard to make the manuscript intelligible to the English reader. I would also like to express my gratitude to the Social Research Center at the American University in Cairo for the varied forms of assistance given to me over the years.

To my wife Laila and my son Hani goes my most profound gratitude. Their unceasing affection and cooperation amid the hardships of the field and the labor of putting this work together were my sustenance, affording and maintaining the only significant meaning in my life.

Finally, due to space limitation I am forced to thank collectively the countless informants, friends, scholars, students, and others who in one way or another have contributed to this book. The ultimate responsibility for errors or inadequacies is, of course, my own.

Since most of the Swahili religious language (written or spoken) is still in classical Arabic, I used the *Encyclopaedia of Islam* system of transliteration, except in the case of QAF where Q was substituted for K. In the use of Swahili terms, I have tried my best to preserve the Lamuan dialect, which varies to some extent from the *Standard Swahili-English Dictionary*. In the case of plurals, I have used an anglicized form, for the convenience of my readers; for example, the plural of *sharif* is *sharifs,* not *ashraf.*

Part One

Lamu Traditional Society:
The Diachronic Dimension

Introduction

Mngwana ni kamba hufa na nauwao.

A free man is like a rope which
decays with the stick to which
it is tied.

Lamu is one of several islands scattered along the East African coast (Map 1). It lies below the Somali border in the Lamu Archipelago. It is not the largest island in that archipelago, but, due to its geographical location, it does contain the largest town in the area, Lamu Town. There are also three small villages on Lamu: to the southeast there is Shella, a small fishing village; to the southwest is Kipungani, another tiny fishing village; and west of Lamu lies a relatively new colony called Matondoni (Map 2). With the exception of Shella, which is only about two miles away, these villages have very little contact with the town.

To the north of Lamu lies Patta Island, which is larger than Lamu and was once the seat of an independent sultanate. Today, Patta Town consists of only a few huts and the ruins of the palace that was formerly the symbol of power on the East African coast.

Lamu is the headquarters of Lamu District, which includes the archipelago and part of the mainland. The district commissioner resides in Lamu Town, and while he is usually from one of the mainland tribes, most of the governmental employees are either from Lamu itself or from Mombasa. The town has a small hospital, two hotels, and a big market which serves the neighboring islands as well as Lamu.

Most of the traders in the market are *Ḥadramis* (or *Ḥadārim*),[1] who settled in Lamu some time ago, and who own most of the wholesale stores. In addition to these large stores, there are also some small retail shops serving different areas.

1. Ḥadramis are the people of Hadramaut, Southern Arabia.

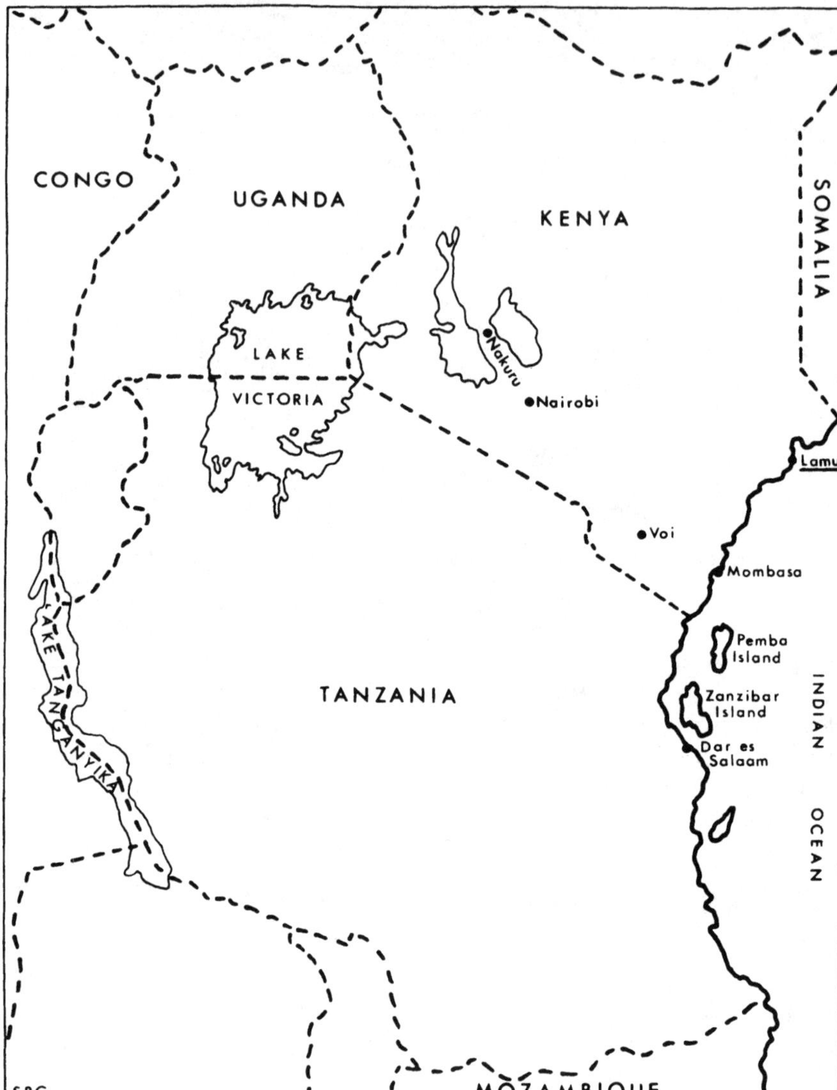

Map 1. Lamu in Relation to East Africa

Map 2. Lamu District

These are owned mostly by *Bajuni.* The Bajuni, as defined by the people of Lamu, are the inhabitants of the neighboring islands. Many Bajuni settled in Lamu during the British rule and worked as sailors, fishermen, or small shop owners.[2]

Of the 6,000 persons in Lamu Town, 3,800 claimed in the 1962 census to be Arabs, while 1,800 said they were Africans. Since most of the latter are the Bajuni who settled in Lamu, and since the Bajuni and the Arabs are all Muslims, we can see that almost all of the inhabitants of the town—approximately 5,600—are Muslims.

Lamu has a historic reputation as a good natural port, and at one time it competed with Mombasa in that respect. During its long history, the island has never been isolated from the outside world, engaging in commercial relations with most of the Indian Ocean trading centers and with South Yemen, Muscat, and Oman. The relations between Lamu and the nearby islands, such as the Comoro Islands, Madagascar, and Zanzibar, however, were colored by their fluctuating political stand toward Lamu. Although Lamu was adamant about maintaining independence as long as possible, it was able to keep some commercial ties with these islands. It is a different story, however, with the surrounding islands such as Mombasa, Patta, and Manda, with whom Lamu's relations have been generally hostile. This was possibly a result of the continuous competition between Lamu and Mombasa for the leadership of the coast. Lamu has tried repeatedly to gain control of the trade coming to East Africa and thus impose its sovereignty all the way down the coast. We still find evidence of these hostile attitudes, especially when the people of Lamu speak about Mombasa.

The minute I set foot in Lamu, I heard the story of Mombasa's historic defeat by the Lamuans. The storytellers usually stress that the people of Lamu, though they were fewer in number and possessed older weapons, were able to defeat Mombasa because of their bravery. In another version of this story, magic is pictured as the decisive factor in the victory. I think the two explanations are both considered valid by most Lamuans.

The people of Lamu do not like to admit that the rivalry between themselves and Mombasa has been due to commercial competition. They prefer to say: "Mombasa wanted, and intended, to dominate Lamu. It tried to turn Lamu into a colony, and to deprive its people of their freedom." In other words, "Mombasa intended to 'enslave us' and deprive us of our pride.

2. The Bajuni began coming to Lamu after the British took over; before that they had not been allowed on the island. They were ruled by the Sultan of Patta, who was a fierce enemy of Lamu. For the Bajuni see: Janet A. Bujra, *Political Action in a Bajuni Village in Kenya* (Ph.d. diss., University of London, 1968).

But who would allow them to do that? Our island was called *Keva Ndreo*, "the island of the proud people." My informants contined: "The people of Lamu do not want anyone to rule them or to be equal to them in courage, war, or pedigree. They refuse to surrender to anyone, and never stop trying to dominate the people of the coast."

It is clear from the above comment that Lamu wanted to rule the East African coast and never be ruled by anyone else on that coast. Lamuans, or their ruling group at least, were satisfied with their way of life and would even go to war to defend it. They tried to protect their internal system by aggressively forcing their life style on any area that threatened them. As we will see, the ruling group of Lamu used religious ideology to support their claim to superiority; Lamu was considered the one real Islamic town, while Mombasa was thought of as having deviated from Islam. Even today, Lamuans maintain this point of view. I once spoke with an informant about a governmental proposal to develop Lamu's port. This would have given the people of Lamu work, while also relieving some of the pressure on the port of Mombasa. I tried to explain these factors to the man, but he replied very simply:

> This kind of proposal is not new. The British made it before. Some British engineers came to Lamu and made a map. When the people heard of that, they made a certain prayer called *Ṣalat al Karb,* the prayer of driving away distress. They made the *Du'a* invocation asking God to drive the government away from their sacred town.

When I pointed out that Mombasa is now a big city and that many people go there for work, the man replied:

> Which is most important, this life or the next? People are fighting for this life, no one is fighting for the hereafter. But this does not mean that this life is better. We think that if we got the modern port here, people from outside would settle here. This means that we would be like Mombasa, where they have British inhabitants, people from the mainland, and, of course, cinemas, bars, etc. In other words, we would lose our religion. We prefer to keep our religion and remain poor rather than be rich and irreligious.

The contemporary inhabitants of Lamu frequently express their fear of losing their traditional way of life; they want to preserve it as long as they can, even if they have to isolate themselves from the outside world. The same informant quoted above, who happens to be a religious leader, pointed out that outside contact would bring innovations, which would inevitably lead to the disappearance of religion. In Mombasa, the chief Muslim judge, the *qadi,* for example, is considered an innovator because he reinterpreted the Shafi'ite version of the Islamic Law concerning the start of Ramadan, the month of fasting, according to Western ideas of time and geography. According to tradition, fasting begins when the new crescent of the moon can actually be seen by the persons in a given locality. Since the crescent moon was seen in Mombasa the night before it was seen in Lamu, the two localities had begun fasting on different dates. The qadi, basing his opinion on the knowledge that the new moon would rise within the same twenty-four hour period in the entire Muslim world, ruled that: "If the crescent is seen in Mombasa, and the news is carried to Lamu (by telephone or radio), then the people of Lamu have to fast, even if they are unable to see the crescent in Lamu." This formal legal opinion given by the chief Muslim judge, the highest Islamic authority in Kenya, was condemned as an innovation, and, according to the same informant, "Every innovation is in error, and every error leads to hell." My informant continued, "Anyone is considered religious as long as he conforms to *our* [Lamu's] tradition."

I do not think that my informant represents only a religious leader's point of view; rather, he expresses the general attitude of Lamu people toward change. This is clear in a letter I received from a Lamuan friend recently. In the letter, he reports an incident which occurred last year concerning Ramadan. This friend, a well-educated man, was convinced that he had to follow the chief judge's legal opinion. So, when it was broadcasted that the crescent moon was seen in Mombasa, he fasted. When the people of Lamu heard of his action, they waited one night until he was alone on his way to the mosque and then accosted him, beating him until he was unable to move. After two weeks, the man met the qadi of Lamu in the market, and was informed that the qadi wanted to see him the following day in court. The next day my friend went to court where he found the judge, a man from a strong native Lamuan group. The court was full of people. When the judge called his name, my friend stood and said he was present. The judge told him to come closer. He did. Then he ordered him to go to the right; he did. Then he ordered him to go to the left, and he did that also. At this point, my friend realized that the judge wanted to show the audience that he was to be obeyed without question. As my friend says in his letter, "The judge wanted to show the people that I am like a donkey. I was about to curse or beat him, but I was afraid. I felt that I had to respect the governmental chair." When the judge spoke again, he said:

> This is the man who fasts one day before us. I made him move at my will. I, as a qadi, and as a man of Lamu, cannot accept any deviation from what we inherited from our forefathers. No one has the right to follow Mombasa. If any one of you

> does that in the future I will torture him. I will send him to jail. This is a warning for everyone sitting in this court.[3]

Then the judge looked at my friend and ordered him to return to his place.

This conservative attitude is the main impetus behind Lamu's struggle against any outside interference. I found such conservatism reiterated in religious symbols and in the Lamuan myth of origin, as well as in various aspects of life from economics to ritual.

As we will see later, Lamu went through many drastic changes in its history, most of which have been enforced by an outside power. But the attitude of the people of Lamu has remained the same. They have never appreciated innovation. In their eyes, anyone who does not follow their way of life cannot be tolerated. The people of Lamu do not consider their island to be merely part of the Muslim world. Rather, they think of it as the leader of the Islamic world, because it alone has preserved Islam in its purity. They feel that from Morocco to Pakistan, the Muslims went astray when they tried to cope with modernization,[4] which is a form of innovation that can only lead to hell.

3. The incident happened on November 23, 1970.

4. This fact is confirmed in an unpublished manuscript by Ḥassan ibn Saiyid Aḥmad al Badawi, one of Lamu's religious leaders, called *Al Ta'asur wal Ibtida': Khata' al Muslimin al Akbar* [Modernization and innovation: the major Muslim error].

1

The Town of Lamu

> We should not, then, draw a distinction
> between "societies with no history" and
> "societies which have histories."
> In fact, every human society has a history,
> and they all go equally far back, since all
> history dates from the birth of mankind.
> —Claude Lévi-Strauss

Examining the diagrammatic map of Lamu (Map 3), one can see that the town is divided into two parts: the northern part, which consists for the most part of old stone houses with flat roofs, is called Mkomani; the southern part, which contains mud houses made of coconut leaves, is called Langoni.

MKOMANI

In Mkomani proper we find eleven out of the nineteen mosques that exist in Lamu. The other eight mosques are scattered around the rest of the town—two are on the fringes of Mkomani; the other six are in Langoni. While the mosques in Mkomani proper are very old, those on the Mkomani borders and in Langoni are relatively new.

Lamu is further subdivided into twenty-seven *mtaa*, locations or quarters.[1] If a person is asked where he lives, he will identify himself first in terms of the section he comes from—Mkomani or Langoni—and then in terms of his location. The number of the locations in each half is unequal. While Mkomani includes about nineteen, Langoni consists of only eight locations. This might

1. As we will see later, a mtaa is defined either by a group's ethnic origin, or by its stratificatory position.

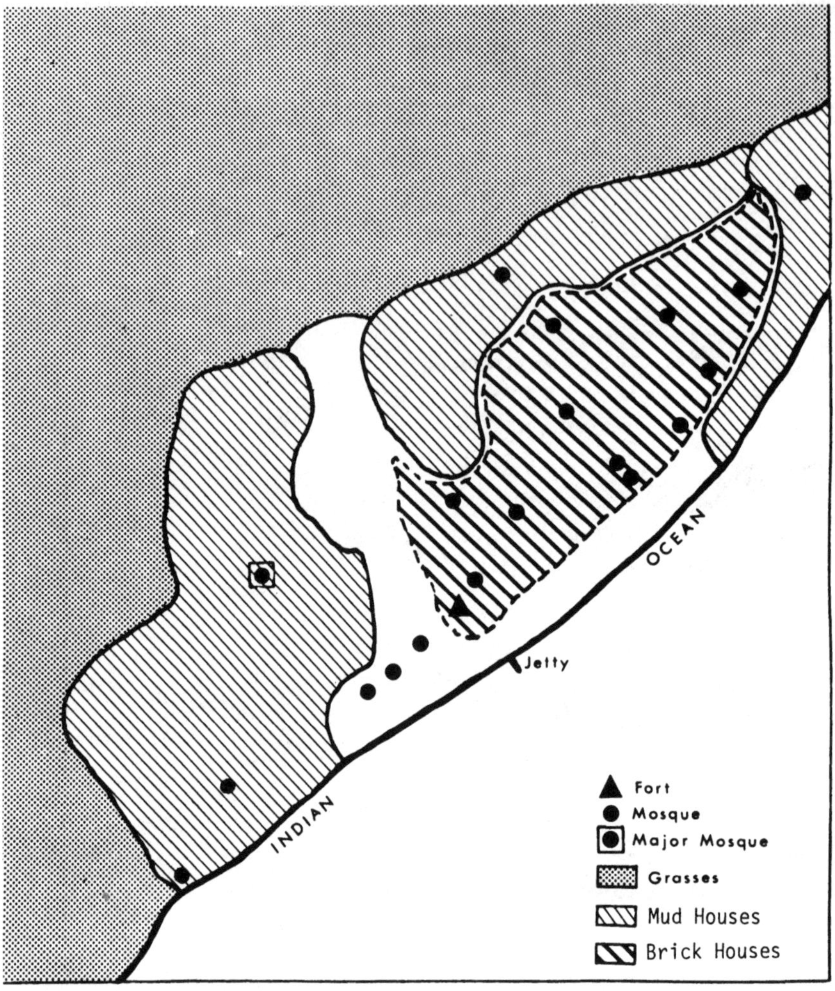

Map 3. Lamu: A Diagrammatic View

indicate that Langoni is ethnically more homogeneous than Mkomani, as we will see later.

On the fringes of Mkomani proper, we find many old mud houses, which form a kind of crescent beginning in the west and going north and then eastward toward the seashore. Neither this crescent nor the buildings on the seashore are considered to be part of Mkomani, since they were not built by Mkomani people. In the upper area live the ex-slaves, while along the shore are the governmental offices which were built by the British.

Mkomani proper contains the following locations:

1. Mkomani	5. Pumwani	9. Bandar Abbasi
2. Bang Hari	6. Kivondoni	10. Turmukoni
3. Kisima cha Ndiani	7. Vyumba	11. Mtamwini
4. Otokoni	8. Kinoni	

The other eight locations, which are part of the Mkomani half of Lamu but not part of Mkomani proper, are:

1. Vuyoni	4. Mkomangoi	7. Kidinitini
2. Tundani	5. Makarani	8. Briki
3. Nairobi	6. Mlimani	

In Mkomani proper, each of the different locations in which the old inhabitants of the town reside has at least one mosque, with the exception of Kivondoni, Vyumba, and Turmukoni. This is interesting because the rulers of Lamu lived in these three areas—first the original rulers, and then the *BuSa'id* rulers from Zanzibar. The BuSa'id, being Ibadi, built or renovated a mosque for themselves, the last mosque in the southern part of Lamu located on the seashore. But why did the old ruling groups not have a mosque in their mtaa?

The people of Lamu say that they deliberately did not want the ruling group to build a mosque of their own, because they thought that if the rulers were confined completely to their own quarters, they would be effectively cut off from the people. If the ruling groups were allowed to build their own mosque, it would be a private mosque, as all mosques essentially are. Then, in order to meet the ruler, a person would have to be invited. On the other hand, if the town built a mosque for the ruler, no invitation would be needed. For these reasons, the rulers were expected to pray in Maskiti Pwani, the Pwani Mosque, which was located in Mtamwini, beside the fort. Like the fort, this mosque was built by all the people of Lamu.

Mtamwini means "the district of the possessors of the town." *Mtaa*, as we have seen, means "district"; Mwini is a distortion of *mwenye*, which means "possessor," so Mtaa Mwenye, or Mtamwini, means the "district of the possessors of Lamu." However, it is more likely that "possessors" refers not to the rulers in particular but to the inhabitants of Mtamwini in general. In fact, in the old times Mtamwini contained a mixture of all the "freer" categories of Lamuans. The "freer" and the less-free categories built the Pwani Mosque in order to serve all the groups, and to impose a political unity on a multiplicity of social categories. The function of that mosque was not to eliminate that multiplicity, but rather to include it within a political unity.

Maskiti Jum'a, the Friday Mosque, on the other hand, was the symbol of the inherent unity, and its function was to express the basic religious unity which lies behind the social multiplicity. Thus, the unity is basic while the multiplicity is accidental. Maskiti Jum'a lies in the northern end of the Mkomani half, in the mtaa of Mkomani. It was built by all the different categories of Lamuan people. The whole town had to perform the Friday service in this mosque. At this service the prayer was preceded by a moral exhortation, with the religious leader standing higher than any of the audience. After this, the *khatib*, or religious leader, led the prayers and made the invocations. On Friday, before the prayer, a *hajib*, a man from the lowest stratum of Lamu society, goes to the mosque and gets a certain staff or stick, and then goes to the khatib's house. When the khatib leaves the house, the ḥajib, carrying the stick, leads the way. He prevents anyone from touching the khatib or coming close to him. When the khatib reaches the mosque, he takes off his shoes and gives them to the ḥajib, who puts them under his arm and then announces the presence of the khatib. Everyone then has to be silent. The khatib enters, not from the main door, but from a special door which leads directly to the niche.[2] He begins by performing a private prayer, then climbs up to the pulpit. Before the khatib begins his religious speech, the ḥajib says loudly, "According to the true tradition [*Ḥadith*], the Prophet said, 'If anyone talks while the khatib is speaking, his action will be nonsensical and this will abrogate his Friday prayer.'" Thus everyone has to sit silently, and any excessive movement is met with disapproval.

The ḥajib's role is essential. For, as we will see later, if he spoke in that commanding tone outside the above context he would have been punished. As a low person, he has to obey the rules of proper behavior. In the Friday context, however, social position was discarded, and the ḥajib spoke to the congregation as one undifferentiated unit. The definition of the ḥajib's position and role is articulated out of a cluster of relations. This cluster of relations depends on the time (Friday prayer), the place (the Jum'a Mosque), and the khatib. On the other hand, the relation of the khatib to the ḥajib, the mosque, and the time

2. A curve in the wall of the mosque which is directed toward Mecca, a direction which the Moslems have to face when they pray (Arabic, *qibla*).

(Friday) articulate the principle of unity over multiplicity which is expressed in other contexts. For example, inside the Jum'a Mosque, there is still a certain flag which cannot be used except in one ritual called *Kuzingu Kuzinguka Ngombe,* the circulation of the bull around the town. This ritual, which will be described later, is led by the khatib and is the most expressive symbol of the ritual unity of the old town of Lamu. The Jum'a Mosque—in one phase of that ritual—will be articulated as the center of purity, a state to which the town must be elevated in order to get rid of its misfortune. In all of these, we find that the Jum'a Mosque, the khatib, the hajib, and the flag, in different combinations, articulate in part the idiom of the religious life in Lamu.

The khatib and the Jum'a Mosque had other functions as well. The khatib used to be consulted before any marriage took place. In the Jum'a Mosque, there was a book called the *Silwa,* in which were written down the names of the various groups, and indications of who was equal (*mkufu*) to whom. If the khatib found that the prospective partners were not equal, then the marriage could not take place. In this context the khatib—like the political leader—used to stress the multiplicity and the inequality of the different groups. In this gray area the authority of the khatib and that of the political leader overlapped, however, and therefore created certain ambiguities.

The separation of the ruling mosque (Pwani Mosque) from the mosque of religious power (Jum'a Mosque) is very interesting sociologically. It is clear that in Lamu the religious authority was originally separated from the executive authority in personnel as well as location. Each of the authorities was to fulfill definite functions, which were aimed at obtaining the maximum good for the old town, Mkomani.

However, there have been many relatively new settlements which have been either built or initiated by the Europeans (*Wa Zungu*). The British built government offices, had a strong hand in the freeing of the slaves, and helped them build homes on the periphery of Mkomani. Their presence was also an encouragement to fishermen to settle on the eastern side. All of these changes, as we will see, disturbed the social structure and social life of the original group of free people, known as the *wangwana* (sing., *mngwana*).

LANGONI

Let us now turn our attention to Langoni, the other half of comtemporary Lamu. Langoni is subdivided into eight mtaa (see Map 4):

1. Girzani: where the Ḥadramis settled and where they have their mosque.

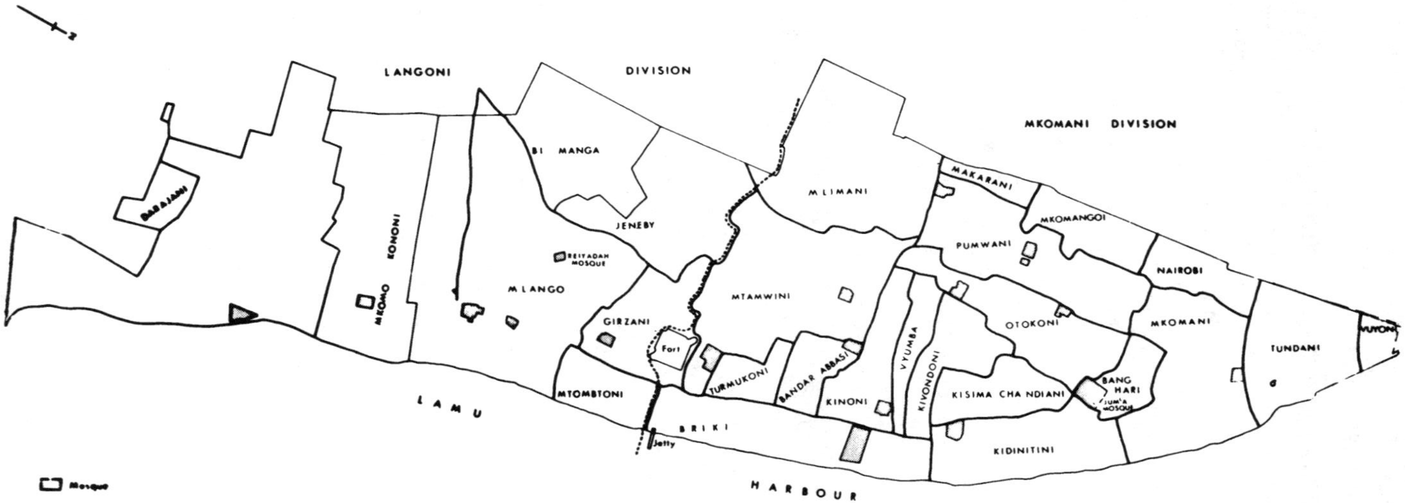

Map 4. Lamu Township

2. Mtombtoni: inhabited by ex-slaves and sailors. It has no mosque.
3. Jeneby: the place where the soldiers of the Sultan of Zanzibar settled. Those soldiers were from Baluchistan.
4. Reiyadah: inhabited by sharifs, ex-slaves, Ḥadramis, Comoro Island people, and Bajuni.
5. Bi Manga: inhabited by ex-slaves.
6. Beit al mal: inhabited by ex-slaves and Bajuni.
7. Darajani: (includes Mkomo Kononi) inhabited by ex-slaves, Comoro Island people, and Bajuni.

From the above it is clear that Langoni is inhabited by ex-slaves, Bajuni, people from the Comoro Islands, Ḥadramis, and the most influential religious leaders of the Reiyadah sharifs.[3] All these groups, with the exception of the ex-slaves, are considered to be *wa geni*, or "strangers," by the established free people, or wangwana, of Lamu. The ex-slaves, however, are called *wa zaliya,* that is, "those born in Lamu." Thus a distinction is made between the "possessors" of the town, the wangwana, and those who are natives. For example, the Ḥadramis are from Ḥadramaut, South Yemen; this is their *watani,* or native country. Even those who have been born in Lamu will still be considered strangers because they have a homeland outside Lamu. The slaves are a different case since they do not claim any other homeland. Thus, while the ex-slaves have no right to interfere in the town's affairs because they do not possess it, the strangers have no right to interfere because they are strangers. Lamu has a proverb which expresses this attitude, "*Mgeni haagui ngoma*," "the stranger is not allowed to beat the drum." This means that the "stranger" is to behave like a guest; if a guest finds a drum hanging on the wall, it would not be proper for him to take it down and beat it.

Therefore, from the people's point of view, none of those who live in Langoni has any right to a voice in the conduct of Lamu's affairs. After all, they are not the "possessors" of the town. The people of Langoni are supposed to keep themselves isolated from what is going on among the wangwana; and this is even expected of the Reiyadah sharifs, a group which will be dealt with at greater length later.

When the wangwana from Mkomani proper speak of Langoni, they do so in a derogatory way. The wangwana look on the Langoni people as lacking in respectability. If someone makes a mistake, the wangwana will say, "He is from Langoni; you should expect that from him." However, the Langoni people nowadays do not easily accept the derogatory attitude of the wangwana. When

3. See the Genealogical Chart, pp. ii-iii.

I asked a Langoni man about the wangwana, he cursed them. Then he added, "*Nyani haiyoni kundule*," which means literally, "A monkey cannot see his anus." In other words, if the wangwana could only see themselves properly, they would be ashamed to speak about Langoni in such a derogatory way. So between Langoni and Mkomani there exist a great deal of factionalism and rivalry. As we shall see, the main issue is power; each half wants to accumulate and manipulate as much power as possible in order to use it against the other. While for a long time Mkomani was clearly more powerful, Langoni has now become the religious and economic center, and the wangwana have begun to lose the basis for their traditional supremacy. When the influential Reiyadah sharifs settled in Langoni and adopted most of the Ḥadrami religious tradition, the wangwana were put on the defensive. By that time their traditional power was fast diminishing. As an example, we find that nowadays the feast prayers are performed not only in Jum'a Mosque, as was traditionally done, but also in the Reiyadah Mosque. Once the head of the Reiyadah Mosque even performed the Jum'a prayer, against all established wangwana tradition.

At the present time, Lamu's wealth lies in Langoni. The majority of the market shops are owned by Ḥadramis who support the Reiyadah sharifs. In turn, the Reiyadah sharifs have been able to obtain the loyalty not only of the ex-slaves, but also of the Bajuni and the Comoro Island people. In other words, those who were traditionally excluded because they were not the "possessors" of Lamu have begun to back the Reiyadah sharifs against the wangwana. The old wangwana ideology that a slave is a slave, "*Mtumwa ni mtumwa*," and therefore cannot have any opinion of his own, has been challenged by the sharifs.

Furthermore, the political changes which have taken place in Kenya are not without significance. For example, the town council now has to be elected, and every adult male in Lamu has been given the right to vote. The wangwana know that if the Reiyadah sharifs do not support them, they will not be elected. And this is true because the majority of the population of Lamu now are either ex-slaves or Ḥadramis; and both groups, as has been said, support the Reiyadah sharifs. Before making any move, the wangwana have to consult the sharifs, and in the 1968 election the names which were confirmed by the Reiyadah sharifs were placed in nomination and were elected.

The old wangwana system which tried to separate religion from politics is not working any more. Now the Reiyadah sharifs manipulate both the religious sphere and the political sphere. In order to bring about that change, the Reiyadah leaders introduced a new religious ideology in which old religious symbols were reinterpreted and in many cases incorporated within the new system. Before we can understand and examine these changes, we have to deal with

Lamu's social structure both diachronically and synchronically.

LAMU FOLK HISTORY

Social Structure and Social Stratification

In this section the origins of the different groups living in Lamu before the BuSa'id rulers took over will be discussed. It is important to note here that, although Lamu's history is a folk history, I treat it as a social fact. For my purposes, it makes no difference that this history has been invented. As far as the people of Lamu are concerned, these events actually took place.[4] Their history is real for them, and through it they judge the existing reality. They might condemn today's way of life, or they might appreciate it; it all depends on the way it meshes with their sense of history.[5] Furthermore, such value judgments not only affect their way of life but also color their total ethos and world view. I do not wish to involve myself in an argument here about what does and does not constitute history; nor do I wish to enter the debate over the difference between primitive and higher societies. It seems obvious to me, for many reasons, that Lamu cannot be dealt with as a primitive society in the traditional sense of that term. Lamu has an extensive oral tradition, and it would be doing the people a grave injustice to speak of them as a people without history. Furthermore, the island has a long tradition of participation in Indian Ocean trade, and an involvement, albeit peripheral, in the history of Islamic culture. It is certainly not an isolated self-contained society. What is important for us here is to discover how the people think about their origins, to define the different groups, and to indicate the social action and cultural orientation which are expected and judged appropriate for them.

In Lamu, deviation from the social norms or neglect of cultural values is not tolerated. Deviators are socially sanctioned and sometimes physically punished.

The Formative Period: The Wangwana Free Men

The general thrust of Lamu's folk history is to incorporate the island's history within the history of Islam. Thus, when the wangwana give an account of their history, they say that the first settlers came to Lamu from Yanbu' in Arabia. They are said to have left their homeland because of the religious hostilities

4. Here I am looking at "history" not as a continuous stream of events defined in themselves and by themselves, but rather as discontinuous events which the natives choose, pick up, and transform into a coherent system.

5. For a different view see: James S. Kirkman, *Men and Monuments on the East African Coast* (London: Lutterworth Press, 1964).

which took place after the murder of Osman, the third Islamic caliph. The first group, when it arrived in Lamu, found the island uninhabited. They settled at a place they called *Hidabu*, (from the Arabic word *haḍaba,* hill), which is located at the southern end of the present Langoni half of the island.

Before long, however, another group of settlers arrived. During the rule of Harun al Rashid (786 - 809 A.D.—170 - 194 A.H.), an army was organized, made up of Syrians, Iraqis, and Persians, and was sent to the East African coast. Part of this army landed on the northern end of Lamu in the place which is now called *Vuyoni.* Neither the southern group of settlers nor the northern group knew of the others' existence. It is said that between them there was a large tract of bush land. The Vuyoni[6] people were very strong; they were trained soldiers, and there were about twelve thousand of them, well equipped with weapons. One day the two groups "discovered" each other. The Hidabu[7] people wanted to subject the Vuyoni people to their rule, claiming that they had possessed the island first. When the Vuyoni people refused to be subject to anybody, war broke out between the two groups.

However, in a place such as Lamu, people have to produce in order to live, and the constant preparation for war meant that no one was able to grow the needed food. The continuous war exhausted both groups, and each of them was eager to establish a peaceful settlement. The Hidabu people decided to send a message to the Vuyoni people asking for peace. Simultaneously, the Vuyoni made the same decision, and the two messengers met halfway in the bush. The Vuyoni messenger was so eager for peace that when he saw the Hidabu messenger he began to speak immediately: "We Vuyoni people are asking for peace. I have been given a letter indicating that we want peace." Hearing that, the Hidabu messenger declared: "As for me I have been given a letter indicating that we will continue to fight to the end." When the messenger from Vuyoni returned, he told his people that the Hidabuans refused peace and were going to fight till the end. The Vuyoni people were exhausted and unable to continue fighting. Therefore, they sent a delegation to Hidabu asking again for peace.

The people of Hidabu wanted to return the visit, so they told the Vuyoni delegates that they would come to Vuyoni and discuss peace terms. The Vuyoni delegates agreed, and they added, "You Hidabu people, on the day of your coming to our place to discuss peace terms, let no man carry arms," and the people from Hidabu agreed. When the Vuyoni delegation returned to their homes, they told their people about the decision. An old Vuyoni man advised

6. Some local traditions refer to them as *Zena.*
7. Some local traditions refer to them as *Sud.*

his people: "Do not put your arms down, because the day of peace is indeed the day of war." But the people of Vuyoni paid no attention to the old man's advice, and they considered his warning a jest. So, on the agreed date, the people of Hidabu came to Vuyoni carrying their weapons, and when they saw that the Vuyoni people were unarmed, they attacked them and utterly destroyed all the Vuyoni men. After the massacre, the Hidabuans set down the peace conditions they desired. The first condition was that the people of Vuyoni should not carry arms or build fences around their settlement. The second condition was that Vuyoni should not wear shoes but rather should go barefooted and should accept as their duty the washing of the dead.

The people of Lamu like to stress the idea that the only survivors of the massacre were "the children and the women." The Vuyonians had no power, so they had to accept all the conditions. They were humiliated, and subsequently were considered inferior. The children left from the Vuyoni group were called *Wa Yumbili Ponde,* or "Wa Yumbili the donkeys," because their fathers were stupid like donkeys. However, the Hidabu people found the Vuyoni women beautiful, even though not equal to them. But, according to the principle of marrying between equals (*mkufu*), the Hidabu people could not actually marry the Vuyoni women. Therefore, they began to cohabit with them without marrying them. A child who came out of this sexual union was called *Wa Yumbili Ngombe,* or "Wa Yumbili the cow," because their mothers were like cows, which do not mind having illicit sexual relations as long as they are satisfied. Nevertheless, the Wa Yumbili Ponde were not equal to Wa Yumbili Ngombe, since the former were the offspring of defeated fathers, while the latter were the offspring of free and victorious fathers. While the Wa Yumbili Ponde had to obey the conditions dictated by the Hidabu group, the Wa Yumbili Ngombe did not have to follow these conditions. Yet, the Wa Yumbili Ngombe were left to live with their mothers in Vuyoni, which meant that under the same roof, and from the same mother, one child would be considered free while the other was considered low and was treated like a slave even by his own half brother.

The Definitive Period: The Distribution of Power

After awhile, some immigrants from Arabia and the Persian Gulf came to the island. They cleared the bush in certain areas and settled there. These newcomers disturbed the political balance; they were necessarily on a higher social level than the Wa Yumbili Ponde, since they had not suffered a defeat.

With the arrival of the new settlers, the Wa Yumbili Ponde found that the time was ripe for them to attempt to better their position. They declared that the defeat of their fathers was due to a trick played by the Hidabu people. The Wa Yumbili Ponde, helped and supported by the newcomers, were about to launch a war against the Hidabu group; however, when the head of the Hidabu, Haji Sa'id, realized that, he said to the newcomers:

> Each year, choose a man from your group, and he will be the ruler for that year. However, for myself, I want to be the one who settles the major problems of the different groups. My word has to be accepted by all of you. For everyday problems, I will allow your man to make the decisions, but the major problems concerning the town as a whole will be mine. I think that the Wa Yumbili should have an office; therefore, I give them the office of the khatibs of the Jum'a. From now on, these religious leaders have to be from the Wa Yumbili Ngombe, so their half brothers, the Wa Yumbili Ponde, cannot say that the Hidabu people are taking everything in their hands.

Both the newcomers and the Wa Yumbili Ngombe accepted the proposal. So, the Wa Yumbili Ponde, finding themselves alone and unable to fight their half brothers and the whole of Lamu besides, accepted the proposal also. Haji Sa'id,emerged as the supreme authority, and he was called the *mngwana wa nyumbe,* which means "the free person who holds the power in the house of government."

Haji Sa'id considered all the people of Lamu to be free people, or wangwana. However, some of them were considered higher and "more free" than others. This meant that the "more free" the group was, the more power it had to take an active part in Lamu's affairs. The Wa Yumbili Ponde were considered wangwana but with very limited freedom, and the newcomers were also considered free, because they had not been defeated. As might be expected, the Wa Yumbili Ngombe were considered "more free" than their brothers, the Wa Yumbili Ponde.

The Hidabu group ruled Lamu for some time. The ruling house was located at Vyumba in the Mkomani half of the island, and the ruler would occupy it during the day and return to Hidabu at night. The newcomers settled in Mtamwini, and the two Wa Yumbili groups lived in Vuyoni. As we have seen, all the different groups in Lamu cooperated in building the Jum'a Mosque which was placed in the northern part of the town so it would be closer to the khatibs. They also cooperated in building the Pwani Mosque, which was to be used by the new settlers and the supreme ruler for everyday prayer. But by themselves the Hidabu people built what is called the *Maskiti Wali Seif* as a place to perform everyday prayer.

Because of the peace which Lamu enjoyed, and as a result of their authority, the Hidabuans grew very rich. They even reached the point where they were washing their children in milk. Even worse, they began to think that all the success they had achieved was due to their own work, and not to God's blessing. But God is powerful; He is the destroyer. One day, after the men from Hidabu left their houses, a sandstorm came, and in a very short time the whole of the Hidabu settlement was covered with sand. All the women and children were killed. This was God's revenge. Having lost their settlement and their women, the men moved to the southern part of Lamu, to the place which is now called Vyumbe. They wanted to marry, but found that there were only two groups from whom they could marry, the newcomers and the Wa Yumbili Ngombe. They preferred the Wa Yumbili Ngombe because they were related to them, and so approached them with marriage proposals. But the women, thinking that the Hidabu people were ill-fated and cursed, refused the proposals. When they were pressed however, they accepted on the condition that the Hidabu group would change its name. The Hidabu males agreed and began to call themselves *Wa Yumbili Pembe*, a name which refers, even today, to the highest stratum of the old society. The offspring of the Hidabu males and the Wa Yumbili Ngombe females constituted a new category which was to rule Lamu in the future. The Wa Yumbili Pembe was eventually subdivided into three groups: the Wangwana Wa Yumbe, the Wa Famao, and the Kinamte. Up to the present, the Wa Yumbili Pembe have been the keepers of Lamu's brass horn or *siwa,* which is blown in the marriage ceremony of the original Lamu people.

The Wa Yumbili Ngombe, after giving their daughters to the Wa Yumbili Pembe, found it shameful to stay in Vuyoni with their brothers, the Wa Yumbili Ponde, so they moved to the Mkomani area beside the Jum'a Mosque. But it was hard for the Wa Yumbili Ponde to stay away from their brothers; so they in turn moved to Pumwani.[8] This place was close enough to Mkomani for them to keep in contact with their brothers, although their brothers refused to let them actually live in Mkomani. It is interesting to note that, even when the Wa Yumbili Ngombe were living in Vuyọni, they refused to marry their half brothers, the Wa Yumbili Ponde: both groups married endogamously. That marriage ought to occur only between equals was an old principle in Lamu. Among the Wa Yumbili Ponde, Wa Yumbili Ngombe, and Wa Yumbili Pembe, we find these principles of stratification:

8. Some people say that this name is derived from *Pa Mwana*, or "the place of the mistress."

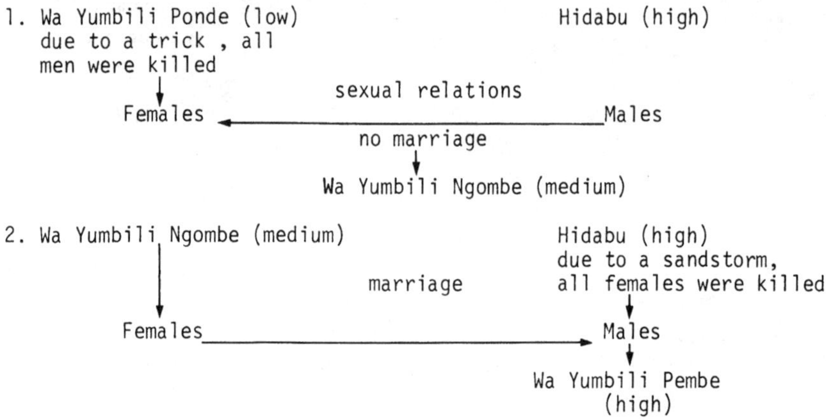

Fig. 1. Principles of Social Stratification

Marriage does not affect the social position of the wife. The Wa Yumbili Ponde females retained their low position, even after they gave birth to the Wa Yumbili Ngombe. The Wa Yumbili Ngombe retained their position after marrying the Hidabu group and begetting Wa Yumbili Pembe. As a result of marriage between the Wa Yumbili Ngombe and the Hidabu group, relations between the Wa Yumbili Ngombe and Wa Yumbili Ponde were severed. This rupture was expressed in the Ngombe group's move to Mkomani, and their refusal to allow the Wa Yumbili Ponde to live with them in the same location. In other words, in order to express their relative superiority, the Wa Yumbili Ngombe separated themselves completely from their maternal group. The Wa Yumbili Ponde were thus forced to become a closed group. They married endogamously because no group wanted to give them their women as wives, or to take wives from them.

However, at a later date, applying the principle that equals marry equals, the Wa Yumbili Pembe stopped taking wives from the Wa Yumbili Ngombe, because the Ngombe girls were not equal to the Pembe girls; and the Wa Yumbili Pembe females were no longer able to marry the Wa Yumbili Ngombe males. Thus the Wa Yumbili Pembe also came to have a very strict endogamous marriage system.

The Wa Yumbili Ngombe and the newcomers were considered equal. Neither had been defeated as the Wa Yumbili Ponde had, and both had limited power. So, being equal, they could intermarry. A Wa Yumbili Ngombe female could marry a male from the newcomers and vice versa. Figure 1 illustrates the principles of stratification that operated among Lamu's social groups at this stage.

Each of the four groups had certain basic roles: the supreme ruler was to be from the Wa Yumbili Pembe; his assistant from the newcomers; the khatibs from the Wa Yumbili Ngombe; the washermen, undertakers, and cleaners from the Wa Yumbili Ponde. However, the members of the Wa Yumbili Pembe group had the right to choose the supreme ruler from among themselves, and no one from the other groups had the right to interfere in that decision. Furthermore, the Wa Yumbili Pembe retained the right to depose the ruler, if they felt he was not able to carry out his duties. After the death of Haji Sa'id, the Wa Yumbili Pembe decided that the ruler should serve only a limited term, not to exceed three years. The newcomers were to choose a person from among themselves each year, and if there was a problem concerning any one of the Lamu groups, this person—whom we will call a "minister"—had to be consulted. He had no right to make a decision, his duty being merely to carry the problem to the supreme ruler, who would then discuss the problem with him. However, whether they agreed or disagreed, the decision of the supreme ruler prevailed. Because the supreme ruler had unopposed authority, the Wa Yumbili Pembe decided that the supreme ruler must be an old man, reasoning that the older the person was, the wiser he would be. The supreme ruler and the minister were thus the symbols of political power. However, neither position was hereditary. Any member of the appropriate group could occupy the office, if he were selected. Thus, in the political sphere, Lamu was similar to a republic.

Another office was filled from among the Wa Yumbili Ngombe, but this one was in the religious sphere, and it was set up differently from the post of supreme ruler. Instruction for this office had to be handed down. A candidate had to be taught; he had to know how to read Arabic; he had to study the religious rules and the different invocations. However, since no one could force the religious leader to pass on this teaching if he did not want to do so, he often chose to teach only his own children. And in turn, his children handed the knowledge down to their own children. The office became *de facto* hereditary, and was thus confined to one unit of the Wa Yumbili Ngombe.

The first such religious leader, or khatib, had three sons to whom he gave instruction, so that when the father died, all three sons wanted to occupy their father's position and enjoy the economic advantages of the office. Finally they decided that each of them would occupy the post for four months of the year, and that whatever he collected during that term would be his own. The khatib's role was not only to lead the Friday prayer, but also to read the Qur'ān, and perform the *Talqin* during the burying ceremony. According to Lamu custom, after burying the corpse, the family of the deceased has to bring a sack of rice and put it beside the grave. The preacher sat on the sack and read from the Qur'ān, and then instructed the dead that "The angels will come to you and ask you 'Who is your prophet?' Tell them 'Mohammed is my Prophet, the Almightly Allah is my God'" and so on. After performing the ceremony, the khatib took the rice for himself. The khatib was also the one who had to read the Qur'ān in the houses of the townspeople, and he was paid for this. It was his responsibility as well to keep the Silwa in which the rules of marriage were recorded. Therefore, if a man wanted to get married, he had to contact the khatib, who would examine his record to determine whether the two parties were equal or not. Depending on his opinion, the marriage might or might not take place. The khatib also received a fee for this.

When the town suffers misfortune or when the death rises extraordinarily, the khatib has to perform certain prayers to preserve the town and drive away misfortune. In other words, the khatib is the religious and ritual expert. However, he is not allowed to interfere in the political sphere.

In summary: the folk historians of Lamu want to stress the idea that the island was unoccupied when the first Arab settlers came. These Arab settlers occupied different locations, and when they discovered each other one group wanted to subjugate the other. As a consequence, war took place. The defeated group was then thought to be of a lower social level than the victorious group. Out of the interaction of these two groups, other groups were formed. At the end, all of the Lamu social groups were known as wangwana, or free people, but there were different grades of freedom and these constituted the social strata of Lamu. Each stratum had an assigned function, but all were directed toward maintaining Lamu's welfare.

The Period of Crisis: Lamu and the Acquisition of Slaves

The folk historians deny categorically that the people of Lamu were involved in capturing slaves. They try to prove this by pointing out that none of the slaves used on Lamu was from the Pokomo or Galla peoples, the two tribes who were geographically quite close to Lamu Island. They reason that if the people of Lamu had been slave captors, they would naturally have operated in the nearby area and would have kept some Pokomo or Galla slaves for themselves. This type of argument might be logical from the Lamuan point of view, and I can neither prove nor disprove it. However, the fact is that the people of Lamu did own slaves, and they used them just as everybody of that time did. The question of the changes brought about in Lamu's social structure as a result of slavery is a fascinating one. As we will see later, the slaves had a tremendous effect on Lamu's social stratification, as well as on the political, economic, and religious systems.

The people of Lamu began to expand to the mainland of Africa late in the eighteenth century. The area was fertile, and they bought slaves to cultivate the land for them. Mombasa was involved in the slave trade and was close to Lamu; however, because of the hostilities between the two, the Lamuans preferred to buy their slaves from Bagamoyo (north of Dar es Salaam), or from Unguja (in Zanzibar). These slaves were mainly from what is now called Tanzania. The people of Lamu thought that the slaves were uncivilized and therefore, of course, unequal. Since the core of civilization for the people of Lamu was Islam, and since the slaves were not Muslims, they were not considered civilized. For the Lamuans, Islam was the miracle by which the pre-Islamic Arabs, the barbarians, were transformed into civilized people. Thus *Astarabu*, which means "civilization," refers exclusively to the Arabs and the Islamic civilization which they developed after converting. The slave was considered a human being, *mwanadamu,* a descendant of Adam; yet, unlike other children of Adam, he was thought to have forgotten the promise he made in heaven to obey God and be a Muslim,[9] and was thus degraded. He was deprived of Islam, which was the only thing that could have made him part of the Astarabu.

As we will see in the Lamuan creation myth,[10] the slaves were believed to be descendants of Ham, the son of Noah, who disobeyed his father. Noah cursed his disobedient son by asking God to make the sons of Ham slaves and servants. In the two myths that I collected, the slaves are considered cursed people; and in both cases, they were cursed because they were disobedient. The so-called traditional Lamuans use both myths to demonstrate that the slaves were unable to support a civilization of their own. They could be taught, but they did not have the faculties to understand what they had been taught, because they could not escape from the curse that condemned them to a position lower than all other human beings. Nevertheless, as part of God's creation, they were granted certain rights. When a slave was bought, he was to be taken in by an old slave trained in taking care of the newly purchased ones. He was to clean the slave, wash him, trim his nails, shave his hair, and also teach him the appropriate social behavior. Because the slaves were to convert to Islam, they were given a minimal amount of Islamic theology. The people of Lamu considered it a waste of time to teach a slave all the finer points of their religion: he need only know

9. See Chapter 4, "The Myth of Creation."

10. In this book I have used the myth of creation, i.e., the creation of Adam and Eve. However, I have also gathered material on the myth of Adam and his descendants, which I have not analyzed thoroughly in the book. I am currently working on that analysis, however.

that "there is no God but Allah," and that "Mohammed is His Prophet." Besides this, he was given some instruction in how to pray. The slave felt obliged to pray, not because he was convinced that prayer was a part of Islam, but rather because it was an appropriate part of his behavior. The slave was taught neither the rules of marriage nor the rules of inheritance.

African slaves were used as currency; they were exchanged between different owners. Thus, if one man wanted to settle his debt with another, slaves could be used as a medium of exchange. If a rich man's son was about to marry, his father might give him some slaves and a piece of land. Slaves were, after all, the main necessities for cultivating the land. And, in turn, if a rich man's daughter was about to marry, her father might give her two or three girls to do her housework. While many slave women were kept in the houses of Lamu to work as servants, most of the men were sent to work on the master's land on the mainland.

Slaves were graded, some being considered superior to others. The slave assigned to cultivation, which was considered hard work, was called *mtwana.* The slave whom the master liked most was kept by him as a *hadimu.* In addition to this, there was a type of slave who did the petty jobs, and he was called *mtumwa.*

The hadimu used to live in the master's house, and sometimes was even given a slave girl as a wife. The offspring resulting from such a marriage was called *mzaliya,* or native, one who was born in Lamu. The Wa Zaliya were considered higher than their own fathers and were trained from childhood to behave appropriately. Growing up with the master's children, the mzaliya was able to acquire some of their knowledge. For example, he used to accompany his master's children to the teacher's house and, though he was not allowed to sit with them and listen to the teacher, he was still able to hear the discussion from outside.

In addition to the African slaves, there were some slaves who were bought from the Comoro Islands. The people of the Comoro Islands fought among themselves, and those who were defeated were sold as slaves. The Comoro people were well known as sailors, and since the Lamuans owned a number of large boats, they bought the Comoro Island slaves to work on them. These Comoro Islanders had been Muslims for a long time before being enslaved, and some of them claimed that they were of Arab origin. This, in fact, raised a sophisticated problem. Were the Comoro slaves really slaves, or not? They were part of the great tradition, i.e., Islam, and they shared in the Astarabu. They were well trained in reading the Qur'ān and even in reciting it by heart. In other words, they maintained that they were part of the civilized world as defined by the Lamu people. The Lamuans realized that they could not treat these people in the same way they treated their African slaves because they clearly were religiously and professionally superior to the Africans. For these reasons, the people of Lamu gave them a special spot in the southern half of the town (Langoni). The Comoro Islanders called this spot *Moi Mwima,* or "the good earth." Later it was also called *Milango,* "the door," because when Lamu people built the wall around their town to protect it from Mombasa, the Comoro Islanders were given the job of closing the door at night. The Comoro Island slaves were allowed to build a mosque for themselves, which they called *Ras al Khiri,* or "the blessed head." The mosque had two doors—one open to the sea, the other open to the town. If the Comoro sailors returned to Lamu at night, they would have to go through the first door and then the second, thus establishing their identity before entering the town.

In their mosque the Comoro Islanders taught their children the Qur'ān and other Islamic sciences. Some of them were so well educated that the masters, that is the wangwana, began to send their children to the Ras al Khiri Mosque to be taught by the Comoro teachers. Thus, the wangwana had different relations with the African slaves and those from the Comoro Islands. While the masters had unrestricted power over the African slaves, their power over the Comoro slaves was limited. As sailors and captains, the latter were given the authority to represent their masters in business encounters. To a great extent, they were left on their own. A master, before giving his boat to a captain, would ask him to read the *Fatiḥa* (the opening verses of the Qur'ān), and to make a promise that he would not betray his master. Then the master would read the Fatiḥa and promise that he would take care of the captain's family if anything happened to him. This ritual recitation of the Fatiḥa indicates that there was a contractual relation between the captain and his master which according to tradition could only be established between two free persons. Thus, from that point of view, the Comoro Islanders were not slaves in the real sense of the word. Furthermore, the wangwana were not allowed to take the Comoro girls as mistresses. Since their fathers were considered Muslims, marriage was the only permissible form of sexual relationship with their daughters. Sexual relations with a Comoro Island girl before marrying her were considered adultery, and any children resulting from the union would be considered illegitimate. Such adulterous relations were condemned by God. Marriage, of course, could only take place between equals, so the wangwana were also prohibited from marrying the Comoro Island girls. Of course, the reverse of the prohibition also prevailed: the Comoro men were not allowed to marry wangwana women. Thus Comoro Islanders were forced to marry endogamously and to exist in Lamu as a closed group.

Because so many were sailors, this special group was able to maintain contacts with their original homeland. In many cases, they were able to go to the Comoro Islands and bring wives back from their home society. In other words, through the Comoro Islanders in Lamu the wangwana were able to maintain strong relations with the Comoro Islands, and with other parts of the East African and South Arabian coasts.

In striking contrast, the African slaves were confined to their masters' estates on the mainland. This land was divided into plots, with each slave cultivating one piece. The size of each piece of land was standardized, and on it the slave had to build a hut for himself and his wife. Every fifteen pieces of land were under the control of a slave headman.

The headman was chosen for his ability to coordinate the work of the slaves and to discipline them strictly. The slaves working under him were bound to obey his orders, and he was given the power to punish them. The headman was supposed to induce the slaves to work hard and to compete with each other. If a slave finished the work on his piece, and he wanted to work another piece, then the headman had to pay him a share of the crop of the extra piece he worked.[11] In addition, each slave was given a piece of land on which to grow his own food.

The slaves were not allowed to visit Lamu Town except at their masters' request. If they did come into town for their masters, they had to leave at night and sleep in the hills east of the town, on the seashore, or south of the town. In other words, slaves were never allowed to sleep in the town—they were never insiders. Such customs, as we will see, were related to the religious and political systems in Lamu.

The masters feared that the African slaves were not loyal to them and that they might help Mombasa or Patta to invade Lamu. Thus, they wanted to keep them ignorant of Lamu's fortifications and military power. Moreover, they felt that the balance between the wangwana groups might be disturbed if the slaves were allowed to be present inside. One group might stage a coup and come to dominate the others.

So, for external and internal political reasons, the African slaves were left outside the town—that is, the male slaves were; this was not the case with the African slave girls. They were sexually accessible, without marriage, to the masters who owned them. If the owner liked a girl, he was able to take her as a *souriya,* or pastime girl. If the souriya got pregnant and delivered a male child

11. Some of the slaves stockpiled these extra shares of the crop, sold them, and bought slaves with the proceeds. Thus the original slave became a slaveholder.

whom the master was sure was his son, then the souriya would be considered *umm-al-walad,* "the mother of the boy," and she would be granted a higher status. For example, the master could not subsequently sell her; the only way to get rid of her would be to divorce her, and let her marry whomever she liked. If the master kept the umm-al-walad souriya, then on his death she would become free. If the sexual relations between the master and his slave brought him a female child, then the status of the slave mother remained the same. The girl child inherited her mother's status and she was married to a hadimu. However, the institution of the souriya played an important role in Lamu's social organization. It created a crisis for the principle of marriage between equals, mkufu.

The male children of a souriya were not considered equal to their half brothers who were born from an equally free male and female. For example, the child of a souriya lived with his mother in the servants' quarters of the master's house and ate the servants' food. Furthermore, his education was not equal to his half brother's, because the teachers refused to accept the two as equal. The male child of a souriya would get only the knowledge suitable for the public. In every respect such a child was not considered a part of his father's wangwana group. However, he did carry his father's name, and he was patrilineally related to his father's group. Since his mother's status was lower than any wangwana group in Lamu, none of these groups wanted to give their daughters to the souriya's sons. As we have said, it was a completely different situation with the daughters of a souriya, who were in no way to be considered part of the father's group—they were considered slaves like their mothers. Thus the male children of souriyas were left without equal females. The only way for the son of a souriya to get a wife was for him to marry a slave who had been granted her freedom. The resulting situation dealt a great blow to the traditional wangwana mkufu marriage principle.

The Jum'a khatib, who registered marriages, had to make a judgment about the appropriate marriage group for the sons of the souriya. He did not know where to place them. The Silwa, the book in which the principles of equal marriages were stated, was not helpful either. The problem became more and more complex and no one could provide an answer. From the religious point of view, the owner of a slave girl could take her as a souriya. No one could negate that; it is clear in the Qur'ān. However, from the social point of view, the children of a souriya could not rightfully be considered equal to their father's group. The khatib faced a conflict; he had to either stand against the souriya relation and in so doing oppose the Qur'ān, or criticize the principle of equal marriage which might lead him to condemn the whole wangwana ideology, which he could not do. The khatib preferred to simply keep silent, and see what happened.

The male children of the souriya created another problem concerning inheritance. Were they to inherit shares equal to those of their half brothers, who were the offspring of an equal marriage? In many cases, the father deprived the sons of the souriya of any inheritance. When he felt that he was about to die, the father might give the sons of a souriya a small portion of his land and some slaves, and then write a will giving the rest of his property to the children of his equal wife. Because the male children of the souriya had a limited knowledge of the Islamic inheritance laws, they were unable to substantiate a claim that this was not right, and the khatib let this pass as an acceptable way of settling the inheritance problem.[12]

The traditional system began to suffer. In the old times, before the souriyas, the children of one man constituted a corporate unit. Even if they were born from different mothers, all were equal to the father, and so equal to each other. They understood themselves to be related through the father to the head of the descent group, the *mza.* For example, if the mza had two sons, then each son would be the head of a *kitumba,* or "unit." However, as they used to say, the mother's side was not to be counted. For example, if X married three wives, and he had children from all of them, then all the children of X were viewed as part of their father's kitumba. If X had brothers Y and Z, then X, Y, and Z were considered, along with their children, as members of the same kitumba. However, X, Y, and Z would each have his own *kwenu,* or household. The kwenu was defined as the place where the younger generation had no power. Thus, if X had three sons living with him, the sons would have no power over their father's decisions in his kwenu. If X was married to and supported three different wives, living in three different houses, then the children of the three wives would constitute one kwenu. If X brought all his children together under one roof, and then they brought their spouses to live in the house, and their children lived together and ate together, this way of living would be called *numba serkali,* a "government house," because the eldest person (the father, if alive) would be seen as the ruler and the younger generations as his subjects. The numba serkali was divided into rooms, and each married couple and their children occupied one room. The inside of the room was called *kwangu* by the

12. This point will be discussed later. However, it should be stated here that when the Reiyadah sharifs came to power, they began to attack that practice. Ḥabib Mansib, a mngwana, made a rule that it was irreligious to know of such a practice and keep silent, and he stated his belief that any khatib who did so would be tortured by God. This marked the end of the khatib's authority. (See Chapter 3, "Lamu and the Rise of the Jamalilil Sharifs.")

husband, " the place in which I have the right to rule." However, outside the rooms, all members of one kwenu, who occupied one numba serkali, had to obey the head or the ruler of that house.

The above description of the traditional extended family stresses the authority of the old over the young. The members of the family were all considered equal, and all had to obey the eldest person in the household. Yet, each room had its own ruler, and as long as the smaller family units in the different rooms accepted the orders of the house, the head had no right to interfere in what was going on in the individual rooms.

The head of the numba serkali had to treat all who lived with him equally. However, the children from a souriya could hardly be treated as equal to the children of a free wife. So even during the lifetime of the head of the numba serkali, the children of his free wife were not allowed to mix with their half brothers, the children of a souriya, who ate different food and dressed in less fine clothing. On the father's death, the children of the souriya were usually forced to leave the house and to live with their mothers, the mother then acting as the head of her own children, though the children of a souriya were patrilineally related to the mza and to a certain kitumba.

As we saw above, Lamu was strictly a patrilineal society; the child inherited his father's name and property. The mngwana woman was considered "a vessel [sufuria]: whatever her husband puts inside her will be kept inside and the child will be like his father," while the souriya was thought to be like "fire [*moto*]: whatever you put inside gets burned." The pot preserves, while the fire burns. The good pot does not change the food you put inside; while in fire, good or bad, food usually gets burned.[13] In reference to this inequality between the children of souriya and the children of a mngwana woman, we found such proverbs as "*ndugu wa kombo si ndugo,*" "the brothers who have the same fathers but not the same mother are not brothers." In other words, the children from one woman and different husbands will make better brothers than those from the same father and different mothers.

Social Stratification and Traditional Education

Lamu's educational system during the slavery period reflected the strict stratification system which colored every aspect of traditional society. Education, at that time, meant the acquisition of religious knowledge, which was exclusively possessed by the wangwana. Though the Comoro Islanders knew the Qur'ān by heart and were somewhat familiar with Islam, they were not

13. This point will be discussed in more detail later (see below pp. 158–59).

recognized by the wangwana as learned people. In Lamu, in order to get this recognition, a person had to be licensed. To be awarded the license, the novice had to spend fifteen or sixteen years with several learned wangwana men. The novice had to be a *mngwana* (the singular of *wangwana*), and he had to be able to pay the teachers. The slave, of course, could not meet any of these conditions.

The teachers, who educated their own children first, and then taught other wangwana as they saw fit, divided knowledge into two parts. One part was considered suitable for any mngwana who could pay, while the other was only offered to the chosen elite. The children of the *'ālim*, as the teacher is called, were, of course, considered part of the chosen elite. The first kind of education was given during the day, while the second was given secretly at night. The elite students were told that this kind of knowledge was not to be taught to the nonelite, and they promised the 'ālim to keep their knowledge secret. The standard wangwana students learned the Arabic language and Arabic grammar, and then were taught to read the Qur'ān. After that came the basic principles of Islam: how to pray over the dead, how to cleanse oneself after defilement, and the wisdom of fasting during the month of Ramadan. This program would take six or seven years, and at this point the nonelite student would stop.

The elite students, however, would continue their education under special learned men, known as *mwenye chouni.* One of the learned men taught them Islamic jurisprudence and the books of the Shafi'ite creed, which was the creed followed by the people of Lamu. Another teacher instructed the elite in the science of *Ḥadith,* or the sayings and actions of the Prophet, and how to differentiate between a strong Ḥadith and a weak one, while a third taught them how to practice "Arabic medicine" which required a knowledge of herbs, the benefits of each kind, and their appropriate uses. Yet another teacher instructed them in the composition of Arabic poetry. At this time the students also began a study of the science of the Qur'ān: the knowlege of why and when individual verses were revealed, and the varying orthodox interpretations of each. When the students finished studying the science of the Qur'ān, which by itself took four or five years, they were qualified to receive the license of mwenye chouni themselves.

At the ceremony for awarding the license, the student and his teachers met at the Jum'a Mosque. After praying together, the student offered the teachers a meal. Following this, the teachers, singly and in the presence of the khatib, declared that so and so, the son of so and so, from the right, and an acceptable, group, and the descendant of an equal father and mother, was granted a license as a mwenye chouni. If the khatib, after consulting his Silwa, found that everything was in order, he would then write the name of the new teacher in the book.

The new 'ālim, as a general rule, could teach any of the sciences which he had acquired, except jurisprudence and the interpretation of the Qur'ān. For these he had to consult his original teachers until they felt he had truly mastered these two fields. When the teachers decided he had, another ceremony was held and this further mastery officially declared. The 'ālim could then give a Fatwa, that is, a legal opinion. By the time all of this had transpired, the new 'ālim was fifty years of age, or older. The teachers reasoned that the older the new 'ālim, the more cautious he would be. Yet even after that, he was not left unsupervised. If the other 'ulama[14] heard that he had deviated or tried to reinterpret something, and that his interpretation did not follow what they had in their books, they could meet and withdraw his license.[15] A 'ālim not only had to keep his knowledge secret, but also was expected to use it to maintain the status quo. If he knew that a new Fatwa might cause antagonism, he had to keep his opinion to himself. The welfare of the community was considered above any other thing, as the wangwana were striving above all else to maintain Lamu society and to keep it without change. Thus, the mwenye chouni, as the Lamu elite, were never unattached from the stratificatory system prevailing in Lamu. They were committed to a certain world view and ethos. They viewed the slaves as every mngwana did, as incapable of understanding sophisticated knowledge.

The Sharifs and Social Stratification

The first sharifs, those who claim to be descendants of the Prophet, arrived in Lamu after the four traditional groups were well established. These first sharifs were the Mahadali sharifs (see the Genealogical Chart), and they came to Lamu from Somalia. When the Lamuans were informed that the Mahdali sharifs were the descendants of the Prophet, they allowed them to settle in the northern part of the town, in Mkomani.

Out of respect, the khatibs allowed the Mahdali sharifs to lead the daily prayers, but they kept for themselves the right to lead the Friday prayer, the feast prayers, and the prayers during the month of Ramadan. However, the Mahdali sharifs were not considered mwenye chouni; the people of Lamu

14. '*Ulama* is the plural of '*ālim*.

15. In fact, a Lamu 'ālim gave a Fatwa that a Muslim can perform his Islamic prayer even in a church. When the Lamu 'ulama heard that, they held a meeting and called the 'ālim in to defend himself. The 'ulama were not convinced that his Fatwa was a valid one, and they withdrew his license.

had enough religious teachers. They were respected because since they claimed to be the descendants of the Prophet, they were thought to have some *baraka,* or power. Their baraka was not demonstrated before or after their arrival in Lamu; yet their claim to descent from the Prophet was respected.

Because the Wa Yumbili Pembe was an endogamous group, the Mahdali sharifs were able to marry only from the Wa Yumbili Ngombe. The sharifs consented to this situation because they considered themselves religious men, and so thought it fitting to marry only from the group that provided Lamu's religious leaders. This meant that the Mahdali sharifs accepted the stratification system which existed at that time.

While the Mahdali sharifs married only from the Wa Yumbili Ngombe group, their daughters married equally from the Wa Yumbili Ngombe and from the group which I have called "newcomers." Those who married the sharif women were asked to treat them with respect, without insulting or harming them. These women were considered part of the Prophet's family and were, therefore, thought to be under the Prophet's protection. If they were insulted, the insult would not remain with them alone; it might ascend to the Prophet himself, who would not accept it and would curse the wrongdoer. Such a curse might harm the husband physically or economically; he might become sick, or lose his wealth. On the other hand, if the husband was good to his sharif wife, the Prophet would be pleased and, therefore, the husband would be blessed. He would succeed in life. Thus the mngwana male who was married to a sharif female had to beware of mistakes all the time. Above all, he did not want to make his sharif wife angry, and as a result the husbands transferred most of their traditional authority to these wives, making them in effect the center of the family. Thus, like the souriya, the sharif wife, because of her social standing, tended to control part of a patrilineal group.

The sharif women were considered wangwana, like their fathers; yet, because of their special relationship with the Prophet, they were thought to be higher than any non-sharif wangwana women. On the other hand, they too were sufurias, or pots; whatever was put inside by the husband did not change. In other words, the child of the sharif female did not inherit his mother's unique social position; instead, the child inherited the qualities of, and belonged to, the father's group.

The Mahdali sharifs were followed by the Ḥusseini sharifs. However, these sharifs were well known in East Africa before they came to Lamu. At one time the people of Patta were under constant attack from the Galla, a mainland African tribe. The people of Patta went to Ḥadramaut, to ask

Sheikh Abu Bakr Ibn Salim [14], the sharif ancestor of the Ḥusseini family, for help.[16] The sheikh agreed to assist them, and sent his son's son Shikhan ibn Hussein to Patta. When Shikhan arrived, he wrote some verses of the Qur'ān on a slip of paper, took some pieces of his father's flag, and asked the Patta people to bury both these things near a shallow place. When this was done, the sea grew deeper and the island moved farther from the mainland. The people of Patta were safe and the Galla were unable to attack. Shikhan settled on Patta and thus the lineage of the Ḥusseini sharifs came to the island. He was known as *Shee Patta,* or the head of the Ḥusseini sharifs. The Ḥusseini sharifs were respected by the kings and people of Patta, until the Nabahani family took over the island. The story is told that Shee Patta had been asked by someone to intervene for him with the Nabahani king and gain forgiveness for him. Shee Patta went to the king and asked him to forgive the man, but the king insulted him and ordered him not to interfere. Shee Patta then said to the king, "God will destroy Patta as you destroyed my reputation." Then the whole Ḥusseini family left Patta to come to Lamu, where they were respected.[17]

The Ḥusseini sharifs had performed many miracles before they came to Lamu; they had demonstrated their baraka, or power. They also had an established genealogy and folk history, and were therefore more than welcomed in Lamu. They were given houses in the Mtamwini mtaa. They married from the Kinamte subgroup, who gave them land and slaves in addition to wives. The Ḥusseini sharifs had been on the top of the system of social stratification in Patta, and they were granted the same position in Lamu. They obtained the wealth needed to support this position from the Kinamte, and received gifts of land and slaves from the rest of the wangwana as well.

The Mahdali sharifs did not have the genealogy, history, or power of the Ḥusseini sharifs, and for these reasons were less respected and less feared. The Mahdali were constantly compared to the Ḥusseini, and their position in the stratificatory system of Lamu was lowered as a result of the Ḥusseini settling there.

The Ḥusseini and Mahdali lived with the other wangwana in the Mkomani half of Lamu. As we have seen, the Ḥusseini were rich in land and slaves, and they were also merchants, like most of the rich wangwana. Furthermore, the Ḥusseini sharifs did not have any relations with the Wa Yumbili Ngombe, or

16. See the Genealogical Chart. Numbers and letters in brackets refer to corresponding numbers and letters on the Genealogical Chart.

17. I was unable to get the exact date of the incident. However, people in Patta and Lamu tell the same story.

with the prayers of the Jum'a Mosque. This was probably due to the fact that their power or baraka had already been proven. They did not need to establish themselves as a religious group, since everyone acknowledged their status even before they came to Lamu.[18]

In conclusion, the ease with which the sharifs fitted into the traditional stratification system of Lamu should be stressed. They quickly conformed to the traditional roles of their respective wangwana groups, and, like everyone else, wanted first of all to maintain the *status quo,* the traditional system.

Traditional Economic Life

In early times Lamu was used only as a natural port for crossing the Indian Ocean from South Arabia to India. The people used to produce a kind of cloth which they sold to those who stopped at the island. However, Lamu's economic life began to flourish after the acquisition of slaves and the cultivation of large areas of land on the mainland. The most important agricultural item was rice. In addition to this, wheat and other grains were grown. The slaves also cut *boriti,* thick poles from the mangrove, which were used by the South Arabians, the Persians, and the Indians to support the ceilings and roofs of their homes.

In search of these items, boats used to come to Lamu during the north and south monsoon seasons.[19] The traders came either from India or from South Arabia.[20] To accommodate their trade, the Lamu people built a market, or *otokuni,* in the place carrying that name (see Map 4). The market lay outside the residential areas of the four groups which constituted the wangwana, and here the merchants of Lamu built huge stores, to which the slaves would carry the crops after they were gathered. Then when the traders from overseas arrived, they would contact the wangwana traders, and, after the business was transacted, the slaves would carry the merchandise to the buyers' boats. Thus, the market functioned mainly as the place where foreign buyers and wangwana traders met and settled their deals. It was not intended to serve the local population. Since each group was self-sufficient, local people did not depend on the market for their everyday needs.

Under no circumstances could the foreign merchants sleep inside the town. Before sunset all had to leave and sleep on their boats. At that time, no one used the market area as a residential location—it was only the town's storage

18. See below, Chapter 3, for more detailed information about the sharifs.

19. A. H. J. Prins, *Sailing from Lamu* (Assen: Van Gorcum, 1965).

20. Chittick Neville, "East African Trade with the Orient," *Islam and the Trade of Asia,* ed. Donald Richards (Philadelphia: University of Pennsylvania Press, 1971).

place. However, since the wangwana would stay in the market area to entertain buyers, during the trading season, they needed a mosque to pray in during the day. To meet this need, they built the Otokuni Mosque, and the prayer leaders in that mosque were the khatibs. This, in fact, indicates that the mosque did not belong to any particular wangwana group. The market mosque was intended to express the unity of the wangwana, in a manner similar to the Jum'a Mosque. Therefore, the leadership of the Otokuni Mosque was delegated to the Wa Yumbili Ngombe, the same group that was given the right to lead prayers in the Jum'a Mosque.

The separation of the market from the residential areas was part of wangwana protocol. It was thought that living in the market might indicate the wangwana's dependency on it, which in turn might lead buyers to think that the wangwana could not live without selling their merchandise. In other words, such an arrangement would make the seller seem lower than the buyer, a concept which the wangwana would not accept. Moreover, each social group was assigned to a certain residential location in Lamu, while the market area was common to all groups. If the market were to be used as a residential area, all groups would have to mix and live together, and that would be a contradiction of the wangwana concept of equals marrying equals and equals living with equals. For all of these reasons, the market was solely a storage area. The wangwana also refused to open shops until customers were waiting, because then they would have to sit there and wait for the buyers, who in turn might feel they had the upper hand. It was also considered unacceptable for a buyer to ask the wangwana to fetch something for him, a request suitable for a slave, but not for a mngwana, who works at no man's command. The market also had its social function. In *baraza,* or meeting places, wangwana met with their friends and conversed about religion, politics, or even love affairs. But as the trading season was over, the market was deserted.

The market was seasonal and peripheral to Lamu's society. It did not initiate any new social concepts, but rather reflected and strengthened the traditional ideology. Traditional ethics controlled the market. Rich or poor, a mngwana was a mngwana; everyone remained in the group into which he was born. There was no place for advancement through personal achievement. Birth determined prestige, occupation, location, education, and even social relations. In this society, wealth was not to be praised for its own sake. The real investment could not be made in this world, but only in the hereafter.

Social Stratification and the Celebration of the Maulidi

One of the most important rituals in Lamu, and indeed in all of East Africa, was the recitation of the *Maulidi,*[21] the celebration of the Prophet's birth. We do not know for sure how or when that celebration was first introduced to Lamu. We do know that there were two ways of reciting the Maulidi: one type of Maulidi was recited by the more advantaged wangwana, i.e., the Wa Yumbili Pembe, the Wa Yumbili Ngombe, and the newcomers; the other Maulidi was recited by the lesser wangwana, the Wa Yumbili Ponde.

The Maulidi of the upper wangwana was known in East Africa as Maulidi Barzanji,[22] and this text was considered to be second only to the Qur'ān itself in its sacredness. Old manuscripts of this service—some over one hundred years old—have been found in Lamu. The Maulidi text was written in classical Arabic and was divided into two parts. The first part is in prose, while the second is in verse. As far as I know, the second part was not read in Lamu.

In the month of *Rabi' al Awwal,* the month in which the Prophet was born, the ruler of Lamu summoned the preachers to come to the Maskiti Pwani to read the Maulidi. The mosque was decorated and painted especially for that occasion, and only the higher groups of wangwana were allowed to attend. This was the beginning of a series of Maulidi celebrations. On the second day the Maulidi had to be read inside the ruler's house, which was decorated and prepared for the occasion. This was considered a private ceremony, and the ruler would invite only those who were his social equals. On the third day the Maulidi was recited in the minister's house.[23] This was also a private ceremony—however, the minister had to invite the ruler. In addition, he could invite anyone from the ruler's group to attend. When these three Maulidis were over, the khatibs were allowed to read the Maulidi in the houses of any of the upper wangwana. However, if two persons wanted to have the Maulidi read on the same day, the one from the higher group was preferred. This arrangement had to be strictly followed, and the rules strictly obeyed. Finally, on the twenty-second of the same month, the preachers invited the ruler, the minister, and their respective groups to a recitation of the Maulidi in the Jum'a Mosque. After this ceremony, the celebration of the Maulidi was over.

The Maulidi Barzanji was a "private" ritual. The only people who were able to read it were either the 'ulama, the mwenye chouni, or the khatibs.

21. *Maulidi* (Swahili); *Mawlid* (Arabic).

22. Jafar ibn Hassan ibn 'Abd al Karim, ibn Mohammed al Hadim ibn Zein al 'Abedin al Barzanji (1690-1766 A. D.—1102-1180 A. H.).

23. A person had been chosen from the newcomers' group to act as a minister.

Furthermore, only licensed persons were allowed to read it, and the only group allowed to give out such licenses were the khatibs. In other words, to be licensed to read the Maulidi Barzanji, the person had to be competent in the Arabic language and a member of the khatib group. If a person were competent in Arabic, but not licensed to read the Maulidi, then his reading would not bring any blessing. The end result of this was that the preacher's group had the exclusive right to recite the Maulidi. Even the sharifs did not read it, since to do so would have required a licensing by the khatibs. The Mahdali group might have accepted this situation, but the Ḥusseini sharifs never would have done so. However, the Mahdali sharifs were ignorant of the Arabic language, and the Ḥusseini sharifs were too involved in trade and already held too much social prestige to be interested in religious participation.

The recitation of this Maulidi was a solemn affair; it was read in a low voice, with everyone sitting quietly in a place corresponding to his social position. If the ruler were present, he sat at the reciter's right hand, with the minister at his left. Next came the old people from each social group, who sat accordingly. Thus this Maulidi was simple and well-organized, and the behavior of the participants highly controlled.

The other Maulidi celebrations however, were quite different. On the mainland the slaves created their own Maulidi, which will be described in the next chapter. The two groups living in Lamu who were not able to use the Maulidi Barzanji were the Wa Yumbili Ponde and the Comoro Island people, and so these two groups celebrated their own Maulidi. Instead of having a private Maulidi, they used to read theirs out in the streets inside their mtaa, with all of the people of the mtaa contributing their efforts. The main street was cleaned and decorated for the occasion. After the last prayer at night, they gathered in their mtaa, sitting on mats spread on the ground, and the oldest person from that mtaa would read the Fatiḥa, burn incense, and bless the Prophet. After finishing, someone might stand and praise the Prophet in Swahili verse which he had prepared especially for the occasion. Another might continue with another verse, also praising the Prophet. This ritual would last for two or three hours. Then, the best poet of the group would stand and describe the world before the Prophet; when he reached the point of the Prophet's birth, all the people would stand up and sing together a Swahili poem welcoming the Prophet's birth. After that, they would sit down again, and the old man who opened the ceremony would read the Fatiḥa and make invocations in Swahili, ending the ritual. This Maulidi was called *Maulidi ya Rama*—the shaking Maulidi.

The Comoro Island people performed this Maulidi, and they invited the Wa Yumbili Ponde to attend, and the Wa Yumbili Ponde reciprocated. Thus the celebration of this Maulidi began to cut across regional boundaries. It also induced competition between the Comoro Islanders and the Wa Yumbili Ponde. For example, if the Comoro Island people held the ceremony and decorated their mtaa in a certain way, the next time the Wa Yumbili Ponde held it they were determined to make better decorations in order to get more praise. The newcomer's group attended both in order to observe and to pass judgment. This competitive attitude was an innovation in a place like Lamu, where everything was prescribed by birth. However, the object or goal of the competition was not to defeat the other group but to gain more praise. Furthermore, each thought the Prophet would be pleased when he saw the elaborate decorations, and if the Prophet were pleased he would bless the audience at the celebration. The participants insisted that during the time when they stood up the Prophet came and attended this Maulidi and looked at those who loved him. This belief expresses the liveliness of the symbol of the Prophet. He was the *sharaf al anam,* the most honored human being, who came to their mtaa and looked on them benevolently. This is why they became emotionally involved. In a highly stratified society such as Lamu, the Maulidi ya Rama and the figure of the sharaf al anam provided the only means through which a low person could give expression to the new society in which he wanted to live. The greatest human being came to their mtaa; even the higher wangwana could not claim that.

The children of the souriyas also attended this Maulidi as observers, and in many cases contributed some of the money for the decorations. They thought that through this they would obtain some blessing. However, because of their position, they were unable to actually join in the Maulidi. Had they done so, they would have lost any claim to being part of the higher wangwana group. The higher wangwana looked down on those who participated in these Maulidi celebrations. They felt this Maulidi to be disorganized; and less worthy of blessing because the participants spoke in Swahili, rather than Arabic, the language honored by God. The loud singing and excited movement of those who participated in this Maulidi was also felt to be inconsistent with the image of quietness which was highly praised as part of the traditional wangwana demeanor. The wangwana used to say "*Mtaratibu hushinda nwenye nguvu,*" "a quiet orderly person usually accomplishes more than a man with strong movements or violence." Quietness, self-control, and the hiding of emotions were all part of the wangwana ethos. But since the Wa Yumbili Ponde and the Comoro Island people had been deprived of the sacred language, the language of the Qur'ān, it seems natural that they would have developed a new language, a language expressing involvement through body movements. When they reached the height of involvement, the participants often cried out or even lost consciousness, and this, from the wangwana point of view, simply proved that the lower people were unable to control themselves.

From the lower social groupings, without a theoretical conscious reflection, a new theology emerged in which the Prophet was the central figure. As we have seen, he was thought of as alive, and given to visiting and blessing. The Prophet was considered above any specific language or descent. Language and descent were the privilege of restricted groups, but love was open to all.

The institutions of the souriya and the Maulidi ya Rama constituted a threat to the established wangwana tradition, and reflected the development of a new world view by the lower wangwana. The development of the new system from the rearrangement of the debris of the traditional one will lead us to the second chapter.

2

The Passing of Traditional Society

Dunia Imezunguka Walo juu hupu moka Mtaya ona mashka Toba tusisahauni Wala musiyadharu Wato tini hendajuu Kwa ulimi sikwaguu Her da Tulewatobani	The world has changed. Do not forget what I told you. Those who were on top came down, those who were down, rose to the top. (If you speak, you will be in trouble. It is better to leave Lamu and go away. We have to repent, let us not forget that. Perhaps, God might accept our pentinence.)

—Ḥamid ibn Sa'id (Lamu poet)

INTRODUCTION

In this chapter, we continue to deal with Lamu's history; however, now we move to relatively recent times, times which are reasonably well-documented. Our aim here is to uncover and analyze some of the organizational changes which had a profound effect on Lamu's traditional system of social stratification, and, as a result, on its political, economic, and religious systems.

LAMU UNDER THE BUSA'ID RULE

The Decline of the Wangwana

As has been said before, Lamu had been in competition with Mombasa for a long time as each tried to extend its power over the coastal towns. However, with the rise of the Mazru'ai family in Mombasa (1741 - 1824 A. D.—1154 - 1240 A.H.)[1] and the success of that family in establishing a pact with the sultan of Patta, Lamu found itself in a very critical position. Now the island was threatened not only from the south but also from the north. Even though the people of Lamu thought they could handle the Mazru'ai soldiers, they knew they could not stand up against a combined army. So, under the leadership of Bwana Zahidi Ngomi, the supreme ruler of Lamu at that time, negotiations began (around 1806) with the BuSa'id sultans of Oman,[2] who were in conflict with the Mazru'ais. As a result of these negotiations, the BuSa'id agreed to supply Lamu with arms and military training. There was one immediate and positive result of this new pressure from Mombasa: Lamu forgot its own internal problems and its people unified against the common enemy.

In 1812, the Mazru'ai and Patta sultanate attacked Lamu from the south, and the people of Lamu went to the defense of their town. However, the attacking force was the stronger and defeated the Lamuans. A slave from the mainland, hearing of the defeat, asked to meet Bwana Zahidi Ngomi and told the leader that he could work magic which would help the Lamuans to defeat the invaders. Everyone scoffed at the idea, but, as Bwana Zahidi Ngomi was an intelligent man, he said to the wangwana, "We have nothing to lose; let him do whatever he wants to do, and then we will see."

The slave got some water and read a magic formula over it. Then he asked Bwana Zahidi Ngomi to give him a drum, and he performed the same operation with it. The slave told the wangwana that he would go before them and splash water on the area occupied by the Mombasa army, and then beat the drum. He told the people of Lamu to attack when they heard the drum. In the morning, the slave was ready. He advanced toward the Mombasa army, and when they saw him coming they thought he was a messenger. When he reached the occupied area, he splashed the water and began to beat upon his drum as planned. The people of Lamu were ready and immediately launched their attack, and the Mombasa army was badly defeated. Nowadays, those who walk on the shore on the southern side of Lamu, which had been occupied by the Mombasa army, will still find fragments of human bone, teeth, or skulls—the last evidence

1. The Mazru'ai family was in and out of power for a long time. Those who know about the changing of alliances on the East African Swahili coast will recognize the difficulty of establishing fixed dates.

2. The BuSa'id family overthrew the Yarubi dynasty in 1741. When this news reached Mombasa, Mohammed ibn Othman al Mazru'ai declared his independence. Then the conflict between the Mazru'ai and the BuSa'id began. The rule of the BuSa'id family over the East African coast lasted until 1964.

of these Mombasa invaders.

As we have said, a historian might well find the story of the slave's spell and his incantations over the water and the drum unacceptable as historical evidence; however, for an anthropologist, the incident is relevant. The mere fact that people still "recall" it is of the utmost importance. First of all, the statement that Lamu's victory was due to a slave's intervention indicates that the wangwana were no longer in control of the situation. Secondly, the incident shows that the slaves were not totally ignorant but had knowledge of *ganga,* or magic, and that this knowledge was considered effective. Thirdly, the story indicates that the wangwana too were threatened, since they felt that the same magic that was effective against Mombasa's army could be used against the wangwana themselves. In other words, the wangwana, who for a long time had preserved their traditional ideology by controlling the educational system, found themselves faced with a new and powerful type of knowledge which they could not control. The wangwana admitted the existence of the slave's knowledge, but they did not admit that it was equal to theirs, and so they had to find a way to explain its effectiveness in the war against the Mazru'ai and Patta sultanate. The handiest explanation was a religious one. Following the distinction made in the Qur'ān between the jin and the angels, the wangwana claimed that while *their* knowledge had been given to them by the angels, the slaves had gotten theirs from the jin. The wangwana claimed that a pact existed between the slaves and the jin; wherever the slaves went, they carried the jin with them. Thus, contrary to what one would expect, the slave's role in the victory over Mombasa did not bring added respect to the slave class, but rather drove the wangwana to be even more conservative in their attitude toward them.

The end result was that the wangwana were threatened not only by Patta and Mombasa but also by their own slaves. So they decided the time had come to seek the protection of the sultan of Oman, who at that time was consolidating his power in East Africa. The sultan, Sayyid Sa'id ibn Sultan al BuSa'id, was more than ready to accept their request. He sent a man to represent him in Lamu, giving him the title of *liwali,* or "governor,"[3] and established a garrison, consisting of Baluchi, Omani, and Muscati soldiers.[4]

These soldiers were not considered to be the social equals of any of the wangwana groups. The Baluchi, in fact, were thought of as a cursed people.

3. This liwali was called Khalaf ibn Nasir.

4. With the rise of the BuSa'id dynasty, Oman began to be divided into two parts: the coastal area, with Muscat as its capital, was under the sultan's rule; the interior, with its capital, Nizwa, was under the imam's rule.

The reason for this, according to the wangwana, was that although the Baluchi had converted to Islam while the Prophet was alive, they had rejected it after a time and returned to their old religion. The Prophet cursed them when he found out about their fickleness, and because of that curse, all the Baluchi, even after returning to Islam, were given tails and for this reason were not allowed to stay inside the town. Thus the Baluchi were not only strangers but also cursed; therefore, their presence inside the town was considered religiously dangerous.

Meanwhile, the liwali, recognizing the factions that existed in his mercenary army, decided to move cautiously. The Baluchi soldiers were considered the most likely to shift their loyalty, while the Omani and Muscati were thought to be more faithful to the sultan. At that time, the real threat was coming once more from the south, from Mombasa. So the liwali placed his more loyal soldiers in the southern parts of the town, in places called Bimanga and Jeneby, while Baluchi soldiers were stationed at Makarani, on the western hills outside the town (see Map 4). This distribution was accepted by the upper wangwana, because it did not necessitate their contact with the sultan's soldiers. The Wa Yumbili Ponde, on the other hand, had extensive contact with the Baluchi, but since the Wa Yumbili Ponde were deprived of any political, religious, or economic rights, they could not protest the presence of their Baluchi neighbors.

The lack of religious unification in the sultan's army was another factor which had to be considered in assigning the soldiers to their posts. The Omani and Muscati soldiers embraced the Ibadi creed,[5] but the Baluchi were Sunnites. The Ibadi and Baluchi beliefs differed in many respects. The Baluchi considered the Ibadi claim that no one could see God face to face to be a heresy; and while the Ibadis insisted that the wrongdoer, Muslim or non-Muslim, would remain eternally in hell, the Baluchi, as Sunnites, believed God's freedom to be unlimited–He could be merciful even to the unbelievers. A wrongdoer, according to man's limited knowledge, might not be considered a wrongdoer by God. For these reasons, the Baluchi regarded the Ibadi as Muslims who had been deluded. At the same time, the Ibadi thought that, although the Baluchi and all other Muslims at most could be called *mwahidin,* or "monotheists," they could never be considered *mu'minun* or "believers."

These theological differences naturally had practical results. For example, the Sunnites thought that personality and political affiliation did not interfere

5. The Ibadi are moderate Kharijites, whose theology was formulated by Abdallah ibn Ibadh, an Iraqi theologian (ca. 661 - 705 A. D.—41 - 87 A. H.). Apparently, the sect was named after him. However, during my field work in Oman (1973), I was told that the name is derived from *abyadh,* which means "white." Therefore, the meaning of *Ibadi* is related to purity, since white indicates purity.

with the performance of the leader of the Jum'a prayer. In other words, even if the leader were unjust or socially corrupt, the people still had to follow him in prayer. Performance of the Jum'a prayer was an absolute duty, and any judgment as to the leader's behavior was Allah's prerogative. Moreover, since the Baluchi soldiers were Sunnites and followed the Hanifite creed, they posed no special orthodoxy problem and were allowed to pray the Jum'a in Lamu's mosque. Although Lamu people were Shafi'ites and not Hanifites, the differences between these two creeds were not significant enough to cause any real difficulty.

But the opposite situation prevailed with the Ibadi creed, whose followers, the Omani and Muscati, were convinced that as true Muslims they should not pray under the direction of an unjust leader who should be deposed. Indeed, the Ibadis made the fighting of the unjust leader the sixth pillar of Islam. Moreover, the Friday prayer, which was an obligatory and essential collective ritual for the Sunnites, was not so for the Ibadis. According to their creed, the Friday prayer was obligatory only in the places assigned to it by the Prophet and the first and second caliphs. Lamu was not such a place, and therefore the Ibadis were to pray individually, an ordinary *dhuhr*, or midday prayer, without all the ritual accompanying the Friday prayer. Because of such differences in ritual, the liwali, who was himself an Ibadi, decided that it was better to keep his Ibadi soldiers outside of town, and so he built them a mosque outside in a place called Darajani (see Map 4).

The wangwana were able to remain isolated from contact with the soldiers, using as an excuse either religious differences, or an old "curse" such as the Baluchi one. However, they were not able to exclude the liwali. The location of the ruler's quarter had nothing to do with religious differences, and, according to tradition, the ruler lived in Vyumbe. So, the liwali had to be given a house in that area, though he was not allowed to marry from the Wa Yumbili Pembe; he was forced to bring his wives from Oman, just as the Ibadi soldiers did.

As the supreme ruler, the liwali took into his hands most of the authority which traditionally belonged to the Wa Yumbili Pembe. All decisions had to be finalized by him and executed not by the newcomers but by the head of the garrison. The liwali did consult the representatives of the Wa Yumbili Pembe and the newcomers, but this was no more than a formal courtesy. In other words, the old political power shifted from the wangwana's hands to those of the liwali; the wangwana lost their decision-making and executive power. Nevertheless, the BuSa'id liwalis did maintain the outer form of the old system; the Wa Yumbili Pembe continued to elect a supreme ruler from among themselves every three years, and the newcomers continued to elect a minister every year, but the liwali used them only as consultants. By the mid-nineteenth century, the Wa Yumbili Pembe were no longer on top of the political system. Now the system was headed by the sultan of Oman, followed by the liwali, then the *jemadar,* or head of the sultan's garrison, and then the wangwana.

The sultan of Oman naturally treated Lamu as a part of his larger domain, and he attached greater importance to the welfare of the whole than to the welfare of the wangwana alone. In other words, in return for protection, Lamu had to conform to the sultan's policy regardless of the consequences for the wangwana. Still, the wangwana were in a better position than they had been before the arrival of the liwali—at least as long as the struggle between the sultan of Oman and the rulers of Mombasa continued. For, if things got too bad, it was at least theoretically possible for the wangwana to ask the Mombasa Mazru'ai rulers to help them against the sultan. The chance of using this leverage was lost, however, when the sultan subdued Mombasa in 1835.

By 1840, the sultan of Oman had moved his capital from Muscat to Zanzibar, and the Lamu wangwana realized that they had truly lost their independence. Mombasa, furthermore, was found to be a more suitable base for the sultan's army, so he transferred the Omani and Muscati soldiers there, leaving only the Baluchi in Lamu.

But relations between the liwali and the head of the Baluchi garrison were bad. The Baluchi, as Sunnites, did not accept the liwali's claim that he represented the imam of the Ibadi or the sultan. Unlike the Ibadi soldiers, the Baluchi had no religious loyalty toward the imam. For them all Ibadis, including the liwali, were Kharijites, who had rebelled against the Islamic caliphs and Islamic authority. In turn, as we have seen, the liwali classified the Baluchi and the people of Lamu alike as monotheists but not believers. These religious and ideological differences were later used by the wangwana to play the Baluchi off against the liwali, and vice versa. Although the difference in creed between the wangwana (who were Shafi'ites) and the Baluchi (who were Hanifites) was only a minor one, it was nevertheless used by the wangwana to keep themselves distinct from the Baluchi. Therefore, the wangwana could, according to their own interest, identify themselves with the Baluchi as Sunnites, or keep themselves distinct as Shafi'ites. In other words, they could shift loyalty as they determined their prospects for maximum gain. Thus the difference between creeds formed the playing field for the wangwana political game.

On the other hand, the liwali found that the wangwana system of stratification could be used as a tool for his own political advantage. Through manipulating the newcomers, the liwali thought that he could affect the status of the Wa Yumbili Ngombe, the custodians of Islam in Lamu, because these groups were related through marriage. As we have seen, the upper social strata in Lamu claimed Arab origins, a fact that the liwalis took advantage of in their effort to get them to take an Arab tribal name connecting them with his own group. Names were adopted by the different existing vitumba, or units. Thus we find one branch of the newcomers calling itself *al Bakri,* another *al Jahadhmi.* Both claimed they came from Oman or Muscat and that they were descended from Joktan; thus they wanted to strengthen their relation with the BuSa'id, who had come from the same area and were also descended from Joktan. This choice of names is of great significance for our understanding of the social situation in Lamu at this time.

The newcomers' claim to be related to the BuSa'id was advantageous for them, but it would never have suited the Wa Yumbili Ngombe. It should be remembered that the religious authorities in Lamu came from the Wa Yumbili Ngombe, and so this group was automatically opposed to the BuSa'id, who followed an opposing creed. The Wa Yumbili Ngombe, therefore, chose the Arab name *al Ma'awi,* claiming to be descendants of Ma'awiya ibn abi Sufian (661 - 680 A. D.—41 - 61 A. H.). There were two reasons for the choice of that particular ancestor: it indicated first that the Wa Yumbili Ngombe were descendants of the first Islamic rulers, the Umayyad dynasty, and second, that they were related to the Adnani, rather than the Joktani, branch of the Arabs, the same branch to which the Prophet belonged. Another advantage to the choice lay in the fact that Ma'awiya ibn abi Sufian was held in particularly low repute by the Ibadis; in fact, they thought he surely had been condemned to hell. So by placing him in a high position and claiming descent from him, the Wa Yumbili Ngombe clearly distinguished themselves from the Ibadis.[6]

In studying a place like Lamu, the anthropologist has to be able to understand the historical connotations of names and to realize that genealogical claims were usually made to express certain symbolically crucial historical relations. By choosing a particular name, one group tried to communicate certain messages to the other groups. Thus the Ma'awi group (the former Wa Yumbili Ngombe) was communicating that it wanted no role in the traditional political system of Lamu and wanted only to continue in its position of religious authority.

6. The division between Joktan and Adnan is not particular to Lamu. In Oman itself the Joktan (mostly Ibadi) are called *Hinawi,* while the Adnan (mostly Sunnites) are called *Ghafiri.*

It is interesting at this point to take a look at the stand of the Wa Yumbili Pembe. This group, as was said before, was divided into three parts, the most important subdivision being the Wangwana Wa Yumbe. Perceiving that al Bakri and al Jahadhmi claimed to be the descendants of Joktan and that their resulting alliance with the BuSa'id would upset the traditional division of authority in Lamu, the Wangwana Wa Yumbe developed a new tactic. Their historians began to claim that their real name was *al Makhzumi,* and that they were called by that name because they were the descendants of Khuzaima. Khuzaima was higher than Huzeil, the father of al Ma'awi. Both Khuzaima and Huzeil were sons of Mudrika, son of Ilias, who was in turn directly related to Adnan (see Fig. 2). The Prophet's genealogical relation to Khuzaima is more direct.

Thus, when the various social groups in Lamu began reinforcing their claim to Arabic ancestry by adopting Arab names, a major shift in social stratification was apparent. Al Ma'awi (the Wa Yumbili Ngombe) and al Makhzumi (the most important subdivision of the Wa Yumbili Pembe) came together under the banner of Adnan, and thus were both to be honored because they claimed descent from the same branch of the Arabs that produced the Prophet. On the other hand, the newcomers called themselves al Bakri or al Jahadhmi. They therefore aligned themselves with the Joktan, rather than the Adnan, side of the Arabs, and thus, at the same time, with the BuSa'id. Their position had to be respected too—but for other reasons. As we have seen, the liwali, the most powerful political figure in Lamu at that time, was BuSa'id. However, power is not the same thing as honor, and Adnan was considered more worthy of honor than Joktan. Thus, al Makhzumi and al Ma'awi were able to claim a higher position in the social hierarchy than the others.

Surprisingly enough, the two other subdivisions of the Wa Yumbili Pembe were not included as equals. The Wa Famao began to shift more toward the BuSa'id, an attitude expalined by the local historians in the following way: They said that Huzeil, the brother of Khuzaima, had another child besides 'Omairah, and he called him Qurish. Qurish was not as good as his brother 'Omairah and his father drove him out. So the delinquent son went to Yemen, where he tried to convince the Yemeni people to attack Mecca, and destroy the *Ka'aba,* the sacred Islamic shrine. However, the Yemeni rulers did not care for his ideas and so they arrested him and his relatives. Qurish succeeded in escaping and went to a Yemeni village called Famia. Those who lived there were called Famao. The Yemeni ruler did not punish the Famao for sheltering Qurish but forgave them and told them to go to East Africa. They came to Lamu. By attributing this history to the Famao subdivision of the Wa Yumbili Pembe, the second division, the Wangwana Wa Yumbe, separated itself from them and gave

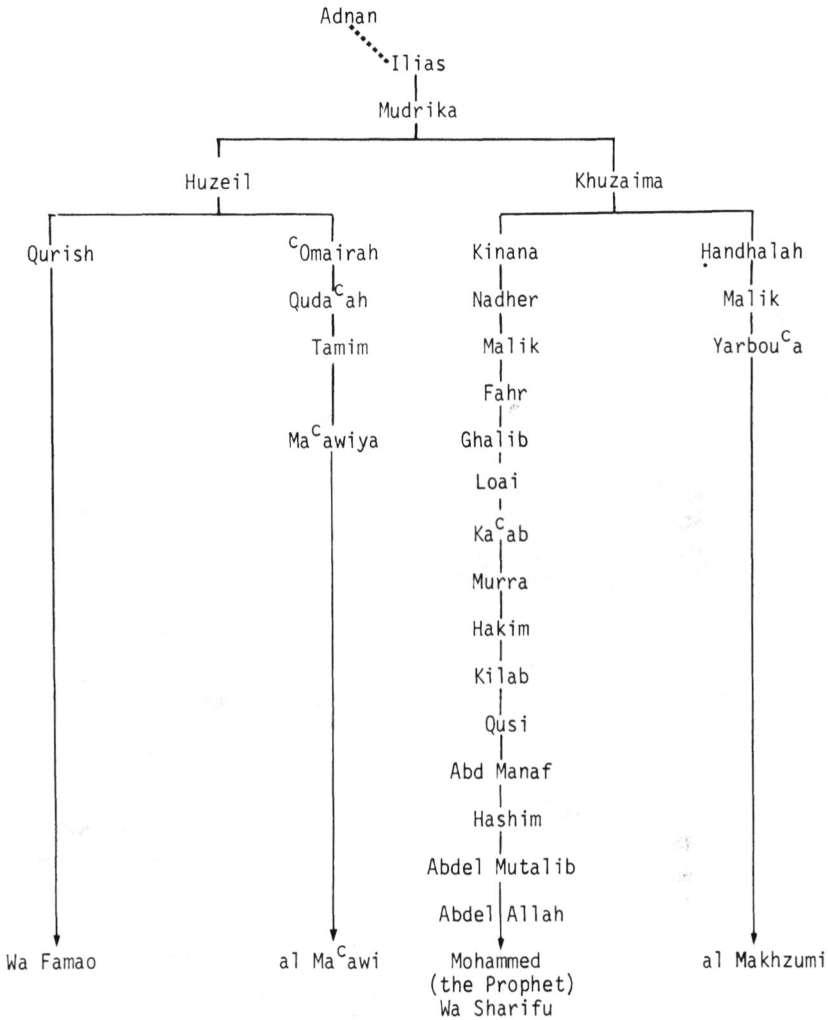

Fig. 2. The Use of Arab Pedrigree in Lamu

substance to its claim that the Famao were the unloyal brothers of the Ma'awi. The Famao were also faulted for being unloyal to the Ka'aba, which was respected by all the descendants of Adnan. In this way history was used to account for the political decline of one branch of the Wa Yumbili Pembe. If they were found unfaithful then, in 1850, it was because they had been unfaithful in the past.

The Kinamte, the third division of the Wa Yumbili Pembe, were considered even worse. They were not Arabs at all.[7] They were said to have come from India. The Kinamte were supposed to have introduced the coconut tree, and since the coconut tree, so the historians thought, could not have come from Arabia but must have come from India, the Kinamte must have an Indian, not an Arab origin.

In conclusion: The BuSa'id presence in Lamu and their political policy contributed to the disintegration of the old, strict stratificatory system, which was based on the assumption that those who constituted one group were by definition equal. By the middle of the nineteenth century, the traditional social patterns in Lamu had undergone a significant reordering (see Fig. 3).

The Basis of the New Stratification

The new system of stratification was not based on power as the old ones had been, although those who were defeated in the original war, i.e., the Wa Yumbili Ponde, still occupied the lowest position. Status now depended primarily on which of the two branches of the Arabs, Adnan or Joktan, the groups claimed as forebears. The Makhzumi—which consisted of three subgroups, the Ba Sheikh, the Bereki, and the Miraji—considered themselves equal to the sharifs because both of them had descended from Khuzaima on the Adnan side. The Ma'awi were considered below the Makhzumi because their common ancestor, Mudrika, father of Khuzaima and Huzeil, was more removed, from the Prophet's line. The Wa Famao position was ambiguous in the new system. They were equal to the al Ma'awi, yet their new alliance with the BuSa'id and their ancestor's disloyalty put them a little below their supposed equals. The BuSa'id, al Bakri, and al Jahadhmi were considered equal, and the inclusion of the Kinamte in this same category is interesting. The unification of the Kinamte, the BuSa'id, and the former newcomers under the Joktan half of the Arabs had the effect of making them all "strangers." In other words, Lamu considered the only real Arabs to be those who came from Adnan; those who came from Joktan, on the

7. This interpretation of the origin of the Wa Yumbili Pembe was written by a man from the Ma'awi group, called Fadhil ibn Omar al Bauri. It is not dated. However, judging from the events, I can say that it is about seventy years old.

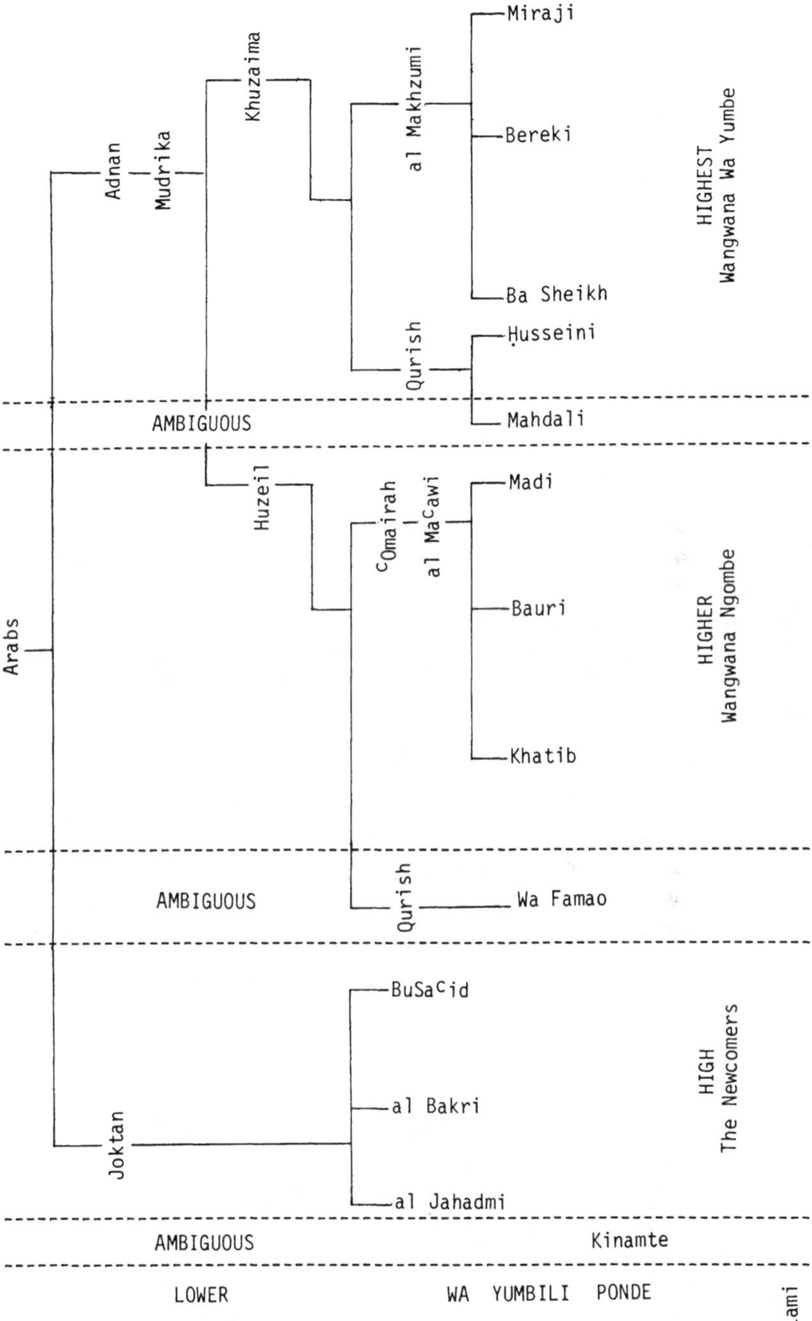

Fig. 3. The Reconstruction of the Old Social Categories

other hand, were considered strangers and unequal to the Adnani Arabs.

This reshuffling of the social groupings created problems, and especially in the field of marriage. The Wa Famao and Kinamte formed, along with the Makhzumi, an endogamous group—the Wa Yumbili Pembe. Although all the members of the group had once been considered equal, now the former two elements declined in status while the sharifs were raised up to a position equal to the Makhzumi, the old Wangwana Wa Yumbe. However, as was said before, the Ḥusseini sharifs took wives from the Kinamte, and the Mahdali sharifs took theirs from the al Khatib. Marriage ties, whether recent or long-standing, created permanent bonds between groups which can be seen clearly in the ritual called *mtanga moja,* or "observing the mourning period together." A group tied together by real and proper marriages, that is marriages between equals, shared the experience of mourning. For example, since the grandmother of the existing Ḥusseini sharifs was from the Kinamte, until now, when one of the Kinamte died, the Ḥusseini sharifs had observed the mourning period, attended the funeral, and served during the recitation of the Qur'ān. Their wives had to be secluded for three days following the death, and were not allowed to use perfumes.

In addition to the mtanga moja, there is another reciprocal mourning arrangement called *kustahi mtanga.* If, for example, the Kinamte group had marriage ties with the Wa Famao, the Kinamte were obliged to observe the rules of the mtanga moja when one of the Wa Famao died. The Ḥusseini, however, who were related to the Kinamte directly, but to the Wa Famao only indirectly, would observe the more limited rules of kustahi mtanga. Kustahi mtanga was based on the idea of showing respect for the feelings of a related group. Thus, the wives of those who observed the kustahi mtanga could go out and visit, but they were not allowed to laugh loudly or to have music in their houses. Meanwhile the men tried to pretend that they were sad. In general, the difference between mtanga moja and kustahi mtanga is the difference between being sad and acting *as if* one were sad.

Institutions such as the mtanga moja and the kustahi mtanga indicate that, while there was a major reshuffling of social groups, the old stratificatory system, based on the principle of equal marriage, continued to exert an influence. Such traditions were not easy to eliminate. However, as the shuffling was accepted and the mtanga moja was adjusted to the new relationships, new possibilities emerged for the so-called equal marriage. The result was ambiguity. For example, the grandfather of the Ḥusseini was either too low to have married a Kinamte woman (according to the old order), or he broke the principle of equality by marrying downward to a Kinamte woman, making it necessary for his children to have to marry downward (according to the new order). The problem could not be solved.

The Wangwana Wa Yumbe, after losing the Kinamte and the Wa Famao as equals, and after losing the executive power to the al Bakri and al Jahadhmi, were unable to obtain any consensus about their position, even from their own historians.

Thus the Wangwana Wa Yumbe, or the Makhzumi, had lost the traditional power on which they based their claim of superiority. Everyone recognized that the real power had shifted to the hands of the BuSa'id. And, as the wangwana proverb says, "*Mnyinga kupata haki ni mwenye nguvu kupenda,*" "the weak person gets his rights only when a strong person backs him or agrees with him." Although no one agreed with the Makhzumi claims to superiority, these claims were perpetuated among the group; the living Makhzumi still speak of Lamu's stratificatory system as if they still retained their former power. Nevertheless, in raising doubts about the old system, the slanted Makhzumi version of history made at least a negative contribution. Makhzumi historians established, for example, that the Kinamte were a lower and non-Arab group, while the Famao were the descendants of a cursed Arab. Also, they planted the suggestion that the BuSa'id, who were then considered the ultimate in Astarabu, were really not equal to the Adnani Arabs.

The BuSa'id and the Principle of Equal Marriage

The BuSa'id remained separate and apart in Lamu as long as Zanzibar was powerful. They had their own mosque and their own burial place, and they even brought their wives from Zanzibar. Some of them, however, wanted to make Lamu their home, but this was not feasible, since the people of Lamu could not marry their daughters to the BuSa'id or take their women as wives because of the religious difference. But when Zanzibar started to lose power and the sultan was no longer the effective ruler of the dominion,[8] the BuSa'id in Lamu began to adopt some of Lamu's customs. They realized that they had to convince the people of Lamu that they were part of the wangwana. At the same time, their Ibadi ideology was weakening. The sultan of Zanzibar, whom they honored as the imam of the Ibadi, was no different from the Ottoman caliph; both were unjust and corrupt. The religious zeal which the old Ibadis had, was lost. So the BuSa'id began to move more and more toward

8. For example, in 1873, the British threatened Sultan Barghash of Zanzibar, and under the threat he signed a decree outlawing the slave trade throughout his dominion. At the same time, a Christian cathedral was built on the site of the slave market in Zanzibar.

the Sunnite creed.

In 1883, the liwali decided that his son should take a wife from the Lamuans. The BuSa'id, of course, thought of themselves as the best Arabs; so, the liwali approached the Ḥusseini sharif family (the highest in rank in Lamu), asking for one of their daughters. But the Ḥusseini, and other groups as well, refused to give a wife to the liwali's son on the grounds that he was not a correct Muslim. The 'ulama were consulted, and they made a formal religious judgment, or Fatwa, that the Ibadis were in fact not correct Muslims. The wangwana thought that this would settle the matter; however, the liwali told them that he and his family would like to change from the Ibadi to the Sunnite and Shafi'ite creed. As the story was told to me, the wangwana were caught; they had given religion as the reason for their refusal, and now that this was no longer to be an issue, they could not switch their position and tell the liwali that he was not their equal; they had to agree. And so the liwali and his family changed their creed.

However, when the marriage was about to take place, a new problem arose. The Ḥusseini, as part of the wangwana, were to use Lamu's brass horn, the siwa, in declaring their marriage, but the wangwana custom was that the siwa of Lamu was to be blown only for equal marriages. Blowing it was a symbolic way of declaring wangwana consent to the marriage. In the case of the Ḥusseini girl marrying a BuSa'id, was the horn to be used or not? There was also another obstacle, which involved the Silwa, the book kept by the preachers of the Jum'a Mosque in which all equal marriages had to be registered, Were the BuSa'id really equal to the Ḥusseinis? Since the BuSa'id were not part of Lamu's traditional groups, the khatib who kept the book had to express his own opinion, which was fast and clear. Following the wangwana principle that the learned men should avoid causing any civil strife, the preacher decided that the BuSa'id should be declared equal to the Ḥusseinis. Two of the Makhzumi subgroups refused to accept that opinion, while the Miraji felt that the other two subgroups had no right to stop the BuSa'id from blowing the siwa. The Wa Famao and Kinamte groups, recalling their old associations with the Wa Yumbili Pembe, backed the Miraji subgroup. The Mahdali sharifs backed the Ḥusseini, and the learned men backed the khatibs. The two subgroups of the Makhzumi then found themselves completely without support, and so they too yielded. The marriage took place; the horn was blown, and the BuSa'id were accepted as equal to the Ḥusseini, the most prestigious Arabs in Lamu.

The BuSa'id issue was a hard blow for the Makhzumi group, It not only indicated that their historians had failed to establish them at the top of the social hierarchy, but it also contributed to division from within. It caused one subgroup, the Miraji, to split from the Makhzumi. Moreover, as a result of this issue, the khatibs revolted against traditional authority for the first time. In the past, they would have supported the Wa Yumbili Pembe; the BuSa'id case was the first issue in which the preachers took a different stance. Furthermore, the debate over BuSa'id status provided an opportunity for the Wa Famao and Kinamte to reinforce their claim to be authentic parts of the Wa Yumbili Pembe. Finally, the acceptance of the BuSa'id as equal to the Wa Yumbili Pembe raised their allies, the al Jahadhmi and al Bakri, along with them.

The second marriage between the BuSa'id and the people of Lamu was between the al Jahadhmi and the BuSa'id. The khatibs took the same stand as before the horn was blown, and the marriage was accepted as correct. Thus the al Jahadhmi were firmly established as equals of the Wa Yumbili Pembe. The end result of all this was that Lamu's complex social stratification was gradually being simplified into only two levels. There were the high and powerful (although not equally powerful) and the low. The low stratum contained, as before, the Wa Yumbili Ponde and the slaves. And, as before, between these two strata were the children of the souriya.

The Baluchi and Social Stratification

The Baluchi soldiers, who, it will be remembered, came to Lamu with the first liwali, lived in the hills behind the town in a place called Makarani and were Muslims whose creed was not significantly different from that of the people of Lamu. The Lamuans called the Baluchi *Bwana Ouya,* i.e., the "little" or "few masters," a name with a political meaning. Since the Baluchi were directly under the liwali, the ruler of Lamu, the *jemadar*, or head of the Baluchi, was known as little master. The Baluchi were confined to Makarani, and none of the other Lamu groups would either give them wives or take wives from them. As a result the Baluchi bought slave girls and kept them as souriyas.

As the idea of adopting Arab names took hold, the Baluchi found a way to improve their lot. They began to use the name of al Ma'awi and, like the khatibs, claimed that they were the descendants of Ma'awiya ibn abi Sufian. This, of course, upset the al Ma'awi group of the Wa Yumbili Ngombe. However, as long as no one from the Lamu wangwana would give wives to the Baluchi, the Wa Yumbili Ngombe thought that the Baluchi claim would die out.

The opportunity the Baluchi were waiting for came in 1885, when the sultan of Witu,[9] backed by the Germans, began to threaten Lamu, Patta, and other

9. I will deal with him later.

parts of the sultan of Zanzibar's dominions. The sultan needed the services of the Baluchi to pacify Witu, and they agreed to help on the condition that their head be given a wife from the wangwana.

The Baluchi head asked to marry the girl whose father was a BuSa'id and mother was a Ḥusseini. The BuSa'id liwali and the Ḥusseini and Kinamte were all in opposition to the marriage. But the Baluchi insisted, and the liwali was caught because the Baluchi would make no move to defend Lamu unless the marriage was performed. The al Ma'awi and the khatibs were equally opposed to the Baluchi demand. So the liwali and the Ḥusseini decided to contact the sultan of Zanzibar and inform him about the matter, thinking that as an Arab, he, too, would refuse to approve. They told the sultan that the head of the Baluchi wanted to marry a BuSa'id–Ḥusseini girl, claiming that because he was also of Arab origin he was equal to the girl. The sultan, needing the Baluchi's help, sent back an answer in favor of the Baluchi. The wangwana resented this tremendously. However, since the liwali realized that the political situation was deteriorating fast, and that the sultan of Witu could invade Lamu at any time, he consented to let his daughter marry the Baluchi leader.

The khatibs refused to record the marriage because, in their view, the spouses were not equal. But the Baluchi demanded that it be recorded, and moreover that the siwa be blown. The liwali, as the supreme ruler, bowed to both demands. The al Ma'awi asked the preacher to refuse. However, the preacher retreated and claimed that, as learned man, he and his family had no right to cause disorder and, therefore, had to obey the liwali. The Ba-Sheikh, revenging the other wangwana groups who refused to back them against the BuSa'id marriage, agreed to blow the horn. The Baluchi leader was married to the BuSa'id girl, and all the wangwana symbols were used in his marriage. The Bwana Ouya name was dropped, and now the Baluchi, as a whole, were known by the name of al Ma'awi. As a result, certain parts of the Wa Yumbili Ngombe refused to remain affiliated with the al Ma'awi category, and so dropped al Ma'awi from their names and began to call themselves *al Bauri* and *al Madi.* Thus the old al Ma'awi category came to consist of al Khatib and the old Bwana Ouya, the Baluchi.

However, the Baluchi use of the name al Ma'awi confused the stratificatory system more than before. By definition, the al Ma'awi were not equal to the Wa Yumbili Pembe, or Makhzumi, so, according to the principle of equal marriage, the al Ma'awi could not marry from the Makhzumi. In other words, the *name* chosen by the Baluchi denoted a category lower than the one from which their leader first married. For the wangwana to accept this was the last blow against the old stratificatory system. The new al Ma'awi had to share all the responsibilities and duties of the group from which they married. For example, if someone died from the BuSa'id, then the al Ma'awi had to share grief with the BuSa'id and observe mtanga moja, while if someone died from the al Ḥusseini, the al Ma'awi observed kustahi mtanga.

Having established their claims to social position, the al Ma'awi (Baluchi) left the hills, and moved into different wangwana areas, such as Mkomani proper, Mtamwini, and Kinoni. The areas of the town which had previously been assigned according to the status of the group began to lose their exclusiveness. The al Bauri, for example, moved out of Mkomani proper and were scattered, and the same thing happened to the al Madi. The structure of the town was changing fast. The old system was now the fond memory of the old people, and they realized that there was nothing to be done to stop Lamu from sinking and dying. As an old man told me, "*Cha kuvunda hakina rubani,*" "If the boat is ordained to sink, the best captain cannot save it."

The new al Ma'awi group was naturally not committed to the old ideology of stratification which the wangwana were trying so hard to maintain. The sole aim of the al Ma'awi was to establish their claim as Arabs, so they could get rid of the stigma concerning their curse. As soon as they had done that, they began to marry the children of the souriyas, who had an ambiguous status. This created another problem. We have already seen that the children of the souriyas had wangwana fathers but slave mothers. The parents were not equal, and therefore these children were not even considered equal to their half brothers, who had been born of equal spouses. Acceptance of the al Ma'awi, who were themselves children of souriyas, as wangwana, strengthened the claim of all souriya children that they, too, should be treated as wangwana.

On the other hand, the Wa Yumbili Ponde, the lowest group, began to argue that they, as the first settlers in Lamu, should be called *al Lami.* They claimed that they were the descendants of Ḥatim al Ta'i[10] and that they were originally from the tribe *al Ta'i*, which descends from Joktan. In other words, they claimed they were related to the BuSa'id, and for this reason they stopped

10. The well-known poet Ḥatim al Ta'i made his tribe very famous because of his generosity. In Arabic, if someone wants to deṣcribe a person as extremely generous, he calls him "*Ḥatimi*," which means he is as generous as Ḥatim al Ta'i. It is interesting to add here that the Ta'i tribe is part of the Joktan division. See 'Abdel Raḥman ibn Ḥamad al Mughiri, *Al Muntakhab fi Nasab Qaba' il al 'Arab* [The chosen description of Arab tribal genealogies] (Damascus: Islamic Office of Printing and Publishing, 1965), pp. 130–36.

performing their traditional duties of street sweeping and corpse washing. They denied the wangwana claim that they had been defeated. In fact, they began to accuse the Makhzumi of having cheated their fathers by breaking their promise to negotiate without arms. They laid all of Lamu's misfortunes at the doorstep of the high wangwana. They even argued that all the present trouble was due to their having mistreated the al Lami: that it was God's revenge. The high wangwana were seen as sinners badly in need of repentance, who wanted to maintain not only what was bad but also what was sinful.

However, the old system still had the backing and support of some influential people—the learned people, the 'ulama, and the khatibs—all of whom were part of the wangwana. If the wangwana were sinners, then the learned people were also, and as a matter of fact they did become suspect. The very ideological basis of society as represented in Lamu by the learned people was tottering. The former corporate unity, where each group had its own quarter of the town and each had certain occupations assigned to it, had ceased to exist.

THE IDEOLOGICAL BASIS OF THE WANGWANA SYSTEM

Under the old system, control of education and the marriage rules—especially the rule that only equals can marry—was used to bring harmony and stability to Lamu society. In this way, the groups kept themselves distinct from one another. Authority and power were strictly controlled by the Wa Yumbili Pembe. Even though religious and executive authority were vested in other groups, in the final analysis these groups depended on the Wa Yumbili Pembe for recognition of their authority. The location of different groups in different areas was further reinforced by the educational system, in which instruction was given according to status.

The Distribution of Hishima

In the traditional system the higher wangwana, in addition to controlling the educational system, also controlled the distribution of *hishima.* Some authors in the past have translated hishima as "respect," but I think this translation is inadequate. Hishima is not only respect, or even honor; it also involves *the maintenance of the position in which respect or honor is due.* In Lamu, a person's position in the stratificatory system was determined by the category to which he belonged, and so every individual had to respect the boundaries of his own position by behaving in the way expected of members of his particular stratum. If a man from a lower stratum were to dress in a big turban and put on a *johos,* or woolen dress—the dress of the BuSa'id—or carry a sword, people would laugh at him. It is as their proverb says: "*Hupija kiemba mutaku wazi,*" "he who puts on the turban—i.e., tries to imitate the Arabs—is not proper or correct because this is behavior not expected from his category." Therefore, in his everyday interactions the individual had to bear in mind that he was acting not as an individual but as a representative of a whole social group. This required him to take considerable pains to preserve hishima and guarantee against its loss.

Members of the higher categories or groups could lose their hishima if they behaved like the lower people, or even treated one of them as an equal. The higher categories also had to keep a distance, even in physical contacts. For example, they did not shake hands with the lower people. If it should happen that a higher person gave his hand to a lower person, the hishima dictated that the lower person must kiss the proffered hand. The way in which the lower person received the higher person's hand was important: the higher person would raise his hand up and then drop it down; the lower person would bow slightly and receive the hand with the palms of his two hands put together, then lower his face to kiss the higher man's hand. If a lower man met an elderly higher person, he had to say "*Shikamu*," which is an abbreviation of "*Nashika miguu yako*," "I hold your feet as a mark of respect." If the higher person established a friendship with a lower person, and spoke to him *as if* he were an equal, then the higher person was behaving against hishima. "*Mfuatana naamwuzi hunuka vumba*," "If a higher man makes a bad [lower] man his friend, then he will be like him." The higher person keeps his hishima only when he acts like a higher person; the lower person keeps his when he acts like a lower person.

Women and the Concept of Hishima

As we saw earlier, the traditional wangwana family was clustered around the father, who had certain rights inside the *numba serkali*, or household. All the persons who lived in one household had to accept the authority of the head of that household. Outside the household, all the married children and their wives and the unmarried children had to behave in the way expected of their category—their behavior had to be in accordance with the rules of hishima. In other words, the young husbands and their wives were to imitate the behavior of the head of the household. If any member of the household deviated from the expected behavior patterns, the head of the household was blamed, and it was he who took action against the wrongdoer. At times offenders were actually expelled from the the household.

However, since the whole household was established on the principle of marriage between equals, even if the head of the household were married to more than one wife, all would be equal to him and thus to each other. Similarly, their children would be equals. This greatly simplified matters, for the same behavior was expected for all members of the household. All members were to respect all the wives of the head of the household, not only because they were married to the head, but also because they came from the categories which tradition dictated should be respected. This was the main hishima principle. Inside the household, the wives of the head might hate (*mashingu*) each other, but they would never show it openly. Being equal to each other, each wife had to care (*kutunga*) for the other. Any dislike had to be not only suppressed but also removed from the heart of the wives; otherwise, they believed, their angels would count it against them. Mashingu was considered more defiling than a dog.[11] Above all, the wives had to keep their husbands out of their quarrels, because if one wife told stories about another, this would cause agitation, and that was condemned by God and considered more harmful than killing a Muslim. So, even if one of the wives knew that the other wife was doing something wrong, she had no right to tell her husband. A whole household would be defiled if mashingu persisted within it. The husband's business would suffer, and he would not be able to keep his wives. Thus, relations between the wives had to be governed by love and respect, if they wanted their household to be blessed.

Inside the household, the first wife was considered to be the head of the younger women. It was she who was supposed to put an end to any misunderstanding which might arise among the wives. She was also the one who divided up the common work in the courtyard. All the wives and the younger women had to respect her and obey her orders. It was her job to see that the women in the household behaved in the expected way. "The Utendi of Mwana Kupona"[12] clearly expresses these values and norms:

> 1. Further, my child, learn how to behave before people of *rank*. When you see them at any place hasten to pay them respect.
> 2. Do not associate with slaves, except during household affairs; they will draw you into disgrace, as perhaps I have told you.
> 3. Go not about with foolish people, who know not how to control themselves; as to persons who are immodest, avoid any contact with them.
> 4. Whenever you see friends, who are *your equals by birth,* if they bid you welcome, hasten to visit them.

11. It is said in Lamu that one day the Prophet found a dog and he brought it to his house. Gabriel, the archangel, refused to enter the Prophet's house, because it was defiled by the dog.

12. "Utendi wa Mwana Kupona" [The advice of Mwana Kupona upon the wifely duty]. See Lyndon Harries (ed. and trans.), *Swahili Poetry* (Oxford: Clarendon Press, 1968); emphasis mine.

Kupona's rules reflect hishima and kutunga principles. As was said before, hishima involved the maintenance of the position in which respect or honor is due: in other words, behavior in a way befitting the position acquired by birth. Kutunga, on the other hand, expressed the necessity of caring for other categories, regardless of their position. Thus, hishima, which keeps the categories distinct and society stable, was balanced by kutunga, which holds the categories together and makes society whole.

The children born in a traditional Lamuan household would be trained not only to respect the members of higher categories and to care for their equals but also to avoid quarreling with their brothers and to obey their stepmothers. A child was to be quiet in the presence of his father and mother. He had to learn to wash himself and to control his hunger and not let it show. This training, which was called *adabu,* or "manners," was considered the mother's duty, and the father did not interfere. The people of Lamu say, "*Aso jundwa na mamaye hufundwa na ulimwengu,*" "[he] who is not taught by his mother will be taught by the world." Since the world does not have the mercy of the mother, this proverb implies that a neglected child will suffer and learn the hard way. Thus, although the child learned from his father the proper respectful behavior of his category toward other people and groups, he learned from his mother the specific rules for manners or polite behavior. Hishima and kutunga were distinguished from adabu, yet all three were needed if a child was to become part of *Astarabu*, or "civilization."

Good manners were considered a reasonable goal for the wangwana categories. However, this was a goal that the lower group had little chance of achieving. Trained in a deprived group, the women did not have the education and economic means to advance more than a short way toward this goal. Nor did the women of the lower group have the time to train their children, because they could not afford slave girls to look after the household. Indeed, they were actually ignorant of adabu because their contact was limited to those who were as low as themselves. In other words, adabu went hand in hand with the principle of marriage between equals. The people closest to the ideal of adabu were from the highest social stratum, and the principle of marriage among equals meant that it remained that way.

Because of her role in the education of the child, the mother was considered very important. A Lamuan child was taught that the mother was the first teacher, and that if it were not for her, he would behave like the *Wa Shenzi,*[13] the uncivilized non-wangwana. The child had to please and satisfy his mother

13. *Wa Shenzi* (plural), *mshenzi* (singular).

(*ridha*); the relations between mother and child were established on the basis of sympathy and consideration (*huruma, kite*). The Lamuans believed that though a mother might mistreat her children, if she died displeased with one of them, that child would never go to paradise.[14]

The child also had to please and satisfy his father. However, the father was not as sympathetic and considerate as the mother; he was not thought of as having the huruma or kite of the mother. If a father became displeased with one of his children, he would never forgive him. The wangwana used to say: "*Radhiya mama hu rudi. Radhiya baba hi rudi*," "You can regain the mother's approbation but you cannot regain that of the father." Because of this the father's dissatisfaction was not condemned as much as the mother's. However, because it could not be regained, the child had to be more careful not to lose his father's approval. The child who lost his father's or mother's approval was assumed to be without manners. This is an interesting judgment for it indicates that he was not well trained as a child, and therefore that in the final analysis it was his mother who was responsible for his deficiencies.

Status and Hishima

Sailors were considered low in the stratificatory system of Lamu because they were accustomed to raising their voices, which a high-ranking man was never to do. He had to speak slowly and in a very low tone, to listen most of the time, and then, when he did speak, to take care not to offend the listener.

The higher persons in Lamu were not allowed to work under any supervision. For example, they could not work as *mgema,* or coconut cutters, because it was the custom of the owners to supervise their cutters, and the implication that the owner might not trust the cutters would be an insult to a person of status. It would not be fitting for the cutter to be directed to "cut this" or "cut that" by the owner standing below.

Higher persons could not work as clerks either, because in such a position they would also have to be under the authority of another person and would have to take orders and obey them. Strangely enough, this is why the high strata never produced a *mu'azin,* or the man who calls for prayer. The mu'azin had to be ordered to call for prayer by the imam, the man who led the prayer. Furthermore, the mu'azin called in a loud voice from the roof of the mosque. All of this made his occupation as unacceptable as that of the mgema. In fact, one

14. They establish this on the prophet's saying, "Paradise is under the feet of the mothers." The local interpretation is that the entry to paradise depends on the mothers' ridha.

of the mosques of the high wangwana supposedly abolished the call for prayer on the grounds that they knew the time and did not need to be reminded. The truth was that the lower people refused to take the job, and since the high wangwana also declined, they had no choice but to abolish it completely. It is the concept of hishima which forbids any high mngwana from working under the authority of another person and from doing any manual labor that would make him dirty, or cause him to have an unpleasant smell.

The high wangwana went about in their johos, or woolen costumes, with swords and colored turbans. This had once been the BuSa'id way of dressing, and the wangwana imitated it. They adopted that mode of dress because it was a symbol of high rank, and as a result the lower people began to call them *zijoho,*[15] "the people who dress in wool." If the son of a vijoho were about to marry, the father would buy him the joho robe, the sword, and the dagger. On the day of his marriage, the father would call all of his equal friends to his house. As a part of the ceremony the bridegroom sat with them for awhile, until a slave came to cut some of the bridegroom's hair, and then carry him off to the bath. After taking his bath, the bridegroom dressed in the joho, and then the oldest member of his group made a turban around the bridegroom's head, which was called *hupija kiemba.* This was the sign that the marriage was indeed a proper one and that the bridegroom was now a full member of his father's group. If a person married without this ceremony, his marriage would not be accepted by his father's group. However, from the day the bridegroom put on the joho, he had the right to go outside in it; he was a vijoho, and according to Astarabu he had to act like one. Acting against the rules of hishima could only show that he was not an Arab and therefore had no claim to Astarabu.

Moreover, hishima also determined the relations which were to exist among the various wangwana categories. The wangwana were supposed to have kutunga for each other. Each category showed this kutunga by maintaining the socially accepted relationships. If a conflict arose between a person belonging to category *A* and a person belonging to category *B*, the conflict had to be limited to the individuals; the other persons in both categories were supposed to refrain from interfering or taking sides. At the same time, the disputing individuals had to try to hide their conflict lest they should lose their hishima. However, each individual subtly tried to gather supporters for his side. Relations between the two conflicting persons might be tense, but they never openly quarreled. If a person revealed his ill will toward another, he too might do the same, and

15. *Zijoho* (plural of *vijoho*).

then secrets which ought not to be spoken of would be uncovered.

The disclosure of secrets would hurt not only the individuals directly involved but also their category and subsequently, the category's hishima. The Lamuans say "*Fulani fanya moto*," which means "he made fire," he "burned" the relations between the two categories and also "burned" their hishima. However, in a small town such as Lamu, everyone knew everyone else's secrets anyway. Stories and rumors went around all the time. It was considered an asset to know the secrets of others. This put everyone under the threat of losing his hishima. Relations among the different wangwana categories had to be maintained and balanced at any cost, because the alternative was to lose kutunga, hishima, and ultimately Astarabu. If that happened, the wangwana would be no better than the slaves they owned.

The Angels of the Right and the Angels of the Left

In this section, I will deal with the nature of the world as the wangwana construct it, and this will lead me to discuss the distinctive features which they use to characterize the different inhabitants of this world. Basic ideas such as purity/impurity, good jin/bad jin, and the difference between jin and human beings will be considered.

The world of the wangwana was not confined to the seen world, nor were the seen and unseen worlds considered completely separate from each other. The unseen world constituted a part of the social reality in which the wangwana lived and interacted. The inhabitants of the unseen world descended in order to observe and evaluate the actions of the wangwana. Every mngwana was thought to have two *malaika,* or angels, one to his right and one to his left. The one on the right recorded the good deeds, while the one on the left recorded the bad ones. Part of the idea of hishima was to behave properly so as not to intimidate the other person's angels. The angels were believed to stay with a person from the dawn prayer to the sunset prayer, at which time they would leave to report above about the person's deeds. This meant that, during the day especially, a person had to be very careful and conscious of his behavior, because his societal actions would be judged not only by his associates, but also by the angels. In similar fashion, the kind of work the mngwana did had to show respect for the angels who accompanied him during the day. If a person respected his angels, he had to respect himself. On the other hand, if he did not respect himself, then the people would not either and his angels would be ashamed of him. If a mngwana worked as a street cleaner, a profession below his rank, his associates would insult him and joke about him. Therefore, he would bring shame not only on himself and his category, but also on his angels.

According to the wangwana, angels were assigned the day a person was born, and they stayed with him until his death, when they returned to the unseen world, to remain until they were sent down to someone else. Usually, the angels were assigned to the same category of persons over and over again. This meant that the angels were stratified in the same way the town was stratified. So, the lower person, when showing respect for someone higher than himself, was in fact showing his respect for the higher angels who lived with that person. Disrespect would hurt not only persons, but also angels. For instance, if a lower person shouted in front of a higher person, this meant that the lower person did not respect the presence of the higher angels. By doing such a thing, the lower person wronged not only the higher angels, but also his own because angels cannot show disrespect for their own superiors.

Women had their angels just as men did. If a man married a lower woman, their angels would not be equal, and the children's would be ambiguous. Did they have the angels of the father's category or the mother's category? No one knew. However, such ambiguity would be sure to be reflected in the ambiguous behavior of others toward the child. Not being able to define the behavior suitable for such a person and his angels caused social confusion. This is why the wangwana insisted on the principle of marriage between equals.

If a higher person associated himself all the time with lower persons, his angels felt out of place; the angels wanted to associate with equals. And this was the argument for every group having its own mtaa, or location.

Offending the angels of another man was a kind of *dhanb,* or sin, which could not be forgiven by God. The only one who could forgive it was the person who had been offended. However, since a man offended his own as well as the other man's angels, he had to have forgiveness from both groups of angels as well as from the man. When this was done, the sin was dropped.[16]

At the same time, sins committed against God's rules were recorded by the angels. These sins consisted of eating forbidden kinds of meat, drinking wine, neglecting the prayers, and not fasting during the month of Ramadan. In other words, the failure to do all the things which God specifically ordered the Muslims to do was a sin against God, which had to be recorded and carried up to Him. God, as the most merciful, could forgive; He is more merciful than the mother to her own children. But there were two things that God would not

16. This is important even today. The story is told of a man who committed adultery with another man's wife, a sin against the husband, which the husband had to forgive. When the husband died, the adulterer came to his grave in front of all the people, and loudly asked the dead person to forgive him because he had slept with his wife.

forgive: unbelief and a statement that there is more than one God. In Lamu if a person did not believe in God, then his category had to punish him by throwing him out. If a man were thrown out because of lack of belief, his wife had to be divorced from him and his children could not keep him name; instead they took the name of his father. His angels were removed, and no one had to respect him. However, unbelief was the only sin against God that had any bearing on the person's hishima. In other words, if a person drank wine, this did not affect his hishima because that was a sin against God, not against another human being. The lower persons could not look down on the drunkard. If they did, they would commit a sin against a human being that could only be forgiven by the drunkard himself.

The second type of sin which was very difficult to have forgiven was a sin committed against the Prophet. Sins against the Prophet had to be forgiven by the Prophet himself, because he was a human being also. Thus, if someone insulted the Prophet, he had to ask the Prophet to forgive him. The Prophet was the mediator between God and the Muslims: his role was to ask God to forgive the Muslims. It was a serious matter for a person to insult the Prophet because then Mohammed would not intervene with God on his behalf, and he would be treated as if he were not a follower of Mohammed. The Prophet, then, had the highest rank and commanded the most respect of any other human being because he had been given the power of intervention.

Beneath the Prophet, there were the angels and those associated with them. The angels were assigned to specific groups by God, and each had a higher or lower place, because God chose to arrange the world in that way. The angels, who were light, obeyed God's orders and stayed with low or high persons without complaint. Human beings had to do the same thing. They had to accept their position, for if they did not they would be sinning against God, questioning God's wisdom and will. *Mtungi Mungu* (real care) ınd *kumcha Mungu* (the real fear of God) meant accepting God's orders. So the relation between a person and God was seen to be built on care and fear. It is interesting to note here that the same root, *tunza,* is used to describe both the care of a person for God and also the care between different groups of persons. The groups, as I have said, had to show kutunga for each other in order to maintain good relations, and again the person had to care for God in order to maintain good relations with Him. In other words, with both God and society, man's relationship depended on hishima. If a person did not care for God, he would be an unbeliever, and if he did not care for society, he would lose his civilization: he would be a *mshenzi,* or uncivilized barbarian.

The Jin and Social Stratification

The wangwana world of the unseen also contained the jin, the first inhabitants of the earth. The jin were not like the angels, for they originally came from fire, as we will see in the myth of creation, while the angels came from light. While the angels are allowed to go up to the seventh sky and enter it, the jin can go up but are not allowed to enter. While the angels are all good, the jin are divided between the malevolent and benevolent. Both kinds exist in this world. The benevolent jin live in towns and imitate the Muslims; the malevolent jin live in dark places, outside of the towns, and are like the Wa Shenzi.[17] Relations between the malevolent jin and the wangwana are dominated by *karaha* (hatred) and *wivu* (envy).

The jin had once been in heaven with God but had been thrown out because of Iblisi. As the head of the jin, Iblisi had not shown enough care to God. He disobeyed God, because he thought that he was better than Adam; he argued with God that fire (of which he was made) was higher than dust. But, God wanted dust to be higher than fire, and, when Iblisi refused to accept the position which God assigned to him, he was punished by being driven out of paradise and transformed into an unseen being. His tribe followed him, and they were also transformed.

But, some of the jin were said to have recently embraced Islam, although the others were still in opposition to God. One of the differences between the Muslim jin and the non-Muslim jin was that while the first could read Arabic, the second could not. "So when a person sleeps, he might see shadows going around. If the person recites the Qur'ān, and the shadows recite with him, then the person will be sure that the shadows are Muslim jin. If the shadows are not Muslim jin, the Qur'ān will destroy them."

The jin imitated those with whom they lived. They were like human beings; in fact, they married humans and had children. They too wanted to live with their equals, but the Muslim jin knew they were not equal to the wangwana, so they would never marry a mngwana woman. If a Muslim jin came in contact with a mngwana woman, he might act as a "brother" but never as a husband. Sometimes a female jin, Muslim or non-Muslim, fell in love with a mngwana male, and in this case, the man would be able to see her, sleep with her, and have children. The following examples are taken from my field notes.

17. In addition to the benevolent/malevolent distinction, jin are also separated into male and female.

There were some people who married jin women, but if it happened to you, and you revealed the secret, you would be harmed. There was someone called Bwana Ali who had a jin wife, and whenever he married other women, they used to die because the jin woman harmed them. She only allowed him to have a concubine (souriya). This became known to people through Bwana Hassani (the Ngazija[18] Mwalimu). One night, during a time when Bwana 'Ali had no human wives, Bwana Hassani went to Bwana 'Ali's house, and he heard 'Ali speaking, and a woman's voice told 'Ali "Hurry, Mwalimu Hassani is calling." Bwana Hassani was astonished, so he opened the door and went inside the room, but no one was there but 'Ali.

Once a man was married to a woman jin, and he had a son by her. This same man had been married to a human being before and he got another son. Once the human son was walking at night, when he met someone who told him not to walk around at this time. Then he asked him whether he recognized him, and the boy told him that he didn't, so the stranger told him that he was his brother from the same father, but a jin mother. The boy told his father in the morning, but the father asked him to keep quiet.

When a mngwana married a non-Muslim jin, he ordered her to convert to Islam and to obey the rules of proper behavior. As a mngwana, he could not live with a mshenzi. She had to follow the rules of the wangwana, especially to be clean and to pray. On the other hand, the non-Muslim male jin, the one who was evil and lived in the bush, could marry a mshenzi woman. The Wa Shenzi and the slaves were "people of the bush," and so were the malevolent jin. The wives of a malevolent male jin were continuously defiled (*najisi*), and continuously committed adultery (*zina*). In fact, the non-wangwana behavior was what attracted the malevolent jin to the Wa Shenzi women. When a male jin saw a woman who was dirty and defiled, he would immediately recognize her as a slave.

When the wangwana spoke of their relations with female jin, they applied their own social rules to them. These rules were concerned not only with marriage,but also with the social hierarchy. According to their way of thinking, it was obvious that a male benevolent jin could not marry a mngwana woman. His status would be lower than hers; he could never be equal to the wangwana groups. However, the benevolent jin was then like the slave souriya who had sexual relations with her master. The children of a mngwana man and a female benevolent jin were as low as their mother.

The situation with the jin was the reverse of what happened between a lower group, such as the Baluchi, and a higher group, such as the BuSa'id. The Baluchi, in order to establish their claim, had to take a wife from a higher group;

18. Ngazija: the local name for the Comoro Islanders.

while the benevolent jin never took wives from the wangwana, because they recognized themselves as lower and never intended to try to set themselves up as equal. As we have seen, the relations between the benevolent female jin and the wangwana males were similar to those between the souriya and their wangwana masters. However, while the children of the benevolent female jin accepted their lower position, the souriya children never did. The benevolent male jin married benevolent female jin who were equal to their mothers; they were never allowed to marry from their father's category.

The social stratification which existed among the wangwana children in the seen world of Lamu did not exist among the jin children. All the jin children were equal to each other, since they followed their mother's lower status while respecting their human fathers and brothers of equal marriage and treating them as higher than themselves.[19] In other words, the human souriya children could not accept both their patrilineal descent and their mother's low status, so they neglected their mother's position and tried to deal with their father's group as if they were equals. They then tried to establish relations with other groups from that position. However, the other groups looked on the souriya children as unequals, and therefore their behavior was judged to be against the hishima principle. According to the prevailing view, the children of a souriya were required to give the wangwana the same respect their mothers, as slaves, used to give. This is what the benevolent jin of wangwana fathers did. They knew themselves to be unequal to their fathers and continued to consider themselves equal to their mothers. In short, the wangwana thought that if they married down, their children would inherit the father's name but the mother's position. But the children of the souriya thought that in inheriting the father's name they were entitled to his position also, and therefore the benevolent jin presented an ideal solution to the wangwana problem. The jin inherited the father's name, but the mother's position; their behavior was equal to the behavior expected from a slave. In other words, they had to respect all the wangwana groups. Marriage between the malevolent jin and the non-wangwana also served to strengthen the wangwana superiority, because in this case there were no restrictions on the marriage of a non-wangwana to a malevolent jin. They could give and take wives from each other, which meant that the non-wangwana and the malevolent jin were equals.

When the marriages between the malevolent jin and the Wa Shenzi took place, both continued to behave in the same way because both were bad. Their

19. The relation between wangwana jin children and their mothers will be discussed later.

children were bad, and they harmed the wangwana. On the other hand, the wangwana offspring from the benevolent female jin, though unseen, circulated around in town and were very helpful to their fathers' groups. Each respected his father's group and extended that respect to all wangwana categories.

The souriya, who were originally Wa Shenzi, might have sexual relationships with their masters and also with a malevolent jin. The malevolent jin knew that this was the best way to harm the wangwana. In such a case, if the souriya got pregnant, the child would be considered to be the result of two males and one female. The malevolent jin and the mngwana father shared the parenthood. Though these children of the souriya belonged to the seen world, their behavior and their orientation were directed against the wangwana. They wanted to destroy that category by initiating social conflict. The wangwana would say that such a person can be known from his continuous actions against others. He usually harms people physically and socially and does not care for society or God. He does not maintain his hishima.

The ambiguity of such offspring created other existential problems. In the first place human beings found it difficult to establish relations with such a person, since his behavior could not be predicted, and, if he did behave wrongly, it would not be advisable to criticize him since he could inflict harm so easily. Such a person lived between two worlds, the seen and the unseen. But he shared in the bad part of the unseen world and was therefore dangerous to those who did not.

The offspring of the Wa Shenzi male and female malevolent jin were unseen, like the offspring of the similar liaison between the mngwana male and the jin female, but they differed from them in that they were harmful. Yet, this type of offspring did not create any social ambiguity, since their behavior was entirely predictable. We can graphically represent the offspring of the various unions expressed above as seen or unseen (see Figure 4).

While the benevolent jin contributed to maintaining the town's solidarity, the children of the souriya were always trying to bring about conflict and hostility in the town, and in this they were backed by the jin who were equal to their mother's category, that is, by the malevolent jin. It was almost as if the souriya children represented the malevolent jin inside the town. Those souriya children who resulted from adultery were the most dangerous group; they brought the town a great deal of suffering. It seemed that both the malevolent jin and the children of souriya had the intention of ruining the town. The wangwana, with the help of their good jin, could defeat the bad jin, but, in order to do that, the children of the souriya and all the slaves—the

Category	Kind of Sexual Relation	Offspring Unseen	Offspring Seen
Male wangwana Female jin	Marriage	+	-
Male wangwana Female non-wangwana (souriya) Malevolent male jin	Adultery	-	+
Male non-wangwana Female malevolent jin	Marriage	+	-

Fig. 4. Wangwana/Jin Relations and Offspring

Wa Shenzi—had to be kept out of town. When the children of the souriya started marrying from the al-Ma'awi group and could not be driven out—when they became part of the town—the wangwana lost their ability to keep their town pure.

THE ECONOMIC BASIS OF THE WANGWANA SYSTEM

The Slaves on the Mainland

The Lamu wangwana kept their slaves exclusively on the mainland. This coincided with their religious ideology, which distinguished between the people of the bush, the Wa Shenzi, and the people of the town, the wangwana. While the people of the town lived in large well-built stone houses, the people of the bush built small mud huts. All religious and intellectual life was naturally inside the town, and the different groups of wangwana enjoyed a surplus of economic resources, derived from the land and slaves, and began to invest that surplus in building new mosques. Such investments were considered most worthwhile, because the builder of the mosque would obtain part of the blessing due those who prayed in the mosque, as long as it was in use. In this way, the builder of a mosque exchanged money for blessings, which for the Lamu people, was the currency of the hereafter. This was the reason that thirteen mosques were built at approximately the same time.

In contrast to the people living in the town, the mainland Muslim slaves were deprived of mosques. They were not even allowed to have a Jum'a mosque. The wangwana thought that it was neither necessary nor proper for the Friday prayer to be performed by the slaves. According to the wangwana, a slave could not lead the Friday prayer, and since no mngwana 'ālim could live in the bush, the Friday prayer seemed obviously out of the question. Consequently, slave religious life was conducted more or less individually, inside the slave's hut.

As we have seen, the slaves of one mngwana were not allowed to marry the slaves of another. The mngwana would assign a wife to each of his slaves, and neither party had a right to object. The children of the slaves were part of the property of the master and, since he was only interested in increasing the number of his slaves, he retained the right to dissolve the marriage of any of his slaves at any time. If a slave wife were taken from one husband to be married to another, her children from the first husband would accompany her to the hut of the new husband. The new husband and all the children, regardless of which father they had, belonged to the owner. Furthermore, when the children reached puberty, the master had the right to sell them or give them away as gifts. In many cases, he would simply transfer them to another part of his estate, where they were to reclaim new land. However, with endogamous marriage, and the successive remarriages of female slaves to one master's male slaves, it soon became very difficult to separate those whom the slave could marry from those whom he had to avoid according to Islamic law. This situation was realized by the wangwana, who did nothing to alleviate it but simply viewed their slaves as bastards, and felt they had further justification for keeping them out of town. In other words, the slaves were stigmatized not only because they were the people of the bush, but also because they were bastards.

In contrast to the wangwana, the slave fathers had no permanent relations with their children. The slave woman might have three or four successive husbands, from whom she would have children. According to the customs of Lamu, the woman had to keep all her children until they reached puberty. The mother was considered the central figure around whom all the children gathered. However, the mother, her children, and her new husband were all controlled by the master. They even used their master's name in their interaction with outside groups. For example, the slaves of the al Ma'awi call themselves by the name *watu Wa Maawi*, people of the al Ma'awi. So their identification was first with the al Ma'awi group, and if asked again they would mention the owner's subgroup name, for example, al Khatib. If questioned further, they would mention their owner's name. However, in all these identifications, they never had a name of their own.

The wangwana used the same mode of identification, but in reverse. If one asked a mngwana to identify himself, he would begin by referring himself to his nearest great-grandfather. For example, he would say, "I am Mohammed ibn Osman." If asked again, he would go up another step saying, "I am a Khatib," and, if pressed again, he would say, "We are al Ma'awi." In other words, he began from his own small unit, and moved up to the big unit. The slave, in contrast, began from the big unit, and moved down to the small unit, which was his master's name.

Further, the slaves were not allowed to use certain proper names, such as Omar, Osman, or Mohammed, because these were considered wangwana names. The slaves' names were usually related to the day on which they were born, names such as Khamisi (Thursday), Jum'a (Friday), or to things which were considered *fali njema* (lucky), such as Faraji (comfort), or Sa'idi (happiness). The most common name was Abdullahi (the slave of God), a name which had another connotation: if a child were considered a bastard, and the mother could not tell whose son he was, then he would be called Abdullahi.[20] The slave girls had their own names too: Maulidi (birth of the Prophet), Simama (the Prophet's intervention), Nasoura (victory), and Rahima (mercifulness). The wangwana females were called Khadija, Fatima, Amina, and 'Aisha, all of which were the names of females related to the Prophet.

It is interesting here to point out the differences within the naming system.[21] All wangwana names were related to the Prophet, his family, and his companions, and slave names almost always called to mind good omens. While wangwana names were considered noble, honorable, and high ranking, slave names referred to attributes of God, the Prophet, or the Muslims who had acquired good omens because of their relation to the Prophet. In other words, the slaves needed the intervention and mercy of the Prophet more than any mngwana; and so names were given to them to remind them of the attributes which they lacked. The lack of these attributes was considered the real difference between the slaves and wangwana.

However, the slaves were distinguished not only by their names but also by the way they dressed. They were not permitted to have a turban, nor, as we

20. *Abdullahi* means "bastard" only in the case of slaves.

21. The Islamic naming system is worthy of the anthropologist's attention. The Ibadis, for example, will never call their children Osman, or 'Ali, or Mu'awiya. All of these names refer to unacceptable persons, who are considered wrongdoers. The Shi'ites, for example, will always use the names of 'Ali and his descendants. However, they will never call a daughter 'Aisha. 'Aisha, the wife of Mohammed, fought and took a stand against 'Ali.

have seen, were they allowed to wear a joho, or woolen dress, or use swords and knives. Their dress was a small piece of cloth around the waist, which left the upper part of the body uncovered. The slave girls were dressed in what is called *kanga,* a colorful piece of cloth covering the body but not the shoulders. They were not allowed to use the *boyboy,* the black dress usually worn by wangwana females. When the slave girls went out, they were covered only with the kanga, which, in fact, was not enough to hide their bodies. Poetry was written describing how pretty the "non-free women" were, how they were able to make a person "lose his mind." Like the jin, they were so attractive that men were unable to avoid following along. The slave women, unlike the wangwana females, supposedly could not control their sexual desires, even when they reached old age. For this reason, they could not be faithful or loyal to one man. They were described as jin or fire; they had to burn all the time in order to exist. This notion of the slave woman can still be found.

The slaves were viewed as low not only in this world but also after death. The dead slave had to be washed by other slaves; no wangwana could touch him. His corpse was referred to by the word *mfu,* which, in Lamu, is also used for dead animals. He was not to be washed with the perfumed material used for the wangwana. The Jum'a preacher was not to perform Talqin, the ceremony in which the dead were told what to say to the angels when they came to his grave. In fact, Talqin was not performed at all for the slaves. Since slaves were the "people of the bush," they had relations with the jin but never with the angels,[22] so the angels would not visit them in their graves. Moreover, the master did not observe a mourning period for his slave; even the slave wife was not allowed to do so.

In summary, the slaves were the main economic power which increased the wangwana's income and helped them to build the mosques and so gather their blessings for many years. However, the slaves were thought of as inferior to the wangwana in every way. They were the people of the bush, the Wa Shenzi, while the wangwana were the people of the town, the people who alone possess Astarabu.

The Establishment of the Sultanate of Witu

When the sultan of Zanzibar captured Patta Island in 1855, the sultan of

22. It is interesting to note here that the custom of Talqin existed in most of the Islamic countries. However, some theologians now see it as non-Islamic in nature, and, therefore, some people have stopped performing it.

Patta, who was from the Nabahani family,[23] fled to the mainland and established what was called the sultanate of Witu. Witu was chosen as the capital of the sultanate because of its strategic position. It controlled the routes linking Lamu with Mombasa and connecting the mainland estates with the island of Lamu. Consequently, if a strong but unfriendly sultanate had been established there, Lamu would either be deprived of its estates, or it would have to pay taxes on commodities transferred through Witu. As it was, the wangwana were pleased with the sultanate, since it was a buffer zone between them and Mombasa. Moreover, any challenge to the BuSa'id power was considered to be in the wangwana favor. For these reasons, the wangwana did not oppose the rule of the Nabahani dynasty over Witu. As long as the new sultanate protected the wangwana interest on the mainland, the relations between the sultanate and the wangwana were favorable.

In their relationship with Witu the wangwana were mainly concerned with economic matters. Their land almost surrounded the new town. In the beginning the sultan of Witu allowed the wangwana to transport crops to Lamu, but did not allow them to transfer any to Mombasa. This regulation was welcomed by the Lamu wangwana; Mombasa suffered from the siege, and the Lamuans were pleased at that.

The wangwana thought that their slaves would not be affected by the newly established town. They predicted that the Nabahani sultan would treat slaves in the same way they did. The sultan was an Arab, like the wangwana, so they assumed that he would keep the slaves outside the town as the Lamuans had traditionally done.

But in 1866 there was a battle at Gongani which signaled the deterioration of relations between the two groups. The sultan of Zanzibar had ordered the wangwana to go and take down the flag of Witu, which had been raised on Gongani. The Lamuan wangwana were not interested in fighting the sultan of Witu, so they contacted him and told him about the orders of the sultan of Zanzibar. The head of the Lamu group agreed with the sultan of Witu that the wangwana would stage an attack, put the flag down, and leave. After they left, the Witu soldiers could return and put their flag up again. They agreed that no

23. The Nabahani family in Patta was part of Joktan, like the BuSa'id. The imam of Oman—before the BuSa'id—was from a branch of the Nabahani family called Ya'riba. When Ahmed ibn Sa'id ibn Mohammed (1749-1783 A. D.—1163-1198 A. H.) the founder of the BuSa'id dynasty, took over the rule, the Nabahani family backed the Ya'riba against the BuSa'id. See 'Abdallah ibn Ḥumayd al Salimi, *Tuḥfat al A'yān bi-Sirat Ahl 'Oman* [A gift given to the chosen concerning the history of the people of Oman], 2 vols., 2d ed. (Cairo: Imam Printing House, 1931), pp. 136–45.

real fight would take place, and that no arms would be fired. On the agreed date, the wangwana attacked Gongani; however, some uninformed Lamuans fired on the Witu soldiers and killed two of them. The Witu army fired back on the wangwana, and killed about seventy of them, leaving the others to flee. The head of the wangwana group was killed, and his hand was cut off and sent to the sultan of Witu. The sultan was angry and told his soldiers that they must not trust any mngwana.

From that date, the sultan of Witu began to play the political game according to his own interests. He disregarded and distrusted the wangwana completely. He needed followers in order to be able to stand not only against the BuSa'id, but also against the wangwana, so he adopted a new policy in which he allowed the slaves to settle in Witu, and also supplied them with protection. As the supreme ruler, he allowed the Lamuan slaves to file complaints against their masters and encouraged them to flee from their wangwana owners. He trained the slaves in the town, gave them arms, and used them as an army.

The sultan of Witu also managed to make use of the conflicting interests of the British and the Germans. While the British were backing the sultan of Zanzibar, the Germans were backing the sultan of Witu, later supplying him with firearms and economic aid. One result was a strong Witu army, which consisted of malcontent, runaway slaves who were encouraged to raid the wangwana estates and force the other slaves to abandon their land. The wangwana of Lamu could not tolerate this situation; and they decided in 1878 to wage an attack on the slave camps around a place called Katawa.[24] The slaves were ready for the fight, and when the wangwana arrived the slaves opened fire. The wangwana had to flee without even being able to carry away their wounded comrades. Lamu lost two of her best and highest-ranking leaders in the fight. It was a defeat so remarkable that, up to the present day, people still remember it with sorrow. The outcome of that battle had far-reaching effects on Lamu's future. The slaves discovered that the wangwana were no better than anyone else; they had run away leaving their dead. Thus, the wangwana as a prestige group ceased to exist. Soon other slaves began either to leave the land or to cultivate it without sending any of the crop back to their defeated masters. Furthermore, the Germans encouraged the slaves to work for them as hired laborers, mainly in the collection of rubber.

In 1885, the German-East Africa Company received a royal charter, and the Germans began to compete openly with the British. They declared their protection for the sultan of Witu, who now had a member of the Mazru'ai family

24. C. H. Stigand, *The Land of Zinj* (New York: Barnes & Noble, 1966), pp. 97–98.

residing with him. The presence of the Germans in Witu had its effect on the wangwana. The Ḥusseini sharif whose daughter had married the BuSa'id (see above, p. 58) negotiated with the Germans, who offered him their protection.[25] When, in 1885, the Baluchi asked to marry the daughter of the BuSa'id, whose mother was Ḥusseini, the Ḥusseini refused. The reason was that the BuSa'id as liwalis were loyal to the sultan of Zanzibar. A conflict took place between the BuSa'id and the Ḥusseini. The BuSa'id Liwali arrested the Ḥusseini sharif and, in the end, killed him. The wife of that sharif was from the Nabahani family and was thus related to the sultan of Witu. So the Germans, who had agreed to protect the Ḥusseini, threatened the sultan, and he was made to bring the liwali to Zanzibar and jail him. As a result of all of this, Lamu was divided internally between those who backed the Germans and those who wanted to maintain relations with the sultan of Zanzibar. The sultan of Zanzibar, trying to keep Lamu under control, ordered six hundred Baluchi to cross the sea and take punitive measures against the sultan of Witu. But the sultan of Witu was able to mobilize three thousand well-trained slaves in the field.

The slave army of Witu emerged as a power which Lamu had to fear, and which enabled the sultan of Witu to impose a tax on products leaving Witu. This was a blow to the people of Lamu, who were still the formal owners of many of the Witu plantations. In 1888, the sultan of Witu established a customs house at the mouth of the Belzoni Canal, and this too affected Lamu, which was already suffering from the export tax. These drastic measures isolated Lamu from commerce and from the outside world. The British tried to convince the Germans that the sultan of Witu had no right to do this, but the Germans insisted on backing him, and they reinforced his position with shipments of arms. However, the relations between the sultan of Witu and the Germans suddenly came to an end. When the Germans found that the cost of collecting rubber was higher than the price they could get from selling it, they dropped their project, and the slaves lost their income. The wangwana land needed a lot of work and the investment of capital to return it to its old productive capacity. The slaves did not have the money to do this, and they were afraid to return to the land.

The British and the Germans concluded a treaty in 1890, "under which the German government agrees to surrender all the land it occupied or claimed . . . placing under British control the sultanate of Witu. . . ." The sultan of Witu had been betrayed, and his natural reaction was to mistreat the Germans who

25. J. H. Clive, *The Political and Historical Records: A Brief History of Tanaland*, (unpublished ms., n. d.), pp. 20–22.

"had sold him and his country to the British, after having encouraged him to resist the demands of both the British and the sultan of Zanzibar." Eventually, some Germans were actually killed by the people of Witu, and the German government asked the British to retaliate. At that time, the British sent troops to maintain order and to arrest the sultan. But the sultan was able to flee, only to die a year later. His brother was then appointed as sultan; however, he was deposed after a short time, and a sultan from outside the Nabahani family was appointed. This put Witu under the direct control of the British and marked the end of the Nabahani dynasty.

The establishment of the Witu sultanate with its slave army severed all relations between the wangwana and their slaves. The slaves were allowed to live in Witu, attend the prayers, and even to fight the wangwana on an equal basis, defeating them twice. They unified behind the sultan because they were afraid the wangwana would pull them back into slavery. For the first time, they were able to achieve a position where they could answer back to their masters without being afraid. However, the sultanate was also a disruptive factor for the slaves. The slaves who used to identify themselves with their masters refused to do so any more. The master's name was a stigma which they wanted to get rid of. But in the meantime they had nothing to replace it. Besides, the continuous military movement had undermined their family structure. Abandoned wives regretted their husbands' involvement; they were more inclined to be satisfied with what they had in the "old" days. So, a number of slaves left Witu for Mombasa, where they could easily get jobs, and where no one was interested in investigating their origins. Those who went to Mombasa were by and large the young who could compete with others for such jobs as carriers, street cleaners, or workers in the gardens around the city. Those who were left in Witu were old men, women, and young children. All of them needed support in order to be able to live; therefore, they approached their old masters in Lamu asking for forgiveness and putting all the blame on the young slaves who left them. The wangwana forgave them and allowed them to live on the old land, but the remaining slaves were unable to cultivate any sizable portion of it, since they lacked the necessary power, organization, and incentive. The reclaimed land began to deteriorate fast; jungle and forest soon covered it.

The British policy was partially responsible for this. The sultans of Zanzibar were manipulated by the British agents, particularly the British representative Sir John Kirk. Theoretically, the British policy concerning Lamu was to break down the traditional system and to try to replace it with a more open one. However, in practice, the British policy was more or less *laissez faire*. The

British tried to convince some investors to buy land and operate plantations in the area, but they failed. A district commissioner of Lamu writes: "After the lapse of a quarter of a century, all that is left of the above enterprises are the two Witu plantations, which together employ only thirty laborers, and the Belzoni estate which only just survived and ran on a profit-sharing basis by Smith, Mackenzi and Co. and Mr. Petly."[26]

In 1893, when the first British district subcommissioner bought the remaining slaves from their owners and freed them, slavery in Lamu came to an end by means of a simple procedure. The subcommissioner would call each owner and his slaves together and order the owner to free each slave by saying to him, "Go, you are free." Then he would pay the owner for his slaves. However, a theological problem arose as a result of this—not only in Lamu, but also in places such as Turkey. In 1830, the sultan of Turkey freed all the white slaves who had kept their original religion, that is those who refused to convert to Islam. He could not free the Muslim slaves, however, because, in adopting Islam, the slave accepted the principle that the master was the only person who could free him, and that could be done only if there was no external force. If there were any force on the will of the master, then he could claim that the act of freeing the slaves was not carried out according to religious rules.

It was the Lamu mwenye chouni who questioned the legality of the sub-district commissioner's action. They concluded that: "No one can free a slave except his master, who had to act under no external force." The subcommissioner was considered the representative not of the sultan of Zanzibar but of the British Government—that is, of a Christian force. Therefore, the mwenye chouni considered the actions of the masters un-Islamic and expected a Muslim slave to reject any freedom which had been obtained by force. However, the slaves of Lamu were not trained to understand such fine points of religious law. As we saw, the wangwana elite refused to offer theological education to anyone but their equals. So, when the slaves were freed by the British, they began to act as free persons, neglecting the legal rights of their masters over them.

The free slaves began to settle in the town of Lamu itself, and the wangwana, under British pressure, accepted the change as inevitable. The slaves were given certain places to live, such as in the southern part of the town in Langoni, or in the hills to the west of the town, in places called Nairobi, Mkomaningoi, Milimani, Bimanga, and Jeneby. In the northern part of the town their area was called Tundani. In each of these locations slaves of different masters lived

26. *Ibid.*, pp. 27–28.

together. The old system of dividing the slaves according to owner was not followed. Thus, the slaves began to intermarry. The slave of one master might marry the slave of another, something which had not been allowed according to the old system. This continuous intermarriage between the slaves of different masters made any ownership claim on the part of the wangwana difficult and obscure. And, being unable to distinguish their own slaves among the others, the wangwana were no longer able to command their slaves' daughters as souriyas.

At the same time, the wangwana were unable to actually marry from among the slaves, not only because of the principle of compatibility of spouses, but also because, to marry a slave, the permission of the master was required if the relation were not to be considered adulterous. The masters, unable to decide who owned whom, began to look at all slave girls as souriyas. In other words, the restriction of personal ownership was neglected. The children from this kind of relationship were called children of a souriya; they had the father's name and the mother's low status.

The wangwana, deprived of their economic resources, were unable to pay the old bride wealth for an equal wife. When they were well-to-do, the bride wealth was very high. The souriya institution was the best alternative in the new economic situation.

The old ideology of marriage between the socially equal lost its power. The Silwa, the book that was kept by the preachers, and in which the names of the socially compatible categories, or socially equal groups, were recorded, was now useless. A Lamu story illustrates this. Once, after the emancipation of the slaves, a man, wanting to marry a certain girl, went to the man in charge of the Silwa. The man told him, "There is no need for the Silwa," but the bridegroom did not understand and said, "Why?" The man told him, "All of you are bastards one way or another and if that is the situation, there is no need to consult the book." The story continues: "The leader of the Friday prayer then carried the book in front of the wangwana, and threw it in the sea, saying that, "The days of the Silwa book have come to an end, and there is no need to keep it, because it will create trouble for all of us."

The Decline of the Wangwana Traditional Family System

The wangwana economic decline affected their numba serkali, or household. The mngwana was not financially able to have more than one equal mngwana wife. However, in addition to her, he could have two or three souriyas, each of them living by herself in her own mud house. The mngwana would go to visit each of the souriyas without any of them knowing that he had had relations with any other. Some of the souriyas refused to have relations without marriage.

Harking back to tradition, they felt a relationship between a mngwana and a slave girl was acceptable only when the master of that girl consented to it. If relations were established without the consent of the master, it was adultery. Legally, the wangwana were unable to establish a normal marriage; therefore, they developed what is called secret marriage, *nikahi ya siri.* Secret marriage, unlike ordinary marriage, did not require publicity; only one person was needed to conduct it. It was very simple: the man who conducted it asked the bride if she agreed to have the bridegroom as a husband, and, if she agreed, then he said, "You so and so are the wife of so and so." He concluded by reading the Fatiḥa, the opening verses of the Qur'ān.

This kind of marriage was condemned by Lamu's religious elite, who said that marriage, following the Prophet, had to be declared and made public. The children, too, had to be declared, so everyone could know those whom he could marry, and those whom he had to avoid. But the wangwana were afraid to declare their secret marriages, because the 'ulama, or learned men, had given a Fatwa that the wangwana could not marry, or even cohabit, with a slave, since the ownership of these slave girls was obscure. Thus, a mngwana who had any relation with a slave girl was committing adultery, and must be punished. The mngwana husband was thus forced to keep his marriage to a slave girl secret. His children from the slave wife had nothing in common with him or with their wangwana brothers. In many cases, they became known to each other only after the father's death. According to Lamuan custom, they could not inherit any of their father's property. In fact, they usually called themselves by their father's name without knowing anything about his group. This makes it very difficult for the anthropologist, because although it appears from the outside that the ideology of the old descent system still exists, there are no judicial or social obligations attached to it.

According to the old system, the strictly defined membership of a group provided and defined the rights of inheritance, and the mutual obligations between members of different groups, therefore, contributed to the survival of the group as a whole. The basic principle on which the group maintained its sociological and ideological coherence was that of marriage between equals. Now things were different; the traditional groups had lost their economic, political, and social control. If, for example, someone claimed that he was al Ma'awi, no power could substantiate or refute that claim, especially because of the existence of the secret marriage system.

The children of the slave wives were left to live with their mothers, and for that reason were not socialized by their fathers. They were not taught the rules of hishima, which ordinarily would have been required of them as carriers of their father's name. The interaction of such children would almost always be with other slaves, and they acquired most of their behavioral patterns from these lower groups. In other words, we find in Lamu today many people who claim a certain name but do not exhibit the behavior that would have been expected from a person with that name in the old times.

Furthermore, the principle of kutunga, which was stressed by the wangwana as the basis for their town's integrity, ceased to be operative. As we saw, that principle was derived from the principle of equal marriage and was backed by a certain religious ideology. The role of the father in the traditional family system was to inculcate such values in the child.

Moreover, the slave wives were given only the minimum economic support by their wangwana husbands. The husbands considered these wives low, and therefore not equal to the wangwana wives. However, the slave wives began to compete with the wangwana women, and in order to get additional income, they became involved in *malaya*, or prostitution. The institution of secret marriage encouraged the practice of prostitution, since no one knew who was married or to whom.[27] The change in dress was also important in facilitating prostitution. The slave girls had come to wear the same dress as the wangwana women, with their faces covered, and only their eyes showing. When they went out to their customers, no one could tell who they were.

The wangwana women, feeling threatened, began to lose interest in the old stable family life as expressed, for example, in the "Utendi wa Mwana Kupona" (see above, p. 64). They began to be involved in prostitution with other wangwana men. This meant that the old principles of hishima, kutunga, and adabu had really come to an end. They were gradually replaced by *setiri,* which means "hiding, or covering up." Everyone had to hide or cover up his mistakes or wrong deeds or those of others. This was especially true with women. "*Tuateni tunyamaye asomwane una nduje*," "Let us keep quiet and silent. He who has no daughter or son might have a brother or sister." Again, "*Aso na mengi, ana machache*," "No one must speak about the mistakes of others, since those who have made no grave error will have made a small one. All of us have our own sins, and we have to be silent; otherwise the society will collapse." In other words, all Lamu people were now equal. As another man told me, "One way or another, we cannot escape the fact that all of us are bastards. This is God's revenge, which we cannot escape. Our grandfathers mistreated everyone;

27. Janet S. Bujra, who worked with the Bajuni, thinks that Lamu is considered a first stop for the Bajuni girls who begin the practice of prostitution. From there they go to Mombasa, where it is more profitable (J. Bujra, personal communication).

now we are suffering." The man who told me this was not an ordinary man, but a descendant of the Ḥusseini sharifs.

The ease of claiming a respectable name has had an effect on the slave mother-child relation. As I have already said, the slave mother was the center of her family. When these girls began to marry wangwana males secretly, they continued to keep their children from the mngwana husband. The children were expected to maintain a close relationship with their mothers. If the child broke from his mother, he would be condemned as an aggressor, and it would be said that he would not go to paradise. This was a dilemma for those children of the mngwana father and the slave mother. In order to justify their claim to their father's name, they were forced to sever relations with their mothers, even though doing so was irreligious. The following quotation from my field notes should clarify this tense situation:

> M. M. is the son of a mngwana. His father was very rich. However, the father married a slave. When the son was born, he lived with his mother, whom the father divorced because of prostitution. When the father died, the boy began to sever his relations with the mother. Due to his relation with the British District Commissioner, he arranged for her transfer from Lamu to another small village. He never visited her or helped her. He never came in touch with his mother's relatives. When the mother grew old, she lost her sight, but he paid no attention. When she died, he didn't participate in her funeral. He did not show grief, or the traditional custom of making *tawsia,* or reading the Qur'ān in the mosque.

When I heard of the death, I expected the traditional ritual to take place in one of the Lamu mosques. But, when nothing happened, I made some inquiries. S. D. explained the matter in the following way:

> M. M. does not want to show that his mother was a slave. He wants to be identified as a mngwana, and to do that he has to neglect and forget his mother. His refusal to support her, or make a tawsia is a real justification for his claim that he is part of his father's category. However, doing that shows also that he is the son of a slave, because no mngwana will neglect his mother . . . the wangwana know that without the mother's *ridha,* i.e., without her approval, you cannot succeed in this life, or in the hereafter.

A mother could punish a negligent son by withdrawing her satisfaction. Without this, the person could not achieve any degree of purity. Neglect of one's mother was a sin, and because this sin was against a human being, God would not forgive the sinner unless the person to whom the harm was done forgave him. In other words, it was the wangwana belief that the son could not be cleansed of his sin until the mother forgave him. This was the irony: the son of a souriya had to dissociate himself from his slave mother in order to make his claim to being a mngwana credible, but that very act was such a gross neglect of duty that it proved him to be non-mngwana. It is clear that a person whose mother was a slave and whose father was a mngwana could never had a well-defined position in society. In order to be a mngwana, he had to behave in a non-wangwana manner.

These changes in society had a great effect on the wangwana concept of hishima. The children raised by their slave mothers might inherit their father's name, but they would not know how to maintain his hishima. They would not know how to control their emotions. When faced with any attack, they would lose their senses, and "burn everything." Such a person might attack the very people he claimed as his own family.

Under the new conditions everyone had to be careful in his relations with others; he could have friends, but at the same time he had to be always suspicious of them. The hishima and Astarabu of which the wangwana were so proud had collapsed. They not only lost their claim of ethnic superiority, but also began to deteriorate to the state of the Wa Shenzi.

THE ḤADRAMIS IN LAMU

The Ḥadramis were those people who came from Ḥadramaut in Southern Arabia. The people in Lamu called them *Wa Shihiri,* or "the people of Shiḥr," which is a coastal town in Ḥadramaut. Because of the political problems and the poverty of their country, the Ḥadramis migrated to different spots all around the Indian Ocean from East Africa to Indonesia,[28] and they came to Lamu as migrant laborers a few years after the BuSa'id. The Ḥadramis in Lamu were extremely poor. They would work as porters, water carriers, or at any other sort of of menial work.[29] They were not even ashamed to beg in the streets. They were despised because of their acceptance of these inferior jobs and their style of dress. The Wa Shihiri used to cover only the lower part of their body with a *kikui,* or small piece of material. The upper part was left uncovered. They had neither head covers nor even sandals on their feet. They were considered the nomads of the Arabs. Thus, *Wa Shihiri* came to be used as a derogatory name.

By describing them as nomads, the wangwana also meant to imply that the

28. Justus M. van der Kroef, "The Arabs in Indonesia," *The Middle Eastern Journal,* VII (1953), 300–323.

29. F. B. Peirce, *Zanzibar: The Island Metropolis of Eastern Africa* (London: T. Fisher Unwin, 1920). p. 125.

Wa Shihiri were not paying enough attention to religious affairs. They were dirty; they had no claim to Astarabu; and they lacked the concepts of hishima and adabu. They even used to sit down with the slaves to chat and exchange joking insults. They were thus in sharp contrast to the *Bi Manga,* the people of Oman, who came as rulers, dressed in the joho, with big turbans, swords, and knives. The Bi Manga were considered urban Arabs who had Astarabu. The BuSa'id family was the highest expression of Arab culture, the Wa Shihiri the lowest. Due to their lowly position, the Wa Shihiri were not allowed to live in the northern part of the town. As strangers, they were confined to the southern part with the Ngazija slaves, to whom they were considered equal.

Because the Wa Shihiri were "strangers," they were not allowed to interfere in Lamu's affairs. The Ḥadramis were not allowed to marry wangwana women, and their daughters were not allowed to marry wangwana males. They were considered to be complete outsiders.

Actually, this low social position was favored by the Ḥadramis themselves. They were not interested in establishing relations with the wangwana; as labor-migrants they were in search of money. And, as part of a tribally organized society, they strove to maintain their relations with their original homeland.[30] They either sent to Ḥadramaut for wives or went there to marry. Keeping themselves on the periphery of Lamu's social arena was important for the economic goals which they wanted to achieve. As strangers, they were allowed the economic freedom which they needed to accumulate money. They were not interested in hishima or in the wangwana ideology.

The Ḥadrami society which the Wa Shihiri left behind them was a highly stratified society, like Lamu. Everyone had a prescribed place, which he could not change. The Ḥadramis who came to Lamu were from the weak (*da'if*) stratum. They belonged to neither the Adnan nor the Joktan divisions, and therefore, "They . . . have the lowest descent status and no ascribed religious status."[31] Thus their position in Lamu's stratificatory system was not new or different from the one they had left behind. This facilitated their adaptation.

The Ḥadrami wives worked in their homes; they made bread and sweets, or did needlework, and then sold these products to the wangwana. They were cautious in their financial affairs, and as soon as they had accumulated some money, they established themselves as bankers. They would go to the mainland

30. W. H. Ingrams estimated that in 1936 the Ḥadramis in Singapore and Indonesia sent about 600,000 shillings to their relatives in Ḥadramaut. See Ingrams, "A Survey of Social and Economic Conditions in the Aden Protectorate" (Asmara, 1949).

31. Abdallah S. Bujra, *The Politics of Stratification: A Study of Political Change in a South Arabian Town* (London: Clarendon Press, 1971), pp. 14–15.

African tribes with a few articles, which they would barter for crops or livestock which they sold on their return to Lamu.

The Ḥadramis often went as far as the Somali borders to contact different tribes, such as the Pokomo, the Orma (Galla), and the Boni. These tribes were generally non-Muslim, and this also suited the Ḥadramis. There is a widespread story of a Ḥadrami merchant who used to take his young son with him on his trading journeys. When the father and son arrived at the site of one of these tribes, the father used all his tricks to sell his goods and to get the highest price for them. One day, the son sat down and talked with the young men of one of these tribes, who began to ask him about religion, and he tried to explain it to them. The father called him and told him that if he continued speaking about Islam and tried to convert the Africans their business would be ruined. Since the tribesmen were non-Muslims, the father explained, he could deceive and cheat them, but if they converted to Islam, he would have to be honest with them. The story goes on to say that the father did not allow his son to accompany him any more.

Such a story indicates that the Ḥadramis had only an economic interest in dealing with the African tribes. Moreover, it indicates that any African who converted to Islam would have to be considered equal to any other Muslim and would have to have been treated in a new way. This means that from the Ḥadramis' point of view, the Africans could achieve a new position simply by adopting Islam. This is in sharp contrast to the wangwana point of view which held that the Africans were incapable of absorbing the ideas and ideals of Islam and Astarabu and, therefore, would never be equal to the Arabs.

The Ḥadramis never adopted any of the wangwana customs surrounding death, birth, or marriage. These occasions were highly significant for the wangwana of Lamu, and they used to spend a lot of money on them. The Ḥadramis, who were very cautious with their money, said, "Leave the money (for inheritors), but do not let it leave you (in your life)." It is better to die and leave money behind than to live without having money.

From this point of view, most of the wangwana customs were considered *tabdhir,* or wasteful and extravagant, by the Ḥadramis. Squandering money was thought to be irrational. Those who spent their money needlessly and irrationally were the "brothers of the devils." Money was considered *na'ma,* or a blessing, by the Ḥadramis, and had to be used carefully. It was to be concealed, so that no one should know how rich another was. If a person showed his wealth, he might be envied by others and the wealth might be lost. In other words, a person should accumulate money, but he ought to behave as if he had little. He must not spend it on luxuries, since the real enjoyments were to be encountered in the hereafter, and not in this world.

As human beings, the Ḥadramis thought they should eat and dress moderately and have little more than a shelter to sleep under at night. This ethic contrasted with that of the wangwana, who had stone houses, slaves, and luxurious food and clothing. The Ḥadramis believed that the wangwana were committing the sin of extravagancy. While the wangwana considered wealth, whose distribution they controlled, to be a means through which they could express their higher rank, the Ḥadramis felt that wealth had nothing to do with rank. The wangwana, then, identified wealth and rank; the Ḥadramis differentiated between the two. In 1968, a Ḥadrami woman died in Lamu, and all the Ḥadramis went to the mosque. One Ḥadrami, who was quite wealthy but low in social position, went to the mosque at that time also. There were some high-ranking Ḥadramis speaking with each other, and this man spoke with them as if he were their equal. When someone told him that he had no right to speak in their presence, the rich Ḥadrami sat down silently.[32]

To summarize the Ḥadrami stratificatory system: The Ḥadramis fall into three strata. First there are the *sada*, or the sharifs, the descendants of the Prophet; second, the *mashaikh,* or traditional religious people and, equal to them, the *qaba'il,* or tribesmen; third, the poor (*masakin*) or the weak (*da'if*). Both the mashaikh and the sada have religious status, while the tribesmen and the "weak" have nothing to do with religion.

When the Ḥadramis came to Lamu, they did not have any sada. However, some of the sheikhs came with them. Together the Ḥadramis built a mosque in the southern half of the town (Langoni), which was called by the name of their religious leader, Ba Wazir. In this mosque they celebrated their religious occasions, which were not substantially different from those of the wangwana, since the Ḥadramis were Shafi'ites like the wangwana. The religious leaders of the Ḥadramis also came to Lamu as migrant laborers, with the aim of making money. They were peddlers, water carriers, and manual workers. These professions did not interfere with their prescribed position as sheikhs, and they officiated at the religious functions in addition to their ordinary work. If a Ḥadrami wanted to marry, the religious leader performed the very simple marriage. He also led the prayers and celebrated Ramadan and the Maulidi. Most of these functions were carried out in Arabic, from texts which the Ḥadramis had brought with them from Ḥadramaut. (I will describe their celebration of the Maulidi later.)

With the accumulation of wealth and the rise of the Witu sultanate, the

32. See Abdallah S. Bujra, *Politics of Stratification.*

Ḥadramis began to open small retail stores to supply Lamu with food. They established their business center at Langoni, and sent for their relatives to come and carry on their old business as peddlers on the mainland. Even though the sultanate of Witu helped them to open their small shops in Lamu, they were not in favor of that sultanate since they had to get their supplies from Mombasa and pay taxes on them to the sultan of Witu. Because of the economic situation, they backed the British and the BuSa'id. They were interested in the maintenance of peaceful conditions in which to sell and transport their goods. They were, as usual, the middlemen, and had to be very careful in their dealings. The Indians in Mombasa were the big wholesale merchants; the Ḥadramis bought from them and sold to the Africans. To carry on their business, they needed a well-established and stable system of government.

When the slaves revolted against the wangwana, the Ḥadramis were the first to extend help to the slaves. With their cash capital, they made deals with the slaves who were still farming the land. The slaves needed cash; the Ḥadramis had it. The Ḥadramis would buy the whole crop, pay the slave some money in advance, and then the crop would be theirs. This credit system suited the slaves and brought great benefits for the Ḥadramis. Still, the Ḥadramis considered trade as their real occupation. The customers, slaves or non-slaves, had to be served in the best way in spite of their social stratum. In other words, they did not mind acting as "servants" for any of their customers, unlike the wangwana who were not ready to accept the idea of serving the customer even if he were equal to them. For example, the wangwana would not serve a Bajuni; the Bajuni were free, yet low. However, the Ḥadramis acknowledged that the Bajuni were the most important customers; they were interested in their purchasing power and had little concern for their stratification.

The Ḥadramis gained from the presence of the British and BuSa'id rule, since through them Lamu opened its doors for more strangers. The Bajuni, who had not been allowed to settle in Lamu before, began to do so at this time. Most of them settled in Langoni. Indians, also, began to come to Lamu. With the increase in the number of settlers, the Langoni market acquired its position as the supplier for the newcomers as well as for the islands around Lamu. While the open market was a boon to the Ḥadramis, the wangwana were not interested in it. They were more interested in manipulating the agricultural production, which they sold directly to the foreign traders. On the other hand, the Langoni market affected the patriarchal relation which existed between the slaves and the wangwana. In the past, the slaves lived only on what the wangwana left for them. They had no other source of income. However, the creation of the

Langoni retail market established a new way for the slaves and for all strangers to support themselves without depending on the wangwana. In earlier days, the wangwana, as the only literate people, had manipulated the old otokoni market because they were the only group who could communicate with the buyers of Arabia, Persia, and India. They knew the secret of foreign trade. Now the presence of the Ḥadramis threatened all that. Firstly, the Ḥadramis had a wider network of relations, especially with other Ḥadramis all over the Indian Ocean. Secondly, they had more readily available cash than the wangwana, who had to depend on the barter system. Thirdly, the Ḥadramis suffered no social consequences from opening the market for every customer. All of these factors afforded the Ḥadramis more freedom to maneuver the market.

Generally, the Ḥadramis' policy was more acceptable to the governments of the sultan and the British than the wangwana's policy. The wangwana had been interested in keeping Lamu in isolation; the Ḥadramis, on the other hand, were interested in opening Lamu up to other East African peoples. This integration, accompanied by peaceful relations, was essential for the progress of the Ḥadramis' business. The decline of the wangwana made the Ḥadramis the strongest economic group in Lamu.

The Ḥadrami Maulidi

As we have said, the Ḥadramis were not allowed to live in the northern part of the town, because they were not considered equal to the wangwana. They were not invited to the wangwana celebrations, such as the Maulidi Barzanji, or the mtaa district celebration of Maulidi ya Rama. They were confined to the southern part of town, Langoni, and the wangwana treated them as a non-stratified group. Yet, the Ḥadramis had a system of stratification, as we said earlier, that was as rigid as Lamu's. Nevertheless, in their religious system, the Ḥadrami sharifs, or *saiyids*,[33] in many cases cut across the social stratificatory system. In Ḥadramaut, if the saiyid was accepted as having *baraka,* or supernatural power, he might get followers from every social stratum. This kind of sharif, in fact, broke the boundaries of both the tribal and the stratificatory system. The sharifs are the *qutb,* or axis, and are stratified according to their powers; one of them is considered a *qutb al aqtab,* or "the axis of the axes." At any given time there cannot be more than one qutb al aqtab. This office can only be held by a sharif; the secret or the trust was so important that no ordinary man would be able to live if he were given it. The sharifs did not die because

33. In Ḥadramaut they call the descendants of the prophet *sada* (singular, *saiyid*). Sometimes I use *saiyids* instead of *sada.*

they were part of the eternal light, the light of Mohammed.

Once a sharif was recognized as a qutb, he would be approached by different tribes and groups both during his life and after his death. After his death, his annual visit would be celebrated by many. The criterion by which a sharif was judged a qutb lay not in his power to make miracles but in his power to gain support or love from the different and opposing groups. In other words, the Ḥadramis say that if God loves a person, then all the people will love him and support him. This public consensus is the Ḥadrami measure of a qutb.

"The axis of the axes," who had to be taken from the Ba'Alwi sharifs, was the highest and the most powerful existing sharif. God would not have anything done in this world without informing "the axis of the axes" in advance. Below him, there were nine *abdal,* or substitutes, who were spread all over the world, and "the axis of the axes" gave them the inspiration appropriate to their capacity and circumstances. Beneath the substitutes, there were seventy-two *nuqaba'* or directors—they are the *walis,* or supporters, or local saints, to be more exact. As I have said, while the qutb and abdal had to be taken from the sharifs, this was not necessary in the case of the walis. When one qutb died, another took his place. The new qutb was decided by God, who restricted his choice to the descendants of Mohammed and to those descendants of the Ba'Alwi sharifs, who were, in turn, the descendants of Ahmed ibn 'Issa al Muhajir, the emigrant, who was from the descent line of Ḥussein, the son of Fatima and 'Ali ibn Abi Talib (see the Genealogical Chart). The qutb position was not hereditary; the only requirement was that the qutb should be taken from the Ba'Alwi sharif group. For example, Saiyid 'Ali bin Mohammed al Ḥabashy[34] was considered the qutb by the Ḥadramis who settled in Lamu, but, when he died, his sons did not inherit that position. Saiyid 'Abdallah al Shatri from Tarim, Ḥadramaut (1873 - 1931 A. D.—1290 - 1350 A. H.) became the qutb (see Map 5). Above all, the qutb had to be religiously well-educated, so, practically speaking, the choice was limited to well-educated Ba'Alwi sharifs.

Beneath the qutb, there were the abdal, who were able to transfer themselves from one place to another; they could be in X, while a shadow of them was in Y at the same time. In their ability to transfer themselves and to take on

34. The saiyid's bibliography can be found in *Riḥlat al Ashwaq al Qawiya ila mawatin al Sādah al 'Alwiya* [The journey of the strong desires to the homeland of the 'Alwy saiyids], by Sheikh Abdallahi ibn Mohammed Bakathir (Cairo: Scientific Press, 1939), pp. 27—28. See also Saiyid Abdullah ibn Mohammed ibn Ḥamid ibn Omar al Saqaf al Alawi, *Tarikh al Shu'ara al Hadramien* [History of the Ḥadrami poets] (Cairo; Scientific Press, n. d.), V, 230—68.

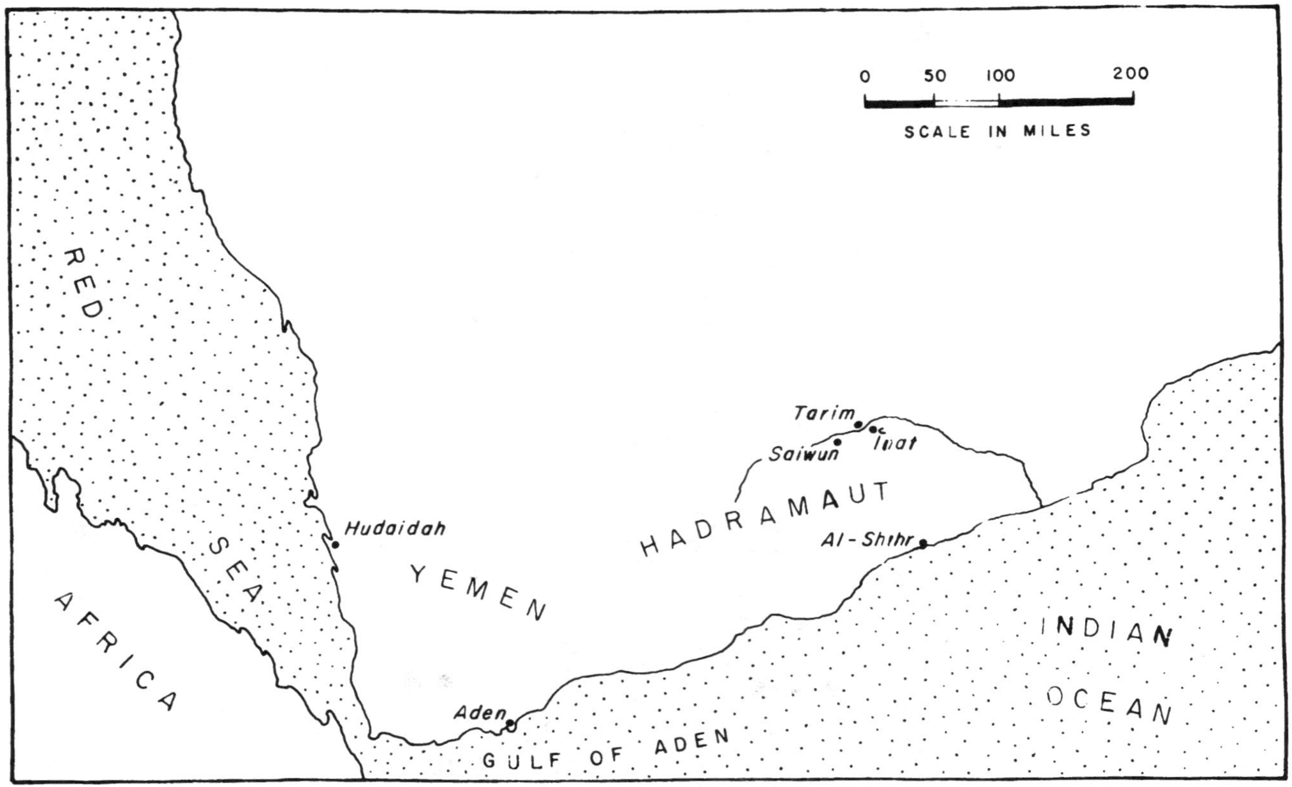

Map 5. South-West Arabia, Yemen, and Ḥadramaut

different shapes, they were like the angels. Their function was to carry the inspirations from the qutb to the nuqaba', the directors. The abdal had to be learned people also, but they could be chosen from any of the descendants of Mohammed. They were not limited to the Ba'Alwi sharifs.

The nuqaba' could be chosen from any Muslim group, and though education was important it was not essential. If the person obeyed God and followed the right path and loved the Prophet, then the Prophet would love him. It is interesting to note here in dealing with these local saints that they were not chosen by God. The decision as to who the nuqaba' were was made according to the amount of love they showed the Prophet. Since the qutb and abdal are the descendants of the Prophet, they love him as their grandfather, and he loves them in return. With the nuqaba', the matter is different; they might, by chance, be descendants of the Prophet, but their love must be expressed if they want the Prophet to love them.

It is clear that Mohammed was the center of the relation between God and the nuqaba'. God loved Mohammed; Mohammed loved his descendants (qutb and abdal); the nuqaba' loved Mohammed, and therefore, they loved his descendants, who loved him. All loved Mohammed because God loved him. However, according to the Ḥadramis, there were two kinds of love. Some people loved Mohammed because they were ordered to do so, while others loved him because they were chosen to. The nuqaba', like other Muslims, loved Mohammed because they were ordered to, and this love was intensified when Mohammed exchanged love with them. This exchange of love converts the ordinary Muslim into a saint. The saint must make a strong effort in order to keep that love; if he is an ordinary man, then there is a greater chance that he will lose that love. If at any point he occupies his heart with any thing other than the Prophet, he might lose the Prophet's love. In other words, the nuqaba' had to keep a minimum relation with this world in order to perpetuate their love, while the qutb and abdal were not under that kind of obligation. While the local saints or nuqaba' had to prove, by their behavior, that they were saints, the qutb and abdal sometimes even behaved in a non-Islamic way in order to hide their position. While unreligious behavior hurts the local saints, that same behavior will strengthen the position of the qutb and abdal. In other words, the local saint was able to achieve a true saintly position only after his death, when he was no longer able to sin. The qutb and abdal achieved that position while they were alive, and what seem to be sins were not counted against them.

At one time, the Ḥadramis in Lamu thought that the qutb al aqtab was

Saiyid ʻAli ibn Mohammed al Ḥabashy, who was living in Saiwun in Ḥadramaut (d. 1914 A. D.–1333 A.H.). Saiyid ʻAli al Ḥabashy established a *sufi*, or mystic order, in Ḥadramaut in which the celebration of the Maulidi was an essential ritual. Every Thursday after the sunset prayer Saiyid ʻAli al Ḥabashy read the Maulidi. He did not use the Maulidi Barzanji; he used another Maulidi written by ʻAbdel Rahman ibn ʻAli al Debʻi,[35] the recitation of which lasted about one hour. The Ḥadramis considered this ritual the center of their religious affiliation.

However, the Maulidi was read not only in the mosque and on Thursdays, but on every happy occasion. It was considered auspicious. When the Ḥadramis married, they read the Maulidi before performing the ceremony, and if they were about to initiate a new business, they did the same. When they circumcised their children they read it; and the circumcision took place exactly at the time when the reader reached the moment of the Prophet's birth. In other words, before any major transition in their life, the Ḥadramis would recite the Maulidi. Between the sections of it, they read *qsa'id,* or religious poetry, either in classical Arabic, or in the Ḥadrami dialect which they called *Ḥumaini.*

The Maulidi ritual was usually led by a sheikh, who began by reading one Fatiḥa as a gift to the Prophet, another for his own saiyids, especially the Ba'Alwi, and then another one for his teachers. The sitting position of the sheikh and the various reciters was very important. The sheikh sat on the right side of the niche with his back to the wall, right and left being defined from the point of view of a person facing the niche. In front of the sheikh there was a *kinara,* or a tray covered with a clean white cloth, on which there was rose water, *ʻudi* (aloe wood), *ubani* (frankincense), *ʻambari* (ambergris), and an incense burner. To his left sat those who had good voices, and could read the qasa'id. In front of him the *muradidin,* or repeaters, sat.

Social stratification was disregarded in this Maulidi because if a daʻif had a good voice he was asked to sit beside the sheikh. Nevertheless, no daʻif or qaba'il was ever permitted to lead the ritual or to recite the Fatiḥa; these were the functions of the sheikhs and the saiyids. If a saiyid were present, the sheikh could not recite the Fatiḥa or burn the incense, since it was thought that the presence of the saiyid screens all who are below him, even the sheikhs. However, the Ḥadramis who settled in Lamu were without any saiyid—therefore, the sheikhs were the leaders of the ritual.

It is interesting to note that although the Ḥusseini sharifs were a branch of the Ba'Alwi sharifs (see the Genealogical Chart), and therefore related to the sharifs

35. ʻAbdel Raḥman ibn ʻAli al Debʻi, *Maulidi al Debʻi* (Bombay: Islamic Press, 1912).

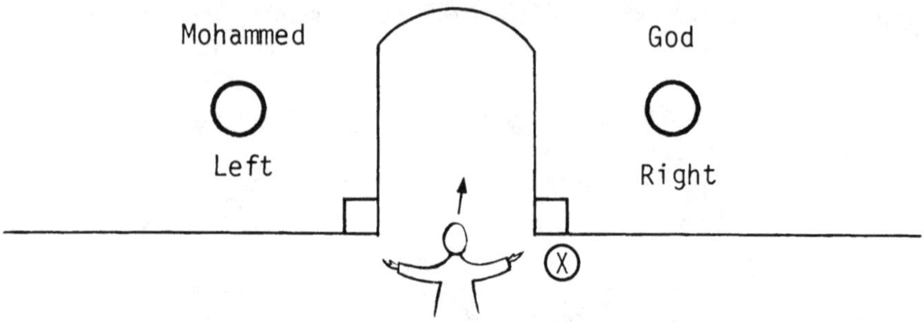

Fig. 5. The Niche: The seating position of the sheikh in the Ḥadrami Maulidi. Situated always in a way that indicates the direction of Mecca, the niche is the most important place in the Islamic mosque. It further organizes the space by determining "left" and "right." X in the diagram illustrates the seating position of the sheikh in the Hadrami Maulidi. Seating arrangements vary according to the social group and the particular ceremony being performed.

of Ḥadramaut, they never respected the Ḥadrami settlers and avoided having contact with them. The Ḥusseini sharifs, in my opinion, were so absorbed in the wangwana ideology that they automatically looked down at the Ḥadramis.

At the same time, the Ḥadramis in Lamu looked down on the Lamu sharifs and considered them inferior to their sharifs in Ḥadramaut. The Lamu sharifs, from the Ḥadramis' point of view, should not have been involved in the secular life of the town, where they worked as traders and businessmen. They were neither well-educated nor endowed with baraka, as Saiyid 'Ali al Ḥabashy and Saiyid 'Omar al 'Attass were. The sharifs of Lamu were called the sharifs of Brava (Brawa),[36] a derogatory name.

On the other hand, the Ḥadramis believed that their sharifs had power, even after death. In fact, without them, the world would collapse. The sharifs were

36. Brawa or Brava is a Somali coastal town. The Ḥadramis say that everyone in Brawa called himself sharif, without showing any sign of his *sharaf,* i.e., honor and credentials.

seen as the *raison d'être* for this world. This is why the Ḥadramis' Maulidi began with a poem praising the sharifs, which called on those sharifs who lived with them or with their fathers, and asked them to intervene with God on their behalf. Thus there was a hierarchy of mediators, the highest of which was the Prophet. However, the Prophet was not God; he could not intervene directly with God. He had to intervene with God through the angels.

The Ḥadramis thought that every supplication to be carried to God had to be carried by the angels. In order to come down, the angels had to smell *ubani,* a substance which irritated them, and so prompted them to come down and carry up the *du'a,* or supplication. However, these angels could not come down except when the Prophet was praised. As part of the believers, the angels were ordered to bless and greet the Prophet. The ubani and praise for the Prophet were both needed in order to get the angels down to the ritual. Thus, in every ritual, the invocation was presented first to the Ḥadrami sharifs, who then asked the Prophet to intervene; then the Prophet asked the angels to come and carry the du'a up to God.

The relation between Mohammed and God and between the Ḥadramis and their sharifs is established on love. The Ḥadramis have to love their sharifs with a love that goes all through them like blood through the body. In one of their poems they express this concept as follows:

> The proof that I love you, descendants of the Prophet, is clear and shining in my heart and in my actions.
>
> Every time I have a distress, you are the first to come to my help.
>
> I have evidence of my real love, which I cannot stop; how could I do that while my soul declared it, even before Adam came to this world?
>
> I am your slave, and this honors me; my heart will never question that.
>
> You are the one who will help me, and whom I trust. You are my hope, my apron, my protectors. You are in front of me all the time. You are my niche, you are my leaders to the right path.
>
> We are the slaves and you are the masters. God purified you and ordered us to bless you.
>
> It is clear that your position is higher than anybody's. God Himself chose Gabriel to be your Father's [Mohammed's] servant.

This elevation of the descendants of the Prophet was not granted to any of Lamu's sharifs. The wangwana treated the sharifs like any of the highest wangwana. They thought that they were to be respected because Mohammed was chosen from them. However, that respect depended on their hishima, kutunga, and Astarabu. Some of the sharifs might have baraka, but this was due to piety rather than to a special relation to the Prophet. In other words, anyone from the wangwana could have baraka, just as the sharifs could.

In both the Maulidi Barzanji (wangwana) and the Maulidi Ḥadrami, the importance of the descendants of the Prophet is expressed. However, the Ḥadramis mentioned the names of saiyids whom they knew, and with whom they had lived, saiyids who were either their predecessors, contemporaries, or successors. These saiyids were the core of the social reality of the Ḥadrami society. Without them, not only the present but also the past and the future would be unimaginable.

As we saw in Maulidi Barzanji, the wangwana behaved according to the hishima principle, which means that stratification had to be strictly followed. The Prophet was thought to praise the wangwana for this. In contrast, the Ḥadramis, in the presence of the Prophet or saiyids, were all slaves, were all low; and that was the reason why social stratification was absent during the Maulidi. The sacred tree threw its shadow equally over all who stood under it and sought its shade.

In both the political and the economic fields, traditional Lamu met changes with which the old wangwana ideology was unable to cope. Economic change was not, I think, the sole cause of the decline of wangwana dominance. Rather, the significant factors lie in marriage and descent, and the ideology connected with them. The wangwana lost faith in their own system, which is clear in the following poem written by Ḥamid ibn Sa'id about fifty years ago.

A Prediction of the Future

> I blow the horn and recall the past. Everything has changed. Those who used to live under thorny trees, now live in great stone houses.
>
> Those who lived under the shadow of [Komba], [mirule], and [mwangati] trees, and used them as their houses, today sit on thrones and wear turbans on their heads. Even those who smelled as animals today smell of jasmine perfume.
>
> The kingdom of Lamu is now in the hands of those who were skinning animals, and who were so low that they dared not eat in the presence of important people. But those important people [wangwana] were like a shining lamp, and, as we know, the lamp rusted. It will never shine again. Those who carried flour sacks on their backs, today are in their glory.
>
> Those people with the thin thighs of rope makers were so poor and low that they used to go around begging, and people used to chase them away. Today they put on turbans with two ends [*mikile*], one end in the front and one end at the back. And

when they speak, people listen to them and think them wise.

Those who used to carry forty pieces of iron on their backs, and at the same time drug the fence-logs. Today their backs bear the best clothes, and their arms carry the best weapons. Those who were not allowed to attend any feasts, are today invited to all.

Those who were ignored and not even allowed to build houses, who used to take shelter under trees, who were afraid even to speak or express their opinions, are today the most revered and respected people. Before anyone is allowed to talk to them, he must ask their permission. Those who were put down in the past, today are free. And they are enjoying themselves.

Those who lived in mud shelters under the rain in the forest, where they used to sleep and find pleasure, today have huge palaces and many blessings. People now welcome them and seek their advice.

Those who used to live and hide in the forest, who were low and unknown, people used to call [*watumbatu*]. Now they are the masters and even famous people beseech them. When famous people gather, the watumbatu are at the head and are gathered about.

The world has changed. Do not forget what I told you. Those who were on top came down, those who were down, rose to the top. (If you speak, you will be in trouble. It is better to leave Lamu and go away. We have to repent, let us not forget that. Perhaps, God might accept our penitence.)

3

Lamu and the Rise of the Jamalilil Sharifs

Hapo uliopo pana shariefu	In this place, we now have a sharif;
Mpani chetezo atiya pefu	Offer him the censer and ubani;
Tusoma Fatiha kwa utatufu	Let him read the Fatiḥa calmly,
Isiwe lahani kwa wenye kusoma.	So that the other readers will not make mistakes.

This chapter will continue to deal with Lamu's steadily changing social structure. In the first two chapters I presented the "*historical*" background of the town of Lamu and also dealt with the radical rearrangements of elements which produced what we conventionally call "social change." At the end of the second chapter, the wangwana ideology was seen as rapidly declining. Those who had established themselves as the real wangwana, and thus as the rightful masters of Lamu, found the genealogical base for their claim of superiority shaken and their economic control dwindling. The increased number of *mwana wa haramu,* or bastards, was one reason for the shift in the traditionally rigorous system of social stratification. Such persons constituted an ambiguous, ill-defined category. On the one hand, they were unable to claim the traditional rights which, as wangwana, they would have received; and yet, on the other hand, they were not really considered slaves either.

The traditional Lamu sharifs suffered from the same inextricable problems. They had been forced to marry their slaves and to take souriyas, and their daughters had married from the wangwana group who were now considered bastards. So, in order to maintain their position in Lamu, the sharifs had to defend their claim to be the descendants of the Prophet. The sharifs considered themselves pure because God had purified the Prophet's lineage and removed the stain of adultery from all who were part of it.

THE LAMU SHARIFS AND THE PROBLEM OF DESCENT

Old sharif familes such as the al Ḥusseini and al Mahadali were part and parcel of the wangwana. When the wangwana were strong and able to protect the principle of marriage between equals, the sharifs accepted this ideology and propagated it. They participated in the wangwana-controlled economic structure and, therefore, met the same fate as the wangwana when the structure toppled. The genealogical claim at the base of their social position was challenged, as was that of the wangwana. But the sharifs tried to save themselves from the accusation that they were bastards by claiming that, as the descendants of the Prophet, they were infallible. They asserted that their children inherited their fathers' qualities, regardless of their mothers' origin. The child of a sharif would be a sharif regardless of the kind of relationship his father had had with his mother. Thus, if a sharif had a souriya, his son from that union would be equal to his son from a free woman whom he had properly married. Even if a sharif had an adulterous relation with a low woman, a son from such a relation would be a sharif. If a sharif had sexual contact with a slave girl, that would automatically change her status, raising her up in the stratificatory system. In Lamu, they expressed this by saying "*Si mgala tena mtu zaliya mwenye*," "she who gives birth to a sharif is no longer a slave." As long as a sharif father agreed that a child was his, that child was due all the rights of a sharif. This was a drastic departure from the wangwana principle of marriage between equals. The new principles of descent moved closer to the position of the children of souriyas, who claimed that they were to be considered wangwana regardless of their mother's origin.

Still, the sharifs kept some of the traditional *mkufu,* or equal marriage ideology, alive. They claimed that the child who had a sharif father and mother was to be considered higher than the child of a sharif and a non-sharif woman. In the first case, the child was called a *mansib,* "of rank or dignity," while the second kind of child was called *sharifu.*

In the past, sharif females had been allowed to marry non-sharif males. However, after the decline of the wangwana, the sharif female could marry a non-sharif male only on the condition that he was not only her equal, but also a *mngwana swa swa,* or a real free man. In other words, the husband of a sharif woman had to be born of a free father and mother. Even if the mother of the sharif girl had been a slave, she was not to marry a man whose mother had been one. All sharifs were part of the Prophet's sacred genealogical tree, and, as such, they were purified. Even if they committed adultery, it would not hurt them, since their purity, coming from Mohammed himself, was considered higher than that of anyone in Lamu. A man who was not really free would not possess hishima, kutunga, or adabu. His behavior would be similar to that of the Wa Shenzi. If such a person married a sharif girl, he might call her names, or leave her without support, or mistreat her. However, if he did that, he would commit a sin not only against his wife but also against the Prophet. The sharif woman, as part of the Prophet's lineage, must not be mistreated. It is said that, when the last day comes, the Prophet will not intervene with God on behalf of a person who has insulted his daughter.

Similarly, following the principle of the sharifs' infallibility, the non-sharif husband could not criticize his sharif wife, even if she committed the gravest sin, since what he considered sinful behavior might not be sinful for the sharifs. In other words, when a non-sharif male married a sharif female, he not only had to act like a mngwana swa swa, but he also had to suspend his role as a man and head of his household. For all these reasons, men thought it was dangerous to marry a sharif woman. If they did, they had to always remain conscious of the fact that they were lower than their wives, and if they forgot, or acted contrary to that realization, then their life in this world and in the hereafter would be ruined.[1] Yet there were some advantages to such a marriage. The prosperity of the non-sharif husband was thought to be due to his wife's sharif descent. After all, the Prophet would not allow his daughters to live in poverty. So the husband of a sharif woman, if he treated her well, would always be *mkundufu,* or rich and dependent on no one; he would be blessed and would possess a good reputation and be loved by others. In other words, he would gain all the pleasures of this life:

> The foremost pleasures of life are three:
> The first health,
> The second to be rich,
> The third to have good luck, and thus
> be loved by all the people.

1. This put certain restrictions on the private sexual life between a mngwana and his sharif wife. The sexual positions, I was told, were to be reversed. The mngwana cannot sleep *over* his wife, but must sleep under her. This is not at all the "normal" sexual position.

It is interesting to note that with this shift in the sharif ideology, the Prophet began to be spoken of as a protective power. In this, the sharifs were clearly very close to the Ḥadramis, which means that they had begun to move away from the wangwana view of the Prophet and his family. The sharifs sought to support their new position through history, referring to the time when their protective powers had enabled them to save Patta. However, when the Ḥusseini sharifs came to Lamu, the wangwana viewed them only as political supporters against Patta. They never stressed the protective powers which they supposedly derived from the Prophet. However, they agreed with the Bajuni that the Ḥusseini sharifs had once had that power. In other words, the wangwana thought that the sharifs were to be respected but not feared. As a mngwana told me, "If they had power, why did they not save themselves, or protect Lamu from what took place?" As far as the wangwana were concerned, the decline of Lamu's social and economic structures was proof enough that the sharifs had no supernatural power.

The Ḥusseini sharifs, trying to preserve their position, soon clashed with the wangwana, and the relations between the two deteriorated. This is expressed in a widespread story:

> In Lamu, there was (and still is) a mosque called *Mwana Lalo.* This mosque was used only by the wangwana. The man who calls for prayer [*mu'azin*] was the only slave allowed inside the mosque. One of the people who used to pray in that mosque was Shee Ahmed Ibn Abu Bakr al Ḥusseini.[2] The imam [leader of prayer] of that mosque was from the wangwana. One day the imam told the mu'azin to call the people to stand up and begin praying. The mu'azin told the imam that Shee Ahmed was still making his ablutions and that he, the mu'azin, wanted to delay the prayer for a few minutes until Shee Ahmed had finished. The imam told the mu'azin that they were not in *'Inat* (where the sharifs came from, i.e., Ḥadramaut), and that they had suffered enough from all the sharifs. Shee Ahmed, when he heard this, left the mosque, and he began to build a new mosque—the Rodha Mosque.

The superiority of the Ḥusseini Sharifs became unacceptable to the wangwana. They began to attack them, and for this they used the Mahdali sharifs. The Mahdali sharifs claimed that they were descendants of the Prophet, but they possessed no document to prove it. Even the Ḥusseini sharifs looked down on them and doubted their claim. But the wangwana used this against all the sharifs; they said that a sharif's descent was as doubtful as anybody else's.

To compound the problem, doubts began to arise about the importance of Islamic education. Some Lamuans sent their children to Mombasa to attend the

2. See the Genealogical Chart.

secular British schools, and one Ḥusseini sharif even sent his son to France. When this boy returned, he was not even able to read the Qur'ān. Unable to remain in Lamu, he moved to Mombasa and lived there. The case of that student is well known, and the wangwana refer to it all the time, especially when they want to give an example of a sharif who does not know his religion. This man used to refer to the Qur'ān as "a book of legends made by the ancestors."

And so the wangwana found many ways to question the claim of the infallibility of the sharifs. The idea that the sharifs were protected by the Prophet, and that they therefore could not make mistakes, slowly fell apart. The sharifs' sufferings were sufficient proof that they were no different from the others. They could not protect themselves, and it was clear that the Prophet did not show up to save his descendants.

The crisis was not confined to the social arena; it also extended to the roots of the sharifs' religious ideology. When the people began to question the sharifs' descent and their relations with the Prophet, they also questioned the role of religion itself. Religion ceased to function as a "control mechanism"; it was unable to explain or justify what was taking place in Lamu, especially in relation to the wangwana.

> Mohammed ibn Seif al BuSa'id was going around telling the people that physical exercises are better than praying. Fasting is not important. He went on to say that if he were appointed as liwali he would close the mosques because they did not contribute anything to Lamu. When a sharif heard what Mohammed ibn Seif al BuSa'id had said, the sharif ruled that Mohammed was an unbeliever [*kafiri*]. When Mohammed died, his father, the liwali of Lamu, asked the same sharif to come and perform the death rituals. The sharif went to the house, and people were sitting around reading the Qur'ān. When they finished, the sharif stood and said, "You have to grant the blessings of your prayers to your fathers or mothers, because the deceased is not a Muslim, and God will not forgive him."[3]

So it was that the traditional sharifs at Lamu were unable to establish their new claims. Although they lived among the wangwana, they refused to reinterpret and reevaluate the sharifs' position. Their relationship to the Ḥadramis and slaves was also affected.

THE ḤADRAMIS AND THE SLAVES

The Ḥadramis and the slaves were despised by both the wangwana and the sharifs. These two groups were similar: neither was considered part of the

3. This sharif will be discussed later.

town's structure, and they had very intensive social interaction with each other. The slaves depended on the Ḥadramis to supply them with credit and jobs. In contrast to the wangwana, the Ḥadramis attributed their success to the power of the sharifs. They thought that the baraka of their sharifs provided them with the real protection which they needed in this faraway town. When I told a second generation Ḥadrami that I was going to visit Saiwun, he gave me the name of his sharif there, whom he called *mansib*, and added, "Tell him that I need him to make some supplications on my behalf." He continued, "Soon he will receive a letter from me. Please tell him that I am still his slave."

The Ḥadramis came from places where the sharifs were well established, and where their claim of supernatural power was never doubted. In Ḥadramaut, the sharifs had a well-defined ideological and social role to play. The sharifs in Lamu, being part of the wangwana, were unable to replace the sharifs of Ḥadramaut. However, when the traditional Lamuan sharifs began to reevaluate and reinterpret their role, they coincidentally moved closer to the Ḥadramis' ideology concerning the sharifs. But the sharifs of Lamu were unable to grasp the sociological direction which would have resulted in gathering the Ḥadramis around them. The ideological elements were present, yet the rearrangement of them was not clear. In other words, even though the Lamu sharifs were able to reinterpret their concepts of descent, the role of the Prophet, and the infallibility of the sharifs, they were not flexible enough to see the similarities between their ideology and that of the lower groups or to make contact with these groups who shared these beliefs. As a part of the wangwana, the sharifs were unable to foresee the power of these lower groups. The sharifs persisted in thinking that the wangwana were the real owners of Lamu, while the lower groups were only strangers.

Meanwhile, most of the newly freed slaves were unable to find a way out of their religious dilemma. If their freedom had not been granted according to Islamic custom as interpreted by the wangwana, then all their actions as free persons would be unacceptable to God. As I said, the slaves were deprived of the angels of the "right" and "left." They were associated with the jin, and thus were considered defiled and Wa Shenzi. They were a burden to the town, a nuisance the wangwana were trying to eliminate.[4]

The wangwana and the sharifs, as the custodians of Shari'a, or Islamic law,

4. I will show more clearly the wangwana views concerning the slaves in the chapter on the wangwana ritual called *Kuzingu Kuzinguka Ngombe,* or "the circulation of the bull around the town" (see Chapter 6). The whole intention of that ritual was to purify the town and get rid of the jin.

declared repeatedly that the free slaves were sinners, and they should repent by returning to their masters and asking them for forgiveness. The slaves were not allowed to attend or participate in any religious ritual, or even to pray in the wangwana mosques. They were the defiled people, the forest people, the people of the bush, those who were without either hishima or kutunga. They were considered part of nature in the crudest sense of the word and were thought to have no laws or manners. It was said that all they ever did was mate and that their sexual drive determined all aspects of their behavior. In short, they represented man in his animalistic aspect. Of course, all these qualities were meant to contrast with those of the wangwana who possessed culture, Astarabu.

The slaves were unable to overcome their dilemma. Paradoxically, if they acted like wangwana and followed the rules of hishima and adabu, they would still be accused of being without hishima. To act even like the lowest wangwana meant that the slaves were improperly raising themselves up to a position equal to that of the wangwana, and such social climbing was obviously against hishima. So, the slaves did not have any place in the wangwana system; they were mere tools. When they came to Lamu, they were unable to adopt any clear behavior code. If the wangwana had their way, they should have continued to act like slaves. "A slave is a slave": even if you give him the best education and the best life, he is unable to acquire the wangwana qualities.

Because the slaves were deprived of all religious education, they were not allowed to read the Maulidi Barzanji. Gradually they developed their own Maulidi, which was called *Maulidi ya ki Swahili,* and which I call here *the competitive Maulidi.* The next section will be devoted to an effort to uncover the assumptions behind the Maulidi.

THE COMPETITIVE MAULIDI OR MAULIDI YA KI SWAHILI

This Maulidi was initiated by the ex-slaves, and there are two ex-slaves whose names are always mentioned in connection with it—Mwalim Jum'ani and Mwalim Bajuri. The competitive Maulidi was read in Swahili, not in Arabic, and was usually performed in the Mkomani area, in the northern half of the town, which is the heart of the wangwana territory. Both Jum'ani and Bajuri used two separate mosques, where the Maulidi was taught, and both mosques were located on the fringes of the wangwana area, where some ex-slaves were settled.

There was a strong competition between Mwalim Jum'ani and Mwalim Bajuri. Both were, for various reasons, backed by wangwana groups, even though their followers were slaves. While Mwalim Jum'ani was backed by the al Lami Wa Yumbili Ponde group, that is, the lowest stratum of the wangwana, Mwalim

Bajuri was backed by the sharifs, the al Ma'awi group, and some of the al Makhzumi group (see Fig. 3). For example, Mwana Atiqa binti Sheikh Abdel el-Raḥman al Ḥusseini supplied Bajuri with money, and Mwana Amina binti Amin al Mahdali composed some of the poetry which he used to recite. Even Ḥabib Mansib Abu Bakr ibn Abd el Raḥman, the well-known sharif scholar, wrote poetry for Bajuri. So, the relation between Bajuri and the highest stratum of Lamu wangwana was a strong one; indeed, Sharif Mansib's wife was also from that stratum, and she too backed Bajuri. Mwalim Jum'ani was backed by the Wa Yumbili Ponde in general, and by one woman of the Wa Yumbili Ngombe in particular—Asha binti Mohammed ibn Osman, who had been the owner of Bajuri, Jum'ani's rival, before he was freed. Jum'ani was not a pure slave. Actually, his father was from the Wa Shihiri, and only his mother was a slave. In other words, Mwalim Jum'ani was from that ambiguous category of persons in Lamu who had a claim of descent without the rights of a proper descendant. These half-slaves were called *Wa Zaliya,* and they were ranked higher than a slave. The Ma Zaliya, if he were liked by his master, might have been used as a house slave rather than as an agricultural worker.

Mwalim Bajuri, on the other hand, was an ex-slave in the full sense of the term, and the origin of the two leaders had a lot to do with those who backed them. The Mahdali and Ḥusseini sharifs and the Wa Yumbili Pembe agreed to back Bajuri, because they saw him as a man who never forgot that he was a slave. He knew his position, accepted his inferior origin, and showed his gratitude to his masters. For example, Bajuri's Maulidi was attended by more people than the other Maulidis, and when Asha binti Osman saw that Mwalim Jum'ani was losing supporters in Mkomani, she wrote a poem for Mwalim Bajuri, part of which said, "*Asotuwa kupata alitabalo*," which means, "He who behaves badly will get what he deserves." When Bajuri got the letter, he went to Asha, and asked her for forgiveness. Bajuri was not a person who liked to "make fire." Jum'ani, on the other hand, as part of the ambiguous descent category, was very proud of himself and acted as if he were a free person. The Wa Yumbili Ponde, who were deprived and put down by the wangwana, found in Jum'ani an excellent tool to use against the higher wangwana. The Maulidi was an ideal occasion for the different wangwana groups to compete with each other, and it also served the purpose of dividing the slaves into two opposing factions.

After the high wangwana lost their position of superiority, they began to compete with each other, using the little wealth which was left to them. The *mashindanu,* or competition, was so strong that the wangwana used to sell their gardens in order to buy the cows for the Maulidi feast and pay for the other

Maulidi expenses. This worked out in favor of the Ḥadramis, who were able to buy some of the wangwana land on Lamu itself.

If Mwalim Jum'ani accepted the invitation of one faction to read the Maulidi, these people would bring two or three cows, slaughter them, and put on a feast. In addition to the food, they also supplied the Maulidi with steam lights, decorations, and other materials used in the Maulidi itself, such as coffee, 'ambari, ubani, rose water, and other things. The Maulidi was usually held in one of the side streets of the area in which this particular group resided, and outsiders would come there to view it. No wangwana participated in reciting the Maulidi on these occasions; they only supplied material support. Different groups would go to observe, the Ḥadramis being among the most regular. When the Maulidi was over, the observers would discuss it, and their judgment would be evaluated by the opposing faction. If they felt that the last Maulidi held by the opposing faction was better than theirs, they would announce their intention to hold a new Maulidi. If faction A had slaughtered three cows, then faction B had to slaughter four or five. If the Maulidi of faction A continued for three days, the Maulidi of faction B would last six. Once a Maulidi was held for nine straight days. At that point, the British subcommissioner found himself obliged to interfere and stop the Maulidi. It seemed unreasonable to him that the Lamuans should engage in this continuous competition and so squander their meager wealth.

The leaders of the two Maulidi were called *fundi,* a word which means "skillful persons," that is, persons specialized in attracting the attention of others. However, calling them fundi had a second, more important, meaning. It indicated that these Maulidi were no longer rituals for the sake of acquiring God's blessings but performances which mainly sought to attract other people's attention. In other words, the most important achievement for the fundi was making a good show and earning the praise of the people. Like a good carpenter who knows how to build a fine table or chair, the fundi of the Maulidi ya ki Swahili knew how to stage a fine performance and earn the praise of everyone. The word *mwalim* was used as a synonym for *fundi. Mwalimu ya Qur'āni,* for example, means the man who is a professional reader of the Qur'ān, or a teacher of the proper method of reading the Qur'ān. However, the words *fundi* or *mwalim* are never used for a learned sharif, or for a man who has *'ilm,* or religious knowledge. In other words, the terms *fundi* and *mwalim* were used in reference to any secular profession, but never for the sacred ones. One informant, who was from the Bajuri group, summarized the above point accurately,

"The Maulidi ya ki Swahili was like Beni;[5] its aim was to attract attention. When we were performing, we knew that we had to perform better than the other group—otherwise we would lose face."

In order to attract more attention at the Maulidi the two fundis began to use the *matari,* or tambourine, and to sing Swahili poems. They were the first to introduce musical instruments to the Maulidi. The ceremonies were further enlivened when Mwalim Bajuri would lose his senses and beat his head and box his chest. He was unable to control himself, especially when the beating of the tambourine speeded up. On this point, my informant agreed with many people of Lamu that a devil (*pepo, sheitani*) rising up into the head of the mwalim was the cause of that strange behavior. This is a very significant explanation, because, as we saw earlier in relation to the Maulidi ya Rama, the shaking Maulidi, although people there were also unable to control their body movements, that was never explained as due to the devil. Here, we find again the influence of the wangwana ideology and its proliferation even among the slaves. The slaves were told that they were impure, and that they were in contact with the devil, and that their uncontrolled behavior was caused by these harmful creatures. In Lamu, any uncontrolled behavior was perceived as inherently harmful. Therefore, there is a sense in which it can be said that the Maulidi ya ki Swahili was held not to acquire recognition in heaven, but to enforce the wangwana ideology concerning the harmful nature of the slaves here on earth.

Moreover, the wangwana thought that their town was pure only as long as the slaves were confined to the mainland. When the slaves moved into town, they brought with them their malevolent jin, who had the power to harm people, especially wangwana. In order to please the jin, the wangwana had to please their agents, the slaves.[6] In other words, through this Maulidi, the wangwana sought to control the effects of the evil spirits by placating their agents with food and other materials.

As was said before, although some people might faint during the Maulidi ya Rama, that was explained by the intensity of the emotional involvement and the expectation of the presence of the Prophet, for the people who recited the Maulidi ya Rama expected the Prophet to actually come. When someone fainted in that Maulidi, people would sprinkle rose water on his face and thus help him

5. Beni was brought to Lamu from Mombasa forty years ago. It is something like Boy Scouts. The teams dressed in uniforms and paraded around certain parts of the town. There was one team at Mkomani and another at Langoni, and they used to compete with each other.

6. I will deal with these concepts in Chapter 6, when I discuss the rituals.

return to his senses. In contrast, when someone fainted in the Maulidi ya ki Swahili, the explanation offered was that the devil had taken hold of him. People would still sprinkle rose water on his face, but, in this context, it was intended to appease the devil and make it quiet, so the devil would allow the man to regain his control. Rose water was used in both cases, but it was given two different meanings, which were in sharp contrast. The idea that interpretation changes as symbols move from one social category to another will be dealt with at length later.

As we have seen, in the Maulidi ya ki Swahili, tambourines were used. However, as a rule, they were not allowed *inside* the mosque. This is an interesting point, for it forces us to ask why this was so. The only other ceremony where tambourines were used was the *ngoma ya pepo,* "the drum of the devil," which used to be performed in the slaves' houses. When the tambourines were introduced into the Maulidi, it appears that their association with the devil was carried along with them. There was a link between slaves, tambourines, and devils. All of these were considered *najisi,* or defiled, and *mbaya,* or bad, while the mosque and the Prophet, by contrast, were *mzuri,* or good, and *safi,* or pure. In the mosque and in the presence of the Prophet, such defiled human beings and things were not allowed. So the tambourine was banned.

Leaving the ideological content of the Maulidi ya ki Swahili aside for the moment, I would like to deal with its social results. The members of the two competitive groups were ex-slaves who were trained by the fundis and used as a chorus. Membership in the choruses was a matter of personal choice. The ex-slaves of one wangwana family might be divided, some joining one group, some the other. This was opposed to what the wangwana expected from their slaves. In the old times, the slaves of one mngwana would act as a group following the direction of the master. Now, each ex-slave could act according to his own preference. The solidarity of the different slave groups was highly disturbed by these competitive games. If a member of one group grew dissatisfied, he had the option of leaving it for the other. The new member would be more than welcome in the other group. The ability to gain more new members was at least partial proof that one group was more successful than the other. But the change and fluctuation in membership created hostilities between the two factions. This was often expressed in the poetry of the Maulidi, where Jum'ani might insult Bajuri, or vice versa. If a quarrel developed, the wangwana supporters of each group would move in to act as mediators, and this, of course, helped the wangwana to maintain their superiority and to keep the slaves dependent on them. The slaves quarrel, and the wangwana interfere. It was an old pattern.

The competition between the two Maulidis was intensified when Mwalim Bajuri transferred his center to Langoni. There he used the Bwana Fadhil Mosque, which was well attended by the Comoro Island people who had settled in Lamu, and which indicates their interest in him and their support. Moreover, the change of locations shifted the competition from Bajuri versus Jum'ani, to Langoni versus Mkomani. However, Bajuri's supporters continued to back him, and invited him to perform the Maulidi in Mkomani, with the intention of defeating the Mkomani group on its home ground. Thus the wangwana notion of the importance of loyalty to one's own locality began to decline. The end result of Bajuri's shift to Langoni was that the recitation was no longer a private affair as in the Maulidi Barzanji, or the Maulidi ya Rama, but was a public celebration which cut across all the traditional boundaries.

Neither group had a fixed date for reading the Maulidi. It could be read at any time and at any place, depending on who had issued the invitation. The Maulidi was usually read in the street in front of the houses of the person or group who was the host. Women attended these ceremonies, though only as observers. Mkomani and Langoni men attended the Maulidi of both groups in order to form their judgments as to which was best. Though the slaves were the players, the wangwana were the observers and, so to speak, the brains of the operation.

The readers of the Maulidi had to dress in white, as in the Maulidi ya Rama. They also used the kinara, rose water, 'ambari, and the incense burner. The Maulidi ceremony began with the recitation of the Fatiḥa and the burning of incense, all of which was done by the head of the group, that is, by either Jum'ani or Bajuri. Then the tambourines were beaten, with the singers repeating the poem: "*Ya Arhama al rahemina, farijan al muslimina*," "Oh, you the most merciful, grant the Muslims forgiveness and help." This was the same poem read at the Maulidi ya Rama, the only addition being that of the two tambourines. The fundi could sing this poem for two or three hours, and their movements were the same as in the Maulidi ya Rama. Yet, they were marked by more tenderness and softness. The fundi moved slowly as if they were dancing. They leaned on each other, swinging. This smoothness of movement (*ulaini*) was highly praised by women.

The rest of the Maulidi also followed the Maulidi ya Rama, except that, again, the movements were softer and the tambourine was used. Sometimes, the fundi would make up his poems on the spot, but more usually they were supplied by his backers, as were the drinks and food. And, in this respect, the Maulidi ya ki-Swahili differed from both the Maulidi Barzanji and the Maulidi ya Rama. Furthermore, the mwalim in the Maulidi ya ki Swahili had a staff whom he could order to take over, if he felt tired. Again, the mwalim was the one who had the right to give orders, and he had to be obeyed. No one could stand and make a poem without being ordered to do so by the mwalim himself—and this was another difference from the Maulidi ya Rama. At the end, the mwalim would make some supplications, as in the Maulidi ya Rama, and then would read the Fatiḥa and send it as a gift to the Prophet. As we have seen, the Maulidi ya ki-Swahili resembled the Maulidi ya Rama; indeed people even sometimes confused the two. However, in terms of social context and intention, as well as in the movements and the use of tambourines, the two Maulidis were quite different.

In this section, the competitive Maulidi has been discussed in some detail. Although the Maulidi was, at least formally, the first religious ceremony to be performed by the slaves, the wangwana were still able to interpret the ceremony in a way which corresponded to their own ideology. That is, they were able to find in it the work of the devil. I would argue that the slaves themselves contributed to the acceptance of this interpretation, and they did so in the ceremony in which tambourines were used, called *ngoma ya pepo.*[7]

In the next section, I will discuss the arrival of a certain sharif who was able, because he was a stranger, not only to perceive the changes which were taking place but also to succeed in bringing together the different elements and rearranging them so that a reinterpretation of religious symbols emerged and a new ideological order was established.

THE ARRIVAL AND SETTLEMENT OF THE JAMALILIL SHARIFS

The history of the Jamalilil sharifs is as obscure as that of the rest of the sharifs who once lived in East Africa. Their own account indicates that they came from Ḥadramaut and settled first in Patta and that the original sharifs in Patta were Ḥusseini and Jamalilil; however, this claim does not coincide with the general oral tradition, which states that the Ḥusseini sharifs were invited there by the people of Patta, but says nothing of the Jamalilil sharifs. Still, when I was in Patta, I did find some very old Jamalilil graves, although I was unable to decipher the dates written on them.

It might be safer to say that the Ḥusseini sharifs, after settling in Patta, invited the Jamalilil sharifs to join them. When the latter arrived, they settled with the Ḥusseinis. I came to this conclusion as a result of the discovery that,

7. This ceremony will not be discussed in this book.

while the Ḥusseinis were allowed to use the Patta horn, or siwa, in their marriages, the Jamalilil were not. According to tradition, the horn was to be used only by those who were considered "owners" of the town. Moreover, I found a letter written by the liwali of Mombasa in 1899 (1371 A. H.) and addressed to Mohammed ibn Fuma Omar al Nabahani, who was the brother of the sultan of Witu, in which the Jamalilil sharifs were mentioned in connection with the siwa. The letter goes as follows:

> To the powerful and honorable Sheikh Mohammed ibn Fuma Omar: I delegate to the governor of Lamu the responsibility to decide the ownership of the Patta horn. Mr. Rogers wrote to the different liwalis [local governors] and other authorities in Lamu [i.e., wangwana], and he asked them about this old treasure. His investigation led him to decide that the siwa was totally owned by the Nabahani family . . . . However, there are others who claimed that horn, i.e., the descendants of Mwenye Basani [Mwenye Bahsani] from Jamalilil, who *made* the horn . . . . Mr. Rogers suggested that you have to obey the law and submit your case to the judges of the Kingdom of Lamu, Faza, and Witu, for a hearing . . . .

This letter is very important, since it clearly states that the Jamalilil made the horn but were not its owners. It also indicates that Mwenye Bahsani was living in Patta at that time.

The fact that the family of Mwenye Bahsani (see the Genealogical Chart [A]) was the one who made the horn indicates that they did not have a religious function at that time. They apparently were only artisans. However, in the oral tradition we find that the Ḥusseini sharifs were the protectors of Patta. They had the power to intervene with the sultan of Patta, and their houses were used as sanctuaries. This contrasts sharply with the position of the Jamalilil sharifs. In other words, while the Ḥusseini sharifs were viewed as the possessors of supernatural power, the Jamalilil were not. They apparently had a position in Patta similar to that of the Mahdali sharifs in Lamu.

The relation between the Jamalilil and the Ḥusseini in Patta was not clear. Yet, some people from Patta told me that the Ḥusseini family protected the Jamalilil sharifs. Still, while the Ḥusseini sharifs were the religious leaders in Patta and took the title of *Shee,* i.e., sheikh, this title was never given to the Jamalilil. There are many incidents, besides the making of the siwa, which indicate that the Jamalilil were craftsmen.

The point which I want to stress is that Jamalilil sharifs were not known as *mwenye chouni,* or 'ulama. Therefore, in the sharifs' stratificatory system they were considered low. They had no power to protect, and they had no *'ilm,* or religious knowledge.

When the Ḥusseini sharifs were humiliated by the sultan of Patta, they left and went to live in Lamu, the traditional enemy of Patta. It seems that the Jamalilil left at the same time. The head of the Jamalilil was Abdallah ibn Hassan ibn Ahmed (see the Genealogical Chart [B]). The Ḥusseini sharif who left Patta was Abu Bakr ibn Ahmed Shee Patta (Sheikh of Patta) [C], and he left Patta during the reign of Bwana Fumo Madi (Mohammed ibn Abu Bakr Nabahani), who ruled from 1777–1809 A. D.—1191–1224 A. H.[8] In Captain Clive's report, we read that

> Bwana Fumo Madi, who was the last of the Patta sultans, exercised undisputed sway over his territory. He gradually got hold over his turbulent townspeople, and the town of Patta was reduced to about forty houses. He even had to besiege his own brothers and order their extermination.

When Abdallah ibn Ḥassan left Patta, he did not follow the Ḥusseini sharifs to Lamu. Instead, he went to the Comoro Islands, where he settled. Unfortunately, this period is obscure. We do not know why the Jamalilil went to the Comoro Islands or exactly where they settled. We know that Abdallah had two male children, 'Ali [D] and 'Alwi [E], and I am told that they were both learned men. Eventually, 'Ali came to Lamu, for what reason we do not know, and he was looked after and supported by the Ḥusseini family. Sharif 'Ali ibn Abdallah lived with one of the Ḥusseini sharifs, Ahmed ibn Abu Bakr [F], who gave him a stone house in the Mkomani half of Lamu and supported him financially. Sharif 'Ali taught in one of the wangwana mosques in the northern area, but he never interfered in Lamu's affairs. In other words, he strictly observed Lamu's wangwana principle that "the stranger is not allowed to beat the drum." The wangwana of Lamu were predictably pleased with Sharif 'Ali's attitude toward them.

In 1866 Sharif 'Ali's brother's son arrived in Lamu from the Comoro Islands. The new sharif was a young man, about fifteen years old. The reason for his departure from the Comoro Islands is not known; however, some people say that he left because his brothers were jealous of his intelligence and tried to kill him. Others say the reason was that he was sick and was sent to Lamu for treatment. A third reason given is that because his father, 'Alwi, was a very severe and hot-tempered man the boy's mother thought it would be better for him to join his

8. *The Political and Historical Records: A Brief History of Tanaland.* Written by Captain J. H. Clive, ex-district commissioner, Lamu, 1933. This typewritten report was given to me by an assistant of Mr. Clive's, who asked me not to publish it now.

uncle in Lamu. A mngwana historian gave me yet a fourth possible explanation; he said that there were many learned men in Lamu, and that the boy wanted to come in order to "drink from Lamu's religious knowledge."

The new young sharif stayed in the northern part of Lamu with his uncle. He attended his uncle's *darassa,* or lessons, as well as the lectures of the learned wangwana 'ulama. He acquainted himself with their views but was very quiet and never asked questions. Some historians say that his silence was due to a language problem, since even though the Comoro Island people understand Swahili, their pronunciation of it is completely different. Whatever the reason, his reticence contributed to his acceptance by the wangwana. He obeyed their rules and abstained from interfering in their affairs.

In 1867, the young sharif was ordered by his father to return to the Comoro Islands. But the boy told the wangwana that he did not want to leave; he used to say to them that, "Lamu is the oasis of religious education." So, he was able to convince some of the wangwana to write to his father in the Comoro Islands, asking him to let the young sharif stay with them. However, in spite of this effort, the father insisted that the boy return. When the boy arrived in his father's village, he refused to participate in the local activities, or speak to anyone. He would close himself up in a room without food or water and read for two to three days. He never laughed or smiled. After a year of this, his father grew worried and consulted appropriate people in his village, who advised him to let the boy return to Lamu. The father agreed and told the boy's mother about his decision, and she informed her son that he could leave. The son was very happy and told his mother that, "In Lamu I find my real life."

The young sharif took the boat back to Lamu, and on board he spent all of his time reading. One day, there was a storm and the boat was about to be swamped, yet the young sharif was so absorbed that he was totally unaware of the storm until a wave hit the boat and he was covered with water. He prayed, and God met his request—the storm suddenly stopped. The people in the boat realized what the young sharif had done, and when the boat arrived in Lamu, the sailors and passengers spread the news. The young sharif, however, kept silent; he neither verified nor refuted the incident, but simply insisted repeatedly that his goal in Lamu was to gather education.

This young sharif's name was Saleḥ ibn 'Alwi Jamalilil [G]. Sharif Saleḥ lived with his father's brother [D] and attended the lectures of different mwenye chouni for five or six years. Sharif Macci taught him Arabic medicine and the way to diagnose different illnesses. Saiyid 'Alwi ibn Abu Bakr ibn Abd el Raḥman taught him *Tafsir,* the interpretation of the Qur'ān. Mohammed ibn Fadil al Bakri gave him two years of Islamic jurisprudence, *Fiqh.* Sheikh Abu Bakr al M'awi taught him Arabic and the science of metrics in poetry. Mansab Abu Bakr ibn Abd el Raḥman taught him the science of Ḥadith.[9]

In every one of these subjects, Sharif Saleḥ was given a special license (*Ijaza*), and these were recorded in the Jum'a Mosque records. When he finished the Tafsir and Fiqh, he was given a general license, with the understanding that his knowledge was to be transmitted only to those who could keep and preserve it, that is, only to wangwana. He was under certain other obligations as well. If, for example, the wangwana discovered that he deviated from their traditional interpretation of the Qur'ān, or if he deviated in his religious opinion, then they could withdraw his license. Without a license, he would be unable to offer any religious advice. And, if he resisted and continued to advise the people, then he would be punished by God and by the wangwana, who would beat him publicly.

THE RISE OF SHARIF SALEḤ: THE FIRST PHASE

Sharif Saleḥ obtained his license around the year 1880. At that time, Lamu was in a state of unrest since, in 1873, the slave markets had been closed, and in 1876 slave traffic on land had been prohibited. These issues led the wangwana 'ulama to serious debates about the theological rights of the sultan and his British advisors. But Saleḥ kept himself out of this problem; he simply abstained from teaching and opened a tailor's shop in the new Langoni market, where he was in continuous contact with the Ḥadramis. His uncle did not like this behavior, and when the young sharif asked to marry the uncle's daughter, he was categorically refused. However, Sharif Saleḥ's behavior did not violate any of the wangwana rules, since he was considered a stranger. The young sharif reinforced his view of himself as a "stranger" whenever he could; and soon he had established relations with the Comoro Island slaves in addition to the Ḥadramis. His small shop became a meeting place for the Ḥadramis and Comoro Islanders.

When his uncle refused to allow him to marry his daughter, the young sharif decided to move from his uncle's house and from the northern half of the town altogether. He lived in a small house in a place called Darajani (see Map 4), and he used to pray in a small Langoni mosque. He was the first sharif to identify himself with the southern half of Lamu. After the last prayer, it was his custom to sit and read the Qur'ān, and before long the Comoro Islanders asked him to initiate a series of lectures for them. He began to lecture in a mosque now called

9. Known in Lamu as "Sharif Mansib." The term *mansib* indicates that he was a sharif from his mother's side and his father's side. Lamu people used the term as a name for him, though his real name was the one used above.

Sheikh Bilad.

The wangwana 'ulama, however, were angered by his move. But Sharif Saleḥ continued to speak politely to them and ask their advice, and he generally treated them as the real owners of the town. He never attacked them, although, as one of his grandchildren told me:

> He saw that the wangwana were discriminating against other groups. He was internally burning, because of the horrible non-Islamic system which was existing in Lamu. The strong people used to devour the weak, and the rich dominated and manipulated the poor. The learned men, mwenye chouni, were silent; they accepted everything the wangwana were doing, and they were interested only in educating their children and those who were able and eligible for education.

So, because the young sharif did not directly attack them, the wangwana allowed him to carry on with his lectures. The Ḥadramis began to attend these lectures and discuss various things with the young sharif, and this led them to make comparisons between their sharifs and Sharif Saleḥ. The young sharif listened more than he gave judgments.

Sharif Saleḥ kept his ties with his father in the Comoro Islands, and he kept him informed about his new lectures. The Comoro Island people who settled in Lamu were mainly sailors, and with their constant coming and going, they kept the young sharif and his father in continuous contact. Once his father sent Sharif Saleḥ a letter saying, "You have to depend on yourself in all your affairs. If you depend on anybody, he might betray you. Be careful, my son." Sharif Saleḥ followed that advice, and he began to move more slowly and to depend more on himself.

When the slaves were emancipated and came to settle in Lamu, he established relationships with them and learned from them that Lamu's real problem lay in the educational system. As I said before, education was only for the powerful elite; the poor, the slaves, and other deprived groups were given only the most basic religious education, and even that was used to support the wangwana point of view. All they learned stressed the idea that social stratification was ordained and decreed by God and that those who claimed to be of Arab descent were closely related to Qurish (Mohammed's tribe), while those who were called Wa Shenzi were not even equipped with the faculties needed to understand sophisticated religious problems. This type of discrimination was the problem which Sharif Saleḥ began to attack. But it was no mean task.

He started by asking the ex-slaves to send their children to an Islamic school which he opened for them. Here he began to teach them not only the fundamentals of Islam but also the most sophisticated problems, and in this he was successful to the extent that the wangwana put pressure on Sheikh Bilad to expel Sharif Saleḥ from his mosque. When he was told that he had to leave the mosque, he accepted the order without asking for protection from anyone, and moved to the outskirts of the southern half of the town to a place called *Dari ya Mtanga,* which means "home of dust." This place, which was owned by Sharif Abu Bakr ibn Abd el-Raḥman, was sandy, and not even good enough for coconut trees. But Sharif Saleḥ liked it because it was adjacent to Lamu's gardens, where the ex-slaves worked as coconut cutters. Sharif Saleḥ built a mud hut there, like those of the coconut cutters, and he used to sit there and talk with the ex-slaves. He spoke to them mainly about religion.

The wangwana were understandably upset by the sharif's behavior and they called him *Sharifu ya Wa Gema,* the "sharif of the coconut cutters," or slaves. Sharif Saleḥ kept his peace, but he stopped going to the town. The wangwana approached Sharif Abu Bakr ibn Abd el Raḥman and asked him to go to Sharif Saleḥ and convince him that his behavior was wrong. They met and Abu Bakr asked Saleḥ why he left the town. But the sharif answered with a question, "Do you think that the wangwana know their religion?" Abu Bakr replied, "Yes." The young sharif questioned him again, "Do you think that the slaves know their religion?" Sharif Abu Bakr said, "No." Sharif Saleḥ said, "As religious men, do we have to teach those who know, or those who do not know?" Sharif Abu Bakr said, "We have to teach those who do not know." Sharif Saleḥ agreed with that and added, "This is the reason for my coming here. The wa gema need me, while the wangwana do not need me. I was ordered by Allah to be here, and I am going to stay here." As the story is told, at the end of that meeting, Sharif Abu Bakr was so ashamed of himself, that in order to apologize to the young sharif, he asked him to take the land of Dari ya Mtanga.

Sharif Abu Bakr, returning to the wangwana, told them, "Saleḥ transferred me from the state of ignorance to that of light. I gave him Dari ya Mtanga, and I am going to protect him." The conversion of Sharif Abu Bakr, the most educated person among the wangwana, was not expected. Those who had marriage relations with the Ḥusseini respected this sharif, and so their opposition was neutralized. As it turned out, Abu Bakr not only supported Sharif Saleḥ, but he himself began to translate some Arabic religious books into Swahili. The wangwana were convinced that Sharif Saleḥ would fail in his plan to educate the slaves, who, they thought, were innately incapable of grasping and understanding religion. So they let him try or, as the wangwana put it, "*Asoskia la mkuu, humindika guu,*" "left him to break his leg." "He who does not listen to the advice of the old, will have his leg broken."

Meanwhile, Sharif Saleḥ now owned land, and on it he built a small mud mosque with a coconut-leaf roof. The slaves were the builders, and they considered it their mosque. The sharif divided the rest of his land into small pieces, and he invited the slaves to build their houses beside his, and around the mosque (see Map 6).

In their attempt to win back the young sharif, the wangwana offered him one of their daughters as a wife, but he refused politely, telling them that he could not support a wangwana woman. Instead, Sharif Saleḥ married from the Comoro Island group, and after that we find that all his wives—and no one could know their number—were from outside the Lamu wangwana. He used to tell his sons, "If you marry from the wangwana, then you have to behave like them. If you do not accept their behavior, then do not marry from them." After the sharif had taken a wife from them, the Comoro Island people formed a group around him. Sharif Saleḥ lived with the slaves, ate with them, and used his medical knowledge to help them. But the sharif still had a long way to go before he would be Lamu's undisputed leader.

Actually, at this time, he was making a continued effort to stay on good terms with the wangwana. This can be seen in his opinion concerning the Comoro Island slaves, who, like all the other slaves, rejected the idea that their former masters had retained certain rights over them. They wanted the sharif to back them in this, so they went to him and reminded him that they had been Muslims before being enslaved, and that, therefore, they should never have been taken and treated as slaves in the first place. After listening to them, the sharif said, "Slavery, by the orders of the sultan, has ended, so no one can claim a slave. However, the wangwana, as the owners of Lamu, must be obeyed; they are our elder brothers, and, for that reason, we have to obey them, respect them, and listen to their advice."

In this answer, the young sharif did not commit himself; he did not give a definite judgment as to whether he felt slavery was good or bad. He did not deal with the theological issue, but he did change the focus of the problem from superior/inferior to elder/younger, and he included himself with the younger, i.e., with the slaves. This neither condemned the wangwana nor made the Comoro Islanders angry, and once again the young sharif had exhibited his ability to keep out of Lamu's affairs. He knew that if he declared his opposition to the wangwana they could hurt him; at the least, they could withdraw his license. Moreover, with only slaves as followers, he had no economic base, and the slaves were still fighting each other through the competitive Maulidi. Saleḥ

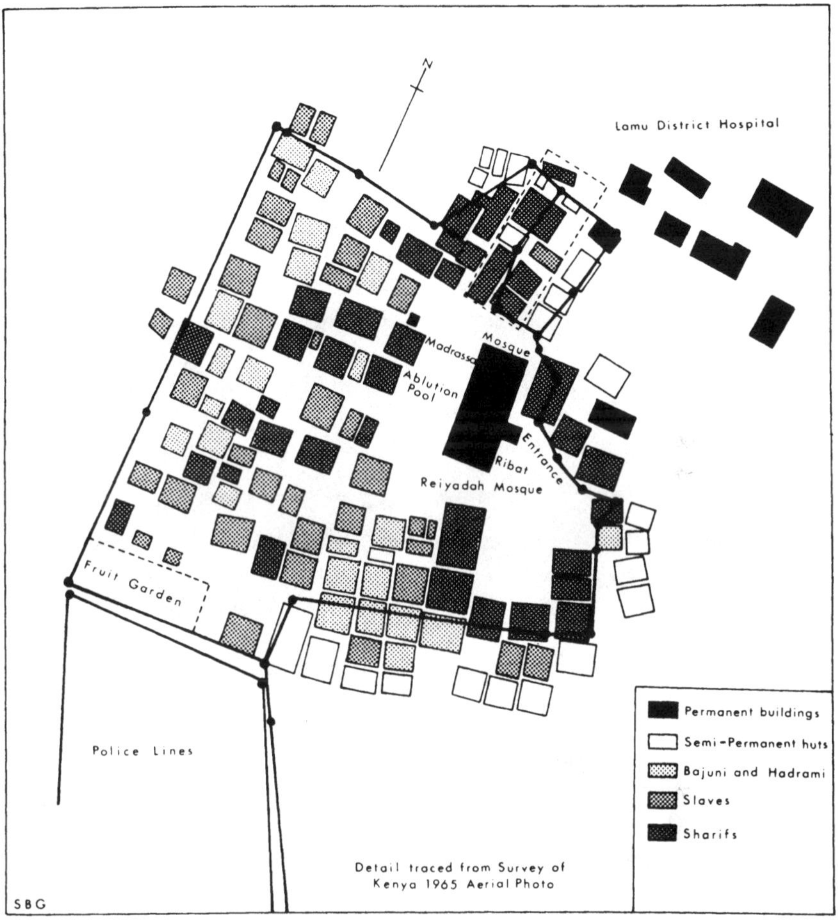

Map 6. The Reiyadah and the Environ

knew that he needed to establish a unified following and a firm economic base before he attacked the wangwana.

THE RISE OF SHARIF SALEḤ: THE SECOND PHASE

As we have seen, at the end of the first phase, the sharif lacked any substantial economic support. At that time the Ḥadramis were the only economically prosperous group in Lamu. However, they were religiously self-sufficient, and so apparently did not need the sharif. They had their sheikhs, their mosque—even their own way of celebrating religious occasions. Yet, as was said before, Sharif Saleḥ was in contact with them. He visited them and attended their celebrations; nevertheless, they did not recognize him as equal to their own sharifs. In other words, they kept their ties with their local sharifs and with their *qutb,* or head sharif, Saiyid 'Ali ibn Mohammed al Ḥabashy.

When Sharif Saleḥ built his small mud mosque at Dari ya Mtanga, he celebrated the Maulidi there.[10] Even though the people who attended that celebration were mainly ex-slaves, Sharif Saleḥ did not use the Maulidi ya ki Swahili. Instead, he used the same Maulidi used by the Ḥadramis, the Maulidi al Deba'i. He often asked the Ḥadramis to come and help him in reading this Arabic Maulidi. The Ḥadramis were willing to do that, since they considered the Maulidi a sacred ritual. Sharif Saleḥ's aim, of course, was to bring the Ḥadramis to Dari ya Mtanga.

The celebration of the Maulidi in his mud mosque was very simple. The usual incense and rose water were employed, and the small decorations were done almost entirely by the slaves, who were very happy to be allowed to celebrate the Maulidi in Arabic, a language traditionally manipulated by the wangwana. However, this was not the only intention of the Maulidi. Sharif Saleḥ, who knew classical Arabic, was unable to read the Ḥadrami colloquial poetry, called *Ḥumaini.* This was considered part of the ritual, so after Sharif Saleḥ had read the Fatiḥa and burned the incense, when it came time to read the poetry, he would withdraw from the ritual and allow the Ḥadramis to conduct it in the way in which they were accustomed. But, perhaps most important, he broke custom by sitting in the back of his humble mosque, on the right side (facing the *qibla,* or niche).

This seating pattern is extremely enlightening. In fact, it is a language in itself, full of meanings. Sharif Saleḥ knew that as a sharif celebrating the Maulidi of his grandfather Mohammed, he had to sit on the left side of the niche. This

10. Sharif Saleḥ began to celebrate the Maulidi in his mosque in 1891 A. D.—1311 A. H.

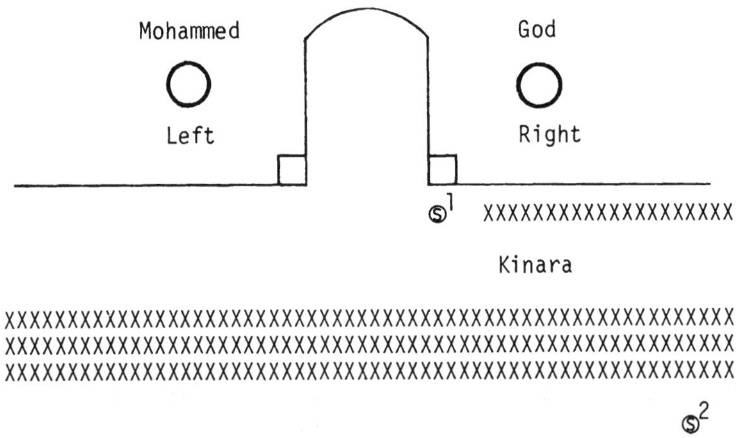

Fig. 6. The mud mosque and the place Sharif Saleh used to sit. Ⓢ[1] indicates his position when he had to read the Fatiha, Ⓢ[2] his position when the Ḥadramis read their poetry

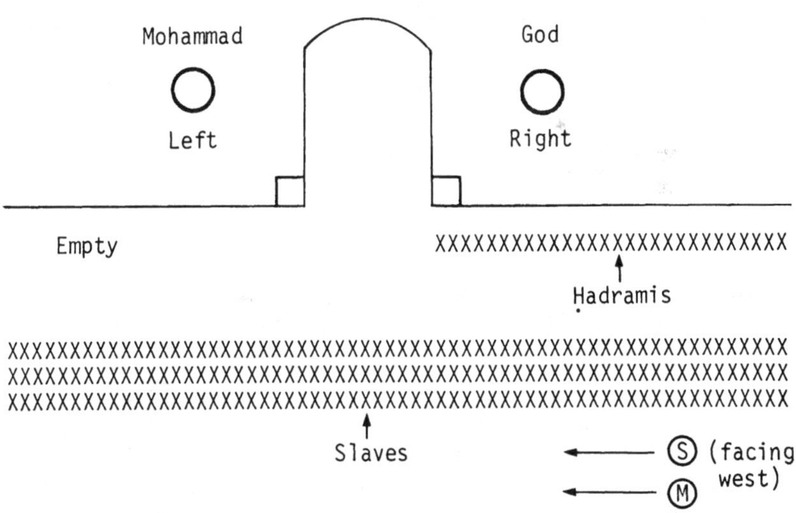

Fig. 7. Sharif Saleḥ's Ⓢ Seating Arrangement with Sharif Manṣib Ⓜ

was the place which had to be occupied by the eldest, or the most respected and important, sharif. Sharif Saleḥ's abstention from using the left-hand position meant that he did not want to preempt the position of the Ḥadrami sharifs. Leaving the sheikhs to conduct the Maulidi indicated that he recognized them as sheikhs. However, the fact that the Ḥadramis allowed the sharif to recite the Fatiḥa meant that they accepted him as higher than their sheikhs. In other words, Sharif Saleḥ did not claim that he would replace the Ḥadrami sharifs, but he did claim that he was higher than they were.

Sharif Saleḥ's choice of a seating place was also appealing to the slaves. Having the sharif seated in the back of the mosque with them was a new experience for the slaves, who were accustomed to maintaining a distance between themselves and the wangwana. However, the sharif distinguished himself not only by the place in which he sat, but also by the way he sat. All the slaves faced the qibla, but the sharif sat parallel to the niche. He neither faced the speakers, nor the slaves. He looked in front of him, a position which kept him inside the slave group and yet distinct from that group. It was, in other words, the same position he tried to maintain with the Ḥadramis.

The second year when Sharif Saleḥ celebrated the Maulidi, he invited Sharif "Mansib" Abu Bakr to attend. When Sharif Mansib came, he sat in the back of the mosque in the same position as Sharif Saleḥ (see Fig. 7). This was an important event, for the first time a wangwana was attending the Ḥadrami Maulidi, he was sitting with the slaves. As a result of this, the wangwana began to attack the Ḥusseini sharifs, especially Sharif Mansib, who stood by Sharif Saleḥ and even said he considered Saleḥ his teacher. People were astonished that a well-educated man like Mansib would recognize that the so-called sharif of the slaves had any education to offer.

Yet Sharif Saleḥ was still not interested in arguing with the wangwana, so he completely stopped going to the northern half of the town. He would sit down in front of his house, either chatting with the slaves, or teaching their children. If one slave stopped attending prayers, Sharif Saleḥ would contact him and tell him that the rest of the group felt his absence, and that he ought to return to pray in the mosque, instead of praying in the house, so that the blessing of his prayer would be shared with others. This kind of approach was new for the slaves. The sharif never accused them of not praying; instead he assumed that they prayed in their houses. And, what is more important, the sharif indicated that a slave had a blessing, and a community of slaves had an even higher blessing. These ideas were new to the slaves. Up to this point, the wangwana had managed to convince even the slaves of the opposite, as we saw in relation to the

Maulidi ya ki Swahili.

The sharif also used his medical knowledge to treat the slaves. He went to their houses, saw their wives and children, and even made sweets to give to the children. Early in the morning, it was his custom to go outside to sweep the area in front of his house. The slaves, seeing him do that, began to imitate him. He told them that Dari ya Mtanga had to be clean because it was their home. If he found dirt even far away from his house, he would carry it back and throw it away. Knowing that the slaves were unable to read the Qur'ān, Sharif Saleḥ would sit down after every prayer and read with them the small verses of the Qur'ān. All read together so no one would be embarrassed. If he found a slave with soiled clothing coming to pray, he would not point out that his clothes were dirty, but instead would go and get one of his own robes and tell the man that he had gained some weight and that his robe was too tight. He tried to teach the slaves without attacking them. *However, he avoided one thing, and he told his children to avoid it also, and that was marrying from the slaves.* The sharif was able to create a new community inside Dari ya Mtanga, and he was the center of that community. It was a slow and hard task, but he accomplished it. The following story was told to me.

> One day a slave woman was sick; the sharif went to her and treated her. When she recovered, she told him: "Thank you, my prophet." He looked at her and said that he was not the Prophet. She listened to him and then said: "If you are not the Prophet, then you must be God." The sharif told her that this was not true either and added, "I am your Muslim brother."

In Lamu, for a sharif to call a slave a brother was something extraordinary. It seems that a new interpretation of traditional religious concepts was taking place. Against the strictly stratified society, there arose a community of mutual brotherhood, a community which cut through the stratificatory system. Sharif Saleḥ, as we will see more clearly later, was not opposed to stratification per se; he was merely opposed to stratification based on the wangwana assumptions.

Soon, the slaves of the northern area began to leave and settle beside the new sharif. The more they heard of his behavior, the more they flocked to his mud mosque. Slaves also began to come from the other islands around Lamu to settle in Dari ya Mtanga. As a result of these migrations, the sharif was able to consolidate his power among the slaves; they followed him without question. These slaves constituted not only the manpower of Lamu but also the buying power. They were hired laborers, and so had to depend on the market for their food supplies. Thus, the Ḥadramis were doubly indebted to them, as laborers and as customers, and through the slaves, relations between the Ḥadramis and Sharif Saleḥ grew stronger. He used to visit their mosque, and they his, and he often expressed his great affection for the Ḥadrami qutb, Saiyid ‘Ali ibn Mohammed al Ḥabashy (see the Genealogical Chart [17]). When the Ḥadramis visited Ḥadramaut, they told the qutb about his admirer and follower in Lamu. Saiyid ‘Ali al Ḥabashy soon began to send messages to Sharif Saleḥ, and before long a strong relationship had been established between the two.

In one of his messages Sharif Saleḥ asked the qutb to license him as a student, and the qutb sent him a letter saying:

> After what I have heard concerning your behavior and your *knowledge* and *love,* I offer you, "child," my general license, and I send you my head cover (*taqia*) as proof of my satisfaction. Obey God in your private and public behavior, and I will ask God to help you.

When Sharif Saleḥ obtained this license, he felt it was possible to act more openly than before. Further messages were exchanged between the two sharifs, and Sharif ‘Ali ibn Mohammed al Ḥabashy advised the Ḥadrami settlers in Lamu to obey and respect Sharif Saleḥ. They were more than willing to do so. In Ḥadramaut, they had been accustomed to having sharifs and sheikhs who mediated in any crisis between the different Ḥadrami groups; but, when they came to Lamu, they had only a few sheikhs, and they were as eager to make money as any other Ḥadrami. So there was no one outside the economic system to whom the Ḥadramis could appeal for neutral arbitration in their disputes. This was the reason that some of the Ḥadramis had become accustomed to contacting the sharifs in Ḥadramaut when they needed an arbitrator. So the Ḥadramis were relieved when Sharif ‘Ali ibn Mohammed al Ḥabashy, who was considered by the Ḥadramis the head of the sharifs, delegated this authority to Sharif Saleḥ in Lamu. This was one step toward reconstructing the traditional Ḥadrami system in Lamu. Nevertheless, there were still some difficulties which had to be taken into account.

For example, in Ḥadramaut, there were a number of sharif lineages, and each had its own *ḥawta,* or sanctuary. These various sharif lineages were in continuous competition. In Ḥuriedah, for example, the ‘Attas sharifs were subdivided into two groups, each headed by a *mansib,*[11] and each with a special function. This competition allowed the Ḥadramis to shift their loyalty according to their

11. Mansibs (sharifs whose father and mother are both sharifs) obviously rank high in the sharifs' system of stratification.

own advantage. Though this was very difficult to do, it was nevertheless theoretically possible, and was consequently important.

Another important point is that the Ḥadramis in Lamu were internally stratified: the mashaikh and the qaba'il were on top, and below them, the da'ifs. This system was resented by the da'ifs, who actually made up the majority of the Ḥadrami community in Lamu. While the Ḥadrami higher stratum disdained certain kinds of labor, the da'ifs were not ashamed of any job as long as it was profitable, and so, in the end, the da'ifs in Lamu became much more wealthy than the qaba'il. The old stratificatory system, then, seemed unjustified to them, and they began to resent the qaba'il superiority. This cleavage inside the Ḥadrami group was very important for Sharif Saleḥ, as we shall see.

The young sharif was not interested in widening the gap between the da'ifs and the non-da'ifs who lived in Lamu. He found that his strength would be most effective if he found a way to unify the Ḥadramis. He sought to establish his claim to neutrality, and so never took sides in any of the Ḥadrami internal affairs. He used to say that, "My message is to teach and not to interfere or take sides." Sharif Saleḥ began to gain a considerable reputation, not only in Lamu but also in Ḥadramaut. And the Dari ya Mtanga area began to include some of the Ḥadramis, who settled there because they wanted to be beside the sharif. They used to say that they loved the sharifs, and, "You have to be with those whom you love." In other words, they felt there were indications that the sharif had supernatural powers, that the Prophet loved him; so the people began to love him also.

In spite of all this success, Sharif Saleḥ continued using the mosque which he had built from mud and coconut leaves. Some Ḥadramis approached him and tried to convince him to collect money from them and build a new mosque, but the sharif refused. He told them that as a sharif he was not going to beg. "If God did not allow us to beg when we were poor, how can we beg for a God who is rich?" He said that, "Everything has a time fixed by God." One day a relative of Sharif 'Ali al Ḥabashy's came from Ḥadramaut to visit Sharif Saleḥ and was invited into the humble mosque. When the Ḥadrami sharif entered the mosque, he asked Sharif Saleḥ to allow him to pray the salutation of the mosque.[12] People sitting around were astonished, for they were not quite convinced that this humble place could really be a mosque. After the Ḥadrami sharif finished, he looked at them and said, "This place will contain the biggest mosque on the Swahili coast." Sharif Saleḥ was pleased, and he did not have to

12. It is an Islamic custom that when a Muslim enters a mosque he has to pray two *rak'as* as a sign of respect for the mosque.

wait long. An Indian, after having quarreled with his wife, divorced her; but then decided that he had been wrong and made a vow that if she returned to him he would spend six hundred pounds on the poor. When his wife returned, the man took the money to Sharif Saleḥ and told him to begin building the mosque. The Ḥadramis and Sharif Saleḥ collected more money and the slaves donated their work. Construction was completed in 1901. Sharif Saleḥ knew that Sharif 'Ali al Ḥabashy in Ḥadramaut had built a mosque and called it al Reiyadah, so Saleḥ called his mosque by the same name. He also changed the name of Dari ya Mtanga to *al Reiyadah,* which means "the sacred meadows."[13]

Sharif Saleḥ, now called Saiyid Saleḥ,[14] built the mosque according to a unique plan; there is none similar to it in Lamu (see Fig. 29). The mosque itself was very small, yet it had a wide courtyard, part of which was a sort of hospice, or *ribat.* In the ribat, students studied and slept. Thus, the new mosque was not only a place of prayer but also an educational center. The children of the slaves and the Ḥadramis came to study the Qur'ān in the morning, while the adults arrived in the evening. Saiyid Saleḥ usually offered the children a meal, and the Ḥadramis contributed money toward this.

The Comoro Islanders were especially assiduous in spreading the news of Saiyid Saleḥ's college, and soon people from many different places were eager to send their children to the new school. In just two years, Saiyid Saleḥ got fifteen foreign students, and it fell to him to support them. But this was not difficult, since contributions came to him from many faraway places. For example, Sheikh Abdallah Bakathir (1859 - 1925 A. D.—1276 - 1344 A. H.), who was working in South Africa, collected money for Saiyid Saleḥ.

Saiyid Saleḥ's son Aḥmed, who was an adult by this time, used to visit the Pokomo tribe in an attempt to get parents there to send their children to Saiyid Saleḥ's school. Saiyid Saleḥ did get some children from that tribe, and they turned out to be his strongest supporters. His efforts were recognized in many places, but the northern part of the town of Lamu still opposed him. To the wangwana, Saiyid Saleḥ was still the "sharif of the slaves." However, his power was now much more substantial, since he was backed by Lamu's slaves and outsiders. The Ḥadramis constituted his economic base, while the ex-slaves made up his manpower.

The building of the mosque symbolized the unity of the inhabitants of the southern part of the town, and Reiyadah was an excellent choice of names, since

13. For another point of view, see Peter Lienhardt, "The Mosque College of Lamu and Its Social Background," *Tanganyika Notes & Records,* LIII (1959), 228—42.

14. The change of title from *sharif* to *saiyid* indicates clearly the Ḥadramis influence. The Ḥadramis call their sharif by the title *saiyid* (master).

it means not only "sacred meadows," but also "paradise." The slaves, who formerly were forbidden to come into town because they were considered defiled, now were living in paradise, the highest and purest place. In the business area, the slaves or sailors might shout and even insult each other, but as soon as they entered the Reiyadah area, they were quiet and polite. In addition to the mosque, the sharif built a new house for himself, but he built it of mud and coconut leaves. He continued his visits to the Ḥadramis, who soon began to call him *ḥabib,* or "beloved," rather than *saiyid* or *sharif.* The slaves called him *Mwenye Mkuu,* "the big master," and no one was ever given this title except him.

When his uncle 'Ali died, Ḥabib Saleḥ refused to follow the wangwana custom of death and burial. For example, when the wangwana carry the *jenaza,* or bier, to the graveyard, they intone, "There is no God but Allah," and they say it in a certain way, so that those who hear it know that the dead person is a wangwana. But, in a pure Ḥadrami funeral, the Ḥadramis carry the bier of the dead, chanting, "There is no God but Allah: there is no God but Allah; there is no God but Allah." And this they also say in a unique way. In the meantime, the children walk in front and say, "Please, God, offer Mohammed your blessings and greetings. God blessed and greeted Mohammed."

Now, the wangwana had considered Sharif 'Ali to be one of them, and they wanted to conduct his funeral according to custom. But Ḥabib Saleḥ insisted that the funeral be done in the Ḥadrami way, and for the first time he declared that the the Ba 'Alwi sharifs were originally Ḥadramis and hence were bound to follow the Ḥadrami custom. So, when 'Ali was buried, there was a problem as to who would make the Talqin, that is, give the directions to the dead. The khatib usually did this for the wangwana, but the Ḥadramis had a sheikh do it. Ḥabib Saleḥ solved the problem by refusing to let anyone but himself perform that service for his uncle. The Ḥadramis accepted that decision because it was the custom in Ḥadramaut for a saiyid to preside at the funeral of another saiyid. Similarly, for the wangwana, the mourning period was forty days, but Ḥabib Saleḥ refused to observe that tradition and instead followed the Ḥadramis' custom of mourning three days for a male relative, and seven for a female. The wangwana also had the custom of secluding the wife of the dead person for three months. During this time, she had to be fed in a certain way, and no one could touch her. Ḥabib Saleḥ refused to carry out this tradition also. Furthermore, when one of the slaves living in the Reiyadah area died, Ḥabib Saleḥ performed the ceremony according to Ḥadrami custom, first praying over the body in the Reiyadah Mosque.

Ḥabib Saleḥ contacted Sharif Mansib Abu Bakr, who owned a large part of the graveyard land in the southern part of town, and asked him for a piece of land in the graveyard. Sharif Mansib gave him a portion for the Jamalilil family, and another for the people who lived in the Reiyadah area. This last piece was divided among the Comoro Island people, the Ḥadramis, and the slaves (see Fig. 8).

The Jamalilil piece was in front of the Ḥusseini graves. When Sharif Saleḥ got the land for the Jamalilil family, he asked the slaves to build a shed on it. The Ḥusseini followed him and built sheds on their own graves.

Ḥabib Saleḥ further strengthened his ties with the Ḥadramis when his son was to marry and he refused to follow the custom of the wangwana sharifs. He declared that his daughters and sons would follow the Ḥadrami custom of paying only twelve Maria Theresa silver dollars (*riyal*), rather than the excessive dowry preferred by the wangwana. Though this idea should have been most suitable to the wangwana, whose economic resources were dwindling, they insisted on the high dowry as a mark of status and disparaged Ḥabib Saleḥ's decision. The BuSa'id at that time were paying more than three thousand shillings as a dowry.

Because he identified himself with the Ḥadramis, they began to invite Ḥabib Saleḥ to complete their marriage contracts, and when they had a Maulidi he was the one to recite the Fatiḥa and burn the ubani. In other words, by this time, the traditional authority of the sheikhs had come to an end; and, since Saleḥ had received his license from the qutb, the sheikhs could not argue with him about his authority. He was now the official representative of the qutb in Lamu.

Sharif Saleḥ was now considered a follower of the Ba 'Alwi path, and especially of the al Ḥabashy order. Both of these orders were Ḥadrami in origin and were headed only by sharifs. I will deal with the Ba 'Alwi path and the al-Ḥabashy order later; however, I would now like to turn to an episode which not only unified the Ḥadramis behind Ḥabib Saleḥ but also divided the wangwana and created discord among their various factions.

THE RISE OF SHARIF SALEḤ: THE THIRD PHASE

Once in the new mosque, Sharif Saleḥ used to celebrate the Maulidi there every year. In 1901, Sharif Mansib Abu Bakr went to visit Ḥadramaut, and he met the qutb 'Ali al Ḥabashy in his home town, Saiwun. The qutb gave him a letter for Ḥabib Saleḥ in Lamu, and significantly enough, in that letter, when he referred to Sharif Mansib, he used the term *walad,* or child, though he called Ḥabib Saleḥ *akh,* or brother. The letter goes as follows:

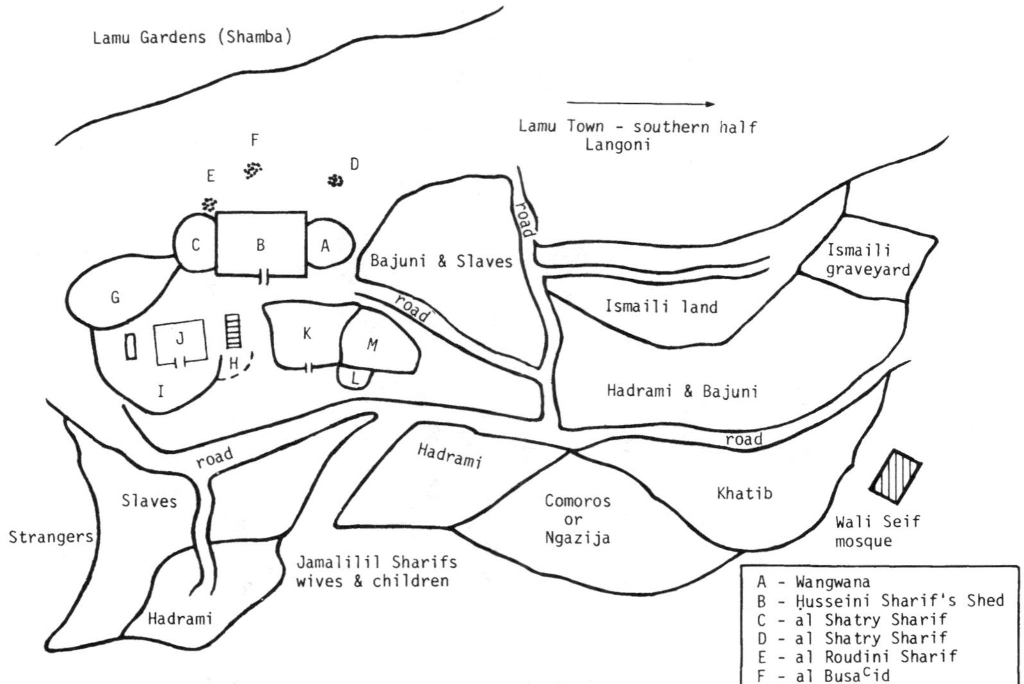

Fig. 8. The Graveyard at Langoni and the Sharifs

> In the name of God, Most Gracious, Most Merciful, I thank God whose power is clear in our actions and in our intentions. I ask God to bless and greet the Prophet's relatives, especially those who follow his path. Now, then, I grant Ḥabib Saleḥ ibn 'Alwi the permission to read these special supplications (Award):
>
> In the name of God, the Most Gracious, Most Merciful. There is no power but Allah. No one can save us except God. [Read it one hundred times.] Then God is our protector. [Read it four hundred and fifty times.] Then you read all the supplications of the Ba 'Alwi sharifs. I tell you, do not stop to increase your religious knowledge, and you have to teach the others. I license you as I had been licensed by my teachers and I give you power to license others on my behalf. I gave *al walad* mansib this letter, which I ask God that you *akhi* will receive safely . . . .

This letter was a turning point in Ḥabib Saleḥ's career, for it brought not only a license, but also the power to give licenses to others whom Ḥabib Saleḥ might feel were qualified. And perhaps more important, the letter referred to Sharif Mansib Abu Bakr, who was considered the highest educated mngwana in Lamu, as a "child," a term which in this context means "novice." Sharif Saleḥ was now considered mature enough to teach others. It should be remembered that Sharif Mansib had been the original teacher of Ḥabib Saleḥ when he first came to Lamu, and now the tables were turned. In the final analysis, this also meant that Lamu's educated people were no longer even equal to Sharif Saleḥ. Sharif Mansib accepted the new reality and was quoted as saying, "I taught Ḥabib Saleḥ, and I am proud that he is teaching me now." But for the wangwana, this acceptance meant that they no longer held the power to withdraw the license from the "sharif of the slaves."

The power of giving licenses made Ḥabib Saleḥ the sole representative of the qutb, not only in Lamu, but in all East Africa. The Ḥadramis began to come to Lamu from faraway places in order to attend the Maulidi of Sharif Saleḥ. The sharif, in turn, asked the residents of the Reiyadah area to treat the strangers like brothers and offer them food and shelter. The ex-slaves, though poor, were happy to exercise their hospitality. The sharif, with donations from the rich Indian Muslims in Mombasa, staged feasts for the Reiyadah residents and the strangers. The Ḥadramis, the slaves, and the sons of Sharif Saleḥ were the ones who slaughtered the cows and cooked the rice. Then all gathered inside the ribat of the mosque to eat. Every household got some food from this feast, which the people considered a blessed meal. At these times Ḥabib Saleḥ would go to the place where the food was cooking and lift the lids of the pans and spit on the food. His saliva was considered blessed, and the stories of those who were cured after eating that food soon spread all over Lamu. The significance of this meal will be discussed in detail later; for now, let it suffice to say that the meal was considered sacred.

The wangwana were irritated at these developments, and they did not like the idea of strangers coming and staying in their town, especially since these visitors paid no attention to the traditional rights of the wangwana. The wangwana felt they alone had the right to invite people to Lamu and that the stranger-sharif who disobeyed their rule had no right "to take down the drum and beat it." As a result of the displeasure of the older people, the young wangwana formed a gang to attack and destroy Sharif Saleḥ's Maulidi. This gang was called *mwitu kumi na mpili,* "the gang of the twelve barbarians," and it was led by Mohammed ibn Abu Bakr, whose nickname was "Kigoma." One year they plotted to get drunk first and then go to the Maulidi and disrupt it. But, as the story goes, "They drank, and went to the mosque, and as soon as the Maulidi began, they got involved in it and forgot that they had come to destroy it." The second time, they planned to kill Sharif Saleḥ and one night went to his house for that purpose. Yet, when they arrived, they found a multitude of snakes ready to bite them, and so they ran. From that day, the gang recognized that the sharif was protected by God, and that no one could hurt him.

The wangwana attacks and failures were useful propaganda and consolidated both the Ḥadramis and the slaves behind Ḥabib Saleḥ. The Ḥadramis viewed them as attacks against their area and their "big master," the man who taught their children and created for them the sacred meadows, the Reiyadah.

After this, the relations between Sharif Saleḥ and the wangwana deteriorated to such a degree that he refused to pray the Jum'a, or Friday prayer, in their mosque. According to the Shafi'ite school, such a refusal was considered a sin. The Shafi'ites insisted that in a small town, such as Lamu, the Friday prayer had to be conducted in one particular mosque. But Sharif Saleḥ declared that he was insulted and mistreated inside the Jum'a Mosque, which the wangwana considered to be solely for their own group. Ḥabib Saleḥ said that he would not order anybody to pray with him but that he would, nevertheless, perform the Jum'a prayer in his own mosque. Sharif Mansib Abu Bakr condemned the wangwana behavior as against hishima and kutunga and declared that he would pray with his teacher. The Ḥusseini followed him, and some of the khatibs also prayed with Ḥabib Saleḥ. Finally, the Wa Yumbili Ponde declared that they would also pray with Sharif Saleḥ, and, after that, the Jum'a Mosque was only used by the Wa Yumbili Pembe and the Wa Yumbili Ngombe. The town was split. The wangwana began to attack each other, and the Ḥusseini were told to go back to "'Inat in Ḥadramaut"; Lamu no longer needed them. The true center of the town was no longer in the north, and even the Jum'a Mosque, the last symbol of the old wangwana authority and power, had been discarded. The wangwana were boycotted by the Ḥadramis, the slaves, and even by some of their own kind.

However, before long, the khatibs found that the division of the Jum'a prayer was not in their interest, and so they tried to convince Sharif Saleḥ to return to pray in the old mosque. He refused at first, but they persisted, and finally, he accepted on the condition that the khatibs would declare that the Jum'a Mosque was owned by all the people of Lamu (*watu wa Lamu*). They agreed to that, and this was a great victory for the sharif, the Ḥadramis, and the slaves. The khatibs' agreement on the neutralization of the Jum'a Mosque was an acknowledgment that Ḥabib Saleḥ's behavior and knowledge were superior to theirs. Dividing the Jum'a prayer was a very unpopular thing in the Shafi'ite school, but no one could convince either the Ḥadramis or the slaves that Ḥabib Saleḥ was wrong.

The wangwana, for their part, were waiting for a chance to attack Ḥabib Saleḥ and chase him out of their town. Their chance arrived in 1909, when the qutb in Ḥadramaut composed a new Maulidi called *Simt al Durar,* "The String of Pearls." Ḥabib Saleḥ, as a representative of the qutb, adopted the new Maulidi, and the Ḥadramis also accepted it, since it was the work of their qutb. Furthermore, it appealed to the slaves, because in it the poetry was accompanied by tambourines and a small drum called *kigoma,* or *mrwas.* The music was part of the ritual, and it thus found its way inside the mosque for the first time. The highest wangwana viewed the Maulidi as part of their hishima and kutunga, an occasion where self-control and quietness were essential features, and they could not accept this heretical innovation. They convinced Sharif Mansib that his teacher had gone astray, and they asked him to contact Ḥabib Saleḥ and tell him to stop that Maulidi; otherwise, they would stop it by force. Sharif Mansib went to Ḥabib Saleḥ and told him that what he was doing was wrong. Ḥabib Saleḥ asked Sharif Mansib whether Abu Bakr ibn Salim[15] was wrong, and Sharif Mansib replied that Abu Bakr ibn Salim, as a qutb, was never wrong. Sharif Saleḥ then reminded him that Abu Bakr ibn Salim beat drums and played music inside the mosque. Moreover, he noted that the new Maulidi was actually composed by the qutb, that he was only imitating the Maulidi of Ḥadramaut. With that, Sharif Mansib apologized to Ḥabib Saleḥ and declared that he had been pushed into his criticism by the wangwana, who only wanted to make trouble. When Sahrif Mansib returned to the higher wangwana, he told them that he now realized that Ḥabib Saleḥ was right and that they were wrong. This left the

15. Abu Bakr ibn Salim was considered a qutb. He was the head of all the Ḥusseini sharifs (see the Genealogical Chart).

higher wangwana no choice, and they began to use force. They attacked the slaves who backed Ḥabib Saleḥ, and physically tortured them.

However, the new Maulidi served the cause of Ḥabib Saleḥ in another way; it brought to his side those slaves who were involved in the Maulidi ya ki Swahili, the one which already made use of the tambourine and drum. These slaves now identified themselves with the sharif who had purified the musical instruments and taken them from the street into the mosque. In fact, Mwalim Bajuri, now in Langoni, detached himself from his wangwana support and asked Ḥabib Saleḥ to allow him to beat the drums. The sharif refused politely, saying that the qutb would send him teachers to train his students in the musical instruments. Yet, the sharif allowed the mwalim to celebrate his own Maulidi in the ribat of the Reiyadah Mosque, the night before the sharif's Maulidi. The mwalim accepted this happily, and again the wangwana lost some of their supporters. The town was now polarized, with the Langoni half against the Mkomani half.

The qutb sent two of his Ḥadrami followers to train the sharif in Lamu. One of the teachers was from the da'ifs, while the second was a personal slave of the qutb, and when they arrived in Lamu Sharif Saleḥ gave them houses in the Reiyadah area. They used to hold the Maulidi every Thursday night after the sunset prayers were over. The students of Reiyadah were required to attend at these times and to practice the recitation of the Maulidi. The teachers sent by the qutb trained two Ḥadramis of Lamu, and when they felt that they were sufficiently accomplished they returned to Ḥadramaut. The two Lamu Ḥadramis trained a third, who in turn instructed a sharif, who then passed his knowledge on to the Jamalilil sharifs. Most of this training was in the use of the tambourines, but the service also involved small drums. Ḥabib Saleḥ usually left these to the slaves, or to anyone who knew how to use them. Sharifs generally did not beat the drum; drum beaters were either adult slaves or their children.

The Maulidi was not the only innovation brought from Ḥadramaut by the teachers. They also introduced the *sama'*, religious songs which the old Lamu Ḥadramis performed in their Ba Wazir Mosque. Now, for the first time, these old poems were accompanied by music. Sama' sessions were held on different public occasions, such as the two Islamic feasts. They were also held to celebrate certain private occasions, such as the return from Mecca after a pilgrimage. Sharif Saleḥ liked to hold the sama' in his house once a month, when he would listen carefully to the singers and sometimes get so carried away that he cried out loud. The musical instruments used in the sama' were the same as those used in the Maulidi, except that the sama' also used a single flute known as the *qasaba.*

Relations between Ḥabib Saleḥ and the Ḥadrami da'ifs grew stronger, and he depended on their economic and religious support more than ever before. Once a Ḥadrami from the qaba'il quarreled with a da'if, and both went to Ḥabib Saleḥ, who finally took the side of the da'if. The qaba'il Ḥadrami was angry, and he stopped going to Reiyadah to pray. Ḥabib Saleḥ left him alone, but after a while he received a letter from the qutb saying, "When you severed your relations with Ḥabib Saleḥ, you lost our blessings. Here in Ḥadramaut, we see Ḥabib Saleḥ at the the grave of the prophet Hud. Return to the Ḥabib and apologize for your mistake.[16] The Ḥadrami returned and apologized, and Ḥabib Saleḥ welcomed him. The Ḥadramis, sheikhs, qaba'il, and da'ifs had to accept his judgment if they did not want to risk the displeasure of their qutb.

However, this statement from the qutb had more far-reaching results. The statement that the qutb and others "see Ḥabib Saleḥ at the grave of the prophet Hud in Ḥadramaut" meant that Ḥabib Saleḥ was now believed to have the power to travel from the African coast to Arabia. He could be seen in two places at the same time, and this made him one of the nine *abdals,* or substitutes. Ḥabib Saleḥ was no longer simply a local saint; he might even be the future qutb. After this the Ḥadramis had to be more considerate and careful; they had to express their utmost respect. So, from that time on, the expenses of the Maulidi, the money needed to maintain the students and the mosque, and unlimited political support were all given to Ḥabib Saleḥ by the Ḥadramis, and they began to call him *Khalifat 'Ali ibn Mohammed al Ḥabashy,* "the successor of 'Ali ibn Mohammed al Ḥabashy."

Realizing that he had indeed succeeded in unifying the Ḥadramis, the slaves, and the strangers, Ḥabib Saleḥ felt he was now ready to deal with the wangwana. The wangwana, who declared they did not want to be ruled by anyone, were still opposed to him and were still trying to destroy his new-found power. They were unable to accept the idea that slaves could celebrate the Maulidi in a mosque or use what they considered defiling musical instruments. Mohammed ibn Abu Bakr, one of their leaders, I was told, used to say:[17]

> This bastard sharif brought the slaves inside the mosque; he taught them, and now he begins to play their instruments. The mosque is the *house of God* in which we have to be quiet and submissive. The "sharif of the slaves" carried the ya ki-Swahili Maulidi into the mosque; he used the tambourines and drums, and

16. All the correspondence with Ḥabib 'Ali al Habashy is kept in the house of Ḥabib Saleḥ. I copied most of these letters by permission of Sharif Bahsan ibn 'Ali Badawi.

17. The source of this account is a well-known local historian who asked me not to mention his name.

> allowed people to faint. The sharif transferred the devil from the streets to the mosque. God curses him and every real Muslim curses him.

But Ḥabib Saleḥ maintained that his Maulidi was not an innovation—that it was like the wangwana Maulidi in all important ways, except that, in his, the Prophet attended and blessed the audience. He claimed that he played the music because the Prophet and the different qutbs liked music, and he had to please them when they were in this world. Kigoma did not care for that explanation and answered the sharif with the following ingenious argument:

> I liked music and I used to play it in my house; yet, my flute was condemned and called defiled, while your flute was considered pure and was praised. I swear by God that my flute and your flute are brothers; they have the same mother and father. Why do you separate the brothers, condemn one and praise the other? This is unfair especially from a sharif who calls a slave "brother."

It is clear that the basic ideas of purity and impurity, which are the cornerstone of Lamu's Islam, had different meanings for the two groups. As we saw before, the wangwana thought that the slaves were the impure element, the people of the forest. The slaves were thought to have established a pact with the devil, and so to be inherently impure; nothing could change them. Ḥabib Saleḥ, on the other hand, viewed purity or impurity as an achievement which had nothing to do with one's connection with the forest or the town. According to Ḥabib Saleḥ, if a slave knew his religion and followed it, he could achieve a degree of purity which might exceed that of the wangwana. Moreover, Ḥabib Saleḥ, himself the center of purity, lived in Langoni with the slaves. He supplied the slaves with a charge of purity which the wangwana could not give. These differing points of view in relation to purity and impurity, which I will deal with at length later, defined the barrier between the wangwana and Ḥabib Saleḥ.

The barrier is illustrated by the following account of a highly significant incident. In 1911, a mngwana was to marry on the same day that Ḥabib Saleḥ was to celebrate the Maulidi. The wangwana prepared their best food and drinks, brought singers from Mombasa, and for the first time, invited the people from Langoni to attend the marriage ceremony. However, this did not worry Ḥabib Saleḥ, and he went ahead with his Maulidi. The mosque filled as usual, and no one attended the marriage ceremony. Kigoma and his followers were furious, because there were not even any slaves to serve the wangwana in the marriage ceremony. So he called together his followers with the intention of taking action. The group went to Reiyadah and set fire to some of the slave houses.

Smoke soon covered the area, and the people inside the mosque realized that their homes were on fire. They began to worry, but Ḥabib Saleḥ stood and said, "Be quiet, and continue with the Maulidi; all of those who continue will be saved by the power of the Almighty God, our Prophet and our qutb. Those who leave have no faith in God's power; they are the hypocrites whom we have to get rid of." With that, the sharif ordered a small boy to take the flag of 'Ali ibn Mohammed al Ḥabashy and put it on the top of the mosque. Then he sat down and continued with the recitation of the Maulidi. The wind carried the fire to the Mkomani half of the town, and the wangwana had to flee for their lives without finishing their marriage ceremony. The story goes on to say that all those people who remained calm and obeyed the sharif were saved; their houses were untouched by fire. But those who left the Maulidi were either burned themselves, or their houses were destroyed.

It is said that, on the same day, a Ḥadrami from Lamu was attending the Maulidi in the mosque of 'Ali ibn Mohammed al Ḥabashy in Saiwun, Ḥadramaut. He reported the following:

> During the Maulidi, the qutb stood up and went to his room. He stayed there for about two hours; we did not know what to do. When the qutb came back, his clothes were dirty, his hands and face were black. We looked at him, and he felt that we wanted to know what happened. After a little pause, the qutb said, "There was a fire in Lamu; my beloved brother Ḥabib Saleḥ called me to put it out, and so I had to leave you." He looked at the Ḥadramis from Lamu and said, "Had the people obeyed Ḥabib Saleḥ, and stayed calm, no one would have been hurt except those who started the fire.

The Ḥadrami from Lamu wrote down the date and what the qutb had said, and when he returned, he told the people what took place in Ḥadramaut, and how 'Ali al Ḥabashy had prevented the fire from spreading. This story strengthened Ḥabib Saleḥ's position, since it substantiated his claim that he had the power to ask for intervention. He had shown an indisputable *karama,*[18] which means that when he asked for help, the supernatural powers intervened because they honored and respected him. The fact that the fire did not burn him but did burn the wangwana and their houses in the Mkomani half of Lamu

18. Many writers do not differentiate between the two concepts of *karamat* and *mu'jizat,* and they translate both words as "miracles." However, according to the Ḥadramis the word *karamat* means "honor" and "generosity." This term is used only for the qutb, who has honor, and who is a relative of the Prophet, who is also highly honored. The qutb, because of his honor, can *ask* the angels, who respect him and whom he respects, to help him do something. The use of the angels is possible as the result of honor. On the other

was taken as a clear indication that the fire had been carried to that area by unseen powers. Ḥabib Saleḥ claimed that the fire was carried away by the benevolent creatures which came to his aid. Since he did not specify which "creatures" these were, people began to say that they were the qutb, the angels, or the benevolent jin. No one asked the ḥabib directly for elaboration; he had only to insinuate. The people who loved him were able to understand him, and actually such an ambiguous statement was needed at that time. Since the society and culture were undergoing such drastic changes, clear-cut statements were of no help, in that they only served to polarize factions within the society.

The slaves thought that Ḥabib Saleḥ's statement meant that because they had stayed and prayed the benevolent powers had come to his aid. The wangwana interpreted the same statement in another way. For them, it meant that Ḥabib Saleḥ was able to manipulate the benevolent jin, and that they would come to help him when he needed them. The Ḥadramis thought that Ḥabib Saleḥ, through the help of their qutb, was able to put out the fire. These three interpretations are still stated by the people who were in Lamu at the time of the fire. It is the job of the anthropologist, then, to accept all three of them as true and analyze their social consequences.

The wangwana were forced by the fire to the realization that the "sharif of the slaves" was highly honored by the unseen powers which seemed to have discarded their authority and to have begun to obey him. In other words, the benevolent jin were thought to have acted as servants to the sharif. It seemed that, as a consequence of their opposition to Ḥabib Saleḥ, the wangwana had lost the support of their "unseen children," the children they had fathered from the benevolent jin females. These children who previously had obeyed the rules of hishima and kutunga began to disobey their fathers and follow Ḥabib Saleḥ. This meant that the last claim of wangwana superiority was destroyed. Souriya marriage had destroyed them economically, and Ḥabib Saleḥ had undermined the base of their religious ideology. The wangwana now had to accept the new authority, even if they did not like it. At this time, the khatib group split from the wangwana and sent their children to be taught by Ḥabib Saleḥ in the Reiyadah Mosque. One of them graduated from the mosque and was given the

---

hand, God had *chosen* some people and *manifested* certain things through them; these were called *mu'jizat.* These persons must also have honor. The qutb has *karama* but he does not have *mu'jizat.* Prophets had *mu'jizat.* According to Sunni Islam, however, there are no prophets after Mohammed, and therefore, no one can make *mu'jizat.* Note that karama also refers to a meal in which honor and respect constitute an important element in the relation between host and guest.

title of sheikh by Sharif Saleḥ. This khatib not only attended the new Maulidi, but beat the tambourine himself. Mohammed ibn ʻAli wrote a poem praising Ḥabib Saleḥ:

> Oh God, Oh God, Oh God
> We ask the Prophet and our beloved ibn ʻAlwi
> Saiyid Saleḥ to intervene in our behalf.
> We ask God to forgive us, and grant his blessings . . .
>
> We ask you for the sake of the descendants of the
> Prophet . . .
>
> And for the sake of our supporters, our leader,
> Our provider . . . . Our light, and the blessings whom
> You sent to Lamu, ibn ʻAlwi Saiyid Saleḥ Jamalilil
> Who renewed Your honorable tradition.
> Who saved the people and led them in the right path.
> He is godly in his name, his personality, his discourse.
> And in his mystical states, and his invocations and customs.
> I am pleased to praise him. He showed us the right path.
> He is the real master, in his education and his actions.
> He is generous and the provider. He is merciful
> And a real adviser.
> He established his mosque on piety and devoutness.
> If the people visit it, they will be cured.
> This is the Reiyadah, the sacred meadows of blessings.
> For the pious it is the real joy for the heart
> Oh God, for the sake of these saints,
> Accept our repentance, and forgive our previous sin.

This poet was not only convinced that Ḥabib Saleḥ was right, but he also felt that he was free in condemning the wangwana for their actions. He admitted that Ḥabib Saleḥ had karama, the honor to ask for intervention, and that Reiyadah was built on piety. The "sharif of the slaves" had succeeded finally in gaining the approval of the wangwana, or at least the majority of them. From that time on, they consulted him before making any decisions. Nevertheless, he still reminded them that he was a stranger. He never wanted to interfere or to criticize the wangwana. His concept of leadership was that if he did the right thing, the people would imitate him without his having to speak out directly.

When some of the Reiyadah students graduated, they opened Qur'ānic schools in Mkomani and Langoni, and these schools were the best propagandists for Ḥabib Saleḥ. Most of the Qur'āni teachers were ex-slaves. One of Ḥabib

Saleḥ's students, who was originally from the Pokomo, returned to his native tribe and became the first Pokomo Muslim there. He succeeded in winning a large number of his people to his side, and they also began to attend the Maulidi in Lamu. The Ḥadramis from Mombasa and other areas as well used to make the trip to Lamu (now called *hija mtoto,* or "the little pilgrimage") for the Maulidi.

After the qutb Ali al Ḥabashy died in 1914 A. D. (1333 A. H.), Ḥabib Saleḥ came to be regarded as the new qutb, and his fame spread to Ḥadramaut, Java, and Zanzibar. The sultan of Zanzibar used to send him letters asking for his blessings. However, such wide fame did not change the ḥabib's way of life. The donations which were sent for his Maulidi were still spent on the celebration as specified, and if some of the money remained Ḥabib Saleḥ would send about twenty-five percent of it to the sons of Qutb 'Ali al Ḥabashy, and then distribute the rest in three equal parts. One part went to education in the mosque, the second to needy people, and the third was shared among the Ḥusseini and Jamalilil female sharifs. The male sharifs were not allowed to keep anything for themselves. After the Maulidi, the ḥabib would once again have no money. He often warned his children about keeping this money, because if they kept it, then the Maulidi would not have been for the sake of the Prophet, but for the sake of the money.

Ḥabib Saleḥ did not license anyone from the islands around Lamu (Bajunis) to make the Maulidi. So, the inhabitants of these islands had to come to Lamu to celebrate it there. Nor did he license the Pokomo, and they too had to come to Lamu to celebrate the Maulidi. Ḥabib Saleḥ refused to press anyone to come to the Maulidi, or, for that matter, even to issue any invitations. He said that the Maulidi was the Prophet's celebration, and that the Prophet therefore invited whomever he wanted.

THE BA 'ALWI ORDER

In this section, I will deal with the Ba 'Alwi order, for this provided the ideological basis for Ḥabib Saleḥ's reinterpretation of Islam in Lamu. The name Ba 'Alwi shows that the order began in Ḥadramaut. *Ba,* meaning "the descendants of," is strictly a Ḥadrami word; and *'Alwi* indicates that the order does not include all the descendants of Ḥassan or Ḥussein, but only the descendants of 'Alwi ibn Abdallah ibn Ahmed. Their ancestor, Ahmed ibn Issa, had come to Ḥadramaut from Iraq through Yemen and settled in Terim. He was continually attacking the Ibadi sect, which was widespread in Ḥadramaut at that time. One of the sharif historians reports that when he arrived in Ḥadramaut, he set out to renew the declining Sunnite tradition and Shafi'ite creed,[19] and was the first to establish the authority of the sharifs in Ḥadramaut.

The Ba 'Alwi order began with 'Alwi ibn Abdallah, who lived in Terim, and was strengthened and reshaped by Mohammed al Faqih al Moqadim, who was called the "great professor." Though Faqih al Moqadim did not have any books, the consensus of the Ba 'Alwi sharifs is that he was the qutb, and that he gave his children and his relatives the essential teachings of the Ba 'Alwi order. In every ceremony his name was mentioned, and supplications were made to him. Both 'Alwi and Faqih al Moqadim stressed two basic principles, which were said to constitute the core of the order—first, knowedge, and second, indifference and obscurity. They differentiated between two kinds of knowledge: indirect knowledge, which included all the traditional Islamic subjects, and direct knowledge, which only the sharifs were capable of gathering, and this because of their special relation to the Prophet. According to the Ba 'Alwi doctrine, the sharifs have a nature different from that of other human beings, which they inherited from their mother Fatima and her father, Mohammed. Mohammed was the purest light, second only to God. Fatima was created from that light, and her sons came out of it after her. These sons were considered the children of Mohammed, not of 'Ali, who was the husband of Fatima. The relation between God and the Prophet was one of love, and the same relation was said to connect the sharifs to the Prophet. Thus it was due to their specially inherited nature and to this love that sharifs were able to gain direct knowledge.

Nevertheless, direct knowledge could not exist in isolation from indirect knowledge. The sharifs still had to master all the traditional Islamic knowledge, but it would then be clearer and more meaningful to them because of their direct knowledge. They might be taught indirect knowledge by a sheikh, that is, a non-sharif, but once in possession of that knowledge they would be able to understand it better than the skeikh had, and, in many cases, they would then become teachers to their former teachers.

As a result of this claim of direct knowledge, the sharifs were thought to be above criticism. There are many cases which illustrate this claim that could be cited here, but one case in which Ḥabib Saleḥ was involved should suffice:

19. Another historian thinks that Ahmed ibn Issa was in fact a moderate Shi'ite. The conversion to Sunni Islam and the Shafi'ite creed might have occurred later. However, we find that Mohammed al Faqih al Moqadim, in one story, attended the lessons delivered by 'Abdallah ibn 'Abd al Rahman ibn Abi 'Abeid, who was a Shafi'ite scholar. See Saleḥ al Ḥamid al 'Alawi, *Tarikh Ḥadramaut* [The history of Ḥadramaut], 2 vols. (Jaddah: Irshad Bookshop, 1968), I, 323–26; II, 720.

> Faraji was a student of Ḥabib Saleḥ. The ḥabib liked him very much. Faraji stayed with the ḥabib day and night. The ḥabib used to pray for a long time before going to his room to sleep. One day Ḥabib Saleḥ went to the water closet, and Faraji waited for him. Faraji heard the ḥabib reciting the Qur'ān inside the water closet Faraji was angry; he could not imagine that a ḥabib who knows that the water closet is a defiled place would read the Qur'ān there. When the ḥabib came out, he looked at Faraji and told him, "Faraji, there are many things which you do not know. You have to be polite. Because if you love me, you have no right to question my behavior. What is right for us might be wrong for you. I know what is in your mind and I forgive you." Faraji was confused, and he was astonished that Ḥabib Saleḥ knew his inner thoughts. He apologized.

Even if a sharif's behavior contradicted the rules as stated in tradition, he could not be criticized, because the sharifs were the only people who had direct knowledge, and hence they might know things which non-sharifs could not know. Moreover, if they were criticized, the Prophet would be angry, and he would come to help and protect his descendants. He might even harm those who dared criticize his sons.

At times, the Ba 'Alwi sharifs gathered non-sharif followers, or *murideen,* around them. They were their admirers and defenders, but these disciples could never reach the position of the sharifs. Even if they became 'ulama, they would not reach the degree of knowledge of even an ignorant sharif. Of course the ignorant sharif was still far below the educated sharif, but since both shared in the nature of the Prophet they surpassed everyone else. Thus direct knowledge was manipulated exclusively by the sharifs, and so, in the Ba 'Alwi order, any status an ordinary person might achieve came only in direct proportion to the amount of love he showed for the sharifs. The more love a person showed, the more blessings he would obtain; the Prophet saw to that. When the Prophet found someone who truly loved his descendants, he would ask God to reward that person.

Related to this were the sharif's ideas of indifference and obscurity. The sharif was not supposed to make an obvious show of his knowledge. For instance, it was not considered proper for him to dress in expensive clothes that would make his status as a sharif immediately apparent. He was supposed to hide the fact of his access to direct knowledge. Therefore, if people loved him, they would do so for the sake of his father Mohammed and out of respect for the Prophet and not because of his personal glamour or appeal. This idea of indifference, or *khumoul,* was crucial. People came to expect the sharifs to act in ways that contradicted their own indirect knowledge, and so it followed that the more indifference a sharif showed the more respect and love he would get.

However, indifference did not mean ignorance, and so the sharif who showed indifference was one who had otherwise proven himself. Some people questioned the knowledge of the Ba 'Alwi sharifs on the basis of the fact that very few books had been written by the members of that order; but the sharifs defended themselves by saying that writing was against the principle of indifference.

In addition, the Ba 'Alwi sharifs stressed the idea of ijaza, or license. The sharifs felt that they had inherited the purity of the one who had founded Islam, that is Mohammed, and therefore they considered themselves the guardians and custodians of religion. Hence, Muslims had to be licensed by them in order to offer effective prayers. When a sharif met one of his admirers, he might say to him, for example, "Say 'there is no God but Allah,' five hundred times after the midday prayer." This was considered a license, and that person's prayers would be more effective because of it. On the other hand, if some of the Ba 'Alwi sharifs composed certain invocations, all the other Ba 'Alwis could use them without a license, because each had received his license from the Prophet. Still, it was a custom that when a young sharif met an old one for the first time, he would ask him about what they called *al ḥadith al awali,* the first saying of the Prophet. The members of the Ba 'Alwi order claimed that the Prophet had revealed to them some of his basic sayings, and that they had the right to pass them on, but only to other sharifs. They kept these ḥadiths among themselves. The Prophet had given his al ḥadith al awali not to every sharif, but only to those who had reached the highest degree of purity, those who exhibited a high degree of karama, or respect.

The concept of karama was essential in the Ba 'Alwi order. Literally, the word means respect, honor, and generosity. The path to karama was difficult and long, and the sharifs were the only ones able to reach it, because of their inherent purity. The path began with indirect knowledge, that of Islamic traditional education, involving such things as the study of the Qur'ān, the Hadith, and the Fiqh. At the end of the course in indirect knowledge, the sharif would be a 'ālim. Others could achieve this state, but the sharif would still be higher than any other non-sharif 'ālim. When indirect knowledge had found its best and purest expression, the 'ālim abandoned the pleasure of worldly things, and b became a *zahid,* or an ascetic, and this stage as well as that of the 'ālim was open to the non-sharifs. However, the difference between the sharif who was both 'ālim and zahid and an ordinary 'ālim who was also an ascetic was that the purity and effectivity of the latter would not be recognized until after his death, that is, until after he had reached the point where he could no longer fall away from the state of purity he had achieved. The sharifs tell many stories of those non-sharif ʻālim-zahid who, at the last moment, made a wrong choice and lost their purity.

> Once there was a ʻālim who was also a zahid, who in order to eliminate all his relations with the world chose a cave in the hills to live in. Every day, God sent him food and water. The man stayed like this for a long time, praying for God and saying the name of the Prophet. One day, a man passed by. The zahid was eating and as soon as he heard the footsteps of the man he hid the good food, and when the man came in, the zahid offered him food which was not so good. The man ate and went away, but God stopped sending food to the zahid.

By concealing the good food, the zahid proved that he was not an ascetic, because he had kept the good food for himself. At the same time, his act proved that he did not trust God as a generous provider. He thought that God would not replace the good food, and this ended his dependency on God. This brought the zahid's relationship with God to an end. The non-sharif ʻālim-zahid lived on the delicate balance of a razor's edge. Not being inherently pure as the sharifs were, he was in constant danger of falling from purity to impurity for only a minor failing.

The Ba ʻAlwi sharifs claimed that they did not suffer from this tension, since they had inherited their purity from the Prophet, who led and protected them and who would not let his descendants fall from favor. Furthermore, they said that if a non-sharif ʻālim-zahid loved and respected them, then the Prophet would love and protect him as well. Such a person would have a chance of becoming one of the seventy-two nuqaba', or directors. The *naqib,* or local saint, might be able to show a karama, but this depended on the love he expressed for his qutb. In other words, the karama of a naqib was only a reflection of that of the qutb. However, the qutb did not know the naqib directly, but only through the *abdal,* or substitutes, who were strictly sharifs and mostly Ba ʻAlwi sharifs.

Relations between the qutb and the Prophet were characterized by love. The qutb loved the Prophet, so that when he requested something from the Prophet the Prophet would ask God, who would, of course, honor the request. Ordinary people simply had to accept this hierarchy or chain of command. If they had a request, they had to approach their local saint (either living or dead), who would in turn approach the qutb through the abdal; the qutb would approach the Prophet; and the Prophet would ask God, who, because of the Prophet's love and honor, would fulfill the request.

The relation between ordinary people and their local saint was symbolized by the *tawasul,* the request to the sharif to intervene with the higher spirits, while that between the local saint and the abdal, qutb, Mohammed, and God was characterized and established first on love, and then on honor. Thus, if an ordinary man brought a request to his local saint and that saint, knowing the man to be sincere, referred the request to the abdal, then the abdal could not neglect it, for to do so would be to cause the local saint to lose his honor. So, the abdal, the qutb, and Mohammed, and even God, are all tied up in this love relation; they are all bound to fulfill the request of the ordinary man.

The sharifs did not say that the ordinary man could not petition God directly—of course he could; but God would look first at the ordinary man's deeds and actions and, according to this evaluation, would either grant or refuse his request. Through the tawasul, the failings of the ordinary man did not remain attached to his request; furthermore, the tawasul enabled him to make good use of the relations between local saints and higher entities. In other words, he put the local saint in an "either/or" position. The saint either granted his request or stood in danger of losing his honor. Honor had to be carefully guarded by the saint, because if he failed once he might lose it forever.

Of course, if the local saint were also a sharif, the Prophet would protect the honor of his descendants, and God would never let him down. In this way, the sharif could maintain his honor both during life and after death. Similarly, because these offices were always filled by sharifs, the abdal and the qutb had their honor secured in life and death. And thus, the ordinary Muslim, if he needed anything, could visit their graves, call their names, and submit his request to them. They would carry the request up to the Prophet, who would carry it to God, who would accept it.

This is why, in Lamu, before holding their main ritual celebration of the Prophet's birth,[20] the Reiyadah sharifs went first to Ḥabib Saleḥ's grave and asked his help in making the Maulidi successful. They read part of the Maulidi beside his grave, and some poems asking the other Ba 'Alwi sharifs for help. When they finished and went into the town, they sang and beat the tambourines and the small drum, and all their songs indicated that their request had been granted, and that the Maulidi was going to be as successful as it had been before. As long as they had made the above *ziyara,* or visit, the Prophet would never fail them. They did not have to wait for the end of the Maulidi, or even until an indication had been given that their request was accepted; they knew that Mohammed's love could not fail and that he would never withdraw his help and assistance.

20. I will deal with the Maulidi of the Reiyadah sharifs in Chapter 8.

The sharifs' infallibility depended on the Prophet's purity, which they inherited through Fatima. Anything belonging to the Prophet was considered exceptionally pure. Even the Prophet's sandal was used for protection because of this purity. In fact, a picure of the sandal can be found in most of the houses and shops of Lamu. In the photograph of the Prophet's sandal (Fig. 9), the writing says, "This is similar to the Prophet's sandal. We do not doubt that looking at it has great benefit; it protects and secures and blesses." The Prophet's sandal is higher than any human being except the sharifs. Because of the sharifs' relations to the Prophet, it was said that they were so pure, they would never go to hell, even if they committed the gravest sins. They were outside the rules which governed ordinary people's lives and behavior. So, if a non-sharif caught a sharif in some failing and attacked him for it, the Prophet would be angry and would take revenge. Thus, if a sharif committed adultery, and a non-sharif knew about it, it was best for him to keep quiet and not tell anyone.

The head of the Muslim qadis, who lived in Mombasa, was continually opposed to the Reiyadah sharifs. He felt that tawasul, the idea of asking the sharifs to intervene with the higher spirits, was not part of "pure" Islam, or Islam as it was in the days of Mohammed. He even questioned the basic idea of the purity of the sharifs. When this chief qadi grew old, he lost his sight, and, of course, the sharifs related that to his previous attacks on them. They said that the Prophet tortured the man by taking his eyesight. The following story told in Lamu is another example of this same way of thinking.

> It is said that when Ḥabib Saleḥ was attacked by a mngwana, he simply looked at the man and said, "We are protected; we are the people who have been mentioned in the Qur'ān." The mngwana laughed and said, "There are many bad people mentioned in the Qur'ān, and you are one of them." At this Ḥabib Saleḥ wept. The man went home, and after awhile began to feel sick. Soon he was not able to speak, his limbs began to droop, and he smelled bad. Finally, he died. When they carried him to the graveyard, no one attended the funeral because of the smell, and, when they dug his grave, they found it full of snakes. So no one was able to bury him, and for three days he was left in the sun to smell. Finally, his relatives went to Ḥabib Saleḥ and asked him to forgive the man. Ḥabib Saleḥ said, "It is not I who has to forgive; the Prophet is the one who is angry. However, I will ask the Prophet to forgive the man, so God will forgive him also." After that, people went to the graveyard, the snakes were gone, and they buried the man.

It is a serious sin to attack or even presume to judge the behavior of a sharif, even if it is obvious that he is wrong. An incident that I witnessed during my stay in Lamu will illustrate this. I quote from my notes:

Fig. 9. The Prophet's Sandal

> Ahmed is a young man who went to Saudi Arabia, where he gathered some basic Islamic knowledge. When he returned home, he helped his father in teaching the Qur'ān to the young children. One day a sharif came to the mosque and tried to have sexual relations with one of the boys, inside the mosque. The boy escaped and went and told his teacher. The young man felt bad for two reasons. First: homosexuality is against Islam as he understood it. Second: the young man thought the the mosque was the "house of God" and, for that reason, the purest place. He went to the sharif and told him to get out of the mosque, and not to come back again. The people did not agree with his behavior, and they stopped sending their children to his lessons. Ahmed was even attacked by some of his family. The sharif declared that Ahmed, being trained in Saudi Arabia, where the anti-sharif Wahabi movement is strong, had lost his faith and had to be expelled from that mosque. The basic issue was lost; the boy was taken as anti-sharif. By the time I was about to leave, he was also leaving for Mombasa to work as a porter in the market. When I met the sharif, I was unable to show him that I knew the real issue; however, he made a statement that "the mosque is pure when we sharifs pray in it. We are the descendants of Mohammed and our religion is from Mohammed, and we are called the nation of Mohammed, not the nation of the mosque. The mosque has no inherent purity. We, as relatives of the Prophet, have that purity. For ordinary people, the mosque will be relatively pure; for us we are purer than the mosque, we are purer than anyone on earth, the whole universe is under Mohammed's shade [*ḥimaya*]."

This sharif was a Mahdali sharif. As for the Jamalilil sharifs, they might condemn homosexuality, but for them the mosque has inherent purity, although not a purity as great as theirs, as we will see later.

The Ba 'Alwi order had no core of members, nor any established way of recruiting them similar to that in the Islamic mystic or sufi orders. Instead it was built on *hub na kurh,* or love and hate: love for the Prophet and his descendants, and hate for all those who were against the Prophet and his descendants. So, virtually anyone who loved correctly and acted accordingly was considered a follower of the Ba 'Alwi order. Some asked for a license in order to make their love more effective, but even after receiving it they remained "lovers" of the Prophet and his descendants, whom they had to praise. Their only other obligation was an unspoken one—to cover their own unusual behavior.

In this respect we can see that the sharifs were similar to the wangwana. They thought that the position they occupied depended mainly on descent, and not on achievement. In other words, we can say that the sharif was a sharif; and poverty or richness, knowledge or ignorance had nothing to do with his position. He inherited the highest purity, and he had to be respected because of it. The sharifs were the representatives of the Prophet, who was the highest expression of Astarabu, and for that reason even the wangwana were unequal to them. The wangwana had to respect the sharifs and care for them. Ḥabib Saleḥ used marriage to express the superiority of the sharifs.

ḤABIB SALEḤ AND MKUFU MARRIAGE

As was said before, Ḥabib Saleḥ refused to marry from either the slaves or the wangwana. He never took a souriya, and he never took a mngwana as a wife. But he did marry, and the number of his wives is not known. As one of his grandsons told me, "Sometimes I meet a woman, and she tells me that she was married to Ḥabib Saleḥ." Ḥabib Saleḥ usually married from outside Lamu. He took wives from the Comoro Islanders and from the Ḥadramis. He was also particularly concerned with preventing his children from marrying non-sharifs. As was said before, the wangwana maintained the principle of equality in marriage; the bride and the bridegroom had to be from groups that were equal according to wangwana definition. Thus the Ḥusseini sharifs were considered equal to the Wa Yumbili Pembe, while the Mahdali sharifs were equal to the Wa Yumbili Ngombe. Though the husband of a sharif woman had to obey the rules of hishima and kutunga more strictly than the husband of non-sharif or wangwana women, nevertheless, the marriage of sharif women to non-sharif men existed in Lamu. But Ḥabib Saleḥ refused to accept it. He declared that a sharif woman could not marry anyone except a sharif man, while a sharif male could marry anyone he chose. Non-sharif men could not marry sharif women because Ḥabib Saleḥ considered them higher than anyone in Lamu. The marriage ideology put forward by Ḥabib Saleḥ occupied a central position in the Ba 'Alwi order. It was part of their religious teaching and folklore.

The Ba 'Alwi believed that the Prophet was created from the light of God and as such was the first of all God's creatures. Mohammed had the highest purity after God. When Adam was created, God presented the Prophet to him. When Adam married Eve, he asked God about the bride wealth, and God told him to "Bless and greet Mohammed, my beloved Prophet." When Adam and Eve "ate" the forbidden fruit, Adam repented by asking God to forgive him "for the sake of his beloved Prophet." In fact, God told Adam that He had only created the world and Adam for the sake of Mohammed.

Adam carried the light of Mohammed in his forehead, and the pure children of Adam, such as Abraham, Moses, and Jesus carried that light in their foreheads also. But none of them could find the womb pure enough to hold that light. In other words, no woman was able to carry the light except Amina bint Wahab. In her the light found the purest womb. She came from a lineage which had never committed adultery; her womb, and her line of descent were pure.

So, Abdullah put the light in her womb, and she carried it without pain, and when she delivered Mohammed he was already circumcized and clean.

The sharifs stressed that Mohammed was not like any other child; he was not the result of sexual intercourse in the ordinary sense. They knew the biological foundation of pregnancy, but refused to apply it to Mohammed. He was the light in the foreheads of the pure children of Adam, and his birth was delayed until a womb was found that was pure enough to carry him. In other words, the birth or material manifestation of the light depended not on the father, but on the mother. The womb of Amina was as pure as the light, and, therefore, it did not change or alter that light, but only preserved it.

Even Mohammed's body was not like ours; it was considered eternal by the sharifs. The purity of Abdullah, the father of Mohammed, was a result of the non-adulterous relation which his forefathers practiced. Abdullah and Amina were equal to each other in this respect; both lineages were free from adultery.

Mohammed himself did not have any male heirs; his only son died as a child. His daughter Fatima was married to 'Ali ibn Abi Talib, the Prophet's father's brother's son. The Ba 'Alwi sharifs say unequivocally that 'Ali was not equal to Fatima, because his family had not abstained from adultery. Thus while Fatima was considered part of Mohammed's house (*ahl al bait*), 'Ali was not. Neverthe-less, the children of Fatima and 'Ali were thought to be from ahl al bait. This was a paradox which the sharifs solved by introducing the story of *ahl al kissa'*,[21] or "the people of the cover." The story goes as follows:

> One day, Mohammed covered himself with a blanket. After a while, Ḥassan and Ḥussein, the sons of 'Ali, entered the room, and they found their grandfather covered with the blanket. They asked their grandfather to allow them in, and the Prophet allowed them to stay under the blanket. When Fatima entered the room, the Prophet asked her to join her children under the blanket. He then sent for 'Ali, and he asked him to join them.[22] The Prophet's wife 'Aisha asked to join, and he said "No, you are not a descendant of Mohammed, while those people are my descendants. Oh, God, bless them and bless their children. Those who love me have to love my descendants, and those who love my descendants will be loved by me and God. Every child carries the name of his father, except the children of Fatima—they carry the name of their mother and my name."

21. Ḥabib Mansib Abu Bakr ibn Abd el Raḥman wrote the story in Swahili poetry. He called it "Kisha Miya" (1850). Also, Ahmed Badawy ibn Mohammed al Ḥusseiny wrote a book called *Ahlul Kissa': Mikisa na ya sifa na tareikh ya sayyidna Ali, Fatima, Hassan na Hussein* (Mombasa: Rodwell Press, 1964).

22. 'Ali was taken under the blanket only after the children and Fatima were there. He was granted that privilege as a result of the honor of Fatima, Ḥassan, and Ḥussein.

Ḥabib Saleḥ, following the Ḥadrami sharifs, said that the story of ahl al kissa' took place after a certain verse of the Qur'ān had been revealed to Mohammed.

> And God only wishes
> to remove all abominations from you,
> Ye Members of the Family,
> and to make you Pure and spotless.[23]

But not all those included under the blanket with Mohammed were equal in purity, for after the verse of the Qur'ān was revealed and Mohammed had performed the ritual with the blanket, he said, "For every child there must be a father, and I am the father and the guardian of Fatima's two children." Again he said, "God created every prophet's children in his back except me. He created my children in 'Ali's back." Moreover, the Prophet once said, "I will leave with you the two most important things: the Qur'ān and my descendants. If you hold very tight to them you will never go astray. The Qur'ān and my descendants are a rope that will not be separated except on the day of judgment.[24]

The story and the Prophet's tradition[25] both indicate that Fatima's two children were not the sons of 'Ali, but the sons of Mohammed. Mohammed's children were in 'Ali's back, and just as Mohammed was light and was pure, so were his children. Fatima, in fact, was not pregnant in the biological sense; she only carried her own brothers. In other words, like Mohammed's father, 'Ali had nothing to do with the birth of his sons. After she delivered her children, Fatima was described as *batul* and *azzahra'*—the "virgin" and the "flower." She was said to have been married in heaven. God was her guardian, while Gabriel was 'Ali's.[26]

The story reads: "There, then, God told Gabriel to be 'Ali's guardian, so he could marry for 'Ali. God acted as the Prophet's daughter's guardian. That child, Mohammed, who was born in Mecca, and was living in Medina."

There are many problems involved here. For instance, it is interesting to note that Fatima's role began to be confused with that of the Prophet. For example,

23. The Qur'ān, 33–34.

24. For these Ḥadith and others, see: Saiyid Ahmed ibn Abi Bakr al 'Alwi, *Tuḥfat al Labib fi Sharḥi Lameyat al Ḥabib,* (Cairo: The Great Arabic Printing House, 1912).

25. Some might question both. For example, in the Ḥadith concerning the two most important things, some say that it goes as follows: "First, the Qur'ān and second my tradition . . . ." However, we are not concerned here with arguing one against the other; rather, we are interested with how the Lamu Reiyadah sharifs used the Ḥadith.

26. The story of Fatima, by Sharif Mohammed ibn Ḥassan ibn Amin ibn Osman al Mahdali, was written around 1802. I have the manuscript.

as her guardian God paid Fatima her bride wealth, which gave her the right to intervene with God on behalf of the Muslim women. Mohammed had been granted the same privilege on behalf of the Muslims in general. No one else was granted that power, and this indicates that Fatima shared the highest degree of purity with her father. A further implication is that 'Ali, who came from a lineage which had committed adultery, could not cohabit with her, because if he did, he would defile her. Therefore, Fatima had to deliver her children while she was still a "flower," a virgin. The children were sacred because they were in fact Fatima's brothers. Still, 'Ali was, in a way, related to the Prophet in that he carried the Prophet's children in his back and communicated that sacred light to Fatima, although without sexual defilement. Out of all of this, the only one who was equal to Fatima in purity was Mohammed, but obviously Mohammed could not give children directly to Fatima, for that would have been incest. A father could not marry his daughter, so 'Ali had to take his place, but the purity of the children was maintained through the mother's virginity.

Ḥabib Saleḥ considered the sharif women to be purer than any non-sharif human being, so if one of them married a non-sharif male, the children inherited their father's qualities. If the husband came from a lineage that had practiced adultery, then he would be defiling the purity of the womb of the sharif woman. In the sharif's minds, this was a grave sin. Since the sharif womb was pure, it rightfully should carry only pure children. But the only people who were equal to the sharif women were the sharif men. The sharif females were assured of their purity through the inheritance of their grandmother, Fatima. However, a non-sharif, even if he himself never commited adultery, could not be sure of his forefathers, and so might still defile the sharif woman, and therefore commit a sin against the Prophet. His children would have to pay for that, and it was said that they would be mentally sick.

This was clear in the case of Ḥabib Saleḥ's father's brother's daughter. As I have said, her father refused to let Ḥabib Saleḥ marry her, giving her instead to a non-sharif Comoro Islander. All but one of the sons of that marriage died very young; the husband turned mad, as did the only surviving son. This was living proof of the truth of the sharif's ideology.

While the sharif women were not allowed to marry non-sharifs, the sharif males could. Male sharifs, as the sons of the Prophet, were thought to be able to transmit their purity to others by touching. If the sharif touched anything, that thing would carry a charge of purity which then could be transmitted to others. Even the leftover bits of food were considered highly pure. Some people, especially the ex-slaves, Comoro Islanders, Ḥadramis, and Bajuni, considered eating or drinking the leftovers of the sharifs as a highly purifying act. People expressed this idea of the contagion of purity in poetry:

Within Lamu I have a lover
His love settled deep in my heart
I would like to touch with my face,
What had been touched by Saiyid Saleḥ's foot.

Among the above-mentioned groups, the purity of the sharif was highly praised, and it was thought that those who loved the sharifs would never go to hell. The Prophet would intercede with God to save them. So religious behavior was judged not only by the standards of the Qur'ān, but also by the amount of love a person showed toward the sharifs. While disobeying God was a sin against God himself, who is merciful, a sin against the sharifs was a sin against Mohammed, who at one time was a human being. Therefore, in the second instance the sinner would not be forgiven by God unless Mohammed forgave him first. The sin against the sharifs, then, was actually more serious than the sin against God, for Mohammed would never forgive those who defiled his daughters, or insulted his sons.

To please the sharifs was a blessing in itself. In the case of a person who had committed a sin against God but maintained good relations with the sharifs, Mohammed might still be able to obtain forgiveness for him. This ideology had been strongly endorsed by the slaves and the Bajuni, who used it as a protection against the consequences of their own sinful behavior. For example, prostitution, which they knew to be sinful, was the main source of income for girls from these groups. However, if before practicing prostitution a girl contacted a Reiyadah sharif and got him to marry her, and if he was the one to deflower her, he would transmit a kind of purity to her womb. After that, she would ask for a divorce. The sharifs entered these marriages willingly, since they were overloaded with women anyway. When the girl was divorced, she went to Lamu or Mombasa to practice prostitution.

The prostitutes claimed that any part of them which had been in close contact with a sharif would never go to hell. This approach suited the customers too; they felt that, if the woman's sex organs had been granted paradise, then coming in touch with her might grant them paradise also. In 1968, when I went with the sharifs to visit the Bajuni Islands, girls sent out their younger brothers to persuade the visiting sharifs to come to their houses. Apparently, they were looking for "husbands." When I asked a young Reiyadah sharif about the number of wives he had, he laughed and told me, "I cannot remember, but they are not less than two hundred. I am still thirty-four. Women like us, and we cannot destroy their faith." When I asked him about what might happen if a woman got pregnant, he answered, "In our tradition, the children have to follow the father, so we take our children. The mother has nothing to do with them."

This strong pressure to have a Reiyadah sharif as a husband created different types of marriages in Lamu and strengthened what the Lamuans called the "secret marriage." And, in fact, it is very difficult to determine the husband of a girl in Lamu. When the women marry secretly, even their families do not know about the husband. The following story, told to me in Lamu, illustrates such a marriage.

Case I: Secret Marriage

Sharif X from Jamilili loved a mngwana girl. He told his sister, who has a religious school for women. She arranged everything. The sharif got married without anyone knowing except his two brothers, who acted as witnesses. The father of the girl did not know. When a young man asked to marry the girl, the father, following the tradition, found that the man was equal, so he agreed on the marriage. When he told the daughter, she did not know how to answer him. She contacted her sharif husband, who was unable and afraid to contact the girl's father. The preacher made the contract for the new marriage. Now, the girl was legally married to two husbands. The young sharif contacted his eldest brother, who was a well-known 'ālim, and told him. The brother said that it was not a real problem. He told the young sharif to contact the sister of the wife and ask her to marry him. According to Islam, if the second girl marries him, then her sister will be automatically divorced. This took place, and now the young sharif is married secretly to the sister of his first wife.

When my informant finished his story, I asked him about his opinion concerning the sharif's behavior. He told me, "He is a sharif. I am not. No one has the right to criticize the sharif's behavior. If he is doing something, we are afraid to judge his actions, because, if we do, we might hurt the Prophet, so it is better to keep quiet." When I pressed him, he said, "I will never do what the sharifs are doing, but I will never criticize them."

In addition to secret marriages, the sharifs introduced a new kind of marriage called *Abi Dawoud.* This kind of marriage was named for Abi Dawoud, who was an influential learned man. Abi Dawoud held that if a girl were legally mature (over twenty-one), and if she liked a man, she could marry that man without any witnesses. The man would perform the marriage, and the wife and husband would be the only ones who knew anything about it.

The wangwana, of course, knew about the sharifs' secret relations with their women, and they did not want to allow their women to marry sharifs, for fear that their women would use that marriage as a step to prostitution. Nevertheless, the wangwana could not stop the secret marriages. The wangwana had lost the control they once had. For example, during the golden age of their influence they claimed that not even the Muslim jin could marry their daughters, because they were unequal to them. They considered their women superior to the jin, and they used the old ideology to keep their women out of contact with any but equal husbands. Then the Jamalilil sharifs came and began to propagate a new ideology concerning their superiority. Male sharifs did not totally accept the principle that their wives had to be equal to them; they thought it was acceptable for them to marry down, and for the children of these "low wives" to marry up. On the other hand, their daughters could marry only from the sharif group. The woman's status, in other words, was believed to have no effect on her children's status. The son of a sharif was a sharif, no matter who the mother was. For the sharifs, a woman was a *sufuria,* a vessel which held the contents given it but did not affect them. Yet, remembering the stories about Amina and Fatima, we see the emphasis on the importance of the womb; the womb had to be pure and to be separated from any adulterous relation. This was the reason why Saiyid Saleḥ directed his children not to marry women from Lamu—wangwana or slaves. He felt it was all right for them to marry from the Ḥadramis or from the free Comoro Islanders. The sharifs who disobeyed this advice suffered. There are two cases in my field notes that show the result of this kind of marriage, one of which took place while I was in the field.

Case II: The Marriage of a Male Sharif to an ex-Slave

A is a young Jamalilil sharif. When he was eighteen, he met a girl whom he loved. The girl's father worked in Mombasa. The young sharif contacted the girl's mother, who was very happy to allow him to have a secret marriage so his family would not know about it, since he was considered young. He married the girl, and he used to spend some time with her. After two years, his father's brother found out about the marriage. When he met the young sharif, he asked him to divorce his wife, because her father was a mwana wa haramu. Her father was essentially a slave of a certain family and he had not been freed in the Islamic way. The young sharif liked the girl, and she was fond of him and never made a mistake. For several days he was unable to decide. Then one day he sat down and wrote a letter to the girl, asking her to forgive him, thanking her for the two years, and then telling her that he had to divorce her. He did not tell her the reasons; he said that "This is our fate." He sent the letter and that was the end of the marriage.

When I asked A about his divorce and the grounds for it, he said, "I loved that girl, but my child would have been a bastard, and this we had to avoid. The sharifs do not like to have their children accused of being bastards." The sharifs always fear that kind of marriage, although it is true that Saiyid Aḥmed al Badawi did take a slave girl as a wife. This slave was given to him as a gift, and he took her as a souriya, and then divorced and freed her. She married after that and still lives in the Reiyadah area.

In the case of marriages with souriyas, the Jamalilil sharifs insisted that their children not only belonged to them, but also had to be socialized by them. Therefore, when they divorced one of their wives, the children were kept in the father's house, where the eldest woman took care of them, trained them, and gave them an elementary education. After this, such a child attended the school in the Reiyadah area where he learned like any other sharif. In other words, he was equal to his brothers; he had the same rights and duties. Furthermore, when his father died, he would inherit like anyone else. In other words, he was a sharif in every respect. He had to visit his mother and take care of her, but his loyalty was toward his father's group. The child of a sharif born of a non-sharif woman would, of course, be higher than those half brothers from the mother's side who had no sharif father.

The son of a sharif, then, inherited his father's status and rank, and as long as the mother was not contaminated by being the product of an adulterous relation, the child would not be affected by her. The mother was a vessel, and had nothing to do with the child's qualities. However, a defiled vessel, like a contaminated cooking pot, would defile the material put into it. All non-sharif women were vessels, but some were clean, and some were defiled. The sharif could use the clean ones, but he had to leave the defiled ones for others.

Sharif girls, however, were not to be understood as vessels. They inherited active purity, which they passed on to their children; and the child of a sharif woman would inherit the purity of his father and mother, and, therefore, he would be a mansib—he would have a position. He would be higher than his non-mansib brothers, although all sharif children have the same basic purity. Still, there are many mansibs who never reached the degree of qutb, while 'Ali ibn Mohammed al Ḥabashy reached the degree of qutb even though his mother was an Abyssinian slave. The following case is an illustration.

Case III: The Marriage of a Sharif Male to a Mngwana Woman

Saiyid Aḥmed al Badawi married from a Khatib family. His wife refused to go to the Reiyadah area to stay there. He was to go to stay with her one night each week. Saiyid Saleḥ was against this marriage; he used to say that "Wangwana women are like charcoal; if they are burning, they destroy, and if they are not burning, and somebody touches them, he will dirty himself." Saiyid Aḥmed al Badawi refused to obey his father, who began to support his other son Eidarous. Eidarous married twice from the Ḥadramis. The mother of Eidarous was from Patta, while the mother of Saiyid Aḥmed was from the Comoro Islanders. All the Comoro Islanders supported Sharif Aḥmed.

Saiyid Aḥmed got a male child, Ḥassan, from his mngwana wife. When Aḥmed married another wife, the mngwana wife was upset. One day he made a promise to grant his mngwana wife whatever she liked. She directly asked him for a divorce, and he was obliged to divorce her. When this happened he tried to take his son. The wife refused because this was not a wangwana custom. The saiyid was unable to convince her. The child was raised in Mkomani, i.e., the wangwana quarter, and he was raised by his mother's family.

At that time, one of the Mahdali sharifs was a student of Ḥabib Saleḥ and Saiyid Aḥmed al Badawi. As soon as this Mahdali sharif, who was called Saiyid Mohammed 'Adnan, finished his education in Reiyadah, the wangwana gave him the responsibility of one of their mosques in Mkomani. When he asked for marriage, he was given the ex-wife of Saiyid Aḥmed al Badawi. From that marriage, which was correct because the Mahdali and the Wa Yumbili Ngombe were equal, according to the wangwana, Saiyid Mohammed 'Adnan got two children. These two male children were raised with their half brother Ḥassan, the son of Aḥmed al Badawi. Saiyid Mohammed 'Adnan taught Ḥassan, who maintained a very limited relation with his father's group.

The wangwana found in that child their best chance. If they could convince him to attack the Reiyadah, then this would mean that the Reiyadah sharifs would cease to be unified, and their internal division could be used by the wangwana. At the same time, he would not be able to attack Saiyid Mohammed 'Adnan, who raised him and taught him. The wangwana and Ḥassan backed Saiyid Mohammed 'Adnan for different reasons. While the wangwana or a part of them were interested in destroying the Reiyadah, Ḥassan tried to be accepted by the Reiyadah sharifs as partially wangwana and partially sharif. The wangwana claimed that Saiyid Mohammed 'Adnan had showed karama . . . they propagated this with the help of Ḥassan, who claimed that Mohammed 'Adnan was a local saint.

The Reiyadah sharifs thought the claim and propaganda contradicted their principle of indifference, or khumoul. They felt that the sharif should have hidden his karama, or at least have been very cautious about using it. Above all, he was not supposed to display it. But, as a Reiyadah sharif told me:

> They were about to advertise that Saiyid Mohammed 'Adnan had a karama in the newspaper; this, in fact, is the sign of "no karama." We never believed in him, and we will never do so in the future. He was a mngwana, and the wangwana are similar to a twig which grew old and no one could straighten it up. It is crooked and it will end crooked. They envied Ḥabib Saleḥ's success, so they wanted to create another sharif to hurt Sharif Saleḥ, but if God wants His light to spread, no one will be able to hinder it, even if that one was a mngwana.

When Ḥabib Saleḥ died in 1937 A. D. (1354 A. H.) (see the Genealogical Chart), Saiyid Aḥmed al Badawi succeeded him as the head of the Reiyadah. But when Aḥmed died in 1941 (1358 H), his brother Eidarous was accused of poisoning him. The eldest son of Saiyid Aḥmed stood against his father's brother, and, in this, he was backed by the Comoro Islanders. The Ḥadramis remained neutral, since both Sharif Eidarous and Sharif Aḥmed had established marriage relations with them. They preferred to wait, even though they were inclined toward Sharif Eidarous, because they respected him for his old age. Eidarous, on the other hand, was openly backed by the slaves and the Bajuni. (His mother was from Patta.) Ḥassan, his stepfather, and the Ḥusseini backed Saiyid Ali (the son of Saiyid Aḥmed) against his father's brother. Saiyid Mohammed 'Adnan claimed that Saiyid 'Ali was better educated than Saiyid Eidarous, a judgment which showed that he did not understand the idea of khumoul. Baḥsan, the son of Saiyid 'Ali ibn Ahmed al Badawi, stood with his grandfather Eidarous against his own father. The wangwana did not interfere directly. One day, Sharif Eidarous saw Sharif Ḥassan in the market, and he took his shoes off and began to beat his brother's son, calling him a mngwana snake, and declaring that he never belonged to Reiyadah. Sharif Eidarous ordered ten ex-slaves to beat Sharif Ḥassan, but they could not because he was a sharif.

Meanwhile, the Comoro Islanders continually insulted the new head of the Reiyadah, calling him a *paka,* or "cat." Instead of addressing him as a sharif, they began calling him "sheikh" in order to degrade him. The new head called together his Bajuni and ex-slaves and they prepared themselves for a fight. One Friday, after the Jum'a prayer, the slaves and the Bajuni caught the Comoro Islanders and began to beat them. The Comoro Islanders were badly defeated, and early the next morning they took their wives, children, and whatever they could carry on their boats and left Lamu for Mambroi, about four miles north of Malindi. This fight is well known as the *Vita vya Mabatini,* "the battle of Mabatini."

Sharif Mohammed 'Adnan, assisted by his wife's son Ḥassan, began to curse and attack Eidarous. They called him the sharif who lost his honor. In retaliation, Eidarous did not allow Saiyid Mohammed 'Adnan or Ḥassan to enter the Reiyadah area. At the same time, he depended mainly on his grandson Baḥsan, whose father was 'Ali ibn Aḥmed al Badawi. The grandson Baḥsan was a mansib, because his mother was the daughter of Eidarous and his father 'Ali was the son of Aḥmed al Badawi. Ḥassan was not even mentioned in this genealogy.

Ḥassan was licensed by Sharif Mohammed 'Adnan and was given a mosque to teach in; in fact, this was Sheikh Bilad Mosque, the same mosque Saiyid

Saleḥ began to teach in when he was licensed. By this time, Sharif Ḥassan was attacking the Reiyadah, and especially Eidarous, openly, and, because he was "under the shade of the sacred tree," no one could stop him. However, Mohammed 'Adnan and Ḥassan could not gather followers as Ḥabib Saleḥ had done. The time was not right, as it had been when Ḥabib Saleḥ began his new movement. The two sharifs failed to establish any relation with Ḥadramaut. Even the qutb of the time, Saiyid 'Omar ibn Sumait, did not approve of their movement, so Saiyid Mohammed 'Adnan remained strictly a mngwana saint. His fame never spread over the sea, or even beyond part of the Mkomani area for that matter.

When he died in 1965, he was buried in the Mkomani graveyard. His sons and their half-brother Ḥassan tried very hard to increase his fame; they even went to Mombasa to invite people to attend the first year's ritual visit, or ziyara, but their success was not outstanding. Sharif Eidarous did not attend, and neither did most of the people from the southern part of Lamu. The Reiyadah sharifs stressed the idea that Mohammed 'Adnan was only a mngwana saint. In 1968, when I was in the field, the sons of Mohammed 'Adnan made a wooden cover for his grave like that of Saiyid Saleḥ and made a ziyara to his grave, and Sharif Ḥassan Aḥmed al Badawi offered a prose composition in praise of Saiyid Mohammed 'Adnan.

In 1968, Ḥabib Eidarous, who was then the head of the Reiyadah, died, and people came from Dar es Salaam, Uganda, Zanzibar, and Ḥadramaut to attend his burial ceremonies. The son of Saiyid Mohammed 'Adnan looked at the thousands of people and spoke the following words exactly:

> The Jamalilil sharifs, no doubt, have a baraka. If you have that baraka, no one can take it from you. The human beings, the jin, and the angels will be your servants. The Mahdali did not get that baraka, and whatever we do, no one will believe us.

This was a true prediction. As soon as the sharif died, Saiyid 'Ali ibn Aḥmed al Badawi was appointed by his brothers as the head of the Reiyadah, and his son Baḥsan was appointed as the manager of all the Reiyadah affairs. In other words, the spiritual leadership was given to Saiyid 'Ali, while the organizational aspects were left to his son. Sharif Ḥassan was called and attended the funeral of Eidarous with his brothers, but he was still considered an outsider. He was a mngwana, not from the Reiyadah. Nevertheless, as soon as he was allowed to go to Reiyadah and pray in the mosque, he began to change his position concerning Saiyid Mohammed 'Adnan, and my last interviews contrasted sharply with my first ones. In the last ones, he admitted that Saiyid Mohammed 'Adnan was an ascetic, or zahid, but not an 'ālim. One day his half-brother Ahmed 'Adnan was praising his father, calling him the master of the sharifs, but when he went out, Sharif Ḥassan told me not to believe him. He said,

> We Jamalilil have the baraka . . . . We have the genealogical relation to the Prophet. The Mahdali have no genealogy, and, in fact, they are not the descendants of Ḥussein, but the descendants of Ḥassan. A child of Jamalilil has more education than any Mahdali, but we prefer indifference.

However, the wangwana at least had succeeded in creating their own saint, and this was one saint who had never declared that he was superior to the wangwana. The Mahdali sharifs were equal to the Wa Yumbili Ngombe, who were given religious education, so the new saint was equal to the khatibs, but he did not try to raise himself higher than his category. One potential problem was postponed, since Saiyid Mohammed 'Adnan did not have any female children, and so it was not possible to predict whether he would have let them marry from the khatibs, or whether he would have allowed them only to marry other sharifs. His sons, however, did have girls, and one of them told me that he would never allow them to marry anyone but a sharif: "We are sharifs, so our girls have to be kept away from the non-sharifs. We marry the wangwana girls, but we must not allow them to marry our girls." In other words, the sons of the saint would not accept the old wangwana ideology of equal marriage. Instead, they followed the central theme of Habib Saleḥ's ideology. They, too, believed that the sharifs were the purest element on earth, and that the universe was created for Mohammed and his descendants. Thus they followed the teaching that other people should praise the sharifs, and, to the extent that they did, the Prophet would intercede for them. As a result of this view, the sharifs had to lead every ceremony—to be present at every social gathering—for their presence was needed to add merit to the religious activity. All religious action depended on them. The verse quoted at the beginning of this chapter aptly describes the mood of Lamu at this time:

> In this place, we now have a
>   sharif;
> Offer him the censer and ubani;
> Let him read the Fatiḥa calmly,
> So that the other readers will
>   not make mistakes.

The conflicting ideologies perpetrated by the traditional wangwana and the Reiyadah sharifs will bear an important relationship to our analysis of the Lamuan myth of creation, which is the subject of the next chapter.

Part Two

Lamu Redefined:
The Synchronic Dimension

4

The Myth of Creation

Ambiwao nganu unazake.

Whoever recounts a story,
adds his share to it.
—Lamu Proverb

THE THEORETICAL POSITION

This chapter deals with Lamu's myth of creation. I am aware that the Lamuan is only one of several versions of the Swahili creation myth, and that the analysis of different versions of any myth is extremely important, as Lévi-Strauss and others have amply demonstrated. Yet, the analysis of a single version in context yields illuminating results which, though less elegant than those issuing from variant/variant analyses, are less subject to criticisms of formalism and are perhaps more appropriate to viewing the living myth as the complex social fact it really is. Accordingly, I have not attempted a side-by-side analysis of the Lamuan myth with, for example, a related version recently analyzed by Professor Jan Knappert.[1] Knappert's concern is primarily with the literary aspects of the myth, and he does not specify the area from which the myth was taken, which effectively prevents its analysis as a living complex.

The structural analysis of myth has come to be almost synonymous with the name Claude Lévi-Strauss, and not without reason, for he has surely made invaluable contributions to its development and refinement. Some, of course,

1. Jan Knappert, *Traditional Swahili Poetry: An Investigation into the Concepts of East African Islam as Reflected in the Utenzi Literature* (Leiden: E. J. Brill, 1967). See also Jan Knappert, *Myths and Legends of the Swahili* (London: Heinemann Educational Books, 1970).

have leveled the accusation of formalism at Lévi-Strauss,[2] claiming that his objective is to leap from the mythic text to simple logico-mathematical formulas, while discarding the more strictly "cultural" context of the myth. Perhaps this is partly true. Buchler and Selby[3] have demonstrated that Lévi-Strauss can be interpreted in this way, and that myth can be analyzed with minimal reference to its cultural context, providing that there exist several versions of variants of *the* myth or *a* myth. The ambiguity of Lévi-Strauss's theoretical writings on the subject is well known—probably more so than the writings themselves—but, suffice it to say, that actual analyses of myths are never without some reference to cultural context.

A first step in the structural analysis of myth is the identification of the smallest meaningful units of the myth (mythemes). The mytheme, while a *meaningful* unit, is to some extent, on a deep structural level, equivalent to the phoneme as discussed by Jakobson.[4] The phoneme, for Jakobson, is a bundle of distinctive features, which exist as relational characteristics. The distinctive features of the mytheme are its function and related subject, which, taken as a whole, are truly useful analytically only in relation to other mythemes, which, by virtue of similar internal relations, comprise a "bundle"—an associative set, or paradigm. These bundles, or paradigms, in turn stand in oppositional relation to each other by varying criteria and in varying combinations. Such relations of bundles may be viewed as occurring on a horizontal plane, as do the words comprising this sentence. Relations of this type—of paradigm to paradigm(s)—are of a contiguous sort, and, if we pursue the linguistic analogy, are syntagmatic. The paradigms themselves may be considered vertical in the sense that their elements are associated by independent relations to a common characteristic. They are therefore non-contiguous and hence not bound to an essentially linear cumulative temporal domain. The deep structural meaning of the myth, then, is generated by relations and sets of relations. It is *meaning* without subjective manipulation.

The identification of mythemes is an exceedingly difficult task. How are we to know what are the very basic units of meaning, especially if we are, willfully or not, working with relatively little contextual material? If we work with translated texts, how can we be certain that what is rendered in English as "he

2. See Kenelin Burridge, "Lévi-Strauss and Myth," in *The Structural Study of Myth and Totemism,* ed. E. Leach (London: Tavistock Publications, 1967).

3. Ira R. Buchler and Henry A. Selby, *A Formal Study of Myth* (Austin: The University of Texas Press, 1968).

4. R. Jakobson and M. Halle, *Fundamentals of Language* (The Hague: Mouton, 1956).

flew to heaven" doesn't really mean "he rose to the clouds" or "he traveled up"? Perhaps the inaccuracies are inconsequential, but they are in any case the result of a preanalytical "analysis" in that the translated text has already been given (usually) Western equivalence lexically and grammatically. Lévi-Strauss has been criticized for relying on intuition, seemingly legitimized by the pervasive assumption that analyst and native share the mental stuff of mythic generation. I am not sure that this is such a bad thing. But surely the problem can be reduced, though certainly not eliminated, by reference to ecological, geographical, and more generally ethnographic data pertaining to the owners of the myth. I cannot, in fact, see how the structural analysis of myth can proceed through the initial identification of mythemes in the absence of considerable knowledge of the cultural context. Meaning, or even what is meaningful, cannot be demonstrated solely on the basis of a translated text.

In other words, to understand the myth analytically is to understand the culture of which it is part. Perhaps, ultimately, this will lead to simple logico-mathematical formulas, but the empirical[5] level of cultural diversity must not be reduced to some irrelevant agglomeration of blatancies whose existence is only occasionally and selectively acknowledged as a convenient heuristic device in the pursuit and verification of some imputed deep structure.

The relation between these two extremes is a dialectic one, and is the work of the unconscious. "The dialectic of superstructures, like that of language, consists in setting up constitutive units . . . to elaborate a system which plays the part of the synthesizing operator between ideas and facts, thereby turning the latter into signs. The mind thus passes from empirical diversity to conceptual simplicity."[6] Analysis should not be so rarified that existential facts, culturally defined, are exempted from the procedures of explanation and understanding.

Although structural analysis is extremely valuable and adds to our understanding of myth, I also feel that there is still a place for Malinowski's currently unfashionable view of myth as a charter for social action. In other words, in addition to the unconscious structure, the myth has a conscious function; it has important social implications for the people who believe in it. For example, the people of Lamu do not call their creation story *ngano,* or "myth." For them it is history, and it is part of their religious belief. It is the sacred part of the

5. Here empiricism means not the naïve empiricism which I criticize later, but the ethnographic richness in which the anthropologist has to immerse himself, guided by a theoretical stand.

6. Claude Lévi-Strauss, *The Savage Mind* (Chicago: University of Chicago Press, 1966), p. 95.

tarikh al kauni, or history of the universe. This history differs from what we might call *maendaleo,* or "evolution."

In the *madrassa,* or main Islamic school, the students study a sort of evolution. A Jamalilil sharif teaches it, and I was able to attend his class and get a copy of his lectures. He says that "evolution is that branch of knowledge from which we know what happened to man and earth." However, he also adds that "our knowledge is limited, and most of what we say here is doubtful." In this statement the difference between myth as *tarikh,* or history, and evolution lies in *i'tiqadi,* or belief. While evolution is doubtful, people believe in the tarikh al kauni. The events are unique and irreversible. Adam lived on earth, and the people of Lamu believe they are his descendants. If anyone in Lamu doubted the existence of Adam, he would be considered a *kafiri,* or "unbeliever"; however, if people doubted evolution, or doubted the idea that there was once a stone age, they would in no way be unbelievers.

Thus myth may well be used as a charter for social action and as justification for the social order.[7] In other words, myth does contribute to the maintenance of an equilibrium without which society might cease to exist. "Myth fulfills in primitive culture an indispensable function: it expresses, enhances, and codifies belief; it safeguards and enforces morality; it vouches for the efficiency of ritual and contains practical rules for the guidance of man."[8] Thus, in this context, myth might be considered a conservative force.

Malinowski saw society as existing in a state of equilibrium or balance. Furthermore, within his system, he was not able to differentiate between signs and symbols. For these reasons, he was led to assert that "myth is not symbolic, but a direct expression of its subject matter . . . . "[9] However, by treating myth as non-symbolic, Malinowski, in fact, missed the most important aspect not only of mythical thought, but also of a whole belief system. His neglect of symbolism was due to his own naïve behavioristic approach. In his stimulus-response model of social action, he could not differentiate between symbols and signs. Consequently, symbolism was viewed by him as the influence of an object, a gesture, or an action upon an organic receptive medium. The relation between the human being and the outside world was thus triadic in nature: subject, sign, and object. Although the determinative characteristic of all symbols is conception, Malinowski said, "that all such definitions are metaphysically tainted, and that,

7. I will discuss this in detail in Chapter 5, and my position should become clearer there.

8. Bronislaw Malinowski, *Magic, Science and Religion* (New York: Anchor Books, 1954), p. 101.

9. *Ibid.*

in reality, symbolism is founded not in a mysterious relation between the sign and the contents of the human mind, but between an object, a gesture, and an action and its influence upon the receptive organism."[10] His ideas concerning communication systems were influenced by this definition of symbols. Within a communication system, Malinowski equated symbols with signs; but this implied that there would be no abstract knowledge, since signs are usually attached to elements of experience and made to stand for these elements in both thought and communication. Consequently, if Malinowski's view were the correct one, one would always be trapped in his immediate world of experience, and knowledge would always be of an instrumental sort. In this schema, actions are determined by the stimulus-response mechanism, and both the stimulus and the response can be observed and easily studied. "Ultimately and as a principle of method in field work, I would insist on the behavioristic approach, because this allows us to describe facts which can be observed."[11]

Malinowski was concerned with those external manifestations which physically appear and could be verified by other objective observers. He wanted to stress that anthropology, like any other science, was limited to a field in which scientists could observe, describe, and verify their findings. Thus he denied that symbols could express and create meanings or concepts by themselves.[12]

The symbol "exists" only in a system, and as part of the articulation of that system. However, "sign," as Malinowski used the term, exists apart from the system. In fact, the major difference between man and the animals lies in man's ability to transcend the world of signs and comprehend the world of symbols. For man, symbols are vehicles for conception, and it is the conception which a symbol makes possible, and not the "thingness" of that symbol, that carries the meaning. Thus symbolism requires four terms: subject, symbol, conception, and object.

Man cannot confront reality immediately. He has so enveloped himself in

10. Bronislaw Malinowski, *A Scientific Theory of Culture* (Durham: The University of North Carolina Press, 1944), p. 139.

11. *Ibid.*, p. 71.

12. Compare this with Durkheim: "Men alone have the faculty of conceiving the ideal, of adding something to the real" (*The Elementary Forms of Religious Life* [New York: Free Press, 1965], p. 469). Again, the material object is not important in itself: "Surely," Durkheim writes, "the soldier who falls while defending his flag does not believe that he sacrifices himself for a bit of cloth" (*ibid.*, p. 260). Also, see E. Leach, "The Epistemological Background to Malinowski's Empiricism," in *Man and Culture*, ed. R. Firth (London: Routledge & Kegan Paul, 1957), p. 132.

symbolic forms, "that he cannot see or know anything except by the interposition of this artificial medium."[13] However, this does not mean that symbols have no relation to reality. Emmet has shown us clearly that the symbolic system is a construction which bears a very definite relation to external reality and which responds to it. The mind does not act like a mirror, but rather carries on "a selective and interpretive activity which builds up symbolic constructions."[14]

Myth is symbolic, and for this reason it can be interpreted differently by various groups of people. Of course, in saying this, we are referring not to the structure of the myth or the fundamental unconscious meaning, but, rather, to the conscious and surface meaning. In other words, the same myth can support different ideologies at different times. The conceptual connotations of the myth are socially defined. For example, when the so-called "Arabs" were ruling East Africa, they formed a closed class and used the myth of creation to enforce this ideological stand. The Africans, on the other hand, were called *Wa Shenzi,* a term that indicated a very low status, which, as we will see, was also justified by the myth. However, now that Africans are the rulers, their social definition has begun to change. This, I suspect, will lead to a reinterpretation of the creation myth. It is conceivable that an anthropologist visiting Lamu today might discover the Wa Shenzi differently defined, and the symbolic elements of the myth bearing a quite new interpretation. But, the myth itself, as part of the Swahili literature, will probably persist without change.

My argument is that the myth should be analyzed not merely in terms of its structure but also in terms of its meaning as a charter for social action. The Lamuan creation myth is not only a logical model but also part and parcel of the social reality shared by the people. The world in which people live and to which they react is not a private world. People express themselves and act toward each other according to the symbolic constructions which constitute their world. These symbolic constructions or forms must have a minimum of shared meaning; otherwise, communication would be impossible. In other words, "cultural acts, the construction, apprehension, and utilization of symbolic forms, are social events like any other; they are as public as marriage and

13. Ernst Cassirer, *An Essay on Man* (New Haven, Conn.: Yale University Press, 1944), p. 43.

14. D. Emmett, *The Nature of Metaphysical Thinking* (London: Macmillan, 1945), p. 95.

as observable as agriculture."[15]

The social and cultural context in which the myth exists and is narrated constitutes an important part of the study of the myth. This has been stated clearly by Victor Turner, who found that "myths are *liminal* phenomena: They are frequently told at a time or in a site that is 'betwixt and between.'"[16] Myths, especially the creation myths, are usually recited during liminal periods, periods of "duration" (*durée*), or unsegmented time in the Bergsonian sense, as opposed to periods which can be measured quantitatively.[17] In periods of duration, the past, the present, and the future are felt not as a succession but as coexistent. This is clear in Lamu, where myth constitutes part of the religious system and must be studied within that context.[18]

In this chapter, I will first recount the Lamuan myth of creation; then, I will offer an analysis of it that deals with the structure of the myth.

THE MYTH

In the beginning, there was *Mungu,* or God. God had no father and no son. He was alive; He was light without darkness and he had existed for all time. We do not know who Mungu—the Most Merciful and the Destroyer—is. Mungu lives above the seventh sky with his favorite creatures. We live in the world beneath the first sky. The center of our world is the blessed land of Mecca, where *peponi,* or paradise, will be ordered by God after the day of judgment.

God was alone, and He took some of His light and made our beloved prophet Mohammed. From the light of the Prophet came the Throne, the Pen, and the Tablet. The Pen was ordered to write but, being ignorant, it did not know what to write and began to sweat. It questioned God and was told to write what was going to happen in the future. With its own sweat the Pen wrote the future on the Tablet.

God then ordered a river of light to encircle His first and favorite creatures, Mohammed, and the Pen, Tablet, and Throne which came from him. Then he ordered a river of fire to encircle the river of light. Because He wanted soldiers, God created angels from the river of light. Simultaneously, the jin were created

15. Clifford Geertz, "Religion as a Cultural System," in *Anthropological Approaches to the Study of Religion,* ed. Michael Banton (London: Tavistock Publications, 1966), p. 5.

16. Victor Turner, "Myths and Symbols," *International Encyclopedia of the Social Sciences,* X (1968), 576.

17. Henri Bergson, *Time and Free Will* (New York: Macmillan, 1910).

18. This aspect of myth will be more thoroughly discussed in Chapter 5.

from the river of fire. The angels and the jin worshipped God, but, while the angels were all identical, the jin were divided into three tribes, each different from the others. God encircled the river of fire with a river of water and surrounded this with a river of snow. God gave the angels power over the river of water and granted the jin power over the wind. Fire and wind worked on water, which evaporated, making steam and bubbles. It was smoky, dark, and moist. The bubbles dried up and became Earth. Rain fell down, and trees came out. All these creatures worshipped God. After some time the trees began to bear fruits which ripened and ripened and then decayed. A bad smell was all over Earth. Earth complained to God and asked that someone be sent to *eat* the fruit before it decayed, so that the odor could be eliminated. *Rahimu,* God the Merciful, sent the first tribe of jin down to live on Earth.

When the jin came down on Earth, they cut stone and dug the ground to build towns. They lived on fruit which they picked from the trees. However, in building their towns, they cut all the trees and were forced to go to the forest when they needed food. Their numbers increased rapidly, making it necessary for them to cut more trees and transform more of the bush into towns. The towns grew bigger, and each town was proud of its strength and began to compete with the others.

The competition resulted in fights, and wars would break out between the towns. However, there were no weapons, and the only way to defeat a town was to cut it off from its food supply in the bush. One town would lay siege to another, depriving the jin inside the town of food, and they would die of hunger. This caused the smell of decay to spread over Earth again; only this time it was worse than before. Earth once again complained to God.

Merciful and generous as He usually is, Mungu ordered the second tribe of jin, called the Ben, to come out of the sea where they had been living and settle on Earth. God ordered these jin to destroy the first tribe. The Ben used weapons and were meat-eaters. Because they hunted and fished, they could not settle in the towns but lived in the bush or on the seashore, continually moving from one place to another. In order to facilitate this constant movement, they divided into small groups.

But since the Ben did not eat the fruits or vegetables, they once more decayed and covered the land with a bad smell. The Ben used to fight among themselves and spread blood over Earth. The smell of blood was also bad, and once more Earth complained to God.

God ordered the last tribe of jin to go down to Earth and do away with the Ben and clean up the blood. This tribe was headed by Iblisi, who was one of

God's favorites. However, in getting rid of the Ben, Iblisi had to kill them, which only produced more blood and more odor. Iblisi killed most of the Ben, but some of them escaped to the sea, where they were safe.

Now, Iblisi and his tribe were alone on Earth. His tribe increased, and he felt proud and powerful. Iblisi became subtle and sophisticated. But Earth never complained about him.

God wanted to create Adam, so he ordered one of his angels, Gabriel, to go down to Earth and bring up some of its dust to Heaven. When Gabriel descended, Earth refused to give up the dust, and swore on him by God's name not to take it. Gabriel was confused, and returned to God empty-handed. God was pleased when He learned the story, and He appointed Gabriel as His first archangel and called him "Trustworthy Spirit."

A second angel, Michael, was sent down. Earth once again refused to give him the dust, and Michael also returned empty-handed. Again, God was pleased and entrusted Michael with the task of providing sustenance for other creatures.

The third angel sent by God was Israfili, and when he returned empty-handed God appointed him as the angel of the trumpet. Israfili was to be the angel who blows the trumpet on the last day, to resurrect the dead.

The last angel sent was 'Azra'il. Like the others, he too was refused the dust, but even when Earth called on God's name, 'Azra'il did not heed his request. He said to Earth: "I have to obey the orders of God. He told me to bring dust, and I will take it by force. This is my function." He grasped the dust and ascended. When God learned of this, he appointed 'Azra'il as the angel of death.

God ordered the angels and the jin to assemble, and showed them the dust. God told them that He was going to make something out of the dust which would live and die on Earth. He asked the angels and the jin to bow to the new creature. Iblisi, sophisticated as he was, told God that the new creature would be bad, corrupt, and a liar. Iblisi looked down on this new creature, who was neither fire nor light but dust, and he knew that dust smelled, especially after being smeared with blood. But God told Iblisi that the creation of Adam was His wish.

The dust was sifted, and the white dust was separated from the rest, which was black and red. The white dust was then brought to God and put beside the Throne. The Prophet's flesh would be made from this dust. The black and red dust were mixed with water from a river near the throne, and God shaped the moistened clay as He wanted it, leaving it beside paradise to dry. Iblisi, eager to see whether the shape was solid or hollow, stuck his finger into it, and this is how the navel was formed.

God gave the figure life, which went from the head down to the feet. The living creature was called *Adamu,* or "Adam."' Adam was very quiet, polite, and thankful. He knew his place and was humble, and he behaved like a free, noble man. The angels were impressed by his behavior and bowed before him.

Iblisi looked at the new creature and felt proud. He refused to bow to him, saying, "How could I bow to something made of a smelly clay? Fire is better than dust." Adam was newly born, and thus a *kitoto,* or child, while Iblisi considered himself mature and old. He disobeyed God, and God told Iblisi: *"Peponi humu andoka, si kea dakika moja,"* "Go from paradise, do not stay here one minute." Iblisi went out. He was angry and vowed to take revenge on the new creature.

Adam lived happily in paradise, the ground of which was made of ambergris. He was satisfied, and he constantly worshipped God. Once God called Adam to come to Him, and Adam obeyed. God ordered something to come out of Adam's back, and creatures like Adam came forth. These were Adam's children. God asked them to promise that they would obey Him and that they would be Muslims. Both Adam and his children made that promise. The children were then returned to Adam's back, and he was dismissed. Adam lived in paradise alone, but now he felt lonely. He needed someone to speak to; he desired a companion.

One day, he slept and dreamt of a beautiful creature sitting beside him. Adam opened his eyes, and found a gracious woman. She was very beautiful, and Adam was full of admiration. Adam came closer and touched her, and found that she was alive. He said "God brought her for me," and called the new creature *Hawia,* or "Eve," which means life. They lived together in paradise, and Adam told her she could eat from all the trees except one, and that one was forbidden because God had ordered it.

Soon Eve began to roam around. She would leave Adam alone for long periods of time, and he became jealous. One day, she told Adam that if they ate the fruit of the forbidden tree they could have *uzazi,* or descendants. Adam refused to disobey God, but Eve continued to argue and urge him. She told him that if they had many descendants, they could exceed the number of the angels. But Adam told her that he was happy, and that he did not want descendants. Eve told Adam that he could not say that he was happy because he had never experienced sadness. Adam asked her about the source of her knowledge, and she replied, "I got it from my friend [*shoga*], whom I met in paradise." Adam cautioned her that this friend might be Iblisi, but Eve replied that Iblisi had been thrown out of paradise, and that he would never be able to reenter it.

Eve began to reproach Adam for his ignorance. She told him that he was created from clay, and he had to return to clay. Yet Adam insisted that Eve's friend was Iblisi, so Eve went and asked her friend whether or not this was true. Without denying it, Iblisi told Eve not to listen to Adam; he told her that Adam was ignorant. Then Iblisi informed Eve that Adam was going to marry a *hurulaini,* or paradise nymph.

Eve was jealous, and she went to Adam and asked him if he was going to marry a paradise nymph. Adam told Eve that there were no paradise nymphs, and he added that Eve was his wife, and that he would never marry again. Eve felt happy, and when she met her friend she told him so. But the friend informed her that Adam was a liar and knew how to deceive her. Eve told her friend that, nevertheless, she could not change Adam's mind.

Iblisi told Eve a secret that would prevent Adam from marrying again. He told her that if she ate from the tree, then Adam would have children, and would not marry another. Iblisi told Eve that the nymph tree was the real reason that Adam did not want to eat the fruit. Iblisi advised Eve to cry and told her that tears were the weapon with which she could conquer a man and make him agree.

Eve did not waste any time. She took Adam to the tree, and they sat under its shade. Momentarily, Iblisi climbed the tree and dropped a fruit. Eve grasped it. Adam was afraid, and Eve began to cry. Adam grew sad, and Eve accused him of not loving her. Adam swore by God that he loved her, and that love of her filled his heart and went all over him. But Eve told him: "If you do not want to eat the fruit, I will eat it and I will depend on myself." Then, she took the fruit and "tasted" it. Adam realized that the sin had been committed and, as a gentleman, he could not allow Eve to be expelled from paradise alone. He grasped the fruit and ate it.

God sent His angels to put the Prophet's dust in Adam's back, and Adam shone. Adam and Eve were driven out of paradise, and the gates were closed.

Adam immediately asked God to forgive him, by the power of his beloved prophet, Mohammed. God the merciful forgave Adam. But Eve refused to ask for forgiveness. She was pregnant, and suffered a great deal. Adam was suffering, too. There were bare, rocky mountains, and there was no one around. Adam regretted his sin, and prepared himself for hardship.

Adam started quarreling with Eve. He blamed her, but she refused to accept his accusations. She asked him why it was her fault, since he wouldn't have eaten the fruit unless he had wanted it also.

Eve was suffering in her pregnancy, and she asked Adam why he also did not bear children. Adam angrily replied: "Because you were the first to taste the fruit, and you asked for children, numerous children."

Adam used to roam around and climb trees, and sometimes the thorns would cut his feet and back and Adam bled. For a long time, he would not eat anything but fruit. He would watch the fish and try to catch them. When he finally learned how to catch them, he would cut each fish down the back and spread it in the sun to dry, for he did not know how to cook.

Eve suffered, but she refused to complain to Adam and hid her regrets. She began to deliver twins, each time a boy and a girl. She suckled the children and took care of them. Meanwhile, Adam learned how to make fire, and began to cook food. He also planted cereals and domesticated goats, sheep, and cows. In addition to these animals that he used to eat, Adam made use of other animals without horns, e.g., the donkey and the camel. Eve depended entirely on Adam. He knew how to do many different things; he was superior to her.

One day an angel came down to Adam and told him that his children had to marry, but that no male child was to marry his own twin sister. Adam informed his children, and all agreed except *Qabil,* or Cain. Cain refused to obey the rules of God. He wanted to marry his own sister, who was supposed to marry *Habil,* or Abel, and so Cain killed his brother Abel. Cain did not know what to do with the corpse. An odor began to spread from the body. God sent down a crow, who found a pigeon. They began to fight in front of Cain and the crow killed the pigeon. Then the crow immediately began to dig a hole, and he put the dead pigeon into it and covered it with dust. So Cain also got up and began to dig a hole, and then he buried his brother. It was God's order that the corpse not be left exposed; burying the dead is the rule of God.

When Eve discovered what had happened, she mourned and wept. She could not keep herself from crying. Adam was sad, but he did not cry, and Eve became angry because Adam did not show his sorrow. But Adam told her that when she asked him to eat the fruit, she was asking for suffering, and he had obeyed her. Now, she must endure suffering. Adam told her that life on Earth must end in death. Eve was astonished, and said that her shoga, or friend, had not told her that. She realized now that her friend had been Iblisi, and that he had deceived her. She admitted her sin to Adam and then asked whether God would accept her repentance. Adam assured her that God was merciful. Eve then asked God to have pity on her and accept her repentance, as he was merciful. Adam told Eve that now there was no doubt that she had repented, and that God had pardoned her. Adam died and left Eve alone.

The myth ends at that point. However, there is one ancillary part that tells about Iblisi and the way in which he reentered paradise after having been expelled. The Lamuan myth deals with this incident in some detail. Iblisi, after leaving paradise, did not go down to Earth; instead, he kept watch beside paradise to eavesdrop on God and find out what he was going to do with the new creature. Iblisi knew that Adam lived in paradise and he knew about Eve; and he was jealous of Adam and insisted on revenge. So, he decided to coerce the children of Adam into disobeying God's orders. If they did that, they would be sent to hell (fire), and Iblisi would not be alone there. Iblisi's tribe went along with him in this decision.

Iblisi disguised himself and took up a position just outside of paradise looking for a way to get inside. The *nyoke,* or serpent, was a paradisaical, beautiful creature. And one day she met the disguised Iblisi, and he asked her to carry him in. But the serpent refused, saying: "If you are allowed to go inside, why do not you go through that gate?" Iblisi told her that he was only obeying God's orders by asking her to carry him in. So, finally, the serpent agreed and put Iblisi in her mouth and brought him into paradise. The serpent was punished for this and was ordered out of paradise. But, because she had carried Iblisi in her mouth, she became pregnant and laid eggs, one of which hatched the *sheitani,* or devil.

ANALYSIS

From the start, we find that the myth of creation makes a sharp distinction between light and fire. While light is continuous and stable, fire is irregular and unstable. The multiplicity of light, expressed as the prophets, the angels, the Throne, and the Tablet, all turn into unity, the unity and simplicity of light itself. Fire, on the other hand, is complex and heterochromatic. Fire produces not only heat and smoke but also different shades of light.[19] But fire can only produce light when it burns and causes smoke, and smoke is connected with darkness. It is clear that fire cannot have a simple definition—as a symbol, it is ambiguous.

This ambiguity is apparent in the myth. Fire (jin) increased and subdivided spontaneously. First, it was divided into three tribes. Then each of these tribes was further subdivided on Earth.[20] The angels that came out of the river of

19. The people of Lamu attribute the division of the jin to these different colors of light. When I asked an informant about this, he said: "If you make fire, don't you get different colored flames?" Then he added, "It is the same with jin."

20. While the myth does not specifically say that the fire creatures are divided into male and female, the people of Lamu speak about male and female jin.

light, on the other hand, were identical, and they did not increase or decrease. They were stable in number and alike in shape and character.

The river of light from which the angels emerged separated the eternal creatures from the ephemeral ones. The angels and the entities encircled by this river are eternal, while the creatures falling outside the circle of the river of light are ephemeral. This gives us the following set of binary oppositions:

Fire	/	Light
Heterogeneity	/	Homogeneity
Flux	/	Stability

Fig. 10. First Set of Binary Oppositions

The circular form of the rivers indicates that they are self-contained and without outlet; thus the outside river contains the inside ones. The last river which contains all the rest is the river of snow. Snow itself is like light, in that it is white and stable. And, in its coldness, it is also opposite to fire, which is hot. However, fire can transform snow into water, and when it does the difference between the river of water and the river of snow vanishes. Heat can also cause water to evaporate. In other words, light does not affect water or snow but fire does. This is the crux of the myth: How could Mungu (light) create something over which He had no power? Fire (jin) is the only element that has the power to initiate transformation. It is the sole positive and effective element.

The myth articulates and discusses the differences between light and fire thoroughly and clearly. After initially setting out these differences, the myth goes on to say that the jin (fire) are also associated with wind. Where does wind come from? Was it created or not? The myth does not say. However, it is logical to connect wind and fire, since both are positively effective elements which have the power of spontaneous change and destruction. Moreover, though wind can strengthen fire, it also can put it out. And, in that sense, wind and ashes have a similar relation to fire; both of them can extinguish it. Thus, even fire is delimited. Although it must burn in order to survive, burning is essentially a form of destruction. The ashes that usually result indicate the strength of fire and, at the same time, its demise. In other words, fire spontaneously creates its own antithesis. The people in Lamu have their own proverb to express this;

they say: "*Moto huzai moto,*" "fire does not beget fire—it begets ashes." Moreover, both wind and ashes produce *moshi,* or smoke. The Lamuan word *moshi* means not only black smoke (which hinders sight), but also white smoke (or steam). While black smoke is the result of wind blowing over fire, white smoke is the result of fire working on water and transforming it into steam, which is water carried by wind. Thus, the creation of Earth was the outcome of all these dialectical relations.

Fire	/	Light
Jin	/	Angels
Wind	/	Water

Fig. 11. Second Set of Binary Oppositions

In the myth wind blows on water, which is transformed into bubbles; bubbles are wind enveloped in water. In other words, when the wind (jin) contacts water (angels), bubbles are the result. But wind and fire (both connected to jin) produce black smoke (darkness). Therefore, the wind enveloped by water is dark wind. This means that the water (light) contains and envelopes dark smoky wind (fire). Thus, light contains and envelopes darkness and bubbles mediate between light and fire.

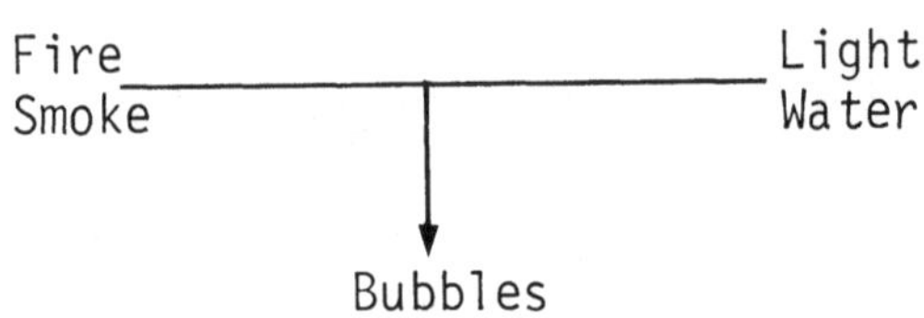

Fig. 12. The Bubbles Mediate

The dialectic continues. The smoke contained inside the bubbles causes water to evaporate (the bubbles "dried"), and the result is white smoke (steam). Water (light) evaporates and is transformed into white smoke. This evaporated water or white smoke results from the division of water into particles that were carried by wind (associated with fire). Again, the unity of the bubbles has been lost—the reverse of the original transformation that produced the bubbles.

Bubbles	=	Wind (smoke, fire) enveloped in water
Vapor	=	Water (whiteness, light) carried by wind

Fig. 13. Bubbles/Vapor

Water (angels), evaporated by heat or fire (jin), transforms smoke (dark) into vapor (white). Earth is the result of this operation. But evaporation also involves the notion of separation: water (down) is separated and carried *up*. In other words, fire has worked on water, and as a result things up are separated from things down. Fire is once again the cause of multiplicity. Wind has carried vapor or water up, and what remains is left down to make Earth. White vapor has been carried up by the wind, while dry and black smoke (fire) has been left down, allowing no life on Earth.

Fire	/	Water
Dry	/	Moist
Death	/	Life

Fig. 14. Third Set of Binary Oppositions

The relation between dryness and death is apparent in the myth. For example, life began on Earth only after rain (water, moisture) came down. Originally, fire had caused water to evaporate, which left Earth dry and lifeless; but, when water came down (rain), vegetation and animals appeared. Vegetables and animals mediate between wetness (up, water, angels) and complete dryness (down, fire, jin).[21] Fire has to destroy, to burn in order to survive, and Earth has to consume water in order to live. Thus, in order to live, both Earth and fire have to consume a third element. But rain (water dropping down from above) is the reverse of vapor (water carried up by the wind). Rain (water) has to

21. This concept shows itself in the way the Lamuans use their plants and animals in rituals. Not only vegetables and animals but also stone and steel are used for religious purposes, that is, as sacrificial material.

penetrate and break through wind in order to bring the dead earth to life. Moisture is the absence of death. The fruits were moist when they were alive, but when they dried, they were dead. The dust from which Adam was made was dry (dead, down), but it was moistened (alive, up).

After observing all these relations, it becomes clearer that in the myth, water, light, and angels are connected with life, while dryness, fire, and jin are connected with death. Added to this is the polarity of the good smell and the bad smell. When the trees were not bearing fruits, they worshipped God and had a good smell; but when they produced fruits, they decayed and smelled bad.

Life	/	Death
Trees	/	Decayed fruits
Good smell	/	Bad smell
Moist	/	Dry

Fig. 15. Fourth Set of Binary Oppositions

This set of relationships is especially clear in the case of the creation of Adam. Three angels fail to carry the *dust* (dry) up into heaven, and each of those who failed is appointed to a job connected with life, while 'Azra'il, who has succeeded in his mission, is appointed as the angel of death. 'Azra'il carries the dry dust (death), and thus becomes the angel of death.

In order for Earth to live, it has to overcome dryness (fire). But, paradoxically, in order to overcome dryness, Earth has to consume and *demolish* water (life): Earth cannot contain water without *demolishing* it. Thus, the creation of Earth cannot solve the basic contradiction. Bubbles cannot continue to mediate between fire/light. Ultimately, Earth fails to mediate between dry/moist. If fire = darkness = death/light = moisture = life, then there is no way in which Earth can mediate between death and life. So we are left with the same basic contradiction.

Thus, the myth tries in another way to overcome this contradiction: Adam was created. Adam was dust (down), and he was dry (dead). Adam was carried up by angels (light). He was *moistened* by river water, and while rain water has to cut through wind (fire), river water is carried by angels (light). So the wind (associated with jin) is excluded entirely from the story of Adam's creation.

This is important, since the exclusion of the wind will leave the river water *stable.* Nevertheless, Adam is dry dust, which has to be moistened by water. But, from the beginning, Adam is different from the other earthly creatures, who have emerged as the result of a combination of heat (fire) transforming water into steam, and water coming down as rain. Adam is given life through the addition of stable water, water which has not already undergone one transformation. This time, Adam's dust, which is multicolored like fire, has been sifted. The white dust is separated from the black and red dust.[22] The unity of the dust (on Earth) turns to multiplicity (in heaven). Adam has been made from the black and red dust, while the white dust has been put under the Throne. The black and red dust are mixed with river water, and, while Earth complains after consuming water, Adam does not complain. Yet it should be remembered that Adam has been made from the same material as Earth; he differs only in that he *lacks* the white dust which had been separated out before he was created. It is important that we now try to find out about this color.

White is connected with snow, which is stable water, and also with steam, which is white smoke (water). Thus we find that white is connected with light and water. Light is eternal; therefore, we can say that Earth has tried to be eternal by consuming light. We can now connect white dust with the eternal, a fact that is stressed in the myth. While the dust (red and black) from which Adam was created has been moistened, the dust (white) from which the prophets were created has never had to be. This conundrum is not an artificial one. The people of Lamu deal with it, and especially when they speak about the

Adam moistened by water ⟶ Ephemeral life

Prophets not moistened by water ⟶ Eternal life

Fig. 16. Eternal Life/Ephemeral Life

Prophet. For example, in a poem which they sing, they state that:

> The evidence and tradition support our belief
> That the Prophet is *alive* and *moist*
> He is like an *unsetting crescent.*

22. These three colors are essential in the ritual life of Lamu. Black and red are usually related to the harmful beings, the jin and the sheitani, while the color white is attributed to the protective beings, the angels, and prophets.

His body is in the grave,
Like a rose which does not decay.
Earth can never consume his flesh,
Or bones. You listener be certain of what I say.

The Prophet's body is eternal. No one in Lamu will admit that the Prophet is dead, while everyone admits that Adam died. The white dust is eternal, while the black and red dust are not. The white dust has been related to light (angels).

White dust	/	Black and red dust
Angels	/	Jin

Fig. 17. Fifth Set of Binary Oppositions

Life, for the Prophet, is not a secondary attribute, as it is for Adam and Earth; instead, life is fundamental to him. Though the Prophet is made from dust as are all other men, his white dust is different from either red or black dust. In other words, the black dust (Earth) has to consume water in order to live, while white dust is able to live without consuming.

In the part of the myth dealing with Adam's delivery of his children from his back, the Prophet is never mentioned. In other words, the Prophet is not to be born from Adam; he is not actually Adam's son. Thus there is a parallel between Adam's separation from Earth and the Prophet's, or the white dust's, separation from Adam. Adam, who is dust and who is so ephemeral, lives in paradise, which is different from Earth. While Earth is the result of a coming together of fire and light, the ground of paradise is made of ambergris.[23]

Ambergris, the excrement of the whale, is usually found along the seashore. The whale is an ambiguous creature. Though it lives in the sea, it carries children and delivers them. Furthermore, whales do not chew their food; so if a man is swallowed by a whale he can live in its stomach. An example of this is Jonah (*Yunis*), the prophet, who is said to have been transported across the sea in a whale's belly. Although paradise is composed of the excrement of the whale, if it is burned (fire), it will give off a pleasant odor. So the floor of paradise has been made of the excrement of a sea creature, a creature which lives in water, and it provides a home for a creature made of dust. Adam lives on the

23. Here we deal with the folk description of paradise. These descriptions are usually given when the people are asked to describe paradise.

excrement of the whale, i.e., inside the stomach of the whale. Since the whale does not chew, Adam is not digested. But Adam, unlike the whale, cannot eat without digestion. He has to chew his food.

This theme is also stressed in the myth. The serpent, who lives in direct contact with ambergris, takes Iblisi in her mouth but does not chew or digest him. So, the serpent, like the whale, is able to eat without digestion. Moreover, she carries Iblisi in her mouth, while the whale carries Adam in his stomach. The creature carried in the mouth, like that carried in the stomach, is alive. Here, it is clear that mouth = stomach.

Eve, the other creature living with Adam, wants to eat the forbidden fruit. However, when Iblisi cuts the fruit and throws it down, Eve only tastes it, or, more precisely, "*midomoni kulitia,*" which means, "she put the fruit between her lips." In other words, she did not bite or swallow it. Thus, the whale, the snake, and Eve all eat without mastication or digestion. Furthermore, just as the whale carries Adam in his stomach, in parallel fashion Eve and the serpent get pregnant. All get something into their stomachs which they will later expel alive. Thus in living in paradise, Adam lives in the "womb" or "stomach" of the whale. And so it is that, while there, he is nourished by the paradisaical rivers of milk and honey—food traditionally fed to infants.

Adam, who has been opposed to eating the fruit, is the one who finally eats and swallows it ("*Adam kala kameza*"). Yet, before eating the fruit, Adam is able to deliver his children from his back. And here the contrast between continence and incontinence is clear. After Adam eats the fruit, he loses the ability to deliver children, while Eve, who at first restrains herself from eating, acquires the ability to deliver children, but only from the front. Before eating the fruit, Adam contains his children not in his stomach but in his back, and he is able to deliver them from there. Eve takes the power to deliver from Adam after Adam eats the fruit.

In the myth, two birds are mentioned outside paradise: the crow (*kunguru*) and the pigeon (*hamamu*). In the myth, Eve is called "pigeon." The pigeon is an earth-bound bird, while the crow is a bird of the heights, of the "up," in fact, a paradisaical bird. God sends him down to earth with an amulet (*hirizi*) for Adam that is designed to make him immortal. But the crow steals that amulet and refuses to deliver it to Adam. According to the people of Lamu, that amulet is the white strip around the crow's neck. The crow steals the amulet but does not swallow or digest it. In fact, the amulet is still around his neck. Similarly, Eve does not swallow the fruit, yet she has the power of delivering children, a power that previously has been Adam's. In other words, both the crow and Eve have stolen eternity from Adam.

In another sense, Eve is also like the serpent, since both of them deliver after "tasting," but without eating. The relation between the serpent and Eve is dominant in Lamu folk poetry. For example, it is traditionally believed that a serpent will never harm a pregnant woman. An old poet actually describes women as serpents:

> You serpent, I swear that you are a bad creature
> I took care of you, and I was kind to you
> Yet, you twisted, and tried to steal my life.

The tree which Eve has "tasted" and which Adam has eaten is in paradise, yet it has been forbidden (*haramu*). Though there are many trees in paradise, only this one tree is mentioned by name and fully described. It is called *sambiruta,* or *hurulaini,* the tree of "nymphs," i.e., of sensual women who grow like fruit. Apparently, neither Adam nor Eve has seen or eaten from the tree before. In the myth, Iblisi states that he is not the one who brought it there; it has been brought by the order of the "Powerful." But, that is questionable, since, as we have seen, the "Powerful," or Mungu, has not directly created either animals or trees. The tree carries the nymphs who are to appear in the afterlife. If we examine the meaning of the name *Hawia,* or "Eve," we find that it means "life." So, while Eve is life, the nymphs are "afterlife." It is clear, furthermore, that Adam gets his children from his back before Eve or "life" is created, i.e., before life. In other words, Eve as life is divided into "before" and "after." Before life (that is, before Eve appears), Adam and his children exist. After life (that is, after Eve appears), the nymphs or beautiful women come out as fruit. But fruit, as we have seen, has to be eaten in order not to decay and smell bad and usher in death. So, Adam eats the fruit, which is a beautiful nymph. Adam, who is a male, and at the time "before life," eats a female from the "afterlife." The "afterlife" is a female like Eve and so is somehow part of Eve (life in general). Thus we can say that by eating the fruit, Adam tries to add to himself that part of Eve which can give him immortality; he tries to eat "afterlife." In other words, he tries, like the crow, to steal immortality.

But what has Eve to do with immortality? In fact, she has a clear relation with immortal beings. For example, she is not a part of the bond which has been established between the children of Adam and God. If we look carefully at the myth, we find that there is a bond between God and all creatures, jin, and angels. The only creatures who have no specific bond with God are the Prophet and Eve. Furthermore, neither the prophet nor Eve is a child of Adam. In addition, and this is unique to the Lamuan myth, Eve is not created from the rib of

Adam; in fact, she has nothing at all to do with Adam. In a Swahili tale called the *Story of Fatima,* Eve's connection with things immortal is further emphasized. Here we find that when Adam marries Eve, he asks God about the bride wealth he has to pay her. In reply God simply tells Adam to pay her "ten thousands of God's blessings on his beloved Prophet." Furthermore, before Adam is driven out of paradise, the angels put the white dust, the light, in his back. The dust, which in the beginning has been separated from Earth, now returns to earth alive. But Adam is not able to spontaneously increase; he has to increase through Eve. Thus, Eve is the one who can give immortality to Adam by bearing his children. But, the children of Adam, by definition, will be a mixture of dust and light. And how can dust mix with light without changing the nature of light itself? Here, we have the same contradiction we had at the be-beginning and at the end of the story of Earth's creation, only it is elevated to a higher level. If Eve is like the prophets, then how can she go out of paradise as a sinner?

When God asks Iblisi (fire) to bow before Adam, Iblisi argues quite logically that he is better than the new creature. He knows that the new creature will kill, destroy, and tell lies. In claiming such knowledge Iblisi is different from the angels, who are completely submissive. For example, when God asks them if they know the names of things, the angels reply: "We do not know anything except what You have taught us." As long as Iblisi is in heaven, he never raises a question, and he too is completely submissive and obedient. But after coming to Earth, Iblisi begins to be proud, subtle, and sophisticated. In other words, he begins to develop ideas of his own. He comes to know the difference between the good and the bad, between prosperity and destruction. He knows differences which are not known in heaven. The proliferation of Iblisi's knowledge is truly amazing, for it consists not only of universal moral judgments but also of the specific knowledge of the secondary qualities of things. For example, Iblisi knows that man will be bad because he has been made of clay, which has a bad smell. Previously, the only mention of a bad smell is Earth's complaint about the rotting fruit. The relation between Iblisi's knowledge and Earth is clear and well established. Iblisi has *learned from Earth.* He has passed the stage of being merely obedient. He has developed a relative, predictive knowledge. He becomes "subtle" and "sophisticated." Iblisi even touches Adam's figure and leaves his trace on it—the navel; but the navel is a sign of pregnancy and birth. So here it is already clear that birth has to follow. Moreover, Iblisi touches the figure to discover if it is solid or void. In other words, he wants to gain knowledge through experience; but experiential knowledge contrasts with God's knowledge, which is eternal and a priori, while Iblisi's knowledge is a posteriori.

Here again we must stress the contrast between the angels and Iblisi. Iblisi knows that the new creature is going to sin—to kill and to destroy. While the angels are pleased with the conditions of the present, Iblisi is speaking about the *future.* So, like God, Iblisi knows the future. For that reason, he is not satisfied with the present. Yet all this happens only after Iblisi leaves paradise; before settling on Earth, he is happy. Through the myth, then, we learn that Iblisi's knowledge (and thus his displeasure) are the outcome of his contact with Earth. Thus, while Adam has gotten his knowledge from above from God, Iblisi has gotten his knowledge from below, from coming into contact with Earth. Adam is satisfied with his knowledge and acquiesces after Eve begins to goad him about the tree of knowledge.

Other trees in Paradise	/ Tree of knowledge in Paradise
Ignorance	/ Knowledge
No descendants	/ Descendants

Fig. 18. Sixth Set of Binary Oppositions

Eve is eager to have knowledge. Trying to convince Adam, she compares their existence to that of animals, who live without intelligence. Then she argues that "to know" means "to know the good and the bad": that is, to have discretion, to be able to choose between alternatives. Eve says that to know happiness, or to know that one is happy, means to know sadness. To know right, we have to know wrong. She means that knowing one half of a pair does not mean knowledge, because knowledge is to know oppositions and to be able to make a choice between them. It seems quite clear that Eve has gotten her arguments from her *shoga,* or friend, Iblisi.

Here, the word *shoga* is of great importance, for it does not simply mean "friend," which in Swahili would usually be rendered as *sahibu* or *rafiki.* The word carries a connotation of transvestism. Thus Iblisi is neither a male nor a female; he is in between. Like the whale, the serpent, the fruit tree, and Adam, Iblisi is an ambiguous creature. He is a transvestite, yet he makes the serpent pregnant. His proper place is outside of paradise, yet he comes inside. The serpent comes in contact with him, and she delivers the sheitani. Eve comes in contact with him and she acquires knowledge, earthly knowledge.

So Adam, who is ephemeral, gets eternal knowledge; while Eve, who is eternal, gets earthly knowledge. Eve has acquired relative knowledge in heaven, but this is not the same thing as the absolute knowledge that has been given to Adam by God. Thus, in relation to Eve and Iblisi, the same theme is repeated. The obedient, ignorant, dependent heavenly creatures are corrupted; they acquire relative knowledge, and along with it disobedience and independence, when they descend to Earth or come into contact with it. These creatures are made from fire, or dust, like Earth. But, creatures made of light—the angels, for instance—can come in contact with Earth without either gaining relative knowledge or becoming corrupted. They are completely ignorant and absolutely submissive from beginning to end. The light entities are either completely obedient, like the angels, or have complete knowledge, like God, while the creatures made of dust are neither completely obedient nor completely knowledgeable. However, even the jin in heaven have relative knowledge. Their division into three tribes means that, between these tribes, there are boundaries and signs of separation. And so they must be differentiated.

Thus Adam, who has been made from dark dust, has been given absolute knowledge. He has been taught by God. While still in heaven Eve and Iblisi, who are eternal creatures, have had relative knowledge, and conversely, Adam, who has been made from dust, contains absolute knowledge, the light. Thus Adam is like Earth, which contains white dust along with the red and black. But Earth complains even when it contains the white dust; it is still striving for life and eternity.

After eating from the tree, Adam and Eve are driven out of paradise. She suffers but refuses to repent because she is not convinced that she has sinned. Eve admits her sin only after Cain kills Abel and Adam tells her that life (*hawia*) on earth has to end in death. Hearing this, she acknowledges her sin and repents. Thus Eve admits she is ignorant, though in paradise she has accused Adam of being the ignorant one. Eve admits her ignorance of earthly life and of eternal life. In other words, Eve has been doubly ignorant. After repenting, she submits to God as a slave, and discards her power of choice. And so, in the end, Eve is both ignorant and obedient, just like the angels.

In heaven, the sinner is Eve; on Earth, the sinner is Cain, a reversal of the paradisaical situation. In heaven, Adam is obedient and Eve disobedient. But on Earth it is Cain who refuses to obey the orders of God which have been delivered to his father. God prohibits twins (male and female) from marrying each other. The older brother is to marry the younger sister, and the younger brother, the elder sister. But Cain refuses, desiring to marry his own twin, and so he kills Abel. As a result of Abel's murder there are two females and one male left. If Cain marries his elder sister, according to divine law, then his twin will have no one to marry. Yet if he marries his twin sister, Abel's sister will not marry. In either case, there will be a female without a husband. Before Eve appears, Adam is alone, and he has no sins. Similarly, on Earth, the daughter of Adam (the sister of Abel) is alone and without sin.

On Earth, Eve stands for complete obedience and submission, the same position occupied by the angels in heaven. However, for Eve to be obedient and submissive, she has to abandon her previous relations with Earth. She has to sever every tie with it, and this contrasts sharply with her situation in heaven. On Earth, she admits her ignorance to Adam, which she would have done in paradise. She discards her power of choice. She is completely dependent on Adam for her living and on God for His forgiveness. In a certain sense, Eve is not different from Adam, for both represent the height of obedience and submission. However, Eve does not have the absolute and superior knowledge of Adam. Thus, on Earth, Adam and Eve have the same relationship as that which exists between God and the angels in heaven. God has knowledge and is superior, while the angels were obedient, submissive, dependent, and ignorant. On Earth, Adam has knowledge and is superior, while Eve is obedient, submissive, dependent, and ignorant. Thus, Adam (Earth) and Eve (immortality) have come to terms. Now there is eternity on Earth and it is not consumed.

In the first part of the myth, Earth (fire) consumes water (white dust, light), and will not release the light until forced to do so. Adam also consumes light (Prophet, white dust), and is unable to deliver it. Adam (= Earth) contains light; the serpent's white eggs (= light) contain the sheitani. Thus, the relations of the first part of the myth restate themselves as:

Adam = Earth = fire containing water (light)

Eggs (white) = bubbles = water (light) containing wind (fire)

Eve = light: (water, life) married to Adam and able to deliver either eternal or ephemeral children; either Earth (black and red dust), or light (white dust)

Fig. 19. Primary Aggregates of Relations

In the beginning, Earth complains that things increase and die; Earth wants

TABLE 1. THE PLOT OF THE MYTH

Unity	Unity in Multiplicity	Multiplicity in Unity	Multiplicity
Light is alone			
			Fire creatures are internally differentiated
	Light creatures are separated but not differentiated		
			Wind comes, creating smoke and steam
			Earth comes out of smoke and steam
		Trees bear fruit, which decay and make bad smell	
	Earth dissatisfied, but refuses to let some dust separate from it		
		Dust is separated from Earth by force	
			Dust is sifted (white, black, red)
Adam alone			
	Iblisi refuses to consider Adam higher than him		
			Eve appears
	Eve refuses to obey Adam		
		Hurulaini is separated from the tree	
	Adam disobeys the rules of avoidance and eats the fruit		
		Children come out from Eve and the serpent	
	Cain disobeys the rules of avoidance and marries his sister		
			Cain kills Abel
		Abel's sister is deprived of her husband. Yet now she can marry any man.	
	Eve dissatisfied		
		Eve is separated from Iblisi	
			Iblisi has no friends
			Adam dies
Eve is alone, yet she cannot marry any one.			

increase without death. Earth suffers because creatures live on it and smell bad (death).

Eve does not consume (water) as the earth has done, yet she is able to deliver light (Prophet). Eve is not only the mother of Adam's sons, but also the mother of the Prophet (light), which Adam (earth) needs in order to be immortal. Earth (= Adam) is not complaining anymore. Death has lost its odor. Eve (= life) mediates between before-life Adam and after-life nymphs.

CONCLUSIONS

In this chapter I have tried to uncover the structure of the creation myth of Lamu. As we will see, although the Lamuan myth is a version of the Semitic myth, it has certain distinct characteristics. Following Lévi-Strauss, I have divided the myth into its mythemes in order to be able to uncover its various strata of meaning. The order of the mythemes cannot be reversed or changed, yet the structural relations are repeated again and again.

The myth plays on the themes of unity/multiplicity, life/death, light/fire, white/black, knowledge/ignorance, obedience/disobedience, nature/culture, up/down, heaven/Earth. I have tried to show that the dominant opposition can be seen as life/death. Eve who is life (up), carries death (down), and so mediates between life and death. She is the one who carries the children who maintain life yet have to die. It may well be that it is this conundrum of death-in-life and life-in-death that the myth is trying to resolve. This Swahili myth, like the others, deals with a basic existential contradiction.

Every repetition is a way to transcend the previous contradiction by putting it in another perspective, but there is no final solution to the basic problems, which also means that there is no final end to the analysis. The myth is not only a structure but also part of a wider semantic field. Even if we accept Lévi-Strauss's idea that myths think themselves in men, without their knowing it, we cannot neglect the content which keeps reemerging out of these structural arrangements. The myth, in my view, is an attempt to say something to someone in some kind of context. In other words, the myth is part of a larger semiological system. The words in that system are not images of reality but a means of communication, which assumes the presences of the Other and tries to be sure that the messages are "properly" decoded. In every culture we find the "text," written or oral, and also we find some interpretation of it.

This leads me to agree with Ricoeur that the Semitic myth, and here he is speaking particularly of the biblical myth, uses a symbolism which, having been interpreted and reinterpreted, is semantically rich and culturally defined:

"Here we find ourselves confronting a theological conception exactly the inverse of that of totemism . . ."[24] Again, speaking of the Semitic myth, Ricoeur says: "The reuse of biblical symbols in our cultural domain rests, on the contrary, on a semantic richness, on a surplus of what is signified, which opens toward new interpretations."[25] The symbols in the myth are regulated by certain semantic relations; it will be impossible to rearrange them. "This is why, in this case, one must speak of semantic regulation by the content and not simply of structural regulation, as in the case of totemism. The structuralist explanation triumphs in synchrony . . . "[26] Myth, writes Ricoeur, is a symbolic expression of the world, and, as such, it is a hermeneutic:

> Whenever a man dreams or raves, another man arises to give an interpretation; what was already discourse, even if incoherent, is brought into coherent discourse by hermeneutics.[27]

Thus, in this myth, we have to pay attention to more than just the deep structure of the mind.

In the following chapter I will try to show that there can be more than one interpretation for the Lamuan myth, and that the time used in the myth is similar to what Turner called "liminal" time and what Bergson called "*durée*."

24. Paul Ricoeur, "Structure et hermeneutique," *Esprit,* XXXI (1963), 596–627. English translation by Kathleen McLaughlin, in *The Conflict of Interpretations,* ed. Don Ihde, trans. Kathleen McLaughlin et al. (Evanston, Ill.: Northwestern University Press, 1974), p. 45.

25. *Ibid.* p. 614. English translation, pp. 47–48.

26. *Ibid.* English translation, p. 48.

27. Ricoeur, *The Symbolism of Evil* (New York: Harper & Row, 1967), p. 350.

5

Myth as a Social Discourse

> If you will follow it [Earth],
> you will lose your light, you
> will be an animal, smelly and
> dirty. And end in a dusty
> house [the grave]. Blessed
> is God, who is the most sublime
> and glorious.
> —from the "Tabaraka dhul 'Ala'
> wal Kibriya'"

Malinowski considered myth a charter for social action. For him, "myth serves principally to establish a sociological charter. The function of the myth, briefly, is to strengthen tradition and endow it with a greater value and prestige by tracing it back to a higher, better, more supernatural reality of initial events. Myth is a constant by-product of living faith, which is in need of miracles; of sociological status, which demands precedent; of moral rule, which requires sanction."[1] The analysis of the Lamuan creation myth as a charter is not only sociologically important, but it is also an essential complement to our structural analysis of the previous chapter. Still, while we cannot neglect Malinowski's point of view, we cannot unconditionally accept it. Thus, I wish to state clearly what I mean when I use the term "charter," and where, in my understanding of the term, I differ from Malinowski

Malinowski's view of myth is related to his model of society. For Malinowski and some other functionalists, myth is a conservative force which is used mainly to enforce, perpetuate, and maintain the *status quo.* Thus Malinowski's social

1. Bronislaw Malinowski, "Myth in Primitive Psychology," in *Magic, Science and Religion* (New York: Anchor Books, 1954), pp. 144–46.

model is what we might call an "integrational" one. According to him, values and norms serve as imperatives which the members of society must accept and to which they must commit themselves if society is to exist. Acting as a charter, myth not only justifies the norms of society and institutionalizes the behavior of its members, but also enforces these values and gives them prestige and "supernatural" force. Values regulate the norms which operate in any institutional sphere; generally they are accepted and internalized, and the individual's behavior is in accordance with them. Anyone who deviates from the accepted mode of behavior, or even questions the values, will be considered pathological. In other words, deviation is not considered a "healthy" phenomenon. For Malinowski, the main purpose of myth is to supply and enforce these integrative imperatives; therefore, myth has the power to keep the society together. Myth convinces the people that their values and norms, their deeds and beliefs, are "all right."

However, if we examine this theory carefully, we will discover that it is based on certain assumptions that are open to question and that it draws certain conclusions which cannot rightfully be deduced. For example, according to Malinowski, if one individual doubted or refused to accept the values of the society, then, according to the above theory, he would have to be sanctioned. Yet, even though this may be true of one individual, it does not necessarily follow that the same thing would happen if a whole group refused to accept the institutional values of the society. Instead, such disagreement might lead to social conflict or war, in which case the consensus of the society would be gone, because each faction would consider its point of view to be the right one. An integrative model such as Malinowski's does not take account of the inevitable existence of social conflict and change.

This deficiency in the model is due to its behavioristic assumptions. For example, Malinowski's inability to differentiate between sign and symbol has deceived him as well as many others. He was convinced that if a myth (stimulus) existed in two societies, then the people of both societies would find the same meaning (response) in the myth. Thus, in a society such as Lamu, with its time-honored stratificatory system, the myth of creation, which according to the wangwana established their right to rule, would theoretically be understood and used in the same way by all the various wangwana groups and even by the slaves. In other words, all the people would have to not only accept the myth but also make a commitment to it and conform their lives to that vision. Malinowski thought that because the language and the semantics of a myth remained the same, all members of the society would have to have the same reaction to it.

This is clear in his maxim: "one word, one meaning," which was expressed, according to Firth, "as his fundamental principle that for each native word we adopt one English 'fixed meaning.'"[2]

In my view it is naïve to assume that there is a one-to-one relationship between the word and its meaning. This assumption should be examined by analyzing the relation between language, thought, and social action. Through such an analysis we will discover that different groups within society have different foci, out of which their particular interpretation of a myth is generated. Thus, the same version of a myth may evoke different reactions and lead to different interpretations. The meaning of a myth as a social discourse depends on the position of the group for whom it is meaningful, and on the claims that group is making against other groups at a particular time and place. In this respect, my view is very close to that of Edmund Leach, who says, "myth and ritual is a language of signs in terms of which claims to rights and status are expressed, but it is a language of argument, not a chorus of harmony."[3] Yet, my own particular understanding of myth also differs from that of Leach in a number of ways.

Leach focuses his attention on the *different versions* of what is essentially the same myth. He tries to see the reason for the differences, because he feels that he cannot simply say that one is more correct than the others. My concern, however, is not with different versions of the myth; instead, I am arguing that the *same written version* of the myth has different meanings for different groups. For example, in Lamu, as we saw in the last chapters, the slaves lived in a world quite different from that of the wangwana. They had different experiences and a different frame of reference in which to explain and justify these experiences. Their basic ideas about life and death, God and the Prophet, purity and impurity were different from those of the wangwana, and so they understood the myth differently. Despite the obvious intention of the wangwana to use the myth in order to manipulate and contain the slaves, we would be naïve if we assumed that the slaves passively accepted the wangwana's ideology without challenge.[4] What the wangwana projected and what actually took place

2. Raymond Firth, "Ethnographic Analysis and Language with Reference to Malinowski's Views," in *Man and Culture,* ed. R. Firth (London: Routledge & Kegan Paul, 1957), p. 106.

3. Edmund Leach, *Political Systems of Highland Burma* (Boston: Beacon Press, 1954), p. 278.

4. It is the social engineers who usually make this assumption. For instance, if they want to introduce something new into a society, they simply assume that the people will perceive it in the same way the engineers do. As an example, when the birth-control pill was introduced in Egypt, social engineers thought that the people would receive it as a

form two different realities, and we have to study both. In some cases, we may find that the interpretations given the myth by different groups coincide; in others there may be two different systems of meanings attached to the same myth. Such is the case in Lamu.

In Lamu, the creation myth does not act as an integrative mechanism. The traditional integrative model of society cannot be made to fit Lamu, a society I consider best described as a field dominated by continuous tensions, which in turn define and redefine the position of the various groups at different points in time. These groups cannot be studied apart from that tension-field, in which social positions and ideologies are polarized at all times. This polarization is expressed against a neutral background upon which these opposites interact. This background is mere potentiality, or essential ambiguity, and therefore it always leaves room for further interpretation and reinterpretation.

In Lamu, myth, ritual, the Qur'ān, and lastly, the sharifs make up that neutral background. It is the stockpile from which opposing groups can draw for both claim and counterclaim. Because of its ambiguity the information in that stockpile can be given different values. For the anthropologist who wants to understand the myth as a social discourse, these values and the dialectical relations between them are the important elements in the myth. In other words, the myth itself will be like a system of mathematical symbols: $p \rightarrow q$ (if p then q). While p and q are variables which can take any value, the relation ($\rightarrow$) is stable. So the myth says: "If (Mohammed is light) then (we will be saved)," and the wangwana will take p to mean, "Mohammed is light, and we are part of Mohammed's tribe; we are his fellow men," and thus q, "we will be saved." The slaves on the other hand will take p to mean "Mohammed is light who is living with us; we love him, and we love his relatives"; and thus q, "we will be saved." The myth mentions only that Mohammed is living light; it does not tell us where he lives—or whether he is or is not separated from the world. However, each group in Lamu feels itself justified in its own interpretation.

In these two interpretations we find, first, that the minimum definition of Mohammed is the same for the two groups; and, second, that Mohammed's intended act of salvation is also accepted by both groups. Nevertheless, while the wangwana took the idea of light and interpreted it according to their concept of descent (light passed on from one generation to the next), the slaves took the

birth-control device. However, the people, one way or another, found that if a barren woman used the pill for some time and then stopped, she would be able to become pregnant. Therefore, the pill was used to increase, not limit, the birth rate.

same idea and interpreted it according to their existential experience (light as warming presence). For the slaves Mohammed was the light that lived among them, and he had to be loved and respected, not through the reflected glory of his descendants, but directly, because he was loved by God. The slaves never mentioned descent. In this particular conflict, the sharifs acted as mediators; they were related to Mohammed, yet they had a strong inclination toward indifference, khumoul. Moreover, as Ḥabib Saleḥ said, "never sit in the chest of a meeting [i.e., never be the head of a meeting], because then the people will neglect you and make you the tail." This means that the sharif has no right to elevate himself over the people, because the people would simply put him down. He must allow the people to do whatever they want; he must be neutral in the minds of the people. Perhaps a particular sharif will mean different things to different people, or perhaps all will agree to give him one value. This is why, as we found in the Ba 'Alwi order, the qutb is a qutb not by appointment but by a general consensus, and he, of course, will deny his position, following the principle of khumoul. In this context, we see that the ambiguity and neutrality of the sharifs is stressed.

At this point, I would like to set forth the wangwana interpretation of the myth of creation, and then outline the slaves' interpretation of the same myth. Both interpretations will, then, define the field of the social discourse.

THE WANGWANA INTERPRETATION

Adam was created from the black and red dust; he was taught by God. God gave Adam the knowledge which made him superior to all other creatures, and he lived in paradise and was happy. However, there came a time when God wanted to examine Adam, to see whether Adam loved him or not. So God created Eve, and Adam, being created from the red and black dust, could not control his sexual drives. He loved Eve, but Eve had been ordered to try to persuade him to eat the fruit of the forbidden tree. Because Adam contained red dust, he was like the Europeans (*Wa Zungu*), who are said to have been made of red dust and consequently know how to play tricks. Adam thought that if he pretended that he did not want to eat the fruit, while letting himself be "persuaded" by Eve, then all the blame would fall on her. She would be the sinner because she was the one who had convinced him to eat. Adam thought that he could deceive God. After Eve took the fruit and put it to her lips, she gave it to Adam, who, after she went first, was all too happy to eat it.

Both Adam and Eve were driven out of paradise. However, before they left, God ordered the light of the Prophet to be put in Adam's back. When Adam left paradise he was guided and controlled by the white dust in his back. In fact, Adam was saved because of it. That dust was inherited not by all the children of Adam, but only by one child at a time, whoever was considered to be the best. Those descendants of Adam who did not have the white dust were involved in murder and adultery and were continually trying to deceive each other. The Lamuans usually introduce a related myth to reinforce this point.

Adam and his children lived in Mecca, which is the center of the world. Because the majority of them were bad, God ordered Noah, the one who at that time had the light in his back, to build a boat. God told him exactly how to build it. When the boat was completed, God told Noah to take onto it a male and female of each kind of animal on Earth. Noah obeyed, and God then sent storms and rain which covered Earth. This was the deluge. After God had cleaned the wicked men from Earth, the water receded, and God ordered Noah to settle down and start anew. Noah did that and he was happy. However, even though Noah carried the white dust in his back, he could only pass it on to one son. Like Adam, he also had the black and red dust in him. He had three male children: Sam, Yafith, and Ham.

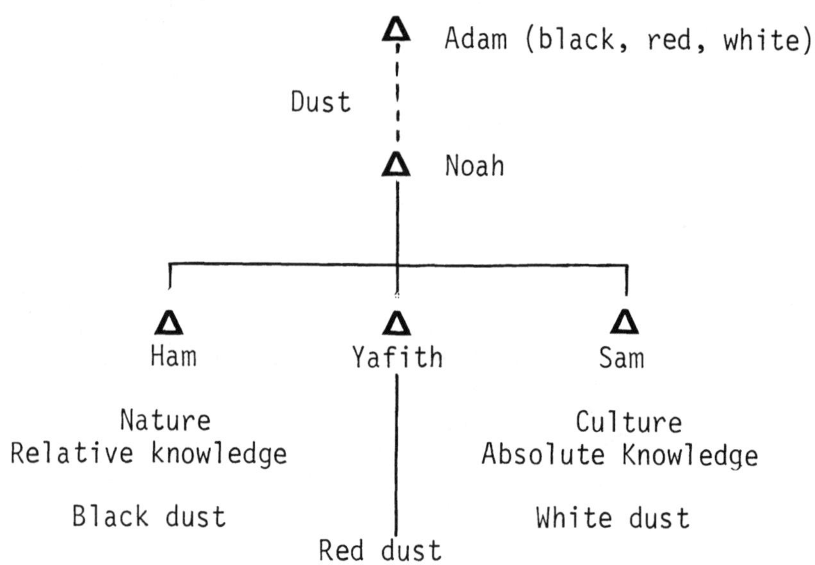

Fig. 20. The Descendants of Adam

Sam was obedient and followed his father's orders. One day, Noah called him, and Sam came directly without delay. His father blessed him and asked God to make all the prophets from that son, and so the children of Sam were all white. When Noah called Ham, he did not come. He disobeyed his father, and Noah cursed him, asking God to make his sons black. Finally, when Noah called Yafith, he did not answer either, so Noah cursed him too, and asked God to make his sons red. The white dust continued in the sons of Sam, yet they contained black and red dust as well, as did *all* the descendants of Adam.

The sons of Sam were obedient and followed their father's will. But the sons of Ham were ashamed of their color, because they knew that their father had been white, and therefore they suspected that their mother had not behaved properly. So they escaped to the forests and lived without religion. And in doing so, they lost all claim to the knowledge which had been given to Adam. Their nature did not accept that knowledge.

The sons of Yafith were unable to keep that knowledge either, and in the end they had to depend on the sons of Sam to deliver it to them. The only things they could claim were tricks and inventions; they never had absolute knowledge. From them came the races Yagog and Magog, which, it is said, will some day be able to destroy Earth.

The light persisted in the sons of Sam; and it passed through Moses and Jesus and then went over to the tribe of Qurish, which was created and elevated in order to bear the prophet Mohammed. This world was created for Mohammed; and the Arabs in general and the Qurish in particular were blessed for the sake of that Prophet.

These additions to the basic myth of creation make an important contribution to the wangwana's understanding of the myth. However, while the basic myth was written and read in the mosque, the additional one was never written, nor was it ever read in the mosque. In other words, it is to a certain extent the non-official myth. In this second myth, the wangwana stress the idea of the three different colors of dust. For them, it was Adam, created from red and black dust, and driven by his sexual impulses, who actually wanted to sin. Here is the first clue to the wangwana's definition of themselves. The slaves (black) and the Europeans (red) are controlled by their earth impulses, but they, the Arabs (white) behave according to the light within them. The polarization is clear: the animalistic impulses, connected with the slaves and the Europeans, are in a state of flux and uncontrolled, while the light, connected with the wangwana, is stable and controlled.

The sons of Adam lost the knowledge which had been given to Adam by God.

The knowledge was light, and therefore existed only in those persons who were prepared to accept the light, that is, in those people whose nature was suitable for knowledge. The sons of Sam were the only ones who were prepared for that knowledge; and eventually the Arabs, from whom the Prophet was chosen, proved to be the best soil for the planting of the light.

But, what is this knowledge? It is the absolute knowledge which Adam possessed before he sinned. It is the knowledge which cannot be separated from obedience. It is not at all like the earthly, or relative, knowledge which Iblisi gained after coming in contact with Earth. For example, after the sons of Ham lost the knowledge, their lives centered around the forest. Because of their nature, they were impure; they did not have light. Due to the fact that they lived in the forest like animals and were dirty and smelly, they were thought to be polluted. The sons of Yafith also shared this pollution. Both only had relative earthly knowledge. Yet, there was a difference between them. While the sons of Ham (black) were attached to the forest, cultivated the land, and lived very close to Earth, the sons of Yafith (red, like fire) knew how to play tricks and to deceive, and were able to change one thing into another, that is, to invent new things. However, both the sons of Ham and the sons of Yafith had to use earthly materials. The sons of Yafith used steel and iron to deceive the people. Since both were deprived of absolute knowledge and since neither produced a prophet, the interpreters concluded that both the black and red dust were bad, dangerous, and defiling. Both the black and red dust were bound to Earth; the two groups lived and acted according to their earthly natures. Their knowledge was relative and depended entirely on comparisons between earthly qualities. Their judgments, which they changed from place to place and time to time, also corresponded to their earthly nature. They were guided by their animal instincts. They represented Adam in his animality. In brief, they stood for nature.

This leads us to the Lamuan concepts of purity and impurity. The white dust was pure—it was light—and, therefore, those who descended from it were pure. The sons of Sam were pure; and the Qurish was the purest tribe on earth, and Mecca, the purest town. However, when the pure come in contact with Earth and subsequently with the earthly creatures, they, like the children of Ham and Yafith, become defiled. And, when the pure are defiled, calamities befall them—failure to achieve a good life, sickness, or even death. But, as we will see later, there are certain rituals which the wangwana perform to ward off these disasters. All these rituals are based on the idea of separation, i.e., separating the wangwana (pure) from the slaves and Europeans (impure). Thus the concepts of purity and impurity play a leading role in wangwana ritual life; they are the idiom of that life.

The impure are, as was said, all those who have been created from the red and black dust, those who have earthly knowledge—in other words, those who are connected with nature; while the pure are those who are given the rules of proper behavior and civilization—i.e., culture. Thus, it appears that the wangwana purification rituals are performed in order to separate culture from nature, the white dust from the black and red dust. This point comes through clearly in a poem which the wangwana read during Ramadan. Ramadan is the month of fasting, during which the malevolent jin and sheitani are not allowed to appear in the town. The town, which according to the wangwana definition extends no further than Mkomani, severs all relations with the outside world. The wangwana keep only minimal contact with the market.

During Ramadan the wangwana day begins with a trip to the mosques to pray. Then, before the afternoon prayer (*'Asr*), they attend the darassa, or religious lecture, in the Maskiti Pwani, the mosque of the Wa Yumbili Pembe. Later, they return to their homes, where they prepare themselves for the sunset prayer (*Maghrib*), which is performed in their mtaa mosques. At the Maghrib, they break their fast and pray, and then they return to their homes to eat. Then, they go out again to the Rodha Mosque, where they pray the last prayer and sit down to read the following poem:

Live pure without doubts and be satisfied,
Be silent and use your mind intelligently
So you might be lucky tomorrow.

Your earth is defiled, when it appeals to you
  it leads
You happily to the clubs (in order to drink);
You are deceived, how much are you going to
try and run (to get what your earth told you
  is good).
Prepare yourself for death when it comes
Do not think that you are eternal in this life.

The deceived will be chained to earth
He will be like a slave for it, trying to catch
  up with it.
It is the calamity. Earth is your enemy, if you
  know that
The son of Adam got blind so you will not see it.

This Ramadan poem is long and is divided into thirty parts. Every night during the month the wangwana sit and read a part of it. One person reads in a very solemn voice full of sorrow and regret. He reads in Arabic, drawing out the vowel sounds. The other wangwana repeat the lines after him in the same tone. Then either the khatib or a Mahdali sharif translates it into Swahili. When the wangwana hear that they will lose everything if they continue to maintain their relation with earth (nature), they cry and shout, "No, no. We do not want that." The whole poem deplores earthly life, and it induces the people to cut their relations with earth, or at least keep them at a minimum. If they do not do so, it is thought that they will be like the slaves who are controlled by their earthly needs. Thus, as a general rule, if a person wants to be saved, he has to minimize his earthly needs and move as close as possible to the world of heaven—not the world of Adam in paradise but the world of the white dust under the Throne. The wangwana feel themselves to be related to that world, since they are related to Sam, to whom Mohammed was related. Mohammed was part of God's light; so ultimately, the wangwana are the descendants of that first light. They are actually related to God. And so it is for that reason that they must have a minimal relationship with this earthly world.

The 'ālim tells the stories of the different peoples who have occupied the earth, and who have been greedy in accumulating power or wealth, and who have built houses and palaces. The most common story is the story of *Namrud:*

> He was very rich, very powerful; he lived a luxurious life. One day the prophet Moses went to him and asked him to pray to God. Namrud said: "Look, I am as powerful as your God, I can give life and cause death." Namrud brought a man sentenced to death and pardoned him. Then he told Moses, "Look, this man was going to die and I gave him life." Moses said, "You are on earth, while God is high in the sky." Namrud ordered a tower to be built so he could climb up and see God. Moses was in despair, so he asked God to take revenge on Namrud. The Almighty God sent a fly which entered Namrud's nose and went up into his head; it was painful, so he had to ask his servants to beat him on the head with their shoes, and this was the only way to calm him down. Namrud died, and his wealth and power vanished.

This little condensed story also reflects the binary opposition between nature and culture, or earth and light, that we saw articulated in the myth of creation. Moses had absolute knowledge and so was totally submissive, while Namrud had only relative knowledge. Namrud tried to build a ladder in order to see God. So, both Iblisi and Namrud tried to use empirical methods in order to gain knowledge. There are many of these stories which are told during

Ramadan, but the theme of all of them is the same: culture/nature, purity/impurity, light (white)/fire (red and black).

As has been said, the wangwana think that both black and red are impure; neither those made from the black dust nor those made from the red can grasp absolute knowledge because of their limited earthly nature. Yet, at the same time, the wangwana say that the sons of Sam can also lose their purity, *if* they are in continuous contact with the impure. In other words, a mngwana in continuous contact with the impure will lose a portion of his purity. At this point it should be stressed that there is a basic difference between purity (*safi*) and impurity (*mchafu*), and the polluted (*najisi*) and the unpolluted (*tahara*). When a man sleeps with his wife, he is polluted and has to take a ritual bath in order to be able to interact, or communicate, with others, or to pray. During his pollution, his field of interaction is limited. For example, he cannot go to the mosque to pray, or touch the Qur'ān, or even fast. Yet as soon as he washes and declares that he is "washing *najasa* from himself," he is considered unpolluted. His field of interaction is open again. The person's pollution or lack of pollution does not affect his basic purity or impurity. Thus the slave might be free from pollution, but still be impure, while the polluted mngwana would retain a basic purity in all circumstances. While washing can get rid of pollution, nothing can get rid of the slave's impurity.

The ideology of the pure and the impure, the polluted and the unpolluted is extremely important for wangwana religious life; in fact it is the cornerstone of their religious ideology. In order to understand wangwana ritual activities and many of their secular attitudes, I find it necessary to examine these complex conceptual constructs further.

The concept of purity and impurity is used, on the one hand, to define the relation between the wangwana and the slaves, and on the other hand, to establish a relationship between the slaves and the malevolent jin. The benevolent jin are the sons of the wangwana, so they have inherited the light from their fathers. The malevolent jin, however, are still earthly in their character. Furthermore, because of their connection with fire, the jin share other qualities with the slaves; both are impure and both are harmful. It is said that a pact exists between the malevolent jin and the slaves, which is designed to hurt the wangwana.

The malevolent jin have known all along that the wangwana are the ones who are on the right path, and will therefore live in paradise and enjoy the blessings of God, while the malevolent jin will live in hell and will never enter and enjoy paradise. This was the reason for the pact between the malevolent jin and the slaves and Europeans. Both the bad jin and their human followers intend to ruin Islam and Astarabu; they do not accept the Qur'ān. The bad earthly nature (*tabia mbaya*) of the jin and their cohorts makes them very powerful and very harmful. They are both polluted and impure; they do not wash and neither do they perform ablutions. They neither read the Qur'ān nor mention the Prophet's name. They are dirty, smelly, and uncivilized; simply put, they are *Wa Shenzi.* They do not live in houses or towns, but in the bush or the trees of the filthy places inside the towns. They especially like to live in dark places where they can perform their tricks and work harm on people who might pass by.

Both the Wa Shenzi and the bad jin must be kept outside the town because both are impure. The wangwana have dealt with the Wa Shenzi by driving them out, keeping them on the mainland and allowing them no means of assimilation. They also felt that the malevolent jin had to be kept in the bush; yet, while the wangwana were able to use physical force to keep the Wa Shenzi out of town, they had different mechanisms to drive the bad jin away and thereby stop them from afflicting death, sickness, and disorder on the town. The most important such ritual action is called *Kuzingu Kuzinguka Ngombe,* i.e., "the circulation of the bull around the town." This ritual is described in detail in Chapter 6.

Purity and impurity are associated with the four cardinal points: north, east, south, and west. The wangwana say that while east and north are the directions of the pure, west and south are those of the impure. The sun comes from the east to fill everything with light. Mecca is north of Lamu, and therefore the qibla, or niche, is in that direction; the north is the birthplace of the light—of Mohammed. On the Last Day, paradise will extend east and north, while hell will be to the west and south. Over and over again we find the same basic polarity: east and north are light, west and south are fire. This cultural definition of directions can even be seen in the architecture of the wangwana houses. The toilets, for example, must be either in the west or south, while the bedrooms and living rooms are usually located in the opposite direction. Furthermore, a host cannot allow his guest to sit facing the south or the west. Also, in ceremonies dealing with marriage, circumcision, birth, or death, the seating arrangements are similarly fixed and the rules must be respected and obeyed.

The rules for seating arrangements are a kind of language—a language that the people use. The anthropologist must work to uncover its structure. The wangwana translate the polarity of east-north/south-west, into the bipolarity of right and left. Thus in every seating arrangement there is an imaginary line which separates the right from the left. And the same evaluation is extended to the human body, where it is symbolized by the right and the left hand. In a formal situation, the seating arrangement is determined by a line defined by the left and right hands of the man who is leading the meeting (*mutasader*). People sit to his left or to his right. In prayers in the mosque and especially in Friday prayer, those who are considered the most important religious or political figures sit to the right of the leader, while the less important persons occupy the left side. The slaves, if allowed to attend at all, are naturally seated on the left side and in the back near the toilets.

The left hand is associated with dirt. People use that hand to wash themselves and to carry unclean objects. When people spit, they even spit on the left side; no one would think of spitting to the right side.

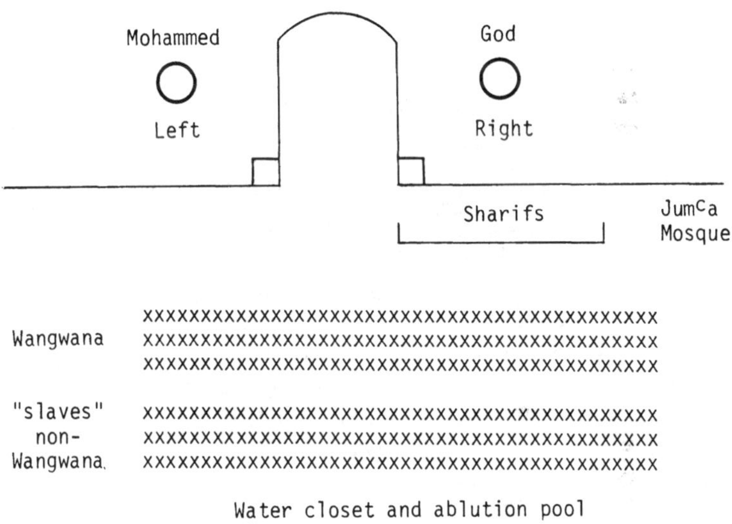

Fig. 21. Arrangement in the Jum^{c}a Mosque

Furthermore, the right and left hand are associated with the right and left foot, so that a person entering the mosque has to step first on his right foot; when he leaves the mosque, the opposite prevails—he has to use the left foot first. When entering the bathroom, one has to enter with the left foot and come out with the right foot. This reversal is important, because, for the people, the mosque is a pure place, while the street is not; so, in coming from the street to the mosque, a person has to use his right foot. Yet, even though the house is not as pure as the mosque, it is still purer than the bathroom, and so, in leaving the bathroom and entering the house one also uses the right foot. Here, in fact, we have a scale of purity/impurity which varies according to the context: for example, the city is pure while the bush is impure, but the street in the city is impure in contrast to the mosque. A word of caution: it would be a mistake to correlate purity with cleanliness, even though the tendency has been to do so. The error of this way of thinking is clear in the case of the *majdhub.*

In Lamu, there are some wangwana called *majdhub,* i.e., "attracted,"[5] who are dirty, half-naked, impolite, and ignorant. They do not pray; they do not wash or cut their nails or hair. They are smelly and in other contexts, might well be called Wa Shenzi. Yet, they are wangwana and highly respected, even feared. In the old times, sailors would invoke their names for protection, and they would make vows (*nadhir*) to them. For example, a sailor might say, "If I return safely to Lamu, I will pay *Shee Mbate* [the name of a majdhub] such and such." According to the people of Lamu, it was usually the case that when the person who made the vow returned to shore, he would find Shee Mbate waiting for him and anxious for his gift. No one knew how the majdhub knew when the sailor would arrive. In other words the wangwana thought a majdhub such as Shee Mbate was very pure, although he was far from cleanliness.

We have to go much deeper to uncover the meaning of purity attributed to one such as Shee Mbate. On the surface, Shee Mbate was like any Wa Shenzi, if not worse; yet Shee Mbate was pure, while the Wa Shenzi were impure. If we return to the myth of creation, we find that the jin began to disobey God when they acquired relative knowledge, that is, knowledge of good and evil, propriety and impropriety, and so forth. In other words, they disobeyed only after acquiring discernment, the knowledge of opposition. This knowledge depended on making a judgment, and thus on making choices. To make these choices, a person must use empirical observation, and he must use logic in order to convince others and himself that his choice is the right one. This contrasts with a state of absolute knowledge, where there is no choice or argument; all things are given directly by God, and His orders must be obeyed. The transformation of the jin from mere obedient creatures to creatures who could make choices, and who consequently had to be convinced, necessitated the acquisition of the power of

5. In the past *majdhub* has been translated as 'possessed," but I think this is incorrect. In possession something or someone (jin) is controlling the person, while the majdhub's mind is attracted to a higher reality. He is not possessed by anything inside.

judgment, i.e., a mind, or *'aql.* This was the power by which they could judge, choose, and become convinced. The 'aql was the power of earthly creatures that enabled them to make choices on the earth. By contrast, culture, as light, did not need choice. It was thought of as homologous with obedience and submission. Taking the point further, Islam corresponded with culture, and the Qur'ān was the highest expression of the divine culture. The Qur'ān and Mohammed were equal, and thus Mohammed's behavior was the Qur'ān in action, or, as the wangwana put it, "Mohammed's nature was the Qur'ān," "*Kȧna khuloqihi al Qur'ān.*" In the life of Mohammed there was no element of choice; Mohammed was completely obedient and absolutely submissive.

Because Adam had acquired 'aql, or the power of choice, his children inherited it from him. However, the sons of Sam acquired light in addition to 'aql. Thus the children of Adam, and their descendants, differed in their degree of purity according to the degree of their dependence on light or on 'aql. A real Muslim had to abandon his mind and live in complete obedience and submission. He did the things he was ordered to do, because he saw no alternative. His action had to be guided by the Qur'ān, and he had to imitate the Prophet. Both of these tasks were easily accomplished by the wangwana because of their genealogical ties to the Prophet, and so the mngwana was an Arab, and the Arabs were the descendants of Sam, who had been given the white dust. The red and black dust had 'aql, or the power of choice, but it was the white dust which made absolute knowledge possible. Those who could claim only black or red dust were attached to nature. They did not have the Qur'ān, and so they had no guidance except that of their own minds, which could not grasp the heavenly world, the world of absolute knowledge, or "culture."

Returning to the majdhub: According to the people of Lamu, he is the mngwana who has no 'aql. Consequently, the majdhub sees things in their original dimension. For instance, the Lamuans say that when he kisses a woman, he does not kiss her for sexual reasons or because he has given in to an impulse; he kisses her because she stands for the partner of Adam, the one who was created by God. For the majdhub, there is no difference between earth and paradise. After all, the rules of defilement and purification came into existence only after Adam became defiled, i.e., made a choice. The majdhub is completely deprived of the power to make a choice, and so, for that very reason, he is quite close to the world of culture, or Astarabu. If the majdhub had been in paradise, his behavior and way of life would have been in perfect accord with the ways of heaven. Other men might say that the majdhub is dirty, but that is because other men differentiate between dirt and cleanliness. But no one can say that the majdhub is impure. The majdhub is the child of God; he is loved by God and is granted a very high position in the heavenly world.

The majdhub is commonly associated with a newborn child. Neither has a mind and yet both are extremely pure. The majdhub's purity depends not on the rules of the book but on his inherent purity. He lives in a paradisaical state, and he is the only mngwana who has a stable position which carries over from his earthly life to his heavenly life, or to life after death. He differs from the ʻālim, the ascetic, or zahid, and the other sons of Sam.

The sons of Sam were also pure in contrast to the Wa Shenzi and the Wa Zungu (Europeans). Yet, the sons of Sam were internally stratified according to the effort each spent in severing his relations with earth and mind. So some could achieve a higher degree of purity than others. But the majdhub was outside this competition, because he was pure from the day of his birth to the day of his death. The sons of Sam, who studied the ʻilm, or knowledge, and tried to apply that knowledge to their life, and who strove for the light and attempted to follow it, were higher in purity than a mngwana who had no religious knowledge and who made no such effort. And this provides another explanation as to why the Wa Yumbili Ponde were considered so low in Lamu society. They were not allowed to obtain religious education, so their behavior had to depend, to a certain extent at least, on their earthly choices. Religious education was only for the Wa Yumbili Pembe and Wa Yumbili Ngombe, who were higher in the traditional stratificatory system.

However, if someone who did receive religious education did not apply this knowledge and did not try to elevate himself from the earthly world, he would be considered lower in purity. Such a person, although technically an ʻālim, would still be in the realm of earthly relations. The difference between him and the ʻālim who applied his knowledge was considerable. The ʻālim who applied his knowledge was not only an ʻālim, but also a zahid. A zahid was a person who had eliminated relations with the world of nature and tried to get inside the world of absolute knowledge and submission, i.e., culture. Nevertheless, the ʻālim and the ʻālim-zahid were both still fallible. If they made any mistake, they would lose everything they had gained. This was due to the fact that they still had ʻaql, minds, which could make a choice; and where a choice can be made, it is possible that that choice will be a wrong one. Thus, the difference between the ʻālim and the ʻālim-zahid, on the one hand, and the majdhub, on the other hand, was that while the majdhub was from the beginning in a state of culture, without the possibility of being debased to a state of nature because he had no ʻaql, the others had ʻaql, and so at any moment could theoretically swing from one side to the other. Any purity or effectivity which the ʿālim-zahid achieved would not be recognized until after his death, that is, until there was no longer a possibility that he would mistakenly exercise his power of choice.

All the above distinctions find their place in the schema shown in Figure 22.

The Sons of Sam	The Sons of Ham and Yafith	
Pure	Intermediate	Impure
Culture	Culture and nature	Nature
Absolute knowledge and submission		Relative knowledge and disobedience. Wa Shenzi
Majdhub		
Zahid-ᶜAlim		
ᶜAlim	Non-religiously educated wangwana. Wa Yumbili Ponde	Wa Zungu

Fig. 22. Purity and Impurity in the Descendants of Adam

On the basis of this diagram, it appears that the sons of Ham and Yafith were totally excluded from the realm of purity. In other words, they were impure by definition. At the same time, it is clear that the sons of Sam would never reach the degree of impurity which the sons of Ham and Yafith did. The sons of Sam might tend toward nature, relative knowledge, and earthly life, but they never lost their purity completely. If we look closely at Lamu's traditional system of stratification, we find that the lower wangwana group, the Wa Yumbili Ponde, occupy an intermediate position. Yet, there is one position open to all wangwana groups—the position of the majdhub. He may be from any category of the wangwana; in other words, he cuts across the whole stratificatory system. Yet, in the end, he has very little effect on that stratificatory system, since he is not allowed to marry. His ambiguous position is underscored by the fact that the majdhub is not considered the son of any particular category. He is related to all of them, since his blessed existence as defined by the wangwana them-

themselves, protects the town. He is purity and light, and the wangwana think they all share in that since they are descended from Sam's light and are related to the Prophet, the highest expression of that light.

However, there is one point that must be considered before bringing this discussion to a close. As was said before, some of the jin converted to Islam, and the wangwana call them the good or benevolent jin. These jin were, of course, originally fire, i.e., red; and the wangwana still consider them lower than themselves, but they are no longer thought to be harmful. In other words, the jin who converted to Islam are considered better than the slaves who had converted. Let me quote from my notebook:

> The Muslim jin establish contact with Muslims; they help them foresee the future, since they knew the future when they listened to God after being driven out of the seventh sky. This is why some Muslim wangwana, e.g., the diviner/magician [*mganga*], have more power than others. They say that the mganga has his *ruhani,* i.e., jin. These Muslim jin do not want to cause any physical or psychological harm. If the wangwana wants his ruhani, then he can call him by using the Qur'ān and incense. There are some men who have contact with a ruhani. When the ruhani comes to the person, he loses his senses, so if the person does or says something, this will be the work of the ruhani. If anyone is sick, the ruhani can visit him. The mganga will burn some ubani, or 'ambari. Then the jin tells the mganga about the cause of the patient's sickness and about the medicine.
>
> When he calls his ruhani, the mganga has to be ritually pure. This goes without saying, since in Lamu, no one can read, touch, or even speak about the Qur'ān unless he is ritually washed. However, the mganga is not only a specialist in diagnosing illness; he might also be involved in protecting the interests of someone, and thus the same ritual could help one and hurt others. However, the mganga says that he does not intentionally use his ruhani to hurt anybody. The ruhani would not accept that since it is not just.

The wangwana explain this by saying that the jin, after converting to Islam, began to imitate the Muslims, and so discarded their old attachments. They lived inside the town and helped the wangwana protect it. Even the children of the wangwana from the benevolent jin females were better than the children of the same men from the souriyas, because they kept the hishima rule. Moreover, the jin were cursed for disobedience once, while the slaves and the Wa Zungu were cursed twice, once with Adam, and once with Noah. All these factors made the benevolent jin better than the slaves; but, of course, they were never equal to the wangwana.

The good jin did not tolerate the bad jin, and worked to keep them outside the town. The good jin had to act like *'askari,* or policemen, in order to protect the Muslim town from the enemies that surrounded it. Their action was like that of the wangwana against the Wa Shenzi. The Wa Shenzi and the bad jin were both impure and defiling, yet the jin proved that after they converted to Islam they could act like true Muslims—that is, like wangwana—which the slaves could never do.

THE WA SHENZI INTERPRETATION

The Wa Shenzi view the myth of creation differently, as we will see. They accept some aspects of the wangwana interpretation but shift them to other dimensions and finally come out with a quite different interpretation of the myth.

Adam was created from red and black dust, but he was taught by God. The Merciful knew that Adam was capable of possessing the knowledge; otherwise He would not have given it to him. Adam was purity and submission. He behaved correctly, and he loved God—until Eve was created. While Eve roamed around, Adam sat worshipping his master. At this point Adam was pure; he had nothing to occupy his heart except the love of God, the Maker and Provider.

Eve, roaming around, discovered Iblisi, whom she liked because his words were like honey. His speech was convincing. She became close to Iblisi, and Adam was jealous. He felt that Eve loved someone else. Eve at the same time could not leave Adam, because he was her husband, so she used to spend time with both Adam and Iblisi. But, while Adam was pure and submissive, Iblisi was not pure. He lost his purity when he disobeyed God. The more Eve neglected Adam, the more love he felt for her. Soon his heart became preoccupied with his love for Eve and he neglected his master. Adam loved Eve so much that, even when he knew that she was seeing Iblisi, he did nothing to stop her. He could have complained or informed God so He would punish Eve.

This love for Eve was Adam's mistake, because it led him away from God. Also, Eve was involved with Iblisi, who was impure, and at the same time, with Adam, who was higher in purity. As a result, Adam began to lose some of his purity, and Iblisi accumulated the purity which Adam lost. In other words, Iblisi began to drain Adam's purity through his contact with Eve. Adam's purity gradually decreased until the day when he ate the forbidden fruit. As soon as Adam ate the fruit, he loved it. So he was in love not only with Eve but also with the fruit. Adam lost most of his knowledge—that knowledge which made him pure—and in the end he was equal to Iblisi. Adam lost his knowledge and purity because these depended on the maintenance of his love for God.

Adam, Eve, and Iblisi were driven out of paradise. But, before God sent

Adam out, he put the white dust—the Prophet's essence—in Adam's back, so Adam would have the light within him on Earth. Iblisi tried to steal this light, and Adam asked God to transfer it from his back to his forehead so it would illuminate the way in front of him. On earth, Adam showed his love for God, and he was obedient and submissive. Meanwhile, Iblisi could not stand to live in the same place as Adam, so Adam lived in Mecca and Iblisi never set foot in that land.

The light which Adam carried was the light of the prophet Mohammed and the light of the Qur'ān. Mohammed and the Qur'ān were together from the beginning; they were never separated or divided from each other. When Adam died, one of his sons carried that light, while the rest were deprived of it. Those who were deprived of it consequently began to deviate from the light and the Qur'ān. Some of Adam's sons were good, while many were not. Henceforth, the same father and mother could have both good and bad children. The good child was he who followed his brother who carried the light, while the bad child was the one who went his own way.

Noah received the light, and he carried the Qur'ān within him. Nevertheless, not all his children were good. Similarly, though Ham was bad and did not obey his father, Ham's children still could have merit. Again, if we look to the sons of Sam, we find that, even though Sam had the light, many of his sons were bad and refused to follow the Prophet's light and the Qur'ān. So, they lived like animals, without any guidance. The children of Ham and Yafith did the same thing; but many of them, when they saw the light of the Prophet and the Qur'ān, converted to Islam, and as a result the Prophet loved them. The best example is Bilal, the African slave, who was loved and respected by the Prophet. He was raised to that position because he loved the Prophet and embraced Islam. The Prophet who possessed all the knowledge did not differentiate among the black, the red, and the white. According to the Wa Shenzi, the real believer was the real lover of light. So Bilal, who contacted the Prophet and got knowledge from the Prophet, was thereby elevated. For the Prophet the black's color in no way hindered his capacity for knowledge.

The light of the Prophet was not inherited by all the children of Sam; only certain ones received it. Because that light could not be divided among the children of Sam, God transferred it to Adam's forehead, and Adam was kept alive until a good child was found to carry it. The good child was the one who loved the light, that is, who loved God and the Prophet. The light was given as a gift in exchange for love, but God, who offered that gift, could withdraw it at any time, if the carrier ceased to merit it. Thus, for the Wa Shenzi, the light was not inherited but was given as a gift to those who deserved it.

Again, when the light went to the Arabs, this was not because they inherited it, but because God wanted to give them His gift. Consequently, the selection of the Prophet from among the Qurish tribe did not indicate that the Arabs in general, or the Qurish tribe in particular, were any better than any of the other sons of Adam. At this point the slaves speak about Mohammed's own less desirable relatives, such as his uncle, Abu Jahl, who turned out to be the strongest enemy of Islam. The slaves insist that there was no relation between Mohammed's purity and the Qurish tribe or the Arabs. Mohammed came from Qurish, because that was God's will. He was the purest person on earth, but that purity had nothing to do with the Qurish or the Arabs. However, those people whom he loved were usually protected by him, and Mohammed loved his daughter's children more than anything else.

After his "death," the light of Mohammed was kept in *barzakh,* which was the world of spirits existing between paradise and earth. All the spirits of the people who died were kept in barzakh, where they could hear and see the people on earth, although those people could neither hear nor see them. The spirits of the dead were not allowed to leave barzakh and come down to earth. But there was one exception to this rule: Mohammed, who could go up to speak to God or come down to visit those who loved him. Mohammed was not dead—he was alive, and he visited the earth. Therefore, no one could claim to have inherited the light of Mohammed. That light was not divisible—it was stable. Mohammed loved the good Muslims; he loved those who loved him, and he particularly loved those of his descendants who loved him more than any earthly thing. So, the slaves conclude that the Prophet might love one sharif more than another because that sharif loved the Prophet more than the others did. However, they do not feel that the Prophet would confine his love to his descendants. According to the Wa Shenzi, the Prophet would exchange love with all those who loved him. The Prophet's love could charge even a piece of stone with power and effectiveness.

Adam's sin was that he loved Eve more than he loved God and the Prophet. And so God punished him by driving him out of paradise, where he had to work in order to live. After that, Adam had no leisure time to spend with Eve telling her how much he loved her. If Adam, who was the father of all human beings and who was taught by God himself, could commit that sin, then anyone—black, white, or red—could do the same, irrespective of his color. And so the slaves reason that neither the presence nor the absence of light is a matter of descent or origin (*asli*). Anyone can follow the light if he so choses.

The above version of the myth coincides with that of the wangwana at many points. Like the wangwana, the Wa Shenzi speak of the light, and of the mixed colors of dust from which Adam was made; yet the meaning they attribute to this differentiation and the conclusions they draw are not at all similar. For example, while the wangwana speak of light as saving the Arabs and making them the privileged people, the slaves speak of the light as a gift which is given to those who deserve it. They feel that, after the death of the Prophet, *his* light was in barzakh, and his love was there for all those who love him without discrimination. This love relation is very important to the slaves, and we should pay some attention to it.

The Wa Shenzi understand the relation between God and the Prophet to be one of love. God loved the Prophet, and the Prophet loved God. At the same time, if someone loved the Prophet, then the Prophet would love him. But as we said before, Adam's sin was that he loved another creature besides God, and yet now it appears that Mohammed could love thousands of people in addition to God. Was this a sin? Here, the slaves say that Adam loved Eve even after he found out about her relationship with Iblisi; he loved her even when she was wrong, and this was the real indication that Adam neglected God's orders. Mohammed, on the other hand, in loving a person who loved him, did not separate himself from the Qur'ān. The person who loved Mohammed would love the Qur'ān, and since the Qur'ān was the word of God, the same person would also love God. Thus there was a connection from Mohammed to the Qur'ān to God, and as soon as this chain of love began from one end, it would carry the person to the other. The real believer is thus a lover in the absolute sense of the term.

The intensity of love is reciprocal. The more love a person shows to the Prophet, the more love the Prophet will have for the person. I have observed many instances where, when the name of the Prophet was mentioned, some of the people would lose consciousness and shout, "God bless him, our Beloved." In one of the mosques where I once prayed, the slave leader sat after the prayer and began to speak about the Prophet, and the Prophet's name was mentioned seven hundred and eighty times in less than thirty minutes. Every time the name was mentioned, all the listeners would shout, "Oh, God bless him, our Beloved." This behavior, as we have seen, is out of keeping with the wangwana principle of hishima and self-control; nevertheless, for the slaves, it is the highest expression of love and merit. "If you love the Prophet, he will love you, and, if he loves you, God will love you. If God loves you, then you will be standing beside the Prophet on the day of judgment."

Such love could turn a person not only into a zahid but even into an 'ālim.

The following story illustrates this:

> The Prophet once came in a dream to someone who was really ignorant, and the Prophet asked him what he wanted. The man said "your love," and the Prophet told him to open his mouth; the man did, and the Prophet spat in it. From that day, the man was one of the most learned in all of Lamu. On his grave, it was written: "The grave of the man who drank from the saliva of the Prophet. The head of the learned men, Sheikh so and so."

In this view of knowledge, the slaves differ considerably from the wangwana. The wangwana restrict 'ilm to that knowledge acquired through study, and particularly that study which in the end produced a license. In other words, for the wangwana, there is a definite procedure and program to be followed in order to obtain knowledge, and this program admits no alternatives. The slaves, on the other hand, insist that 'ilm can be obtained directly from the Prophet. According to them, all the knowledge in the books is only one drop of the Prophet's knowledge, but if the Prophet loves someone he might endow him with 'ilm. So, for the wangwana, knowledge equals light, which can only be possessed by the wangwana, who alone are suitable for it. But, the slaves think that if knowledge is light, and the Prophet is the highest light, then he can pass it on to anyone he choses. They think that all the sons of Adam are suitable for that knowledge, if only they can show the Prophet that they love him.

For the slaves, there is no such thing as inherent purity, except for the original light of God and those who have come directly out of Him, that is, the Prophet and angels. For them, the rest of the creatures fluctuate between purity and impurity. For example, Iblisi, who was pure at one time, eventually lost that purity. Similarly, Adam was once pure but lost it. So, even the carrier of the Prophet's light, who had to be high in purity, could be debased and have the light taken from him. For purity is not different from love of the pure elements. The more love you have, the more purity is attributed to you. Purity is the reflection of the Prophet's light inside a person's heart; and thus a child is pure because his heart is not yet occupied with other kinds of affairs. When the child grows up, he can keep his heart clean by filling it with love for the Prophet, or he can allow it to become occupied with other affairs and so lose his original purity. According to the Wa Shenzi, every human being—black, white, or red—is born with a high degree of purity, and he has the option of either keeping or losing it. The wangwana and non-wangwana are equal in this respect; descent, origin, and occupation have nothing to do with it. The Prophet himself was a shepherd and a trader. Many of the Prophet's companions worked with their hands, but this did not interfere with their love and respect for the Prophet. Thus, for the slaves, purity and impurity are two ends of a continuum, and people are placed along it according to the amount of love they have for the Prophet. The slaves feel that even Iblisi, or a jin, can repent and come to be treated like any Muslim. Therefore, in their eyes, purity is an achievement and not a matter of inheritance. They see every Muslim as continually trying to augment his purity—and, having reached a higher degree, as moving on toward an even higher one, and so on. For the slaves, the acquisition of purity is a never-ending process; and the possibilities for it are as wide, vast, and limitless as the mercy of God and the love of the Prophet.

When the benevolent jin converted to Islam, they converted for the sake of the Prophet and not for the sake of the wangwana. They loved the Prophet, and God the Merciful accepted them and allowed them to live with the Muslims. The benevolent jin identified themselves with the good Muslims, and this is why, after the coming of the Jamalilil sharifs, they left the Mkomani area and congregated around the Reiyadah. The jin shifted from the wangwana mtaa to the sharifs' mtaa. A story from my field notes illustrates this:

> Once the district commissioner of Lamu was pushed by the wangwana to take action against Ḥabib Saleḥ. The district commissioner did not want to take action until he saw whether Ḥabib Saleḥ had followers or not. One of the wangwana hired all the slaves who would normally have been in the mosque and sent them out to cut their coconuts, and so there were very few people to pray in Reiyadah on that day. The wangwana told the commissioner to go and see the mosque, expecting that he would find it empty and conclude that Ḥabib Saleḥ had no followers. He went with Ḥamid ibn Sud the Busa'idi, and looked through the window into the mosque. Then he looked at Ḥamid and said, "All these people inside the mosque, and you tell me that the man has no followers." Ḥamid looked, and there was no one except Ḥabib Saleḥ inside the mosque, so he told the commissioner that there was only Ḥabib Saleḥ. The commissioner got angry and said, "I see more than five hundred people and you say one. Do you want to tell me that I am blind?" In fact, all those who were inside were the jin who came to help Ḥabib Saleḥ against the wangwana. The benevolent jin follow the good Muslims, regardless of their being a mngwana or non-mngwana.

The above ideology coincides with that of the Jamalilil sharifs to a certain extent. As we have seen, the Jamalilil speak of love as one of their key principles, and they leave the door open for local saints who are outside the sharif descent groups. According to the Jamalilil sharifs, the nuqaba', or local saints, could be chosen from any group regardless of color or race. In other words, even a slave might achieve that degree of purity, while a mngwana might not.

It all depends on the love a person shows for the Prophet. Again, according to the sharifs, even the position of the qutb is theoretically open to everyone; but they say that an ordinary person would not be able to bear that degree of purity—if he were chosen for the office, he would soon die. In other words, the sharifs are at least able to consider the possibility of achieving a high degree of purity, while the wangwana close that door completely. However, the sharifs are like the wangwana in stressing their descent and claiming that they cannot be treated like others, because they have a basic degree of purity which they had inherited from the Prophet and which they cannot lose, regardless of their actions. In other words, they are infallible. However, both the sharifs and the slaves stress the idea that the Prophet is alive in barzakh, sharing his love with all who love him and especially with his descendants. And both accept the fact that the Prophet, as the head of all the sharifs, does not want anyone to criticize or insult them, because that insult would eventually attach to him. If we speak of basic purity, then, we find that the slaves think that all persons are born pure and that, generally speaking, the amount of purity decreases with age, although each person actually has the choice of maintaining or relinquishing his purity. And even the wangwana are no exception to this general rule. In contrast, the sharifs take the position of the wangwana on the issue of basic purity, but they never have treated the slaves as the wangwana do.

The wangwana, beginning from the assumption that the slaves are inherently impure, avoid touching them, especially if they are dead. A corpse of a free man is called *maiti.* However, if the dead person was a slave, his corpse is referred to as *mfu,* or "decaying cadaver." His body is not washed, or even touched, by the wangwana. And so when a slave dies, no one will wash the body, except other slaves. He is considered impure, defiled, and smelly, and if there is no slave around to wash him, he is simply wrapped in matting *jambi* and buried as he is. A slave is not considered worth washing, since nothing can remove his impurity. He is inherently impure and touching him is not only defiling—this is the case with any dead person—but actually causes the person who touches him to lose some of his own purity. In this case, the word *mfu* is doubly interesting, for it is the word used in reference to dead animals. Thus the corpse of the slave is equal to the body of a dead animal. Both are polluted, impure, and smelly. Muslims do eat beef, but they have to slaughter the cows themselves in order to be able to eat them. If a cow dies a natural death, then it is not only polluted, but if eaten it will impart impurity to the one who consumed it. Thus, the same rules apply to the corpse of a slave; it is defiling and, if touched, it can cause a person to lose some of his purity.

Despite this wangwana attitude, if a slave dies and there is no one to wash him, a Jamalilil sharif will do it.. They say that it is against Islam to bury a Muslim without washing him; in fact, it is a very serious sin. So when a slave dies, the sharifs refer to his body by the word *maiti* and refuse to call him by any other name. Furthermore, the sharifs supply the shroud, or *sanda,* and pay for it themselves. They consider their work as worthy of merit. However, we must not interpret the sharifs' action as due to their inherited purity; because, as we have seen, the wangwana use the idea of their inherited purity as an excuse for avoiding any contact with the corpse of a slave. I think that the sharifs share with the slaves the basic concept that a Muslim achieves his own degree of purity regardless of color or ethnicity. Yet, the sharifs still claim they have a minimum amount of purity that they can *never* lose.

No one in Lamu would express these basic concepts in the above systematic way; yet, as anthropologists, we are not entitled to simply observe a situation but must try to understand it in order to discover not only the basic conscious concepts at work but the deeper "grammar" that the people use without being able to consciously systematize it. We are dealing here with what Noam Chomsky calls "the deep structure" behind which lies the grammar of the language.[6] I hope that we can discover the "grammar" that underlies Lamu's religious thought and action. The natives who make use of that structure do not need to build elaborate theories out of it; they have the rules unconsciously in their minds, and it is the job of the anthropologist alone to discover these rules and point out how they work. It is not an easy task, but it can be done.[7]

6. See for example, Noam Chomsky's "Language and the Mind," in *Changing Perspectives on Man,* ed. Ben Rothblatt (Chicago: University of Chicago Press, 1968).

7. Nur Yalman, "The Structure of Sinhalese Healing Rituals," in *Religion in South Asia,* ed. E. B. Harper (Seattle, Wash.: Asia Society, 1964).

6

Ritual and Transcendental Time

> We, like Earth, are created to vanish and die
> Those who will follow it, will not gain.
> Our life, even if we are inclined to love it,
> Will end, and we will lose it.
> Blessed is God, Who is the Most Sublime and Glorious.
> —From the "Tabaraka dhul 'Ala' wal Kibriya"

In this chapter, I will explore the relation between myth and ritual. Lévi-Strauss, in the Finale of *L'Homme nu,*[1] discusses this topic in some detail and responds to those critics who challenge him to relate ritual to the operations of the mind as he does with myth.

In his response Lévi-Strauss argues that ritual must be viewed as part of a semiological system. In studying ritual anthropologists have to focus their attention on discovering the distinctive features which distinguish ritual language from other forms of communication. In ritual the use of body movements, the spoken language, and the ritual objects together comprise a system. The arrangement and rearrangement of the above-mentioned elements must follow certain rules which are obedient to the structure of the mind. This arrangement and rearrangement of the same ritual elements allow for a large amount of redundancy through which "noise" is eliminated, and meaning, as the ultimate

1. Claude Lévi-Strauss, *L'Homme nu* (Paris: Librairie Plon, 1971).

structural arrangement of all the elements, is achieved.

Emotional involvement in the ritual is the result of that successful journey at the end of which the participants feel that they have achieved their goal, a goal which might be the inverse of that of the myth.

This is clear in the Lamuan case. In the Lamuan myth, Adam's death leaves Eve alone with no suitable husband. Eve returns to a unity which stops the flow of multiplicity; she is not able to produce successors who can be used as markers of the segments of time. In other words, in myth, unity is the final articulation of the problems of multiplicity.

Ritual, on the other hand, is a reversal of that state. In the following ritual, it is clear from the analysis that the participants intend to return the indivisible unity (or, the Qur'ān = the Word of God) to its origin, and so regain their normal state: the state of multiplicity in which they experience the divisibility of time and space. Prior to the ritual (during the whole month of fasting), there is a strong dialectical tension between two structural arrangements of time. Through the ritual the participants succeed in replacing one arrangement for the other, and as a result they return to normal relations which can be apprehended and understood within a secular time and space.

THE RITUAL CONTEXT OF MYTH

Lamu's myth of creation does not exist in a vacuum. It is a part of Lamuan religious life and is narrated in a religious context, to which we now turn. Our consideration of this context will help us to evaluate some of the concepts expressed by Victor Turner in his article on "Myths and Symbols," which has already been mentioned.[2]

The myth starts from a certain point in time, i.e., when God was alone. God's time is different from ours; God's day is equal to fifty thousand of our years. Though this measure is not actually included in the myth, when the people mention the day of judgment, *siku ya hukmu,* they say that it is equal to fifty thousand of our years. Thus, it seems that the people differentiate between two kinds of time: time as we know it, which is connected with the movement of the sun; and transcendental time, which is ordained and fixed by God.

Transcendental time was set in motion when God ordered Israfili to sound the trumpet. The trumpet was supposed to speak and bid the dead arise (*inukani nyote pia*) and wait for God's judgment. Another example of

2. Victor Turner, "Myths and Symbols," *International Encyclopedia of the Social Sciences, X (1968),* 576.

transcendental time was expressed in the myth when God created the Pen; he asked it to write what was going to happen. In both cases, we find that the present, the past, and the future were intermingled. In the case of the trumpet, the *past* actions of human beings would be made *present* (they would be judged). In the case of the Tablet, the present (what is being written) constitutes both future and past. It is clear, then, that this time does not correspond to our secular time.

In addition, there was another ordinary way of measuring time, which applied the deeply rooted principle of the priority of the "cause" over the effect. For example, the father had to be prior to the son. The elder had to be prior to the younger, and so forth. These relationships were established on the principle of order and progression of descent, and this system necessarily involved a time element. Though this means of measuring time might be adequate in our world, it would not be in the other world. On the day of judgment, the order of descent would be absent: a son would not pay attention to his father; a wife would not recognize her husband; and everyone would be concerned only about himself. The only exceptions to this total confusion would be those children who had died before puberty, and the prophets, especially Mohammed. These exceptions will be explained in another place; the intention here is only to show that, as far as the people of Lamu are concerned, *transcendental* or *sacred time* is different from conventional time and that, in Lamu, people recognize that difference although they do not analyze it.

If we focus our attention on the transcendental time of the myth, we find it is not empty; yet neither is it composed of similar units which we would call hours, minutes, or seconds. Instead, it is a time of transformation, in which things change from one state to another: the ignorant get knowledge (Tablet); the obedient become disobedient (Iblisi); smelly dust is transformed into a human being (Adam); and unity (Adam) brings multiplicity (Eve). In each case, the realization of the new state is sudden and abrupt. There are no gradual or accumulated changes that ease into the new and final state. In other words, in that kind of time, things "are" and "are not"; everything is becoming. Existence and non-existence are intermingled. Everything is becoming; nothing is fixed. This liminality is the basic characteristic of sacred time. Such liminality is also characteristic of the town during the month of Ramadan, the time when the myth is read.

This month of fasting has a high degree of religious importance in Lamu. Ramadan, the ninth month of the Islamic year, is called *mwizi wa tumu,* or "the month of commandment," while the others are called *mlanti.* In contrast to the

Islamic year which begins with the month of Muharam, the Swahili year begins with the month of Shawal, which is the tenth month of the Islamic year. Shawal is called *mfungua kiwanda,* i.e., "the first month," and therefore Ramadan is at the end of the Swahili year.

The point which must be stressed from the beginning is that in Ramadan, the bad jin and sheitani do not appear. Ramadan is the month of minimal secular or earthly involvement; and the relation between that and the maximum amount of of purity in the town during that month constitutes the real protective power which stops the invasion of Iblisi, the bad jin, and the sheitani. In this month, the malevolent jin are defeated and the town lives in a state of sacredness and purity. Similarly, if the situation is reversed, we would find that the minimal amount of purity existing in the other months is attributed to the invasion of the bad jin and sheitani. It is clear, then, that the good jin depend on human purity for their protective power and that any decrease in human purity decreases the ability of the good jin to protect the town. So, Ramadan is separated from the rest of the year, and its time is different from that of the other months. Let us now briefly describe this "different sort of time," and then discuss its structure.

The beginning of the month of Ramadan must be declared by Lamu's religious leaders, the mwenye chouni, and they depend on the direct proof of seeing the new crescent moon with their own eyes. On the twenty-ninth of the month preceding Ramadan, the *madrassa,* i.e., the Islamic school, closes, and on that day, the *mandari,* a sort of picnic, takes place.

The Mandari

The mandari is a ritual picnic, which takes place on the day before Ramadan. It is sponsored by the religious leaders and includes all of Lamu's male children. Early in the morning, the children gather in front of the Reiyadah Mosque. They put on their white *kanzus* and *kufias,* dresses and hats, and wait in front of the mosque until the youngest leader of the Reiyadah (a sharif) comes out of the mosque carrying a flag. The flag is red with white borders. On the flag, the words *Ya Ḥabib 'Ali al Ḥabashy,* "Oh, Beloved 'Ali al Ḥabashy," are written in Arabic. As soon as the flag comes out, the children arrange themselves in lines, four children to a row, with the youngest children in the front, and the oldest in the back. One of the elder children is chosen by the leader to beat a small drum called a *kigoma,* while the leader himself beats the tambourine. The leader begins singing a *nashid,* or hymn. This nashid praises the Prophet who brought Islam, the essence of all religions, to earth.

Pray on the one who delivered the essence of messages
Mohammed, the essence of purity, who was chosen by God.
He was the chosen, and he contained all the virtues.
In paradise, he lives
And everytime, when the northern wind blows,
My hearts leaves me and travels to his residence.
I am far from those whom I love,
Which was against my intention.
I am alone and have no one to talk with except the stars.
Sleep deserted me, and all the time my eyes are wide open.
I made a vow that, if those whom I love would visit me
Then, I will discard all my possessions
Because I do not really love anything except him
And I want him to be satisfied with me.

Hand in hand the children swing from side to side and repeat the words after the singer. They walk through the southern part of town until they reach one of the gardens (*chamba*). The children clean off the ground under one of the big mango trees, and then spread their mats and sit down.

Later, other religious leaders, mostly sharifs from Reiyadah, arrive and sit down with the children. The children try to imitate the sharif's way of beating the tambourine, or his singing, and in that spirit they continue until the food is ready.

The first meal is *chakula ya sbuhi,* breakfast, and consists of cooked goat meat and banana. The goats are bought some time before the mandari and are kept in the house of the mother of the current leader of Reiyadah, where they are slaughtered early in the morning of the feast. Then the meat is carried to the garden by the elder children, where it is cooked along with the banana. The breakfast is distributed on trays from the Reiyadah Mosque.

The children and the sharifs cluster around the trays and eat together. Food is plentiful, and the children are told to eat more and more until they are satisfied. After they finish eating, they wash their trays, and everyone moves toward the beach. On the beach, the young children take off all their clothes and swim, while the sharifs and the older children strip down to their underpants. Everyone plays together, splashing water, singing songs, and making fun. The children's attitude toward the sharifs at this time is utterly informal. Around noon, the sharifs come out of the water and dress; others follow and soon all return to the garden. As soon as they arrive, the eldest of the Jamalilil sharifs opens the cooking pot and spits in it, and then the call for prayer is made. This is the noon prayer; yet, instead of calling the children to pray, which is what usually happens, they allow them to continue playing. After the prayer, the sharifs and the children sit down on the mats on which they prayed before. And once again the sharifs and children laugh, play, and eat together in a quite informal fashion.

Meanwhile, any adult non-sharifs who happen to be present (wangwana, slaves, and strangers) eat by themselves. Actually, no adult who is not a sharif, except for the cook and the teacher of the Qur'ān, is invited. However, if such a person passes by he might be asked to the meal, but he joins the madrassa Qur'ān teacher, who is not a sharif, and they eat together. Again, the food is served on trays, five persons to one tray, with the sharifs and the children intermingling. However, this does not mean that at each of the trays there necessarily has to be a sharif. The only hard and fast rule is that non-sharif adults are segregated.

The children at the mandari are mixed. They include sharif children and the children of the wangwana, as well as the children of the slaves. In other words, any differentiation based on descent that would normally play a role in Lamu society is not observed in this ritual at all. The only restriction is that they are not allowed to eat with the non-sharif adults.

In the afternoon, women appear around the chamba, and the sharifs go to meet them. Each woman brings a gift (*zwadi*) for her child. The sharifs take the gift and present it to the child with the indication that his mother brought it for him. In one case, the father of one of the boys was present, but when his wife came, he did not take the gift and give it to his own son; instead, a sharif went and got the gift and gave it to the child. When I inquired about this, I was told that this was the custom; on this day the sharifs *have* to carry the gifts to the children.

Before sunset, the children are once more arranged by the sharifs in order of age, and they return to Lamu by the same roads they used that morning. However, this time, the children are the singers, while the sharifs are busy taking care of the little ones.

> Oh, descendants of Ba 'Alwi plead for us
> By your power all our misfortune will vanish
> You are the closest people to God
> By your help everything can be achieved.
>
> Oh, you Faqih Moqadim, you the son of Mohammed
> The son of 'Ali
> You are the leader, and you are respected
> By his Almighty God.

This poem is a request for the Ba 'Alwi sharifs to intervene to clear away all misfortunes and protect the town. If we compare this poem with the one which is sung by the sharifs, we find that while the sharifs call on their grandfather, the Prophet himself, the children, many of whom are not sharifs, call on the descendants of the daughter of the Prophet, i.e., the Ba 'Alwi sharifs. The first poem is a description of the Prophet's virtues and his love, for which the luxuries of life must be discarded. The second poem is a plea for help, and it is addressed to the Ba 'Alwi sharifs. Thus it appears that while the relationship between the sharifs and Mohammed is one of love, that between the non-sharifs and the sharifs is one of tawasul, which, as we have seen, ultimately turns out to be one of love also. People who love the relatives of the Prophet eventually demonstrate their love for the Prophet himself.

When the procession returns to the Reiyadah Mosque, the flag is taken down and folded and then returned to its place inside. Then the children are picked up by their relatives, and the ceremony ends.

When the sunset prayer (*maghrib*) in the Reiyadah Mosque is over, people congratulate each other for the month of Ramadan. People greet the Reiyadah sharifs by kissing their hands. After that prayer, the sharifs' movements are severely restricted. During Ramadan, they are not seen in the marketplace or near the seashore. They lead prayers, give lectures, and conduct certain rituals but refrain from getting involved in the secular life of Lamu. Their main activity is that of giving darassa, or lectures. Although all the darassa are delivered by the sharifs, they occur at different times. During Ramadan, there are three lectures given daily in Lamu: one at Maskiti Pwani by a Reiyadah sharif after midday prayer; the second at the Reiyadah hospice, or ribat, by a Reiyadah sharif after the *'Asr*, or afternoon prayer; and the third in the Rodha Mosque by a Mahdali sharif after 'Isha' prayer. The most popular darassa is that held after midday prayer.

The Darassa

The darassa delivered in Maskiti Pwani is the most important one. The leader of this darassa is Saiyid Ḥassan ibn Ahmed al Badawi. Along with him some of his half-brothers, the sons of Ahmed al Badawi, lead parts of the darassa.[3] The situation is unique in that the leader of this darassa is a Jamalilil from his father's side and a mngwana from his mother's side (see Case II, Chapter 3), and at the

3. In this darassa the ideology of the Jamalilil sharifs is well expressed. The darassa itself is dominated by the Reiyadah sharifs. The darassa held at the Reiyadah mosque is so similar to that held in Maskiti Pwani that I found it sufficient to describe one of them.

same time is also related to the Mahdali sharifs.

The mosque in which this darassa takes place does not belong to any group in particular; it was built to serve all the different groups on the island. Maskiti Pwani is located at the southern end of Mkomani, quite close to Langoni. In fact, the area where the mosque is situated is peculiar, because some people actually consider it to be the boundary between Mkomani and Langoni. The people who attend this darassa come from all the different groups living on the island. Any male, child or adult, can attend, and they do come from all over the island, something that would only happen during Ramadan. In Lamu, each mosque has one particular group attached to it; they are called *rawatib,* or those who pray regularly in one mosque. However, during Ramadan, the restrictions of rawatib are abandoned, and most of the people desert their mosque for others, usually to hear a particular darassa.

The darassa in Maskiti Pwani is held after the noon prayer, a prayer which is led by a non-sharif. After the darassa, people gather at the right side of the mosque. Here, right and left correspond to the right and left hands of a person facing the niche, or qibla. In some mosques, there are two circles, one on each side of the niche; on the one at the right is written "Allah," and on the one at the left the name of Mohammed appears. The seating arrangement during this darassa is extremely important. It is necessary to go into this arrangement more deeply if we are to understand the significance of the ritual. The mosque as ritual space reflects what is taking place in Lamu society as a whole. In Lamu, seating arrangements are a language in themselves and one that has to be understood in order to communicate with the people. Any mistake in the place one sits could seriously jeopardize the anthropologist's work.

The eldest sharif, Ḥassan ibn Ahmed al Badawi, who is half Jamalilil and half wangwana and who is the organizer of the darassa, sits in the center against the right-hand wall [A]. Beside him to his right, sits his brother [B]. To his left-hand side sits Ḥassan's sister's son [C], who is also a sharif because his father is a sharif. The area beside C is left empty; next to B sit various other sharifs. Both B and C are Reiyadah sharifs. Thus, the whole area is occupied solely by sharifs. In front of the sharifs, there is a stand on which they place the Qur'ān. There is an empty space between the Qur'ān and the place where the children sit, all dressed in white. The older children sit in front, while the younger ones stay in the back. Behind the children, there is another empty space, behind which the wangwana and non-wangwana sit in no particular order. When a new person arrives, he sits in the closest place; the people make space for him without distinguishing between wangwana and non-wangwana.

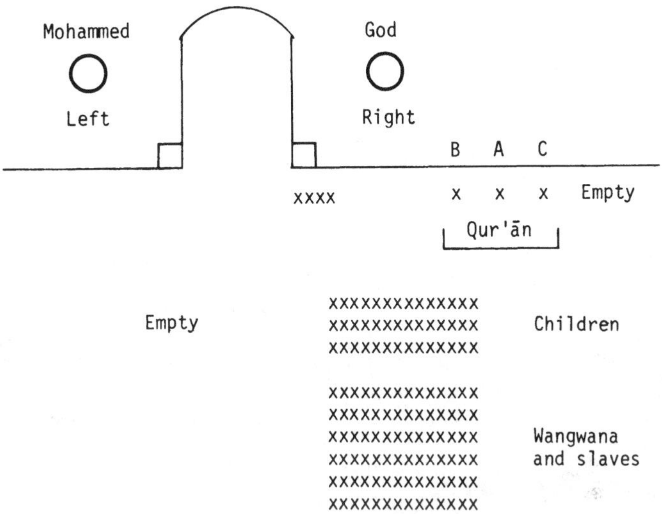

Fig. 23. The seating arrangement in Maskiti Pwani for the Darassa during Ramadan

This seating arrangement contrasts with that in the Jum'a Mosque (see Fig. 21). In this mosque, where all Lamuans have to perform their Friday prayer, the children have no assigned place. They are scattered all over the mosque. There, the wangwana sit in the first three rows, while the sharifs sit only on the right side of the first row. The non-wangwana sit in the back of the mosque, and behind them are the ablution pool and the lavatories. Thus, in the Jum'a Mosque, wangwana and non-wangwana are completely separated. The difference between these seating arrangements is important, as we will see later.

In Maskiti Pwani, when everyone is seated and ready for the darassa, the leader tells the children to begin, and they begin by singing a poem without any musical accompaniment. This is a special song for Ramadan:

> Ramadan, the month of devotion and good deeds,
> The month of godliness, virtue, and merit,
> A month by which the souls are purified from their offenses
> By the reading of the Qur'ān and being obedient
> Ramadan the school of superiority and divine guidance,

> The institute of ethics and obedience.
> In the month of Ramadan, God sent us His word,
> His Qur'ān, which obliterated the deep darkness.

When they finish, the leader [A] hands the Qur'ān to one of the children and asks him to read certain verses, after which the darassa begins.

> In the name of God, the Merciful, the Compassionate, God said the truth, and His eminent Prophet delivered the message of God. We are witnesses to what our God, our Master, our Owner, our Benefactor, has told us. We praise our God, the Sublime, and the most Generous. Oh God, let us use the Qur'ān fruitfully; make the Qur'ān our guide. Oh God, make the Qur'ān the light which will lead us in our life and after-life. Oh God, remind us of what we might forget of it. Teach us its hidden meanings, and help us to read it all night and day. Oh God, forgive us, our parents, our teachers, and religious leaders and all the Muslims. Be merciful to us, Oh God, You are the Origin of Mercy.
>
> In the name of God the Merciful, the Compassionate. God blesses and greets the Prophet, our master Mohammed, the stem and origin of the tree of light. Mohammed the sparkle of the Merciful Hand. He is preeminent of a human nature; the most honorable of the bodily forms; the essence of God's secrets, and the container of all the chosen knowledge . . . . Now let us go to our topic. The true word is God's word (the Qur'ān); the best guidance comes from following the Prophet's footsteps. The worst thing is innovation. Every innovation is a heresy, and every heresy, a deviation from the right path, and this leads to hell. The interpretation said . . .

At this point, the sharif begins explaining the Qur'ān's text, using the traditional Islamic commentators, translating the Arabic text into Swahili, and then making his comments on it. When he uses examples, he takes them from the life of Lamu itself. Yet, he is not allowed to mention names or to refer directly to certain persons. He has to make his remarks as general as he can, and yet it requires little effort to identify the object of his discourse, especially for those who know what is going on in Lamu. For example, in speaking about marriage, he said on one occasion: "We ought to be kind to our women; they are our partners; they carry our children. If some of you complain about your wives, then I will say as God said: good men will have good wives and bad men will have bad wives." The point here is that those men who complain are bad anyway, so God gave them bad women. But it might also mean that, if a good man found himself with a bad wife, he ought to divorce her. Those listeners who know about the current marriage problems in Lamu would understand that the sharif is referring to certain specific persons. Others who do not know anything of these problems would understand this statement only as a part of general religious education.

In this darassa, when sharif [A] finishes, sharif [B] begins his lecture. He is an expert on the life of the Prophet, and he selects and speaks on the things and events from his life that are especially relevant. For example, one of his lectures was on the Prophet's modesty (*utulivu*).

> The Prophet never acted like Abu Lahab, who was arrogant [*eneya kiburi*] and proud. Abu Lahab was like a man who eats with his left hand. He knows that his hand is dirty, and he is told that his hand is dirty, yet he persists, not because he is right, but because he wants to hurt Mohammed. The Prophet is unpolluted; he is pure, and those who follow him are pure. Islam is the core of purity, and anyone who loves Mohammed is pure and will enter paradise. Mohammed will intervene with God on behalf of his followers and he will not do so unless they are pure.
>
> The Prophet used to fast days and days, and he was happy with that, because he knew that this was the way to please God. He never complained. But look at the people now; they are happy when the day comes to an end, because they are hungry; they are like animals, while the Prophet was never hungry, because he was close to God. We have to remember God and thank Him that He sent us Mohammed, who led us from darkness to light. Also, we have to remember God; He will help us to forget our hunger. If we remember God all the time, we will never be hungry. Adam was forgiven when he mentioned the name of Mohammed and asked God for forgiveness. The name of the Prophet and his deeds are light . . . . Let us ask God to forgive us and our parents for the sake of our beloved Prophet Mohammed.

The third sharif [C] reads parts of the myth and comments on them. His aim is to point out the wisdom of God and the relevance of the existence of Iblisi and and his jin followers. "God would have abolished them, but He left them as a means by which He could examine the loyalty of human beings. God created Adam and the world in order to transfer the light of the Prophet to the world . . . . "

Thus the darassa draws to a close. It only remains for the children to sing another song, in which they thank their teachers who have taken the trouble to teach them.

> Oh, God, for the sake of your chosen Prophet
> Let us achieve our goals [acquiring knowledge]
> Forgive all our past deeds, You are the Most generous
> Forgive our parents, oh God, and our children
> God, forgive all the Muslims, Amen, Amen
> Oh, God, listen to us
> We praise You in the beginning and at the end.
> We bless and greet our beloved Prophet,
> May God bless and greet him infinitely

And also his relatives and companions
And those who descended from him.
Finally, we praise those who are teaching us.
They preserved the knowledge, and they handed it down to us.

When the children finish their song, the leader [A] asks all the people to read the Fatiḥa, the opening chapter of the Qur'ān, and to send it as a gift to the Prophet and to all Muslims. When this is done, the darassa is over. The leader stands up and people approach him, and one by one they kiss his right hand. After that all the sharifs go home, but they do not go through the main market street; instead they go through the small alleys behind the town. This is something which they could never do except in Ramadan.

The Darassa in the Rodha Mosque

The Rodha Mosque is located in the Mkomani area. It is the mosque of the wangwana and their followers, the Mahdali sharifs. The leader of that mosque is a sharif from the Mahdali (see Case II, Chapter 3). Here the darassa is held after the 'Isha' prayers, and the wangwana form the greatest percentage of listeners. The seating arrangement is very informative:

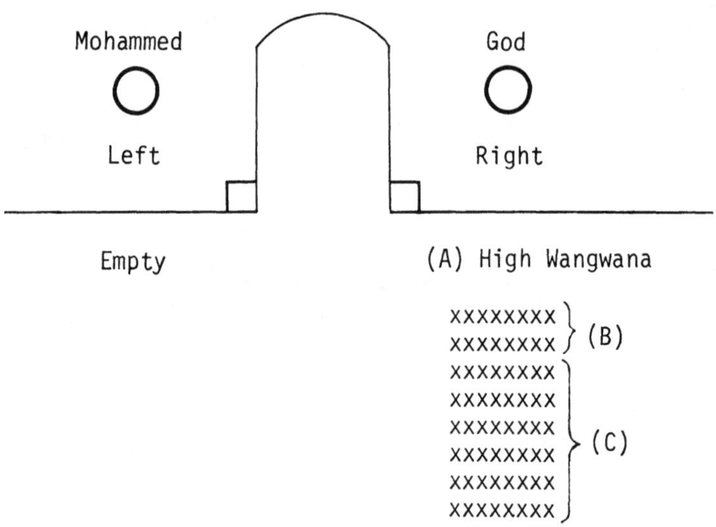

Fig. 24. The Arrangement in Rodha Mosque

The leader [A] sits with other high wangwana on the right side of the niche. When I was in Lamu, this sharif had no one to help him in the darassa. He had only one brother, who lived on the mainland, and the rest of the Mahdali sharifs were uneducated. Even his half brother, the son of Ahmed al Badawi, would not attend his darassa; and neither would the Jamalilil sharifs. The group that does attend consists of the wangwana and their children, and some strangers.

The children [B] sit facing the leader, in a row perpendicular to his left hand. There is a small empty space between A and B. Directly behind B sit some other wangwana [C]. There is no space left between the wangwana and the children. The wangwana are mixed together, and social stratification is absent.

The darassa is organized for the interpretation and translation of certain poems. The same myth of creation that we have already examined in detail is read; however, the leader also selects other stories from many different places to use as examples. In general, the lectures are oriented toward stories, proverbs, and wisdom.

This darassa begins with a sharif child reading part of the poem called "*Tabaraka dhul 'Ala' wal Kibriya'*," "Blessed is God, who is the Most Sublime and Glorious," The child reads the poem in a certain prescribed rhythm and all the people answer him:

> I begin by thanking my Master,
> I thank Him for the blessings He offered us,
> Blessed is God, who is the Most Sublime and Glorious.
>
> We like earth are created to vanish and die
> Those who will follow it, will not gain.
> Our life, even if we are inclined to live it, will
> End, and we will lose it.
> Blessed is God, who is the Most Sublime and Glorious.
>
> If you follow it, you will lose your light,
> You will be an animal, smelly and dirty
> And end in a dusty house (the grave).
> Blessed is God, who is the Most Sublime and Glorious.
>
> We will die, and we will leave it.
> Some people will be sorry for our departure
> And they might cry.
> But after ten days they will forget us
> And we will be rotten bones. Think of
> That, you who worship life.
> Blessed is God, who is the Most Sublime and Glorious.

The listeners cry and declare that they are wrong. The rhythm of the reading and the whole atmosphere of the darassa make a strong statement against involvement in the world. The real Muslim emerges as the one who is able to discard the natural world and depend on the cultural world as defined by God in the Qur'ān and as explained by Mohammed. In that atmosphere the sharif begins his darassa. The following is a summary of one I happened to hear on one occasion:

> God is the Most Merciful and Gracious. He gave us eyes, ears, and tongues, not to use against His will but to use to enforce His orders and His will. If we look around us, we will find birds. Look how they eat, and how they carry the food to their offspring. The mother bird eats, then flies to her children and vomits the food she ate in front of her children, so they can eat it.
>
> Meanwhile, look at cats; if they are hungry, they will eat the food, and they will never think of their kittens. Why and from where have these differences arisen? It is God who gave the birds these ideas, while He did not give them to cats.
>
> But, also He gave us the Qur'ān, and He taught Adam, so we are not like cats. We love our children; we praise our Prophet, and we have to follow God's orders. If we will not do that, we will be like the cat who leaves her kitten to die of hunger while she is overfed. If we neglect the Qur'ān and the Prophet's tradition, then we will be similar to the cat. We might marry our mothers or sisters or even daughters; there is nothing to stop us from doing these things except the orders of God. Once a man went to the Prophet and he told him, "Mohammed, I planted a flower, and it grew up to be beautiful and healthy, and then, someone told me that I had to give it to another person, because I could not keep it for myself. But I did not like that idea at all; I took it for myself." The Prophet, all wisdom, knew that the man was speaking about his daughter, so the Prophet asked the man, "What is your religion?" The man answered, "I do not have one." The Prophet looked at him and said, "Do whatever you want, because you are no more than an animal." Without religion we are all animals. This world in which we live is not real. We are here only to be examined.
>
> For that reason, God left Iblisi in this world to deceive us. If we conquer him, then we will be saved. Our worldly life is not real.
>
> Let us suppose that a wealthy man died leaving his wife a big house and a lot of lands. Let us suppose that that wife gave birth to a child on the same day her husband died; she would, then, be allowed to marry again on that same day, because she would not have to wait for *'adda* [a period of four months and ten days during which every woman has to remain unmarried in order to be sure that she is not pregnant from the previous husband]. When she married, all the money, all wealth, would be transferred to the new husband. Even the clothing of the deceased husband would be used by the new one. Where is reality here? Nothing is real. This world is a joke, a laugh, but while some think that it is laughing with them, in fact, it is laughing at them. The only reality is that light brought to us by our Prophet, which, if we follow, will give us paradise, which is as real as God promised us; we accept his promise.

After his lecture is finished, the people read the Fatiḥa and send it to the Prophet as a gift, and ask God to help them to overcome this deceiving world. The sharif then stands up; but very few people approach him to kiss his hand.

The Friday Service in the Reiyadah Mosque

This service is important since it is exclusively a sharif service;[4] no one joins in it except the Jamalilil sharifs. The wangwana sharifs pray their Ramadan night prayers (*tarawiḥ*) after the 'Isha' prayers, that is, around 8:00 P.M., but the Reiyadah sharifs perform the tarawiḥ after midnight. The prayers are the same in any case, but in the Reiyadah Mosque they are held on Thursday night (which is really early Friday morning). After the Reiyadah sharifs finish their prayers, which are conducted outside the mosque, they go inside and sit down to read certain poems and beat their tambourines and drums. This ceremony is private; it is only for the sharifs and their sons, and no one else may attend. Again, much is to be learned by focusing on the seating arrangement. Instead of sitting on the right side of the niche, the sharifs sit on the left side, far from the niche, with their backs to it.

The sharifs and their children read certain poems praising the Prophet. However, everything read during this service has had to be composed by the Ba 'Alwi sharifs. One example is the *Ratib al Ḥaddad*, or the devotional superrogatory exercises of Ḥaddad.[5] The ritual is performed quickly, and the singing is carried totally by the adult sharifs [A]; while the young children [B] act only as a chorus or repeaters. In this ritual, the younger children sit in the first row while the older ones [C], the musicians, sit in the back. Thus the musical instruments are played not by the adult sharifs, but by older children, and the younger children, the chorus, are seated in between the musical instruments and the adult sharifs [A]. Moreover, the space between the adult sharifs and the younger children is eliminated.

The End of Ramadan in the Reiyadah Mosque

When the people see the new moon, they end their fasting, and the following day they celebrate the feast. But before that, on the night on which they see the new moon, they hold a ritual called *iḥya'*, the "revival." At this point, it would be helpful to describe that ritual as it is performed in the Reiyadah Mosque.

4. During Ramadan the Reiyadah Mosque is closed; people perform their everyday prayer and Ramadan night prayers in the hospice on the right side of the niche.

5. The author is Saiyid Abdallah ibn 'Alwi ibn Mohammed ibn Ahmed ibn Abdallah al Ḥaddad al 'Alwi. He is considered a leader of the Ba 'Alwi order.

After the 'Isha' prayer, the sharifs' followers from all over Lamu gather inside the mosque. They divide themselves into eight groups, each group forming a

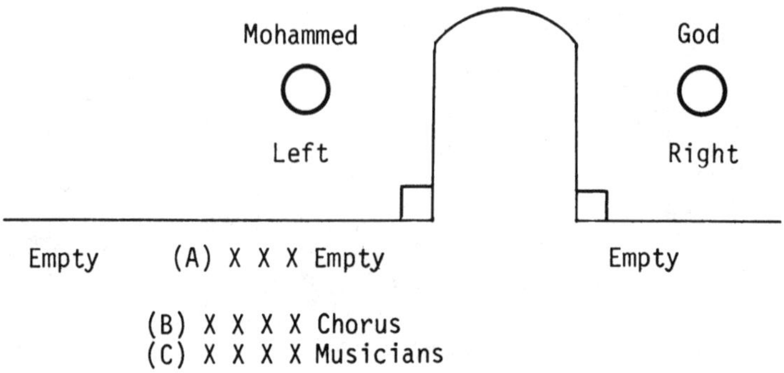

Fig. 25. The Arrangement for the Friday Service in the Reiyadha Mosque

circle made up of seven or more persons. The circles are a mixture of sharifs, wangwana, slaves, and children. The Qur'ān is divided into eight parts, and one is assigned to each circle. Actually, the Qur'ān is traditionally divided into sixty *ḥizb* or parts, so each of the circles would have about seven and one-half of these parts to read. Each member of every group reads one-quarter of a part and then passes the Qur'ān to the person sitting on his right side. Thus, the Qur'ān moves counterclockwise. During the reading, popcorn and sweet coffee are distributed, but they rotate in a clockwise direction. Moreover, if a sharif is sitting in one of the circles, he is the last to receive the coffee or popcorn. Everyone is served before the sharifs. Each circle has only one cup, so when a person finishes, he fills it for the next person, who, in turn, has to refill it for the person on his right, until it reaches the sharif.

The seating arrangement is quite different from that of the darassa. Sharifs share the following circles with non-sharifs: 4–5–6–7–8. Circles 1–2–3 are composed entirely of non-sharifs. In circles 4–5–6–7–8, the non-sharifs begin the recitation.

Meanwhile the leader of the Reiyadah sharifs sits on the left side of the qibla, alone, dressed in his best clothes. He does not participate directly in the ritual.

However, at the end, he has to make the invocation called "The Conclusion of the Great Qur'ān." Directly before that, the sharif in group 8 sends his empty cup of coffee and an empty basket to the sharif in group 7, who sends it to the

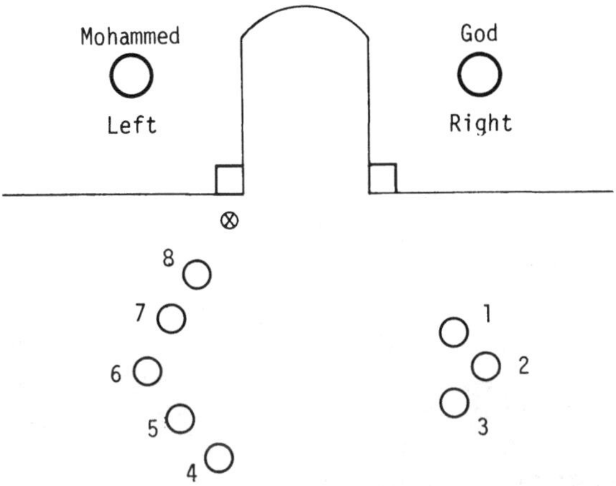

Fig. 26. Seating Arrangement During the Ihya'

sharif in group 6, and so on, until the basket and cup arrive at group 1. As the leader of the sharifs begins reading the "conclusion," the cup and basket are returned, but this time they are full. Each group has put in its leftover coffee and popcorn. When the head of the Reiyadah sharifs reaches the end of the prayer, the sharif in group 8 gives him the cup and the popcorn. He drinks the coffee and eats the leftover popcorn, and then leaves the mosque. After that, no one touches him, and he contacts no one.

As I have said, the Qur'ān is divided into eight parts, with each group reading approximately seven and one-half parts. Each group is told where to begin and where to end, and all begin reading together, at the same time. Thus, if group 1 begins from the first verse of the Qur'ān, group 2 begins at the verse that immediately follows the one where the first group would eventually end. In other words, if we can image the Qur'ān as a straight line, then when group 1 begins at point A, group 2 begins at B at the same time. All the groups read simultaneously, and all are supposed to finish at the same moment. All the groups try to finish as fast as they can and everyone puts out great effort to achieve greater speed in reading. It is especially interesting that the Qur'ān, which is usually read in sequence, is on this occasion read concurrently, apparently with the aim of eliminating the time factor. In other words, it is as if

The Qur'ān

A B C D E F G H

---

1 2 3 4 5 6 7 8

Fig. 27. Diachronic Arrangement of the Qur'ān

the people are reading the Qur'ān in one indivisible act, without the interference of time as we know it. They want to overcome the linearity of the Qur'ān and the succession of time segments as we normally perceive them. The unity and indivisibility of the light is manifested in the Qur'ān through this ritual.

At any rate, if we look at the participating groups which represent all Lamu's strata, we will find that they achieve another sort of unity through reading the Qur'ān as whole, a unity which is the ideal of social life. Each group is related to the group beside it, which is related to another group. The relation of group B to group C depends on the relation between groups C and D, while all depend on the head of the Reiyadah sharifs, who sits by himself, separated from everyone, even his own relatives.

As was said, the head of the Reiyadah sharifs sits on the left side of the niche under Mohammed, and in front of him the whole Qur'ān is recited in one simultaneous act. The whole community, oblivious to social divisions, is unified in front of him. The head of the Reiyadah makes the invocations for all the different groups. At that time, no one could dispute the authority and power of that head, who is seated under the shade of the Prophet. The head of the Reiyadah is symbolically returning to his ancestor (Mohammed) and reasserting his kinship ties directly with the Prophet. Thus, through the Prophet, the head of the Reiyadah establishes a relation with God.

As we will see later, during Ramadan, the sharifs maintain only a minimal relationship with the Prophet. Their intensive activity is directed toward establishing a relation with the Qur'ān (*dhikr*)[6] and God. Thus when Ramadan

6. The Qur'ān as dhikr is the eternal word of God; it is undivided and stable like Light and it is also pure.

ends they are eager to reestablish the old kinship ties with the Prophet, that light

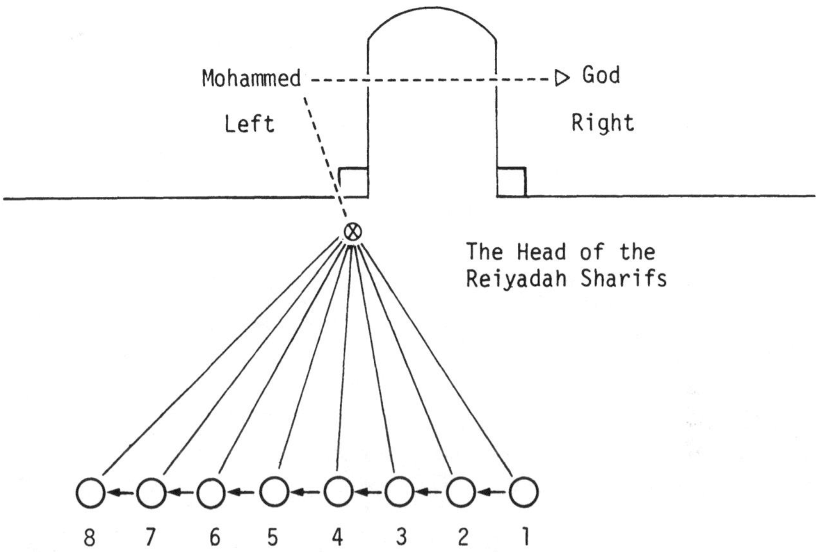

Fig. 28. The Qur'ān as Synchronic

who had lived on earth and mixed with the people.

The ritual in the Reiyadah Mosque reaches its climax when all finish reading the Qur'ān and chant in one voice, "God is great, God is greater, God is the greatest of anyone. We praise God for His blessing. He sent us our beloved Prophet. There is no God but Allah." Then, the head of the Reiyadah sharifs reads the prayer asking God to accept their good deeds for the sake of the final prophet Mohammed, the Leader and the Guide. Now Ramadan is over; the month of devotion and supplication has come to an end. Then, the head of the Reiyadah sharifs leaves; he does not stop or give his hand to anyone, and no one tries to approach him. He returns to one of his houses.

We will later be returning to a discussion of the iḥya' in conjunction with other rituals.

The Sama'

On the first day of the feast, after the 'Asr prayer, the Reiyadah sharifs hold what is called *sama' salafi,* a name which refers to the traditional religious songs. This ritual is held not inside the mosque but in the *ribat,* or hospice (see Figure 29).

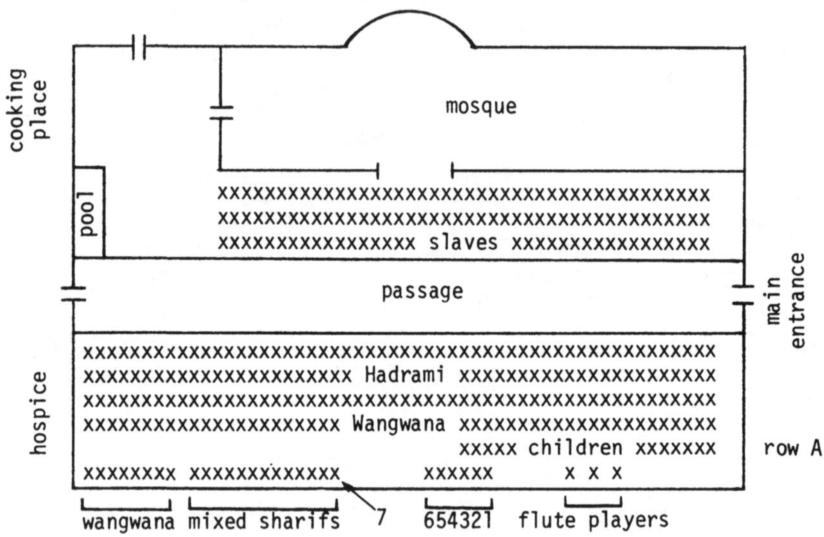

Fig. 29. The Sama^{c} in Reiyadha

In the sama', the head of the Reiyadah sharifs sits directly facing the center of the niche. To his right sit the Jamalilil sharifs and to his left sit the Ḥusseini, al Roudini, and al Mahdali sharifs. Next to the Mahdali sharifs sit the wangwana, and in front of the Reiyadah sharifs, in the first row, sit some of the children of Lamu from various social and ethnic groups. In this arrangement, the children of the slaves are seated among the wangwana and Ḥadrami children. Yet, directly behind them sit the wangwana, and behind the wangwana, the Hadramis. Behind the Ḥadramis there is an empty space, and the adult slaves are seated on the other side of that space. No one sits inside the mosque; it is closed.

The sama' begins with a reading of the Fatiḥa by sharif 7, who sits on the left side of the niche. Then the head of the Reiyadah sharifs puts in the censer incense that is a mixture of ubani and 'udi. After that the flute is played. There are three flutes; two are played by the sons of the Jamalilil sharifs and one by a slave. This slave is the best flute player in Lamu. The tambourines follow the flute, and they, in turn, are followed by the two small drums. The sharifs are the only persons with the right to beat the tambourines, and the small drums are beaten by the children only. When the music stops, the sharifs, accompanied by 2, who is of dubious descent (*mwana wa haramu*), sing together the following song:

> We begin by calling the name of God our Master
> Whom we thank for the blessing which He bestowed on us
> We pleaded with Him for help in all our affairs
> He is the Helper of the creatures, and the Master of
> the universe
> We plead to God by all the names which were mentioned
> [in the Qur'ān]
> And by all those names which were hidden
> We plead to Him by all the books which He sent
> By the Qur'ān, which is the cure to the believers
> By the angels, whom we ask God to allow us to meet
> By the righteous and all the prophets and messengers
> We plead to be protected
> We plead by the relatives of the prophets and messengers
> And by those who followed them on the right path
> We plead by the 'ulama [i.e., the learned people who
> know the orders of God]
> We plead by the saints and the pious men
> Especially the real leader Wajih al Din the crown
> of the knowers
> His rank was very high
> His knowledge was not only concerned with the legalistic
> aspect of Islam, but also with its certainty
> When you remember the Eidarous, who was a real qutb,
> Your heart is purified and ready to accept what the right
> people say.

There are two tambourines, and they are beaten by any two of the sharifs 1–3–4–5–6, but they never cross to the left-hand side of the head of the Reiyadah sharifs. They are always on his right-hand side. The kigoma could be beaten by any child, but he has to be in row A, so he can be seen by the tambourine beaters. In row A are found children and also adults. They are no longer separated as they were during Ramadan. When the music ends, one of the sharifs sings a poem without any musical accompaniment. He begins by saying, "Oh God, bless and greet our master Mohammed and his relatives and his companions." The people answer, "Oh God, bless and greet him." The sharif then says, "Ya Hooh," and the people repeat it after him. Then, he begins reading the following poem:

> Let me listen to the religious songs which please the heart
> Remember whatever my pen writes for you.
> When God ordered that we have to come together, this
>   was a happy event.
> God was so gracious that he gave us what we need, and
>   the desert turned green.

The singer prolongs the last word, and the people say in the same rhythm, "There is no God, but God," *La ilaha illa Allah.*

> It is good for those who will follow me
> It is good for those who have a heart which is aware
>   of the secret that I uncovered.
> I amongst those *lovers,* ask you to be involved in love.
> By all these we plead to God
> To forgive the sins of all who are present
> And be merciful to them.
> We end the poem by asking God
> To bestow his protection on us, so no one will be
>   able to hurt us.
> Now, the Throne covers us, and God's eye is looking after us.
> Then we conclude by greeting and blessing the Prophet,
> Mohammed the leader of us all, and our best advocate.
> Oh God, we ask you by Your Most Holy Name
> And by the power of the chosen Prophet to free us
> From grief and release us from suffering.
> Oh God, we ask you for the sake of the five [ahl al kissa'] [7]
> For the sake of those who had been covered by the
>   Prophet, to look at us
> Oh God, for the sake of Mohammed forgive us
> And for the sake of Ḥabashy look at us.

The people listen attentively and quietly to the song and its accompanying music. The sound of the flute constitutes the background against which the tambourines and drums are contrasted. The flute is the most important

7. See above, p. 152.

instrument, because it establishes the successive rhythm. Next in importance to the flute are the two small drums, because they regulate the beat of the tambourines. If the drums are not exact, then the tambourines cannot be either. Though it is said that the adult sharifs do not beat the drums in the main ceremonies, I found that toward the end one of the sharifs took one of the drums and beat it. However, the sharif who did this was usually not the leader of the ceremony. The tambourine, on the other hand, is played only by a sharif—sometimes by the leader of the Reiyadah. Again, the singer prolongs the last word, and the people say again, "There is no God, but God."

> Those who went through this path got their beams of light
> from me.
> No one can say that he knows better than me.
> Oh God, fulfill our wishes, and improve everything
> And guide us and help us to follow the Prophet and
> his companions.

When the singer finishes, he says "Praise be to God, the Master of the universe," and then another poem (with music) is sung, and when it ends, another poem (without music) is read by a non-sharif. The non-sharif singer, however, has to be invited to sit beside the sharif before reading the poem. The ceremony ends with a non-musical poem, where, instead of saying, "Praise be to God, the Master of the universe," the singer says, "God by His grace will bless our gathering. He will forgive us for the sake of the chosen prophet Mohammed, His final messenger, the leader of those who follow the right path, Amen." The Reiyadah leader then makes his invocations in a very low voice, and at the same time puts more aloe wood in the censer, and then asks the oldest sharif present to read the Fatiḥa. This old sharif says: "To Mohammed, the chosen, in order to have our wishes fulfilled . . . Fatiḥa." Then, everyone reads the Fatiḥa, and when the sharif leader stands, the people do also and go to him to kiss his hand; and they do the same thing with the younger sharifs. The sharifs then leave the mosque and begin a round of visits to various houses in Lamu to which they were invited. The first day is only for blood relatives. The sharifs are accompanied by their followers, and in every house a sweet meat known as *ḥalwa* is served, and this is followed by either tea or coffee. The owner of each house asks the head of the sharifs to read the Fatiḥa for him, but first one of the young sharifs recites the Fatiḥa in a loud voice to get the people's attention. Then the leader of the sharifs, who is still somewhat separated, again reads the Fatiḥa, while the owner of the house distributes perfume. Sometimes this perfume is accompanied by betel leaves (*tambuu*). After this short ceremony, the sharifs leave for another house where everything is repeated; and so it continues until sunset. The second day, the sharifs visit non-relatives, mostly Ḥadramis, slaves, and Bajuni. In other words, most of these visits are centered in the Langoni half of Lamu, in the southern part of the town. Nevertheless, most of the wangwana attend the iḥya' and the sama'.

The sama' continues in the Reiyadah Mosque for three days, and, on the third day, when it is finished, rose water is distributed to the people and sprinkled around. After that, the sharifs hand out plates of ḥalwa which are carried around by the Reiyadah followers. Each person cuts off a piece of ḥalwa and eats it, followed by unsweetened coffee. The distribution of the ḥalwa begins with the head of the Reiyadah and then moves to the person on his right. After this small ceremony is over, the sharifs walk about in the town, as they did on the second day. However, they are not visiting anyone in particular this time; they shake hands with people, sit in the coffee houses, and visit their Ḥadrami traders. They are greeted and their hands are kissed. But all this takes place in the street and they do not enter any houses.

ANALYSIS

Before I begin my analysis of the material, it is necessary to say a word about the sharifs' conception of purity and impurity.[8] An understanding of these ideas is crucial to an understanding of the rituals, especially those performed during Ramadan. Since the sharifs' views on purity and impurity are expressed most directly within the rituals themselves, we can uncover much through analysis of these rituals. Nevertheless, for the sake of clarity, I would like to lay them out here and then from time to time refer back to them. Actually, this sharif ideology has already been touched upon—for example, when we spoke of Ḥabib Saleḥ refusing to accept the wangwana idea about washing the bodies of dead slaves. The wangwana thought the slaves were impure, and so they refused to wash their corpses. Ḥabib Saleḥ, however, used to wash the dead of the slaves. He declared that while any dead body was in itself *defiling* to any living Muslim, the dead Muslim was *pure* regardless of origin and color. Ḥabib Saleḥ believed that as soon as any person converted to Islam he became pure, regardless of his origin or color. Here, Ḥabib Saleḥ made use of the distinction between impurity and defilement that we have already discussed in some detail.

8. From here on, when speaking about "sharifs," with no mention of the name of a particular branch, I will be referring to the Jamalilil or Reiyadah sharifs.

The wangwana ideology concerning purity and impurity is based on a distinction the wangwana make between the sons of Sam (pure), and the sons of Yafith and Ham (impure). The wangwana view purity and impurity as inherited properties, and they claim that purity is exclusively for those who own hishima and kutunga. The slaves, they believe, are inherently impure and have neither hishima nor kutunga. At the same time, the wangwana believe that there are different grades of purity, and that, while basic purity is inherited, it is possible to achieve higher levels beyond that. Religious knowledge is considered to be one way to achieve this goal; another is to withdraw from the world and abstain from joining everyday affairs. At the same time, the wangwana believe that impure things can have an adverse effect on pure ones. Thus, if impure elements such as slaves or malevolent jin come in contact with pure elements, the pure will suffer. But since the impure elements can only intrude when the pure are in their lowest state of purity, there are certain rituals performed by the wangwana to elevate the town to a higher level of purity, and at the same time to neutralize, though not eliminate, any impurity that might be present. This will become clearer in the following chapter when we deal with one of the wangwana rituals that is intended to neutralize the impurity of the jin and the slaves. Through such rituals, the wangwana are able to protect their town from the Wa Shenzi.

But now let us return to the Jamalilil sharifs, for whom the question of purity and impurity is distinct from that of descent, and who have therefore been able to use their ideology to unify Lamu and to destroy the basis of the old stratificatory system. The Jamalilil sharifs have challenged the wangwana idea that purity is inherited and remains the private property of one group. The sharifs have declared that all Muslims have purity regardless of descent or origin. Yet, the sharifs still claim that they, as sharifs, have a degree of purity higher than anyone else's because they are the descendants of the Prophet.

These concepts concerning purity are crucial; they have profoundly affected Lamu's religious and social life. The sharifs consider all non-sharifs (Muslim and non-Muslim alike) as having been born pure. However, the sharifs are said to be the only group to be born with such a high degree of purity. Furthermore, non-sharifs can lose their purity; they can become impure, while the sharifs can lose *some* of their purity but would never be without that basic amount which has been handed down to them through descent. The sharifs share in the light of the Prophet, and this is part of God's light, which is the origin of purity.

The impure are all those who refuse to recognize the existence of God. All those who worship trees or animals are impure. These people are out of God's mercy, and they only continue to exist because of God's grace. While God's mercy (*rahima*) extends only to His slaves—that is, to those who worship Him—God's grace (*ne'ma, 'ezzi*) is bestowed on everything, alive or dead. Iblisi, the malevolent jin, and even such creatures as ants, are allowed to exist only because of that grace. God could have annihilated Iblisi but instead, through grace, He allowed him to live.

God is merciful to all His worshippers, and these worshippers are the pure ones. According to the sharifs, the impure are all those creatures who live only because of God's grace. Such creatures as the malevolent jin have a brain which could have led them to gain God's mercy, but they have never used that brain properly, and similarly all those Africans who have known about Islam, yet have not converted to it and have preferred instead their own religion or Christianity, are also impure. The old Christians who lived before Mohammed and whose descendants have continued up until now as Christian are, nevertheless, considered pure. The sharifs make this distinction clear. Once someone from Lamu asked a sharif whether it was religiously allowable for him to marry a Christian Pokomo or not; the sharif answered, "It is not allowable; she is impure, and if you marry her, God will not bless your children."

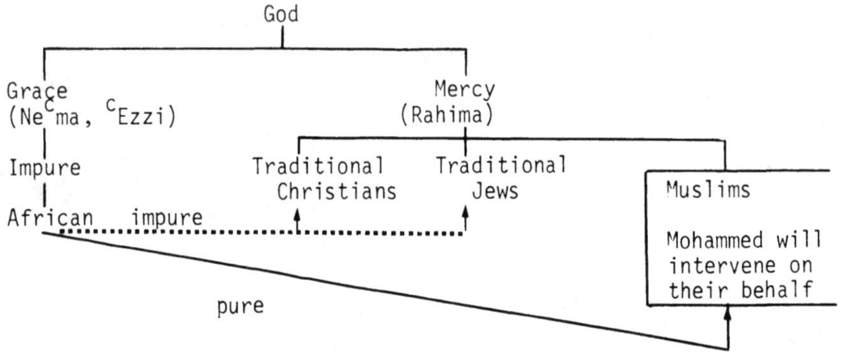

Fig. 30. The Distribution of God's Grace and Mercy

Again, while the Muslim can eat the food of traditional Christians, he is not allowed to eat the food of newly converted Christians. The newly converted are impure, and all impure creatures are always defiled.

According to the sharifs, pure creatures are sometimes defiled and other times undefiled, but they can easily get rid of their defilement by means of a ritual bath or through ablution. For example, sexual intercourse defiles a pure man and requires the taking of a ritual bath afterward. On the other hand, sleeping or breaking wind would also defile, but the pure man would only have to make ablutions to take away that defilement. Washing the dead is defiling, and the person who performs that task needs a ritual bath. Touching a person's sexual parts is defiling, but for this ablution is all that is needed. If a man touches a woman, he has to make ablution. All the cases where defilement could be eliminated by ablution are called cases of "minor defilement," while all the cases in which a ritual bath is necessary are called "great defilement." In other words, the sharifs recognize degrees of defilement—at least among the pure. Defilement and undefilement alike are characteristics of the pure. A pure man might or might not be defiled, but an impure man is always defiled. There are no degrees of impurity. Impure creatures are all equal in their impurity.

Nevertheless, just as the sharifs recognize degrees of defilement, so they recognize different degrees of purity. The qutb has a very high degree of purity, and the local saints under him are also high in purity. If the qutb and local saints are sharifs, then like all sharifs, they have a minimal stable amount of purity which they have inherited from the Prophet. The sharif can invest his purity and yet be sure from the beginning that he is not going to lose his capital—while another Muslim, who might also try to invest his purity, knows all along that he might lose it all in the process.

According to the sharifs, Muslims have a degree of purity regardless of origin or descent, and they can build on it so that even a slave might be able to gain a degree of purity higher than a wangwana. A person can increase his purity by learning the path of love. Thus, if a slave loves a local saint, and through that loves the Prophet and all those who are related to him, then the Prophet will be that slave's guide in this life and in the hereafter. The Prophet, who was sent to the world as part of God's mercy, will take him under his wing. It has been said that on the day of judgment, when all worldly relations such as kinship and social stratification are void and meaningless, love of the Prophet will be the only relation left. The Prophet will extend his protection to those who love him and care for his descendants.

The sharifs believe that all Muslims, by virtue of being Muslims, are under

God's mercy and therefore pure. However, through the love of the Prophet, the Muslims have the *shafa'ah,* the right to ask the Prophet to intervene on their behalf and ask God to forgive them. It is the shafa'ah that makes the Muslims different from any other group that enjoys God's mercy. The only way a Muslim can lose his purity is by denying God's existence, or by insulting the Prophet. If a Muslim does this, he loses the right to ask the Prophet to intervene on his behalf. He would be in a similar situation if he converted to another religion such as Christianity. He would still lose God's mercy, because he had once known the true path but had left it for another. The Muslim who converts to another religion is impure. He is equal to those who worship fetishes.

All Muslims, according to the sharifs, are pure; yet, they have different degrees of purity corresponding to the amount of love they show toward the Prophet and his descendants. The more a person loves the Prophet, the more he will be loved by God. Such a person's actions are entirely directed by that love. However, such love is hard to maintain, since the highest degree of love can be achieved only if a person denies all his relations with this world—and this means that he has to be literally transferred from it. As a matter of fact, if a non-sharif reaches that degree of love, he will die immediately. Such love is said to be the heaviest burden and the "secret of all secrets," (*sir al asrar*). As we have seen, al Ghazali,[9] the great mystic, could not survive one minute after he reached that highest degree of purity. Therefore, for all practical purposes, ordinary Muslims have to be satisfied with only a limited amount of purity. If their purity increases beyond a certain point, they will be in danger. The sharifs are the only ones who can carry that purity and therefore, if by any means some Muslims get a higher degree of purity, then they have to transfer their unneeded purity to the sharifs.

The sharifs, possessors of the highest purity, can do things no one else can. They are the owners of the Qur'ān; they alone can carry it as *dhikr,* or divine word. The sharifs can transform the Qur'ān from a mere book to the living word that expresses itself through them. They are the only ones capable of this, because the highest degree of purity, which is inherent in the Qur'ān, can find a corresponding amount of purity only in the sharifs. Through the Qur'ān, the sharifs could overcome all misfortune and defeat all impurity.

According to the sharifs the jin are impure, and if they come into contact with a Muslim, he will suffer. Such a mixture of purity and impurity creates

9. Abu Hamed Muhammad ibn Muhammad al Tūsi, known as al Ghazali, a great Islamic scholar and mystic (1058–1111 A. D.—450–505 A. H.).

sickness that can only be cured by the Qur'ān and the sharifs. That is why the sharifs insist that the Qur'ān "cures." It cures by defeating and driving away the impure element that causes the sickness. It also protects. The sharifs, with their high purity, can defeat the impurity of the jin by their mere presence, or by touch. The saliva of the sharif is considered pure, and if touched or swallowed by a sick person, it drives the impure element away. However, if the attack of impurity is an especially powerful one, and if the sharif's purity comes in direct contact with the afflicted person, the two contending powers might kill the patient. Therefore, in any ritual intended to eliminate impurity, the sharif has first to lose part of his purity, and he generally accomplishes this by coming in contact with people who are lower than he is. After lowering his charge, so to speak, he can then touch the sick person. In such situations the sick person has to be defiled also in order to better his chances for survival.

The sharifs agree that impure elements can attack one who is pure, such as a Muslim. But, they insist, any Muslim has to be in his lowest state of purity in order for such an attack to occur. And even if such an attack does take place, the sharifs believe that their purity can easily drive away impure elements. In this belief, the sharifs differ from the slaves. The slaves, like the sharifs, believe that the jin are impure and that they can attack the pure. However, according to the slaves, if a jin attacks a Muslim, that jin will possess his head, and there is no way to get rid of him. The jin will remain inside the Muslim's head, and is separated from him only after death. The only recourse is to appease the jin and give him what he wants in the hope that he will be gentle with the man whom he possesses.

The slaves classify the jin according to their place of origin, or watani. Some are Arabs, some are Somalis, some are Africans from the tribes of the interior, but none are Swahili. Each of these different groups of jin speaks the language of his native land, and in the ceremony performed in order to appease a jin, his own particular language is spoken. Similarly, each kind of jin wants to be given certain gifts. For example, the Arab jin like certain sea herbs. These jin, who are usually from Oman, like sick persons to dress in white with turban and sword. Thus, even if a patient is a woman, she has to put on these clothes, which are strictly for men in ordinary life. The ceremony for appeasing the jin is called *ngoma ya pepo,* or *ngoma ya sheitani.* Thirty years ago this ceremony was widely practiced in Lamu, but now it is not likely to happen more than once or twice a year.[10] This shows that the sharif ideology concerning the

10. Though the ngoma ya sheitani is full of symbolic aspects, which I think are important to analyze, I have neglected to do such an analysis here. I will deal with that

effectivity of their purity in defeating impurity has gained more support than the possession theory of the slaves.

It is also interesting that the slaves are the leaders of the ngoma ya sheitani, and that the wangwana men and women have been the main participants. This indicates that the wangwana ideology concerning purity and impurity is in a state of drastic decline. However, there is a place in the wangwana ideology that could be interpreted as allowing for the pure to be attacked by impure elements such as the jin. This we will see in the next chapter.

With this background, let us turn to the sharifs and try to analyze their rituals for the month of Ramadan. To do this we have to keep in mind their ideas concerning purity and impurity.

When the month of Ramadan begins, the sharifs separate from other adult non-sharifs, and yet they establish close relations with children of all strata. In the mandari, the children and the Jamalilil sharifs take a bath together, after which they eat together, as one group, while the wangwana and the slaves eat separately. This separation, however, does not take place in the first meal of the mandari, but only during the second. The difference between the first and the second meal is that the second takes place after bathing, and the sharif spits in the food. When the children consume this food, they are separated from everyone except the sharifs. The reason for this separation emerges more clearly in relation to the gift-giving involved in the mandari. The children are not allowed to go and take the gifts from their mothers; the sharifs have to act as intermediaries even if a boy's father is present. In that ceremony, the Jamalilil sharifs become the link between the *wangwana* and the *slaves* on the one hand, and the *children* on the other hand.

Children ←——→ Sharifs ←——→ Wangwana and Slaves

Fig. 31. Sharifs as Mediators in the Mandari

---

ceremony in a separate paper. The ngoma ya sheitani might be compared with the *zar.* I feel that the zar is a ceremony that has not yet been analyzed properly. It has been discussed from the psychological and even sociological points of view, but it has not been analyzed as a part of a wider symbolic system, i.e., culture. In other words, the relations between the symbols used in it and the messages are still unanalyzed.

After eating the food which has been charged with the sharifs' purity, the children are separated from everyone except the sharifs. At that point, the children are given a gift brought to them by their mothers. In order for the sharif to carry the gift to the child, he has to be in contact with a person from the outside world who has not shared in the sacred meal. Moreover, such a contact necessarily results in defilement. Thus, in contacting the women, the sharifs become defiled. So while the children are pure and undefiled, the sharifs are pure and defiled, and it is in this state that the sharifs have to return to the town. Still, immediately after the second meal, the sharifs enjoy a state of purity without defilement.

Those sharifs who join the mandari are the junior sharifs. The senior sharifs, especially the head of the Reiyadah, do not participate in the mandari. In fact, two or three days before Ramadan, the head of the Reiyadah disappears and during that time is not seen in the market or around the town. He prays by himself and has very limited contact with other people, even of his own group. The younger sharifs bring him food from the market and carry his messages to other people, but he himself is completely secluded.

Thus, here also, we find that the junior sharifs act as a link—this time between the head of the Reiyadah sharifs and the outside world. After the second meal, the head of the sharifs and the children have the same relationship with both the junior sharifs and the wangwana and slaves. Neither the children nor the head of the sharifs can contact the outside world except through the junior sharifs. However, the children are separated because they ate the food which was mixed with the sharif's purifying saliva, while the head of the Reiyadah Jamalilil sharifs is separated without eating any special food. We can say, therefore, that the spittle adds something to the children which makes them more like the head of the Reiyadah sharifs. And thus if we are able to discover the reason for their separation, we will also understand the separation of the head of the Reiyadah sharifs.

The children are separated from all others but the sharifs after they have eaten the food in which the sharif spat. Before eating this meal they have a bath; and after they eat the food, they are given a gift. Taking this ritual one element at a time, let us now define what a child (*kijana*) is, and then discuss the meaning of the bath.

In Lamu, a kijana, or child, is different from a *mtoto mchanga,* or little baby. The kijana is not a little baby, yet neither is he a *mtoto mzima,* an adult. The kijana differs from the baby in that he possesses senses and can express himself. From the religious point of view, the kijana is in the first stages of learning religion. Nevertheless, he is not yet completely responsible for his actions, since his brain, or ʻaql, is not yet well developed. And it is chiefly in that respect that he differs from the adult. The adult is responsible for his actions, his brain is developed, and he can choose for himself. He knows what is right and what is wrong. The child, on the other hand, has an undeveloped ʻaql and, therefore, has no power of choice. A child has to obey and accept orders without discussing them. This is why the child has to be protected. This inability to choose is important, since it is also one of the acknowledged characteristics of prophets and angels. However, while the prophets and angels disdain the power of choice, the child is only temporarily dependent on someone else to make choices for him. Nevertheless, if we separate the child from those who usually make choices for him, then we have a human being without the power of choice. The child is then as pure as the angels and prophets. In Lamu, this is one of the highest degrees of purity.

The children in Lamu achieve that purity only after taking a bath with the sharifs; the bath ritually cleanses both from defilement. Then the children eat the food containing the sharif's spittle. The sharif's spittle is considered very pure and efficacious. If someone is sick, his relatives often approach a sharif with a cup in their hands and ask him to spit in the cup; this is then given to the sick man. This is called the Prophet's cup (*kombe ya Mtumi*), and it is only effective if the spittle is that of a sharif. Sickness is caused either by the evil eye (*husuda*), or by the interference of malevolent jin; both are said to disturb the balance of the body and cause sickness. The Prophet's cup helps to get rid of the sickness by driving away the original cause of the disturbance. The cause of sickness is impurity, whether it comes from the evil eye or a malevolent jin. The sharif's spittle restores the person's purity and causes him to overcome his sickness. There is a relation between that spittle and the Qur'ān. When the sharif spits, he reads certain verses of the Qur'ān. The Qur'ān and the saliva of the sharif are both light; both share in the eternal light, which exists at a very high degree of purity.

Thus, when the children eat the food that has been mixed with the spittle, they too reach a high degree of purity, a purity which the wangwana and the slaves who eat the same food could never achieve, since they do not share in the ritual bath. Thus, the children, like the head of the Reiyadah sharifs, are separated from their own relatives and from society in general. However, the separation of the children expresses something more than that. They are chosen to be separated and classified with the sharifs because they alone, of all the groups, are most similar to them.

In Lamu, people characterize the relation between God and the vijana[11] as one of love. The vijana are loved by God, and in turn they love Him, even though they are not able to express that love in words. These ideas are expressed in the idiom of purity. For example, when one of the vijana dies, he is not washed. The people say that a child will go directly to heaven and become there one of the birds of paradise. God allows children to intervene on behalf of their parents, and to ask Him for mercy. For this reason, the people of Lamu have the elaborate ritual of *'aqiqa,* that ritual through which the living establish a relation with their dead male children. If a child dies when he is young, around seven or eight years old, his parents have to make the aqiqa for him. A cow has to be slaughtered and food has to be prepared for the people who read parts of the Qur'ān during the ritual. After the meal the people name the child, in this way establishing a realtion between the child and his parents. Even if the parents are divorced, they have to come together on that day and sit beside each other and feed each other. The man puts the food in the mouth of the woman, and vice versa. The ritual is elaborate, and I will not describe it in detail here. The point that I want to stress is that the male children are considered pure and believed to have the right of intervention, the right to ask God to bestow mercy on their parents and to forgive them. As we have already seen, this right of intervention, or shafa'ah, was originally given only to Mohammed. But now, it appears that the dead vijana and Mohammed both have it. Besides, while the Prophet lives in the barzakh, or intermediate realm, the dead vijana live in paradise. In other words, they have no need for resurrection. They are already in paradise and can intervene with God at any time, while the Prophet is able to petition God only after the resurrection. Generally speaking, then, the vijana, when separated from this world, have a high degree of purity tantamount to that of the Prophet. They are loved by God and can intervene just as the Prophet can.

In the course of time these conditions change. When the vijana grow older and develop the power of choice, their purity decreases and they no longer have this close relationship with God. However, as was apparent in the myth, all "choice" is connected with earth and therefore with the world of relative knowledge—in the end, with nature. As the children grow older, they move closer to nature and further away from absolute knowledge or culture. Still, there are degrees of involvement in both nature and culture. And as long as a particular child does not yet have the power of choice among relative things (*nature*), he is

11. *Vijana* is the plural form of *kijana.*

recognized as one who is closer than most to heaven and culture. The vijana are pure; they are like Adam in paradise before the creation of Eve. They are connected with God through absolute knowledge, and so if they die while still in that state they cease to be the children of their parents until the aqiqa ritual is performed reconnecting them. Before that ritual they would be directly related to God; they would be His children. And He would love them as He did Mohammed. In other words, both Mohammed and the dead vijana are thought to have ritual kinship with God.

The sharifs have a very high degree of purity, but they have a brain which, if used, lowers that purity and makes it less effective. Naturally, in everyday life, the sharifs have to use their brains to interact with other people. But this means that the amount of purity they have at such times is not very different from that of ordinary people. In Ramadan, the month of the Qur'ān and the month of God, everything is elevated in purity, and so, the sharifs, in order to be able to communicate with Mohammed or God, have to be separated from their society where they would be forced to "make choices." At the beginning of the month of Ramadan, after the sunset prayer, the Reiyadah sharifs visit their head and then begin their separation from society. They discard their power of choice, something which the head of Reiyadah has already achieved days before Ramadan, so that when the younger sharifs visit him, they get a charge of his purity. And so it is that during Ramadan the sharifs have especially high purity, higher even than the children.

It is important to note the difference between the sharifs and the children. The sharifs, as I have said, think they have a minimal amount of purity that they cannot lose. This stable, basic amount of purity has come to them because they are the sons of Mohammed. Still, they can increase this purity through religious education and other means which we have already outlined. By contrast, the children have no way to increase their purity; in fact, the older they get, the less purity they have, because it is inevitable that their brains develop and become capable of the power of choice. Thus, while the sharifs have a stable amount of purity, the vijana necessarily have a dwindling amount. But the sharif's amount of purity can be increased—and to do that he has to be like Mohammed under the Throne, as pure as light, and as obedient as the angels.

Mohammed under the Throne had no relation with this world (for it was not yet created). So when the sharifs want to achieve such a high degree of purity, they have to be separated completely from all social life. But this is practically impossible since they are living on earth. Additionally, even separation involves the concept of making a choice. In other words, they have to make a choice not to make a choice. This is a contradiction, and so the only way to separate themselves without making a choice is to come in contact with the only pure group which has no power of choice—the vijana. The ceremony of the mandari involves a kind of substitution. The vijana have to take the sharifs' place, and the sharifs have to act like the vijana—they have to act like children. The vijana need someone to make choices for them on this earth while they are still without that power. And, in turn, during Ramadan, the sharifs need to become children of God as the dead vijana would be.

The gifts which are given to the children by their mothers reflect this view of things. The sharifs have the right to intervene between the society and the children. (They carry the gifts.) But, in order to do that, they first have to be defiled. Still their head remains pure and without defilement, like the children after the sacred meal and before they receive the gift. The gift is defiling. It defiles the sharifs, and this is intentionally done, for, if the sharifs are to be left in that high state of purity, they, and the vijana, might die. The only way to get out of this dangerous situation is to be defiled. In the mandari, the saving defilement is transferred from society at large to the sharifs and from the sharifs to the children.

The fear of allowing pure ones such as the children and the sharifs to remain in a high state of purity without defilement is found in other contexts. To make this clear, let me explain some specific cases. For example, immediately after the birth of a male child, the call for a prayer (*adhan*) is made in the child's right ear, while the call for people to stand for prayer (*iqama*) is made in his left ear. In the call for prayer, God and Mohammed are the only figures mentioned, but the iqama calls all the Muslims to leave everything and come to perform their prayers. Thus the call in the left ear is related to this world. Another example: the baby who is born pure has his face covered with black (*muru*). This is done after the baby is washed. After covering his face with muru, the child is given to his mother. The mother is still bleeding and thus is defiled; the child becomes defiled through contact with her.

The baby, like the sharifs and vijana, is in a very critical ritual state. He is marginal, or *liminaire*, existing on the "threshold." They are neither in nor out; their position is uncertain and unstable, and therefore, dangerous and contagious. If the vijana and sharifs turned to absolute purity, they would not be able to live in our world. Absolute purity is achieved only after death, not before it. So to increase the amount of their purity would automatically transfer them to a certain degree from this world to the next. To stop them from moving in that direction, they have to be defiled. This is the reason why an earthly object (the gift) has to be given to the sharifs in order to defile them, and why the sharifs give it in turn to the vijana. Both the sharifs and the vijana are in precarious positions. So before the sharifs and the children return to the town, they must be defiled.

When the sharifs enter the town, they go to their mosque and make ablutions and pray. Then, they go and visit their leader. After this visit, which as we have seen charges them with purity, the sharifs are separated from everyone, even the children, and in fact, at that point, they are all symbolically dead. They are the dead vijana, or children of God. To increase the degree of purity more than that they actually would have to die.

The sharifs have to maintain a position where they could symbolically express that they are still alive. And, here lies the meaning of the sharifs' weekly change of position from the right side of the niche to the left side. At the right side they express their relationship with God and at the same time make the point that they are extremely pure. They are in contact with the origin of all eternal light. However, on Thursday nights they sit on the left side of the niche, thus reestablishing their relationship with Mohammed, who has lived on earth, and is their ancestor. They thereby stress the idea that their light is subordinate to the light of Mohammed. In other words, they stress the idea of descent, and this is an earthly concept. In addition, they use musical instruments which, as they say, express the same joy (*furaha*) and satisfaction which Mohammed expressed for these same musical instruments when he was alive on earth. The musical instruments, and the joy and satisfaction as well, are all related to Mohammed in his earthly life. Consequently, in a symbolic way the sharifs express their earthly nature. The change of position keeps the sharifs in contact with the world and reduces the degree of purity they accumulated during the week to a safe level.

Nevertheless, during Ramadan the sharifs achieve a degree of purity higher than that of the qutb. They reach that height by being incorporated and unified with the vijana. The group is divided into those who have a stable amount of purity (the sharifs and the dead vijana) and those who are eventually going to lose their purity (the living vijana). While the sharifs are completely separated from the wider society after they visit their leader, the children have to come in contact with their parents after they return to their houses. Thus, while the sharifs have a direct relationship with the center of stable purity, the vijana are the only members of the society who have high amounts of unstable purity. So in this case the children serve as the channel through which a certain amount of purity is transferred to the parents.

The important difference between those who have stable amounts of purity and those who have unstable amounts is recognized in the mandari meal. The sharifs, who have a stable amount of purity, spit in the food, which is then eaten by those who have an unstable amount of purity. Thus the children are able to share in the stable purity of the sharifs and yet are still like their fathers in that they have an unstable amount of purity. Through separation, the sharifs accumulate a degree of purity which is higher than that of anyone else. They are, for that reason, dangerous even to the children who share a high degree of purity with them.

This degree of purity is intensified in the mosque when the sharifs sit on the right side under the Throne with the Qur'ān. It is a seating position which the sharifs occupy only during Ramadan. The sharif's relation with the children is intensified, and the children are elevated to a higher degree, while the ordinary people are lower than both the sharifs and the children. In the darassa, each degree of purity is recognized in the seating arrangement in the mosque, and each group is separated from the other by the space left between them. The children are separated from the sharifs, and the ordinary people are separated from their own children. Kinship and hishima have no role to play in this; the wangwana and the slaves share the same place: they sit side by side. The sharifs have the highest purity and consequently are the only group encompassing the Qur'ān. In the darassa we find that there is a space that separates the children from the sharifs, and also one that separates the sharifs from the wangwana. These empty spaces between the different groups are extremely relevant; they have an important function—to keep contact between the groups at a minimum. In the mosque, where purity is intensified, any contact is dangerous, and therefore these open spaces are necessary. In the mosque we have a continuum of purity realized in front of our eyes. Over the head of the sharifs there is the sign of God; the young children sit facing them; the wangwana sit behind the children, and in the back of the wangwana are the toilets, the area of continuous defilement. In this situation, it is also plain that purity and impurity are the opposite ends of a continuum and not two separate and inherited entities.

The sharifs observe their Friday ritual inside the Reiyadah Mosque. This is a ceremony exclusively for the sharifs, and in it we find that they sit on the left side of the niche, with the space between them and their children eliminated. In this ritual we are dealing with sharifs who share in a minimum amount of purity which they can never lose. Secondly, when the adult sharifs sit on the left side of the niche, they are trying to reduce the amount of purity which they have accumulated. For these reasons, contact between the sharifs and the children is not dangerous.

Now let us turn our attention to the Rodha Mosque. As we have seen, the Rodha Mosque is one of the mosques in the Mkomani half of the town, and it is used exclusively by the wangwana. The leader of darassa there is a sharif from the Mahdali family. In fact, he is the half brother of one of the Reiyadah sharifs. The Mahdali sharifs, it will be remembered, consider themselves to be part of the wangwana. During the darassa the sharif-leader sits with his back against the right side of the niche. There is a very small space left between him and the children who sit in a line perpendicular to his left hand. Directly behind the children sit the wangwana, with no space separating them from the children.

If we compare the seating at this darassa (Fig. 24) with that of the Reiyadah sharifs (Fig. 23), we find that the Reiyadah sharifs sit facing a middle group of children, while the Mahdali sharifs sit at right angles to them. In other words, if we turn the row of Reiyadah sharifs around, we will still have two separate rows which cannot be included in each other; while, if we do this with the Mahdali sharif, he will be included in the children's row. This is very important, since, if we consider as well the lack of separating spaces between the different groups, we find that we have a very nice expression of the wangwana's idea of purity.

The wangwana believe that the sharifs have no purity which is different from their own. In fact, for the wangwana, being an Arab is enough to assure purity. From this perspective the sharif and the mngwana have the same amount of purity. The sharif sits in the place of an 'ālim. His position does not convey the idea that he is inherently higher in purity than the wangwana, but simply that he is higher because he is an 'ālim. In other words, if there were an 'ālim other than the Mahdali sharif to give the darassa, then he would sit directly in the same place.

The wangwana believe that during Ramadan both the sharifs and the wangwana discard nature, both therefore achieving the same degree of purity. The sharif and the wangwana alike come from the white dust and both share in the same purity. However, because the sharif as an 'ālim does not get involved in everyday life, in ordinary times he has a higher purity than the wangwana; but during Ramadan, when the wangwana also discard their relative knowledge, all are equal to the sharif.

Besides, in the wangwana mosque, all the children are wangwana children. This is different from the situation in the darassa of the Reiyadah sharifs, where the children of the wangwana sit beside the children of the slaves. In Reiyadah, purity and impurity have nothing to do with origin, color, or ethnicity, and the only separate and distinct group in the Reiyadah darassa is that of the Jamalilil sharifs.

Nevertheless, both the Reiyadah sharifs and the wangwana think that the month of Ramadan elevates them to a relatively higher degree of purity, one which they do not normally have. Yet, while the Reiyadah sharifs have a ritual meal, after which they are set apart from everyone, the wangwana and their sharifs have no such meal. In fact, those wangwana who are usually set apart from the others following the traditional stratificatory system are mixed together in Ramadan. The fact that they are all pure overcomes all social stratification. The sharifs, on the other hand, who claim that they are higher in purity, are set apart in Ramadan and have to avoid contact with non-sharifs, even though on ordinary days they have to act as equals. In this scheme all the non-sharifs, wangwana and slave alike, are classified together as unequal. And this represents, surely, the greatest threat to the old wangwana stratificatory system.

The Reiyadah sharifs believe that all non-sharif adults can be elevated in purity by means of their own spittle. Through that spittle, they give the children something of themselves, some of their own purity, which the children pass on to their parents. And thus all of Lamu is elevated in purity by these junior sharifs. During Ramadan, the junior sharifs maintain a continuous relation with the center of purity and obtain their purity through him. Through the darassa they are able to transfer a part of their purity to the others, but this has to be done through a highly pure medium—the children. So, during Ramadan, the sharifs are the donors who contribute to the high ritual status of the town as a whole. The children are the only group who have the power to carry that purity and deliver it to all people who live in Lamu. In other words, during Ramadan, the children do the job that is the sharifs' on ordinary days. But the amount of purity received by the non-sharifs depends on the amount that the children can carry. During Ramadan, the children are treated with respect and love. Assuming the position of the sharifs in ordinary times, the children become an asset, and the necessity to please and satisfy them sometimes works hardship on the father and mother. This is clearly the case in relation to the gift given to the children. If the mother does not have anough money, she has to borrow it, and no one can refuse to give her money to buy the gift. The children have to be pleased, so they will carry the purity from the sharifs to their family.

The wangwana, on the other hand, believe that they have inherent purity and that by the mere act of discarding relative knowledge and abandoning their relations with the world, they can raise themselves up to the highest level of purity. They do not need any such ritual as the mandari. The month of

Ramadan is not considered by them to be essentially different from other months, yet by their activities and by the goal of purity which they set for themselves during that month, they change it into a sacred month.

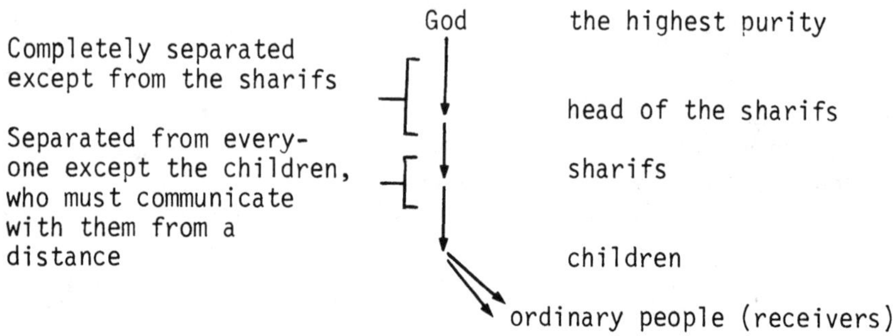

Fig. 32. The Distribution of Purity During Ramadan

Now let us turn to the rituals that end the month of Ramadan. Such rituals are not performed in the wangwana mosques. They are solely sharif rituals. In the iḥya' ritual the head of the Reiyadah sharifs sits on the left side of the niche, and all the junior Jamalilil sharifs who participate in the ritual also sit on the left side. Yet while the junior sharifs mix with children and adults from all of Lamu's social categories, the head of the Reiyadah is still set apart. In this ritual, the junior sharifs mix with non-sharifs for the first time, and for the first time the head of the sharifs sits on the left side of the niche in the presence of other people. This ritual marks the transition of the sharifs from seclusion and separation to their everyday position. The junior sharifs also make that transition. In fact, they are the ones who have to channel the transition of their leader. They not only change their seating position but also come in contact with other people who have been previously excluded. Now the head of the sharifs sits on the left side under the Prophet's light, which is eternal yet still connected with earth through the humanity of the Prophet. In the iḥya', the sharifs have to make that transition from the eternal to the ephemeral. The time expressed in that transition is different from the time that we normally experience—it is a duration or indivisible time. It is like mythical time, when things "are" and "are not" simultaneously. For that reason, we find many items of the ritual reversed. For example, in ordinary times, the sharifs, if any are present, have to begin the rituals. It is considered very bad for an ordinary person to presume to begin a ritual in the presence of a sharif. But, in the iḥya', the ordinary persons have to begin the rituals. At that time, no sharif is allowed to initiate the recitation of the Qur'ān. The sharifs have to give their recitation after the non-sharifs. The order of offering the food is also reversed. The sharifs drink coffee and eat popcorn after all the members of the circle clearly indicate that something is to be transferred from the non-sharifs to the sharifs. Here it is also relevant to point out that while the junior sharifs drink more than one cup of coffee and eat more than one portion of popcorn, the head of the sharifs drinks only one cup of coffee and eats only once from the popcorn. Usually, the head has the first cup of coffee and the best of the popcorn, but in the iḥya' he is given the heeltaps of everyone's coffee and the leftover popcorn. This is the exact reverse of what the junior sharifs did in the mandari.

In these two rituals saliva plays important but reversed roles. In the mandari the sharif puts his saliva in the food and then the participants eat it, while in the iḥya' the sharif drinks the remains of the coffee which has been in contact with the saliva of all the participants. In the mandari, the sharif gives the participants a pot full of food, while in the iḥya' they give him the leftovers. As I said before, the Jamalilil sharifs, and especially their head, are considered purer than anyone else. Yet the participants in the iḥya' give them, and their leader, the leftovers of the popcorn, and the coffee cups that have been in contact with people who are in no way equal to them in purity. Furthermore, in the course of the iḥya', the sharifs inside each of the circles 4–5–6–7–8 drink from the coffee cups after the non-sharifs have used them.

In these circles, sharifs and non-sharifs are seated together. Toward the end of the ritual, the cup in group 8 is given to the sharif in group 7; it then passes from group to group in this manner until it ends up in group 1. There, a non-sharif puts the leftover coffee from his group into his cup, and then gives it to group 2; someone there does the same thing. The same process is repeated in each of the circles through the eighth and final one. Then the last sharif gives the cup to the head of the Reiyadah sharifs. The head of the Reiyadah drinks from the cup, which contains the leftover coffee of all the groups. He drinks the leftovers of those who have no stable amount of purity, as well as those who, like himself, do have it because they are sharifs. An empty basket is passed around in a counterclockwise direction and then filled in a clockwise movement with what is left of the popcorn. In both cases, the head of the sharifs is given something which has to be discarded or discharged by those persons doing the giving. Though the participants are lower in purity in comparison to the head of the sharifs, they are still pure and undefiled.

At this point in the analysis, it is necessary to return to the part of the ritual which takes place before the food is given to the head of the Reiyadah. At that time the Qur'ān is read by each group and moves around the circle in a counterclockwise fashion, while the food inside each group moves clockwise.

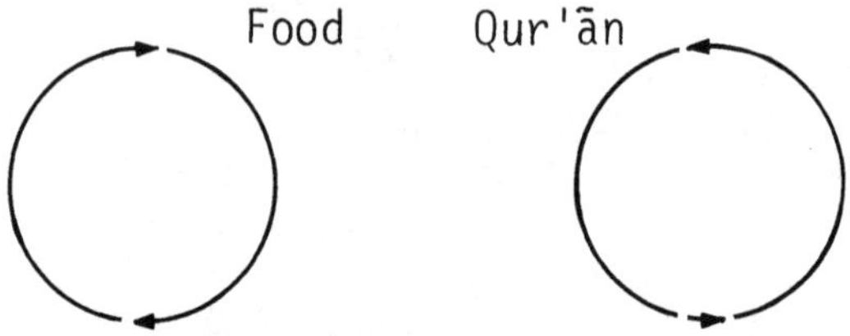

Fig. 33. The Movement of the Qur'ān and Food Inside Each Group

Inside each group, when a person finishes reciting his section of the Qur'ān, he always passes it to his right, while the food is always passed to the left. However, the Qur'ān recitation *as a whole* goes from right to left, i.e., in a clockwise direction. After the Qur'ān and the food have been circulated, the Reiyadah sharif makes the invocations.

Thus, in the iḥya' ritual we have five movements: (1) the movement of the Qur'ān inside each circle, which is counterclockwise; (2) the movement of the empty cup and basket, which is counterclockwise; (3) the movements of the full cup and baset, which are clockwise; (4) the movement of the Qur'ān, as a whole, also in a clockwise direction; (5) and finally, the movement of food inside each circle, which is clockwise.

From the above, we can observe that the recitation of the Qur'ān inside each group goes in the same direction as the empty cup and basket, while the full cup and basket rotate in the same direction as the original distribution of the Qur'ān.

Now let us look closely at each of these five movements. The recitation of the Qur'ān inside each circle (1) indicates that the Qur'ān can be divided into small parts; where one person stops reading another begins. Here each individual is distinguished by the temporal sequence of the recitation, he is either "before" or "after." And in this respect, the second movement (2) resembles the first

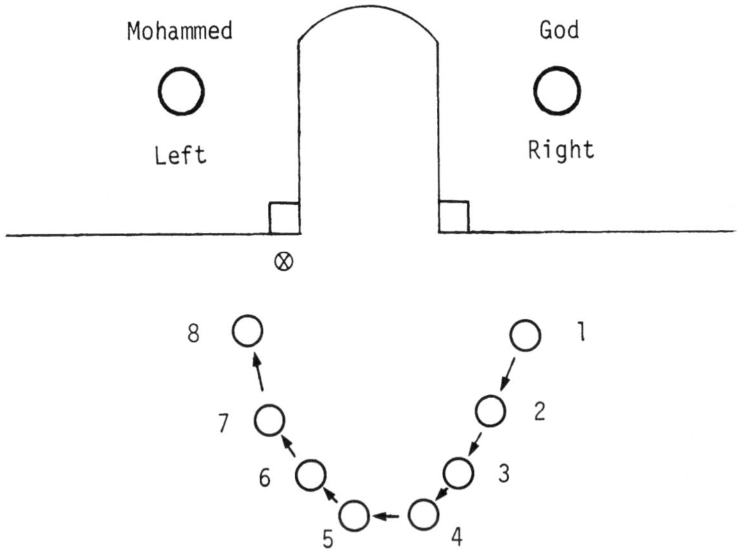

Fig. 34. The Recitation of the Qur'ān in the Iḥya

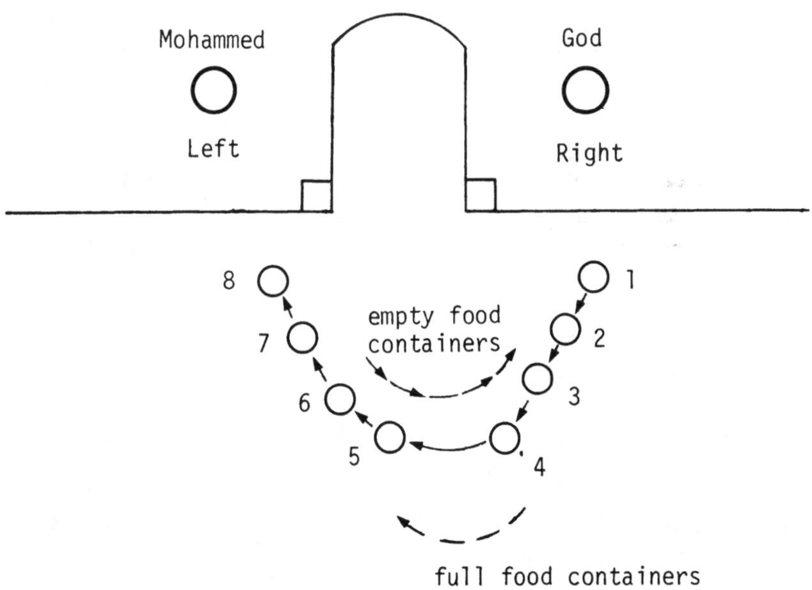

Fig. 35. The Movements of the Qur'ān and Food in the Iḥya

(1)—only in the second the distinguishable elements are groups rather than individuals. The cup and the basket have to pass from one group to the next in a sequence; yet when they are empty, those who receive them are still full (charged), and the cup and basket cannot be filled until they reverse their direction. Thus, we have the cup and basket before being filled (discharged) and the cup and basket after being filled (charged). And, after they have been filled, those persons who have been full (charged) are left empty. So, while clockwise movement indicates that the group is still full (charged), the counterclockwise movement indicates that it is empty (discharged).

The ritual of iḥya' begins with a counterclockwise movement (charged, full), but ends with a clockwise one (discharged, empty) that involves all the groups. All the clockwise or discharging movements (3)(4)(5) are movements that have *not* been initiated by a sharif; instead they are directed toward and *end with* a sharif. Of the counterclockwise or charging movement, (1) is not initiated by a sharif, while (2) is. This may indicate that both the non-sharifs and the junior sharifs are full or charged. In (3)(4)(5), we find that the non-sharifs end their movements with a sharif or discharge something into him. The food inside each group is given to a non-sharif first; then the rest is eaten by a sharif. No movement ends with a non-sharif except that of the empty basket and cup, but these are to be filled and sent back to a sharif, leaving the givers empty, or discharged. Even the junior sharifs give (discharge) the rest of their coffee and popcorn to the head of the sharifs. The only movement initiated by the junior sharifs is the one of the empty cup and basket. It goes from left to right. This movement comes immediately before the end of the ritual, after the whole Qur'ān has been read.

As I have said, during Ramadan, the sharifs sit on the right side of the niche under the Throne, in direct relation to the highest purity. After Ramadan, the sharifs send an empty basket and cup to the non-sharifs, who sit close to that sacred place. This movement of the empty basket and cup initiated by the sharifs resembles the movement of the recitation of the Qur'ān inside each group. So it is appropriate to ask if there is any relation between the divisibility of the Qur'ān and that which the junior sharifs and the non-sharifs want to discharge. The only thing which all participants have in common is a degree of purity which is higher than the amount needed for ordinary life, the ordinary life in which sharifs and non-sharifs have to come in close contact with each other.

During Ramadan, people are classified and separated from each other on the basis of the amount of purity they have. At the beginning of Ramadan, the sharifs and the children form one group, yet the sharifs are still so pure that they have to be separated from the rest of society. However, by the time Ramadan ends the ordinary people have accumulated a degree of purity which enables them to sit beside the sharifs. They sit on the left side of the mosque, while the sharifs sit on the right side. There is some danger that the sharifs' proximity to the highest purity could intensify their purity to such a degree that they might hurt the non-sharifs. Thus, by sending the empty cup and basket, the junior sharifs express symbolically their intention to discard the unneeded amount of purity which keeps them out of contact with ordinary people. As a group, the sharifs are united and elevated in purity through their direct connection with the highest purity, and the Qur'ān is the one thing that connects them and unifies them as a group. During Ramadan, the sharifs have a superadded charge of purity; they are not only the people of the house whom God keeps clean, but also the owners of the Qur'ān. After it is over they want to return to their ordinary life as sharifs with a stable amount of purity.

By dividing up and initiating the recitation of the Qur'ān in their groups, the non-sharifs express to the sharifs that this is the highest position they can have if they want the ordinary people to communicate with them without being endangered. If the sharifs did not return to their ordinary life, things would have to be reversed.[12] This action is performed by the non-sharifs while the sharifs are still seated on the right side of the niche, and therefore it is an appeal to God to let the sharifs return to their ordinary life, so they can keep everything in its suitable predestined place. At this point, the sharifs, who are loved by the Prophet and who are rightfully the leaders, are the followers. In this state of extremely high purity they can lead no one without harming him. It is necessary for them to return to their normal state if anyone is to communicate with them.

Now, if we look at movements (1) and (2), we find that they express division and multiplicity. The Qur'ān, which as the word of God is indivisible, is divided up among at least fifty people. The coffee and popcorn are also distributed among just as many persons. By way of contrast, the other movements (3)(4)(5) express a unity which cannot be easily divided. If we begin from (5), we find that the multiplicity of food and coffee is the factor that unifies not only the members of one group, but all the groups, since all eat the same popcorn and drink the same coffee. In the final step of the ritual (3), the unity of

12. The reversal would be impossible since it would hurt the Prophet and his descendants, which as I said before, is considered on of the most harmful sins.

the eight groups is expressed in the unity of the food and coffee which are given to the head of the sharifs. No one could distinguish among the various pieces of popcorn given by the different groups and say that this or that popcorn is given by this or that group. And, of course, the same is true with the coffee.

Let us now turn our attention to movement (4). As I have already shown, in Ramadan the purity of the sharifs depends on their relation with the highest light, their relation with God and the Qur'ān. During Ramadan, they call themselves "the owners of the Qur'ān," and not the descendants of the Prophet. Of course, being the descendants of the Prophet is what gave them the chance to be the owners of the Qur'ān, but in Ramadan they stand *primarily* in relation with God and the Qur'ān and not with the Prophet, as is usually the case. This is the reason why the weekly Maulidi is not celebrated at all during Ramadan. In that month the Prophet functions no longer as an end in himself but only as a means. The sharifs' high degree of purity is the result of this special relation with God and the Qur'ān. During Ramadan, the sharifs are able to give some of their purity to the non-sharifs through the children. And, through the children, part of the sharifs' purity is transferred to all those ordinary people who attend the darassa, and even to the wider circle of all those who live in the Reiyadah and Langoni mtaa. In this way, the sharifs are able to transmit their purity to a very wide group of Lamuans.

At the end of Ramadan, all those who have any relation with the sharifs have to attend the iḥya'. They all read the Qur'ān as one indivisible group, in one indivisible moment. Those who read the first parts of the Qur'ān are seated in those circles on the right side of the niche, while those who read the last parts are in the circles on the left side of the niche. The head of the Reiyadah sharifs sits down under the shade of Mohammed with the Qur'ān, as a single unit, in front of him. The movement of the reading is directed toward him. The highest purity returns as one unit to that person who alone is able to communicate with the highest reality and who is able to bring this purity down to earth. In the iḥya', all the groups give that purity back to him. They discharge it in front of him. Even the junior sharifs participate, for they too want to return their superadded purity to their head. When the people finish with the recitation, they shout together: "There is no God but Allah, there is no God but Allah, there is no God but Allah. Allah is great." (*La ilaha illa Allah, La ilaha illa Allah, La ilaha illa Allah. Allah Akbar.*)

The head of the Reiyadah sharifs has to read the invocations, which are called the "conclusion of the great Qur'ān." Then he is given the popcorn and coffee. The sequence of these two actions is important. The sharif is first given the

Qur'ān as a whole and then he is given the popcorn and coffee which have been collected from every group. All the groups empty their unneeded purity into him, and they give him the Qur'ān as an indivisible unit. The sharif is then charged with more purity than he had before the ritual began. And, for that reason, he must be separated; he is quite dangerous. Other rituals have to be performed in order to get him out of his forced seclusion, as we will see.

Yet, the junior sharifs feel relief after they have passed onto their head the superadded purity which has kept them out of contact with ordinary people for a whole month. The sharifs, like everyone else, look forward to the month of Ramadan; nevertheless, they are always eager to have it come to an end. All the people, including the sharifs, want to return to their ordinary life, and I think one of my friends from Lamu was not wrong when, speaking about the iḥya', he said: "Ramadan is over and people are happy to return to their old life." In fact, the word "iḥya'" is derived from *ḥaya*,[13] which means life; so the iḥya' ritual is one marking the return to life.

In order to go even further into the meaning of the iḥya' ritual, I would like to refer to another ritual that is usually performed by the sharifs during ordinary times. The ritual which we will now consider is performed for those sick persons who have been afflicted with an impure power. The sharif is brought in to drive this power away, so the sick person can return to his normal life. In other words, this ritual, which is called *ku zinguka*[14] or *kuta hijabu*, is performed in order to help a sick person separate the impure element from himself and overcome it. The separation of the impure element is the primary reason for the ritual. This ritual appears to be the reverse of the iḥya'. If we compare the two rituals, we might be able to uncover their common deep structure.

The curing ritual is performed by a junior sharif who is accompanied by seven adult non-sharif males. First of all, the sick person takes a ritual bath; then he has to be dressed in white, and to sit facing the north. The sharif sits behind the sick person, around whom the seven non-sharifs form a semicircle. The sharif begins the ritual by reciting certain parts of the Qur'ān. Then the man to his right takes up the reading and passes it in this fashion through all seven non-sharifs back to the sharif. Before the end of the recitation, a bowl of raw rice is sent to the room and is given to the person who sits to the left of the sharif. That person receives the bowl with his right hand and takes some of the rice

13. The name Eve (Hawia) is derived from the same root.

14. In Chapter 7, I will deal with a ritual called *Kuzingu Kuzinguka Ngombe;* the reader must not confuse the *Ku Zinguka* with the above ritual since they—as we will see—are different.

with his left, and then passes it to the person sitting on his left, and so on. When the bowl is given to the sharif, however, he takes the rice with his right hand. At a certain point, the sharif begins to throw rice on the sick person, using his right hand, and this movement is picked up by the person to his right who does the same thing, only using his left hand and so on. While the bowl of rice rotates around the group in a clockwise direction, the action of throwing the rice goes counterclockwise. This is followed by the sharif spitting on the sick person, a movement that is repeated by the non-sharifs, again in a counterclockwise direction. The ritual concludes with everyone calling God three times, "*La ilaha illa Allah, Allah Akbar,*" and then saying, "Oh, God, make it easy for us, You are merciful and great." After that the sharif and seven non-sharifs read together certain verses of the Qur'ān. Finally, the sharif makes the invocation. Rose water is then sprinkled on the sick person, the sharif, and all others present. The sick person then leaves the room to take a ritual bath; this is a necessary step before he can resume his ordinary life.

In the above ritual we find four movements:

(1) the sharif begins the recitation of the Qur'ān, and it moves counterclockwise (full, separation);

(2) the rice is received by a non-sharif, and moves clockwise (empty, unification);

(3) the sharif throws the rice and the others follow counterclockwise (full, separation);

(4) the sharif spits and the others follow counterclockwise (full, separation).

In contrast to the iḥya', the Ku Zinguka ritual begins with a sharif reciting the Qur'ān, and then passing it around counterclockwise (1). Also, while in the iḥya' the sharifs initiate one movement (that of the empty cup and the empty basket), in the ku zinguka the sharif initiates three of the movements (1)(3)(4). All the movements initiated by the sharif are counterclockwise, and the one initiated by a non-sharif is clockwise.

The counterclockwise movements in the iḥya' are all designed to separate and divide the giver from the receiver. The movement of the empty basket and the empty cup separates the groups with the sharifs from the groups without the sharifs. Also, in the iḥya', a person passes an empty cup and basket to someone who has a full cup and basket. Both the giver and the receiver could have filled the cup, but they do not; they have to wait for the cup and the basket to return full. As the cup and basket are filled, they go around the circle, again in a clockwise movement. So the counterclockwise movement leaves the giver and the receiver with their own cups still full, while the clockwise movement leaves them with empty cups.

The aim of the iḥya' is to separate something from the participants and give it back to the only one who could handle it. The head of the Reiyadah sharifs is the only one who can carry the excess purity, and, therefore, all the movements indicating the intention of discharging something and unifying it in him, i.e., all clockwise movements, are directed either to that head or to one of his junior representatives. The other movements are counterclockwise and directed toward the non-sharifs. We find again that the counterclockwise movements are intended to separate something from the performers and carry it to the one person for whom the ritual is performed.

In the ku zinguka, the sharif begins the ritual with a counterclockwise movement. In fact, all the counterclockwise movements in the whole ritual are begun by the sharif. Thus, at the beginning of the ritual the sharif as much as announces that he is the only one who is full, and therefore the only one who can discharge something onto the sick person. The movement of the bowl of rice in a clockwise fashion indicates that the non-sharifs are empty—although through that movement, they become united. This is the sole movement initiated by a non-sharif.

Throughout the ritual the stress is put on the sharif. The sharif is full, and he has to separate something from himself. He throws the rice, which he carries in his right (purified) hand. This indicates that he separates and throws something pure; the non-sharifs follow suit, but throw the rice on the sick person with the left (defiled) hand. The sharif donates purity and absence of defilement. The non-sharifs donate defilement. Again, the sharif spits on the sick person, and we know that the sharif's saliva is highly pure. The others spit on the person but their saliva is highly defiling. So, while the sharif gives the person purity, the others defile him. These are the crucial elements in the ritual. Purity has to overcome impurity. The presence of these two forces is clear in the manner in which each person grasps the rice. While the sharif does it with his right hand, the others do it with their left hands.

The question now is: Why are the seven non-sharifs included in the ritual in the first place? The high purity of the sharif is dangerous if it comes into direct contact with the impurity of the sick person. So, the non-sharifs' presence is important; they have the job of defiling the pure material thrown by the sharif, rice or saliva. Defilement is not the opposite of purity, and so the two do not cancel out each other; instead, defilement prevents the sick person from being completely destroyed by the high purity of the sharif. In other words, defilement facilitates the unification of the purity of the sharif in the sick person.

For the people of Lamu, the contact of purity and defilement is the core of human life on earth. The sharifs are the only people who can intentionally play with purity—give it out and take it in. They are the children of God, the children of Mohammed, and the owners of the Qur'ān. They leave very few resources for others to manipulate.

At the end of the ritual, rose water is used, which indicates that the impure power has been driven away, and that the whole group, including the sharif, is in a normal state. There is one more step for the sick person, however; he has to have a ritual bath in order to get rid of the defilement caused by the impure elements, the defilement of the saliva of the non-sharifs. The purity of the sharif is able to overcome the impurity of the jin; or, harking back to the language of the creation myth, one could say that light defeats fire once more.

In the above analysis, I have tried to show that ritual movement has meanings and to demonstrate what these meanings are. If we understand the language of the rituals, then we will be able not only to decode what we observe, but also to predict the kinds of movements which are likely to be used in other rituals. Furthermore, if we analyze the sama' ritual and compare it with the iḥya' and the ku zinguka, we will be able to define the ritual status of the sharifs in general and of the head of the Reiyadah sharifs in particular. Through that, we should be able to penetrate the patterning of relations in the community.

In the sama', the head of the Reiyadah sharifs sits facing the middle of the niche, and to his right sit the junior Reiyadah sharifs, while the Ḥusseini, the Mahdali, and the wangwana sit on his left. In this ritual, the Fatiḥa is read by the Roudini sharif (7) (Fig. 29). The incense is put into the fire by the head of the Reiyadah sharifs. The ritual begins with these two sharifs (7) and ⊗ working together, even though the Reiyadah sharif has to wait for the Roudini sharif and the others to read the Fatiḥa, before he can put in the incense. To end the ritual, the head of the Reiyadah sharifs makes the invocation, and then the Roudini sharif (7) reads the Fatiḥa along with the others. And, in this case, the roles are reversed; the Roudini sharif cannot read the Fatiḥa until the Reiyadah sharif has made the invocation. In both cases we have a succession of movements, with the second movement dependent on the realization of the first. It is clear that the time involved here is strictly of the divisible kind.

The ritual begins with a recitation of the Fatiḥa by the Roudini sharif (7), and then turns to the burning of the incense by the head of the Reiyadah sharifs. Thus the action moves from the left side of the niche to the middle of the niche, where the head of the Reiyadah sharifs sits. At this point, however, the movement does not pass on to the right side of the niche.

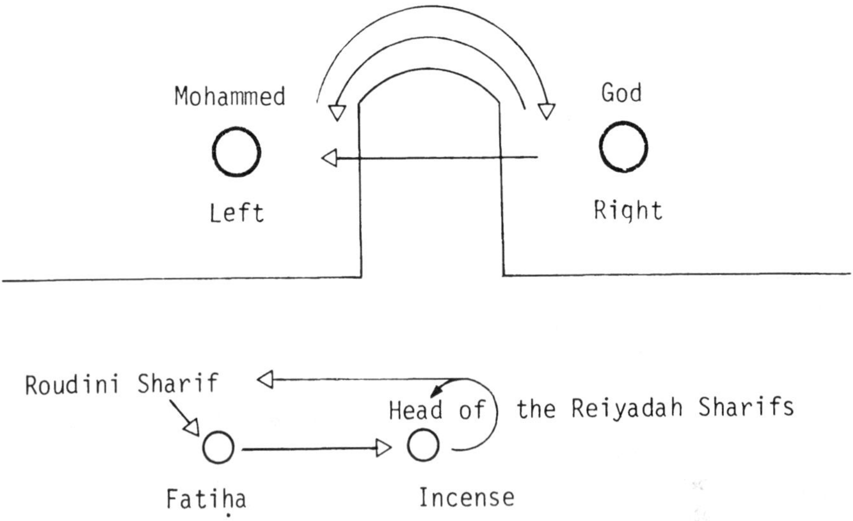

Fig. 36. The Beginning of the Sama^{c}

At the end of the ritual, the head of the Reiyadah sharifs makes the invocation, and then the Roudini sharif recites the Fatiḥa. Thus the movement reverses, passing from the middle of the niche to the left.

The Roudini sharif recites the Fatiḥa at the beginning and end of the ritual; the head of the Reiyadah sharifs burns incense in the beginning and makes the invocation at the end. These movements to the right and left can be translated into the two basic clockwise and counterclockwise movements. In Lamu, all movement is divided into movement of the right or left, and, because of the Lamuans' basic orientation to north, this distinction coincides with that between clockwise and counterclockwise. Thus clockwise and counterclockwise can be identified with the left and the right sides of the niche. The movement from left to right is clockwise, while that from right to left is counterclockwise. After all, Mecca is the center of purity and thus provides the direction by which left and right must be defined. The initial reading of the Fatiḥa by the Roudini sharif (7) initiates a clockwise movement, while his final reading of the Fatiḥa comes at the end of a counterclockwise movement.

The incense is also important in this ritual, because it too carries part of the "message." In Lamu, the use of ubani incense along with invocations usually means that angels are involved. The people of Lamu say that when ubani incense is burned its smell disturbs the angels, and so they come down to earth. They are thus in a position to carry the invocation up to God. On the other hand, *'udi*, or aloe, is usually used in situations where the people anticipate the presence of the Prophet. The fragrant smell of 'udi is an expression of the love and respect which the people have for the Prophet. Now, in the beginning of the sama', mixtures of ubani and 'udi are burned. This part of the ritual appears to have a double intention: to disturb the angels and bring them down, and also to send up a fragrance suitable for the Prophet. In Lamu, the people never burn ubani in order to bring the Prophet. In fact, ubani is never used in the Maulidi, the celebration of the Prophet's birth. If it were used, it would be considered an error. In this celebration, either 'udi or ambergris has to be used. Similarly, ubani is used only when a person wants his invocations to be carried up by the angels. In other words, ambergris and 'udi bring the Prophet *down* into the midst of the people, while the final purpose of the ubani is to send the angels *up* with the people's messages to God.

In the sama', a mixture of 'udi and ubani is used. At the same time, the head of the Reiyadah sharifs sits neither on the left nor right, but facing the middle of the niche. Furthermore, he is facing Mecca, the reverse of his usual position not only in Ramadan but also on ordinary days. Even in the iḥya' the sharif faces south. Again, in the sama' the head of the Reiyadah sharifs sits among the people, while in the iḥya' he sits alone, and in fact for the whole month of Ramadan, he remains as secluded as possible.

The mixture of the incense and the in-between position that the sharif occupies in the presence of the Prophet and the angels are both geared toward bringing him out of seclusion. In the iḥya', the sharif is still in direct relation with the Qur'ān; he is given the burden of carrying the highest purity. The whole ritual is aimed at putting off on him the superadded purity that places the other participants in a precarious position. But, in the iḥya', neither the Prophet nor the ubani that indicates his presence is in evidence. Through his invocations, the head of the Reiyadah sharifs hands the Qur'ān to the angels, and when he does this the Prophet resumes his position as intermediary between God and man. After handing the Qur'ān to the angels, the head of the sharifs is able to resume his relation with society. The mixture of ubani and aloe wood is thus a sign of this double movement, at once surrendering the Qur'ān and reaffirming the presence of Mohammed.

We also find in the iḥya' ritual that the head of the sharifs is given something, and that that something serves to keep him secluded from the rest of the people. The Qur'ān that is ritually handed to the head of the Reiyadah sharifs is not the divisible Qur'ān; it is the Qur'ān as the eternal word of God. In Lamu sharifs and non-sharifs alike recognize a distinction between the Qur'ān as the eternal word of God (light-purity), which they call *dhikr,* and the Qur'ān as a physical entity which has been printed and put into use. While the Qur'ān as a book may be destroyed, the Qur'ān as dhikr cannot and would never be destroyed, for it is always kept and preserved in heaven.

If we look to the clockwise and counterclockwise movements in these rituals, we may find more support for the theory that their purpose is to return the sharif to ordinary life and reinstate the Prophet as the link between God and the people. The sama' ritual begins by a clockwise movement, which indicates that the intention of the ritual is to empty something in order to facilitate unification. The head of the Reiyadah sharifs makes the invocations, and the movement is counterclockwise, which means that he is full and wants to be separated from something.

The ritual ends on the third day, with the ḥalwa moving from the sharif to the people seated on his right, an indication that he is now empty. This movement is the same as that made by the non-sharif in the ku zinguka when he distributes the rice bowl. Both movements are declarations of emptiness. Yet, in the iḥya' the head of the Reiyadah sharifs is given the coffee and the popcorn as the climax of a clockwise movement. In that case the givers discharge something onto the sharif—an excess amount of purity that they do not need and that is potentially harmful to them. But after the sharif gives the Qur'ān back to the angels and the Prophet is once again present, he discharges these blessings into the eaters. So, through the Prophet and his blessings, the sharif is finally able to contact the people. Now the Prophet and the Prophet's love are the means of unifying the people.

In this respect, the seating arrangement in the sama' is very important. The children sit on the right side of the niche, with their backs to Mecca and their faces to the south, the same position that the sharifs occupy during Ramadan. Because the children have not yet developed a "brain," 'aql, they cannot make choices. In other words, they still exist in a state of simple obedience, and, for that reason, occupy the same place the sharifs occupy during Ramadan. As a matter of fact, the children sit in the same place that the sharifs do during their darassa at Maskiti Pwani, with one important exception. Instead of having the non-sharifs seated in front of them, they have the young sharifs and a representative of the ex-slaves and a mngwana of dubious origin. The rest of the group sits behind.

Yet, as I have said, the interaction between the sharifs and the children is still very important. The ritual space between them has to be eliminated. And this is done through music. The children beat the drums, while the sharifs beat the tambourines. But musically the tambourine is controlled by the drums. So the children are in fact the ones who control the beating of the tambourine, and thus the children and the sharifs become as one. Near the end of the third day of the ritual, the head of the Reiyadah sharifs takes a tambourine and beats it, following the lead of the children. After a while, a sharif takes a drum and beats it, and he is accompanied by a non-sharif child. The flute remains in the background.

Music also expresses the idea of successive time or passing time. It is unrepeatable, gone before we can view it. It is like the fleeting arrow of time. The head of the Reiyadah sharifs plays the music with the children; then a sharif (not a child sharif but an adult) beats the drum with the children.

So, at the end of the third day, everyone returns to a state of relative purity; people may resume normal relations with one another. This objective is apparent in the distribution of rose water, which in Lamu is used on every occasion where people are restored to their customary positions. At the end of the ku zinguka, rose water is used in this way. Also, after the customary period of mourning (*mtanga*) rose water has to be used. And, of course, in the celebration of the Prophet's birth (Maulidi), the rose water plays an important role. Even in the Maulidi ya ki Swahili, where the leader often goes into a swoon, rose water is used to calm his jin and restore him to normal relations with the community.

Let us now deal with the seating arrangement of the various groups. If we look at the sama', we find that the powerful Jamalilil sharifs sit to the right of the head of the Reiyadah sharifs. All those sharifs who sit to the right of the Reiyadah sharif are the well-educated descendants of Ḥabib Saleḥ. On the left-hand side sit the other sharifs, arranged not according to their education or power, but according to their age. The oldest sharif sits directly next to the head of the Reiyadah sharifs, and then the younger sharifs follow him. This arrangement has far-reaching implications. First of all, it indicates that those other sharifs are not equal to the Reiyadah sharifs in their education, since if they were considered equal they would be seated with them. There is one non-sharif who sits in the group with the Jamalilil sharifs, and he is a mngwana of contested status, but he is really considered a learned man by everyone in Lamu. So when the Reiyadah sharifs allow him to sit with them they are stating that this "dubious" mngwana is able to sit with them because of his education.

The choice of a *mwana wa haramu,* or "dubious" mngwana, one who is related to an ambiguous and undefined category, is quite interesting. He could claim that he is a mngwana, but, at the same time, his slave maternal uncles could claim that he is part of their category. His status is contested, and it is left to the different groups to define him. One obvious advantage is that the slaves sitting in the back of the mosque could claim him as a part of their group. This claim is made not in order to pull that person down to their level but to prove that the slaves, or Wa Shenzi, are not basically different from the wangwana. Such a claim, of course, is tantamount to an attack on the wangwana ideology concerning the role of the souriya in childbearing. The wangwana believe that the slave womb is defiling and that, like a bad cooking vessel, it burns and defiles the contents. If this ideology is in fact correct, then there is no way for the son of a souriya to achieve a high enough degree of education to sit beside the sharifs.

The mixing of children of all social groups also enforces the slaves' point of view. If the slave children are allowed to sit with the children of the wangwana and sharifs, and if they are treated as equally pure, then to the slaves this means that the sharifs do not agree with the wangwana's interpretation of purity and impurity. The slaves interpret this as an indication that all children are equal in purity. In other words, they feel that color and origin do not play an important role for the Reiyadha sharifs.

The fact that, in the sama' ritual held in the ribat of the Reiyadah Mosque, the slaves are seated near the mosque is also relevant. They consider the mosque where Ḥabib Saleḥ used to pray and which they helped to build as the most sacred place, and thus they consider themselves privileged to sit near it. In addition, the Reiyadah sharifs propagate the idea that if a person has a guest, then the host has to offer the guest the best of everything. So, by sitting in the back, the slaves enforce the idea that they are the hosts at the Reiyadah Mosque while the wangwana are their guests.

The slaves are not only identified with the Reiyadah mtaa, but also are proud of it. For this reason, if any person comes into that mtaa, he is treated like a guest. Thus, when the wangwana come to the Reiyadah mtaa and to the mosque, they have to be served, but not because they are wangwana but because they are guests. The name of the mtaa even contributes to this way of thinking. In one sense, *Reiyadah* means "paradise," and the owners of paradise have to be generous to everyone.

The Ḥadramis view their seating position differently. They consider the Jamalilil sharifs to be their own sharifs. The Jamalilil sharifs were licensed by the Ḥadrami qutb, and thus Ḥabib Saleḥ was their qutb. The Ba 'Alwi sharifs' orders are not to be judged by any mortal creature. For the Ba 'Alwi, the sharifs are the light and the integrative power in the world and thus must be obeyed. At the same time, the Ḥadramis consider the Jamalilil sharifs their representatives, and if they are the leaders then the Ḥadrami also are leaders.

Once inside the mosque and enacting the rituals, the highly stratified society is unified and acts as a whole. However, everyone needs a sacred month and a sacred time in order to achieve a degree of purity which could never be reached in everyday life. In other words, Ramadan is the month of liminality during which the society experiences the ideal state of existence and an intensive feeling of sacred time. During that month the wangwana, the slaves, and the Ḥadramis are all united through the purity that is carried to them by their children, who obtain it from the sharifs. Even those wangwana who attend the Rodha Mosque darassa also attend the Reiyadah sharifs' darassa. And while in the Rodha Mosque they might perpetuate the old stratificatory system, when they attend the Reiyadah sharifs' darassa, they attend it as equal to all the members of the group with which they sit.

The above three rituals are either directed toward or led by the sharifs. In one of them, the ku zinguka, the aim and purpose of the ritual is actually verbalized. People state that the ritual is performed in order to enable the sick person to return to his normal relations with society. To make this possible the sharif has to separate out the impurity that is causing the sickness. The goals of the other rituals are not verbalized by the people of Lamu. But, through a study of the social context of these rituals, the kind of time involved in the ritual and the ritual status (the different degrees of purity or impurity) of the participants, one can discover the connections between these rituals and discern the subconscious goals, those goals that the actors might not be able to verbalize.

Some rituals, such as the iḥya', are performed only once a year. Others, the ku zinguka for instance, can be done many times. However, the ku zinguka cannot be performed during Ramadan, and the iḥya' cannot ever be done *except* at the end of Ramadan. So, we feel safe in saying that the iḥya' is a ritual which "ends sacred time," while the mandari is a ritual which "begins sacred time." The ku zinguka is a ritual which can be performed only in ordinary times. After all, the impure elements which could afflict people and so might have to be separated out do not use their power during the month of Ramadan because the

Qur'an is present and it is highly pure. Thus the month of Ramadan is so pure it will conquer and drive away impurity. In other words, the purity of the sharifs replaces the purity of the month of Ramadan, and these two, each in its own way, are the only effective powers against impurity.

Now, if we look to the three rituals we find that all of them begin with a movement which is either clockwise or counterclockwise. These two movements indicate, among other things, the language of the ritual which people know subconsciously without necessarily being able to verbalize it. Analyzing a number of the rituals led by the sharifs or carried out in their presence, I came to the following conclusions, which I will call the grammar of the sharif rituals. As we will see later, this grammar strictly follows the rules of purity and impurity as professed by the sharifs.

1. If a sharif comes in contact with a group of ordinary people who are in a state of normal purity, or who are lower than that in purity, then all the sharifs' movements will be counterclockwise. In this case, the non-sharifs will never make the opening movement, and when they do move, their movements will be in a clockwise direction. (Ku zinguka, for example.)

2. If a sharif who is in a state of purity higher than usual contacts a group of ordinary people who are also in a state of purity higher than usual, the sharif will never initiate a clockwise movement. His movements will be counterclockwise. The other group will be free to move in both directions. (Iḥya'.)

3. If the sharifs come together and one of them is in a higher state of purity than usual, and if these sharifs contact an ordinary group that is in its normal state of purity, then the sharifs will be free to move in both directions. The ordinary group will never initiate any movement. (Sama'.)

4. In any ritual we have to differentiate between the initiator of the ritual, that is, the person who begins the ritual, and the receiver, that is, the one who receives the results of the ritual. The former usually makes the first move. The latter has no right to initiate any movement at all.

5. If the initiator of a ritual begins the ritual with a counterclockwise movement, then the ritual is intended either to separate the initiator from the receiver, or to separate something from the initiator and give it to the receiver.

6. The sharifs are the only initiators of a ritual that begins with a clockwise movement. These rituals are intended to endow the receivers (who have to be non-sharifs) with something only the sharifs have.

At this point a further distinction may be helpful. In the three rituals we have both stable and unstable purity. The iḥya' is intended to separate the unstable or superadded purity, which is not needed, from both the junior sharifs and the ordinary people, and give it to the head of Reiyadah. After this is done, the junior sharifs are left with their stable purity and the ordinary people with that purity they normally have in the course of everyday affairs. In other words, the junior sharifs return to the ritual status which they had before Ramadan; and the ordinary people return to their normal status also. The junior sharifs are reinstated to their former position, which leaves them still higher than anyone else. In ordinary times, the people live under the wing of the sharifs, who are in relation with the Prophet.

The sick person who is the focus of the ku zinguka ritual has been continuously defiled by being in contact with the impure. The sharif does not intend to aggregate that person with himself. In fact, the movements which the sharif makes are both counterclockwise. By that the sharif states that the ritual is one of separation. The sharif cannot be aggregated with the sick person or with the seven non-sharifs, because they are all without stable purity. The sharif is the only person who possesses it. The sharif spits on the sick not to transfer stable purity to the sick person, but to separate the impure element from him. The purity of the spittle is used to drive away the impure element. The only clockwise movement is made by those who own unstable purity and are therefore like the sick person. So when the sharif drives away the impure element, the sick person is able to aggregate with those who have unstable purity, that is, with the seven non-sharifs who also participate in the ritual. The sharif is different and separate, and this is why the rose water comes after the spittle. The spittle changes the person's status by driving away the impure element; rose water is always indicative of a change in status.

The sama' ritual is the one through which the head of Reiyadah is reinstated and regains his former position. According to rule (3) of the grammar of these rituals, the head of the Reiyadah is still higher in unstable purity than anyone else, even the other sharifs. But the ritual is initiated by a sharif who has nothing more than the stable purity, and so it begins in a clockwise movement. The only group which does not initiate any movement is that made up of the ordinary people. These ordinary people are the receivers. In the sama', after the head of the Reiyadah sharifs burns the incense, the purity of the Qur'ān is carried up by the angels. Then, after two days, the ḥalwa is passed from the sharif to the ordinary people. Here also, as in the ku zinguka, the ordinary people cannot be aggregated with the sharifs; the people lack the stable purity and so would be in danger in such contact. But, the head of the sharifs can be aggregated with the Prophet and also with other sharifs, and through their light the people in Lamu will be protected. Finally, in the sama', the receivers of light are not the sharifs who have the light already in them, but the people who are under their shade. So the ritual is intended to protect and save the people by reinstating the head of the Reiyadah sharifs to his customary superior position.

In summary, we can see clearly that the sharifs are the only group that begin a ritual with a clockwise movement. The sharifs have a stable purity which the others do not have, and, when a ritual is begun by them with a clockwise movement, it means that the sharifs have something to give the people, something which the people could not obtain otherwise. But the sharifs are also the only group that can drive out the impure powers and keep the town successful and prosperous. Thus, if the people love the sharifs, then the Prophet will love the people for their sake; and if the Prophet loves the people, then the people will be saved in this life and in the hereafter. The Prophet's love is the center of the world, and without it the world would collapse.

During Ramadan, the sharifs and the whole society live under the protection and guidance of God's word. But the word of God is of such high purity that the people are not able to act in ordinary circumstances. It comes down for the sake of the month of Ramadan, and it has to be removed after that time. People know that the word of God can stay with them only one month, while the Prophet remains with them the rest of the year. The mode of life during that month, as pure light and absolute obedience, is so removed from nature that people are unable to work, eat, or even sleep. To live in this world of nature, people need intermediaries, the Prophet and the sharifs.

During Ramadan, the Prophet occupies a secondary place compared to the Qur'ān. However, when Ramadan ends, the Qur'ān has to return to its place, and the Prophet must return to his place also. The purpose of the sama' ritual is to make that very exchange. The angels come down to take the Qur'ān, and the Prophet comes down to bless the people. This exchange is made possible by the sharifs who link the "world up" with the "world down." In other words, they link culture with nature, and also stable purity with unstable purity. The whole universe is connected through them, and these connections are established on love.

I began this chapter by showing that the myth can have different interpretations. These interpretations may conflict with each other at certain points, and they may coincide on other points. Such interpretations are important to the social anthropologist, because they constitute part of the ideology that shapes the social definition of the different groups doing the interpreting.

The Lamuan myth of creation, however, does not exist in a vacuum. It has a social context which is part and parcel of that myth. The time that the myth expresses is seen to be similar to the sense of time experienced during Ramadan. While, during Ramadan, the town of Lamu is similar to the paradise of the myth, the relation of the sharifs to culture and nature is similar to the relation found to exist between Adam and Iblisi.[15]

In the Ramadan rituals, we find that the strict stratification system is partly removed. People live in a state as pure as that of Adam before he came in contact with Eve or Iblisi. At that time, the Qur'ān was the center of life; Mohammed was not needed. But when Adam committed the sin, he was punished and driven away from paradise. Adam was pardoned when he asked God to forgive him for the sake of Mohammed. Thus, outside of paradise Mohammed was needed. He had the power to intervene (*shafa'ah*). And so, after Ramadan, that is, after Lamu had ceased to be paradise, the people needed Mohammed once again.

The sharifs consider all the people of Lamu to be equal; and they believe that each can achieve a degree of purity either high or low, depending on the amount of love he expresses for the sharifs. Yet, they also declare that no one is equal to them, since they share through descent in the light of Mohammed. They may take the people "under their shade," but the people will never be equal to them. Their rituals express their ideology and propagate it. Yet the sharifs build the case for their superiority not on descent alone, but also on the idea that they have power, and without that power, the word and the universe would cease to exist. They have widened the definition of purity so as to include everyone, while at the same time separating themselves from the mass of people and securely situating themselves at the top of the ladder.

15. As we saw in the myth, Eve mediated between life and death, she was *becoming*. Mohammed mediated between light and darkness, with life thus equaling light, and death equaling darkness. Both Mohammed and Eve mediated between life and death, and the sharifs followed Mohammed as mediators between life and death and between light and darkness.

7

Lamu Redefined: The New Tenants

Mvundati ni mwarati.

He who destroys a town is its resident.

—Old Lamu Proverb

Mohammed's name is the "Mahi"; or the one who cleans, and takes away our sins. Remember his name always and you will be saved.

"Wa'z al Fouad," or "The Heart Warning"

—Amina, the daugher of Saiyid Amin

In this chapter and the next I will deal with two important rituals that take place in Lamu. These two rituals clearly reflect the difference between the wangwana's and the sharifs' ideology. Through the analysis we will be able to discover their different ways of defining the town and of classifying its inhabitants. For both groups the definition of the town centers around basic ideas of purity and impurity; it is not a geographical but a ritual definition, a point of view which has been generally neglected by Islamic scholars.[1]

Both rituals are performed in Lamu, yet the first, which is called *Kuzingu Kuzinguka Ngombe*, i.e., "the circulation of the bull around the town," is strictly a wangwana ritual, while the second, which is described in the next chapter, the Maulidi, or celebration of the Prophet's birth, is led by the Reiyadah

1. Xavier de Planhol, *The World of Islam* (Ithaca, N.Y.: Cornell University Press, 1959), p. 23.

sharifs. Within the context of these two rituals, Lamu is defined and redefined, a process that maintains an ongoing dialectic between the wangwana and the sharifs.

THE CIRCULATION OF THE BULL AROUND THE TOWN

As we have already seen, the wangwana distinguish between two types of jin: the malevolent jin, who live in the bush outside the town, and the benevolent jin, who converted to Islam and thus can live inside the town. The malevolent jin are considered harmful and anti-wangwana; in other words, they are against Astarabu, or culture. They hate the Muslims and are continuously engaged in attempts to harm them. Sometimes, they invade the town to kill the Muslims and destroy their religion. These jin are impure and thus always polluted. As such, they cannot live near anyone or anything that is not also impure and continuously defiled.

Thus, the malevolent jin can be called upon and put to work only by impure human beings. These impure human beings are, of course, the Wa Shenzi, or the people of the bush. The ex-slaves are considered Wa Shenzi and are thought to be in relation with the malevolent jin. The Wa Shenzi males marry female jin, and the Wa Shenzi females marry male jin. Yet in both cases defilement must be the *continuous* state of the human beings involved. If a non-wangwana male marries a female malevolent jin, he has to follow the rules of his wife, the rules of defilement (*unajisi*). The following accounts are taken from my field notes.

> We had a man called Bwana Kai. He got married to a jin woman. She told him that he had to live aloof from people, and she even stopped him from working. From time to time she was able to bring him a quantity of ambergris to sell. The proceeds were spent on food and clothes. *He was not allowed to eat beef or to drink certain drinks. She ordered him to eat meat uncooked, and much of his food he had to eat raw.* This man died because he disobeyed the jin. She *caused* his death.
>
> Mwana Fatuma was a slave, and when she was freed she left and settled in the western part of the town. She did not want to marry, but was a prostitute [*malaya*]. She used to go around the town in order to persuade men to commit adultery with her. However, she refused to *marry* a rich man, because, as she used to say, she was married to an important jin. Certain days each week she did not go out or allow any man inside . . . these were the days of the jin.

The malevolent jin could be summoned by a Wa Shenzi (*mganga*) or magician by killing a chicken and burning its heart, intestines, and liver. When the jin smells this odor, he comes. Different jin like different colors; among their favorites are black, red, and gray. Some of them are said to be especially fond of multicolored chickens. White chickens, however, are never used to summon the jin. As we will see later, color and smell are the most important characteristics in Lamu rituals.

The Wa Shenzi mganga usually uses his magical powers in the service of evil. He does not cure but only injures. Hence, the person who employs him has to be very secretive. For instance, the mganga can only be approached at night. In Lamu, most divorce cases are attributed to this type of magician, as are many types of sickness. The following case is a good example of the magician's use of the malevolent jin.

> Fatima was married and lived with her husband in Mombasa. The husband was a minor governmental worker. He could not afford to have a house of his own, so he rented a room in a first-floor flat. There were other people who lived in other rooms. All the occupants had to use the same water closet. One of the occupants was a woman who had a bad relationship with her mother's sister. This occupant was also called Fatima. We will refer to them as Fatima (1) and Fatima (2). One day, Fatima (1) was out, while her husband was home. Fatima (2) was also out. Around 8:00 P.M., someone knocked on the door and Fatima (1)'s husband opened the door and found Fatima (2)'s mother's sister. He allowed her in. She went to the bathroom which is used by all the occupants; then, after awhile, she left.
>
> Fatima (1) came home and went into the bathroom; and as soon as she entered it, she began to scream. The husband went to see her, but she tried to kill him. She tried to kill her children too. She refused to eat or to wash. The husband took her to the hospital, but they refused to allow her in, since she was not physically sick. She returned home but began to behave in a dangerous way. Then she was taken to a sharif, who wrote her a *komba,*[2] which is prepared by writing verses of the Qur'ān with saffron and rose water on a plate. The writings were then washed off with water, and the water was taken as a medicine. This was intended to clean the patient and clear her of the devilish deed of the jin. But it was not effective.
>
> The husband then thought of consulting a man who had his own ruhani. He went to a mwalim, or Islamic school teacher, whose ruhani declared that a bad jin was involved in the affair. But he did not want to divulge the name of the magician who was responsible. The magic had to be cleared away by "bad medicine." The Muslim jin could not do that.
>
> The husband began to think of what had happened that night. He remembered that Fatima (2)'s mother's sister had visited her. But he could not approach her directly and accuse her of making bad *ganga* (magic) against his wife. There was no reason for the old lady to do that. He sent his wife to Lamu. He went to Mombasa to try by indirect ways to discover the name of the mngwana who had done the evil and to find out why he had done it.
>
> Before I left Kenya, I met the husband in Mombasa, and he told me that the jin

2. *Komba* (plural, *kikombe*) means "cup."

> had been directed to Fatima (2), but Fatima (1) had arrived first and had gone to the bathroom where the magic was laid, and the jin could not differentiate between the two women.

This case shows clearly that harm was intentional from the beginning. It is said that the harm was accidentally afflicted on an innocent person. Yet everyone knows the bad jin are, in fact, able to distinguish between the two persons. Most likely, that jin simply chose not to distinguish between the two persons, because he had a bad nature (*tabiya mbaya*). The jin intended to harm any Muslim he could and thereby do his best to destroy Islam and Astarabu.

As we have said, benevolent jin are those jin who have converted to Islam, and who have been in contact with the wangwana for a long time. The wangwana differentiate between two types of benevolent jin: those who have converted to Islam but originally had been malevolent jin, and those who are the result of the marriages of wangwana males to female jin. Those malevolent jin who have converted to Islam are unable to overcome or change their original impurity. In fact, they are like the Wa Shenzi who convert to Islam; both remain essentially impure. The other benevolent jin, unlike the souriya children known as mwana wa haramu, do not create any social problem. They follow the principles of hishima and kutunga. Like the mwana wa haramu, they are ambiguous. They share in the light of Sam, which is in their fathers, though they are born to impure mothers. Still, unlike the mwana wa haramu, the relations between the wangwana jin children and their mother's group are always bad. While the mwana wa haramu create many problems for their father's relatives, the wangwana jin children create more for their mother's original group.

Thus, in the final analysis, the wangwana see three categories of jin: first, the malevolent jin, who are impure and defiled; then, the jin who converted to Islam and from whom the wangwana take wives; lastly, the descendants of the wangwana from these wives. While the jin who converted to Islam can never overcome their original impurity, the jin children of the wangwana and their jin wives are considered pure. Though their fathers are pure, their mothers are not. Yet, as I have said before, these jin children accept their mother's lower status and for that reason are able to maintain their hishima and kutunga. But the wangwana claim that, even though they accept the social status of their mothers, they never accept their mother's impurity. The wangwana claim that their jin children follow the fathers and thus are as pure as they are.

In order to maintain this claim, the wangwana argue that their benevolent jin children are continually fighting a battle with the malevolent jin, and even fight against their own mothers. In other words, the wangwana believe that in order to prove their claims to purity, their jin children drive their own mothers back into the bush. Thus the wangwana project an image of their jin children as the ones who clean the town and protect it from all kinds of impurity.

The wangwana stand by these claims, thus insisting on the ritual status of their jin descendants. But I think we have a paradox here. The wangwana, by permitting the transference of their purity to children who are born of an unequal wife, a jin wife, contradict their reasoning in assigning their children from souriyas to a position lower than themselves. In other words, if the status of the mother makes no difference, why are their souriya children prevented from inheriting their qualities and being equal to their half brothers from equal marriages? The wangwana claim that this is due to the nature of the souriya womb, which is like fire, burning whatever is thrown into it. But the jin females are also said to be fire. How can they give birth to children who are as pure as their fathers? The people of Lamu usually avoid such questions by pointing to another fact. The wangwana claim that the behavior of the mwana wa haramu indicates that they are actually trying to destroy the wangwana, and therefore Islam. The behavior of the mwana wa haramu, they say, is similar to the behavior of the malevolent jin, while the benevolent jin children of the wangwana obviously try to protect and strengthen the wangwana, and therefore Islam.

Still, the jin children face the same paradox as the mwana wa haramu; i.e., in order to be accepted as wangwana, they have to sever their relations with their mothers, in fact, with all slaves, an act that is contrary to basic tenets of hishima and kutunga. The wangwana jin children have to drive their mothers, as well as all the other jin who have converted to Islam but are not the issue of a wangwana marriage, out of the town. But, to do that, they need their father's help. The fathers have to get the slaves out of town and leave them in the bush.

The wangwana claim that an accumulation of impurity inside the town makes it subject to easy attack by the bad jin. When the boundaries separating purity from impurity and the town from the bush vanish, the bad jin are able to penetrate the town and do harm to it. When the number of deaths in the town rises above the usual number or when the children get sick, or people lose their minds, or when fire or flood strikes the town, the wangwana explain such events as the work of the malevolent jin. The circulation of the bull around the town is intended to drive away these jin.

The Social Arrangement

The khatib of the Jum'a Mosque is responsible for arranging the ritual of Kuzingu Kuzinguka Ngombe. The khatib consults the owners of the town, that is, the wangwana. After that, he contacts the diviner, or *mwalim ya ramli,* who uses certain special techniques to diagnose the cause of the misfortune that befalls the town.

Mwalimu ya Ramli and Divination

One of the first persons involved in the initial stages of the ritual is the mwalimu ya ramli. He is responsible for deciding the color of the bull to be sacrificed and the place from which it has to be brought. The diviner is said to be an expert in what is called *raml,* a word which means sand. However, in reality, sand is not used at all; raml actually refers to the method and not the material used by the diviner. Let me quote from my notes:

> Shee 'Abdalla is a young sharif; he is about thirty years old. He speaks Arabic with great difficulty. He owns a small shop in which he sells rice, oil, onions, sugar, etc. However, the shop is mainly used as his office for practicing magic [*ganga*] and divination [*ugazi-falak*]. He says that ganga is divided into white, or "religious" magic, and black *pagaa* or *Shenzi* magic. The sharif gave me the following information about his work:
>
> The customers for white magic, which includes divination, are mainly the wangwana; they think that the Qur'ān does not prohibit this. I have to use the Qur'ān to convince these people that I am not a black magician. Before consulting the raml, I have to make ablutions and perform prayers. This will put me in contact with my jin. My jin was born in Lamu; he is the son of a mngwana. He is very kind. When I read Yasin,[3] my jin will read with me. We are different from those African Wa Shenzi who cannot read or write in Arabic, and who are not ritually clean when they make their divination. They usually use malevolent jin, who want only to do harm. Our raml requires knowledge; we have to learn it from someone who knows it. Maḥfouz Lu, who was a Somali, taught me. We do raml by writing on paper and making accounts and shapes. Also, in our raml, we need to be cautious; we must not use it for any bad intention. The Wa Shenzi use their magic without fear. They try to imitate the shapes we make, but they do it by writing on the ground. Raml came to use through the Prophet, so those who do not know the Prophet will not be able to use it. We begin by making King Solomon's seal which looks like this:

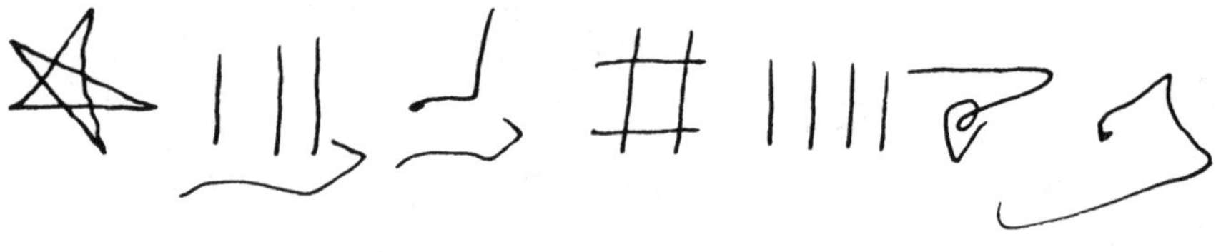

3. Qur'ān, Sura 36.

After this the magician draws, at random, a series of parallel lines (//////). When he has drawn four vertical lines in the same way, these will constitute the first shape; for example:

```
///////
///////
//////
//////
```

The diviner then draws these shapes four times, i.e., they become four sets:

```
  1       2       3       4
//////  /////   /////   ////////
/////   /////   //////  ///////
/////   /////   //////  /////
/////   /////   //////  /////////
```

He then connects each parallel line with the one next to it (#); for example;

```
# # #
# # /
# # /
# # /
```

If all the pairs are connected without any odd line left, the group will be represented by (—). If there is an odd line left, the set is represented by a (.). In the above case, for example, we obtain the following:

```
—
.
.
.
```

The magician then carries out the same procedure for all four shapes, and the result is as follows:

```
        1         2          3           4
(a)     -         .          .           -
(b)     .         .          -           .    Mothers
(c)     .         .          -           .
(d)     .         .          -           .
      Life      Wealth   Brotherhood  Parents
```

Fig. 37. First Stage of Divination

Second Stage

The first configuration is called the "Mothers" and from the recombination of the above we get the "Daughters." The principle rule is to put (a), (b), (c), (d), horizontally.

```
   5          6          7          8
   -          .          .          .
   .          .          .          .    Daughters
   .          -          -          -
   -          .          .          .
Children   Illness   Marriage   Death
```

Fig. 38. Second Stage of Divination

```
-   .   .   -   -   .   .   .
.   .   -   .   .   .   .   .
.   .   -   .   .   -   -   -
.   .   -   .   -   .   .   .
1   2   3   4   5   6   7   8

    Mothers         Daughters
```

Fig. 39. First and Second Stages Combined

Third Stage

Taking rows 1 and 2, 3 and 4, 5 and 6, 7 and 8, and applying the rule of odd (.) and even(—), we will obtain the next forms, which are called "Granddaughters."

The diviner then uses these configurations to answer specific questions. For example, if the petitioner is suffering from an illness, 6 will tell him what type of illness it is; in this particular case it is fever. Yet all the forms also signify natural symbols, e.g., fire, air, water, and dust. Fire and air are in friendly relations, as are water and dust. Yet, fire and air are enemies of water and dust.

9	10	11	12
.	.	.	-
-	.	-	-
-	.	.	-
-	.	.	-
Travel	Authority	Hope	Enemies

Fig. 40. Third Stage of Divination

This is important since if, for example, a person wants to see the relation between illness (6) and life (1), the answer is deciphered in this way: (6) = fire, while (1) = air, which means that if the illness is treated, recovery can be expected.

The following table (Table 2) is used to decipher the different forms. It gives meanings for all possible combinations of (.)'s and (—)'s in groups of four.

This table is used mainly to diagnose the cause of some sickness or bad luck that has befallen an individual. However, when the town is the petitioner, the diviner is not asked to define the *cause* of its trouble, because the cause is well known—it is the bad jin. And neither is the diviner asked to determine the date or the time when the bull for the Kuzingu Kuzinguka Ngombe is to be slaughtered, for the slaughtering must always take place on a Friday before the Jum'a prayers. The diviner's role in this ritual is to determine the color of the bull, and the area in which it has to be purchased. To determine the color of the bull, the diviner has to treat the town as if it were a single person and set out the forms as in any other consultation. If the town's problem centers around an increase in the death rate, then he has to compare the form of life and the form of death and take the result and see what color is connected with it. If he were using our example, he would have to compare form (1) with form (8) (see Figure 41). The resulting new form indicates the color as shown in the above table: the bull has to be black; and because the last form points to bad luck, the bull has to be purchased from people who live either south or west and on the mainland.

Acquiring the Bull

After the color of the animal has been determined in the above way, the

TABLE 2. DIVINATION CHART (Cont'd.)

Symbol	Name	Luck	Natural Symbol	Color Preference	Diagnosis	Sacrifice
· – – –	Nasra Kharga	Good luck	Fire	Yellow	Pepo - Possession	Cow - Goat
· – – ·	^{c}Agla	Bad luck	Dust	Black	Sexual disease	Glass
– · · –	Egtima^{c}	Mixed	Air	Black	Anxiety	Singing birds - Monkeys
– – · ·	Nasra Dakhla	Good luck	Dust	Red	Pepo - Possession	Cow - Goat
· · · ·	Tariq	Good luck	Water	Green	Severe internal colds	Sea weeds - Birds
· – · –	Qabd al Kharig	Bad luck	Water	Black	Pain of limbs	Singing birds - Monkeys
– – – –	Gam^{c}ah	Mixed	Fire	Green	Bardi ya	Insects
– · – ·	Qabd al Dakhil	Good luck	Air	Yellow	Bisi Blood disease	Cow - Goats

TABLE 2. DIVINATION CHART (Cont'd.)

Symbol	Name	Luck	Natural Symbol	Color Preference	Diagnosis	Sacrifice
. - - -	Nasra Kharga	Good luck	Fire	Yellow	Pepo - Possession	Cow - Goat
. - - .	^{c}Agla	Bad luck	Dust	Black	Sexual disease	Glass
- . . -	Egtima^{c}	Mixed	Air	Black	Anxiety	Singing birds - Monkeys
- - . .	Nasra Dakhla	Good luck	Dust	Red	Pepo - Possession	Cow - Goat
. . . .	Tariq	Good luck	Water	Green	Severe internal colds	Sea weeds - Birds
. - . -	Qabd al Kharig	Bad luck	Water	Black	Pain of limbs	Singing birds - Monkeys
- - - -	Gam^{c}ah	Mixed	Fire	Green	Bardi ya	Insects
- . - .	Qabd al Dakhil	Good luck	Air	Yellow	Bisi Blood disease	Cow - Goats

khatib of the Jum'a Mosque begins collecting the money needed to buy the

form (1)	with form (8)	and the result would be:
-	.	.
.	.	-
.	-	.
.	.	-

Fig. 41. Comparing the Forms of Life and Death

bull. The wangwana are the only ones allowed to contribute. The khatib uses his personal judgment to eliminate all those false wangwana known as the mwana wa haramu. However, in a place like Lamu, where making such fine distinctions is extremely difficult, it is to be expected that many persons from the ambiguous group will be unintentionally included. Nevertheless, the ideal is to include none of them.

The Ḥadramis and ex-slaves (Wa Shenzi) are also kept from contributing. The slaves were originally the people of the bush, and they are at least partially responsible for the proliferation of impure jin inside the town and therefore cannot contribute to the welfare of the town. Furthermore, the Wa Shenzi's involvement in secular activities is inevitable, since they do not own anything and have to work in order to earn their income. This means that they necessarily make economic choices and use their "brain" all the time. In other words, the ex-slaves move according to their "brain," and not according to the rules of culture. For all these reasons, they are not allowed to contribute money for this ritual. However, as we will see later, they do play a crucial role in it.

The bull has to be brought from the mainland, in a particular direction to be determined by the diviner. He tells the khatib to buy the bull from a place south, north, east, or west of the town. The khatib goes to the mainland and buys the bull from the assigned place. It is then carried in a boat to Lamu. As soon as it arrives at the jetty, it has to be turned over to a wangwana child, who leads it to the vicinity of the Jum'a Mosque, where it is tied near the door on the west side. One of the slaves who lives in Mkomani is charged with feeding the bull and supplying it with water. The water is provided from the mosque well.

During the night, the Jum'a khatib and other wangwana gather in the Jum'a

Mosque and all read Yasin, afterward making the following invocation, "Oh God, make it easy for us and fulfill our wishes; we are your obedient servants;

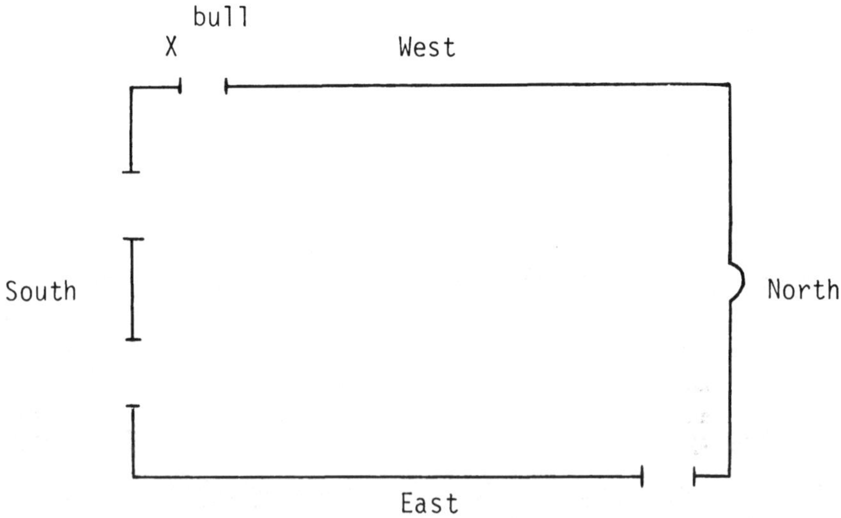

Fig. 42. Positioning of the Bull

please save us from what we fear. Oh God, you are the Merciful and the Powerful." Then, they read the Fatiḥa and send it as a gift to the Prophet. Finally each goes to his home.

The Rituals inside the Mosque

Early in the morning all the children of the Mkomani half of Lamu, including the children of the slaves, gather in front of the Jum'a Mosque, with the Qur'ān teachers supervising them. There are no drums, nor are there any other musical instruments. For a while all remain silent; then the teachers distribute parts of the Qur'ān among themselves, and read it concurrently, with the children following them. When they are about to conclude their reading, the khatib appears and goes inside the mosque to fetch the sacred flag out of its box. This particular flag is used only on the occasion of this ritual. It was originally sent to Lamu by the qutb of Ḥadramaut, Sheikh Abu Bakr ibn Salim, the grandfather of the Ḥusseini sharifs, in order to protect Lamu from invasion by the Wa Shenzi. This must have been sometime around 1550 because Sheikh Abu Bakr ibn Salim died in 1584 (see the Genealogical Chart). No one is to touch the flag except the khatib; all defilement must be kept from it and it is never to be allowed to touch the floor. On this flag, which is made of green cloth, is written the Arabic sentence: "There is no God but Allah, and Mohammed is the messenger of Allah."

Before the flag can be fastened to the pole, the pole must be carefully washed by the khatib. After the flag is tied on, the pole is given to a wangwana child, who carries it out the west door.

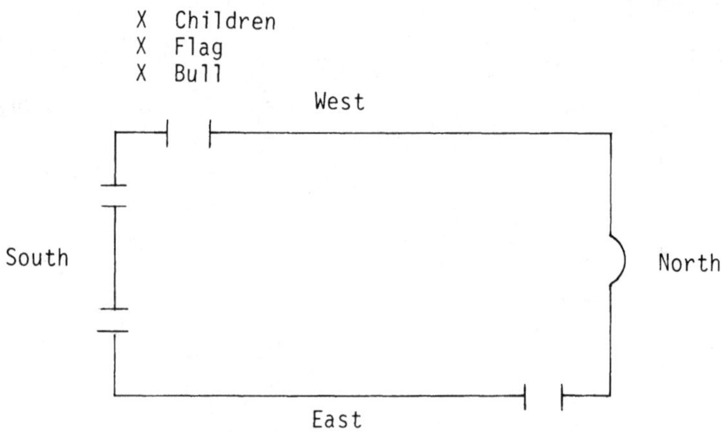

Fig. 43. Order of the Procession

When the flag has been sent out, the wangwana gather inside the mosque and form five circles. The first is headed by the khatib, and the participants in this circle read the Maulidi Barzanji. The second group reads the Burda;[4] the third reads the supplication of the Nabahani; the fourth reads the invocation of Ahl Badr (*Du'a' Ahl Badr*);[5] the fifth is assigned the *Taib al Asma'*, the most

4. The burda is the poem composed by al Bousiri in praise of the Prophet. The story is that al Bousiri was seriously sick. He lost his hope for recovery, and one night he dreamt of the Prophet, who gave him the poem. In the morning, al Bousiri recorded the poem, and he was cured. *Burda* also means Mohammed's outer garment. The Prophet covered al Bousiri with that garment.

5. Ahl Badr are those Islamic martyrs who were killed in the battle of Badr, the first Islamic battle, where the unbelievers were killed and God said, "So it was not ye who slew them, but God slew them; thou didst not cast when thou didst cast, but God cast." (Qur'ān, 8:17.)

pleasant and kind names (of God).[6] All of this literature is read in Arabic.

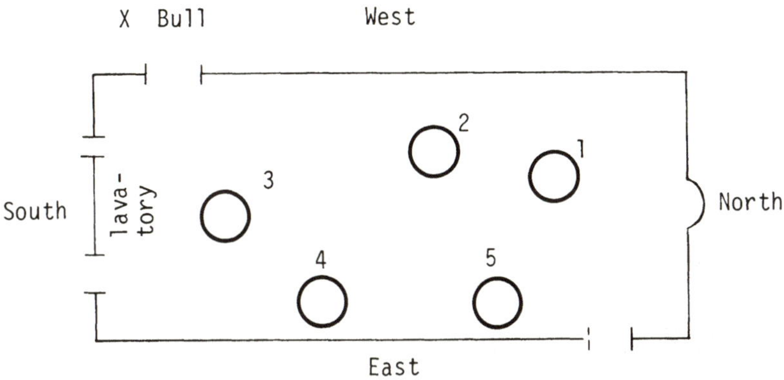

Fig. 44. Ceremonies Inside the Mosque Before the Circulation of the Bull Around the Town

The first group is considered the leading group, because it is led by the khatib, the traditional religious authority of the wangwana.

Let us now turn to the ritual materials that are used by the different groups. The first circle reads the Barzanji Maulidi and uses rose water. The second circle uses aloe wood incense but no rose water, and the three other groups burn frankincense (ubani). All groups read their special literature concurrently; however, when the first circle comes to the part of the Maulidi where it says that the Prophet is about to be born, all the circles stand up and read a poem praising the Prophet, and rose water is distributed to all the groups. It is sprinkled first on the khatib, then on the person standing to his left and so on. In other words, inside the circle, it moves in a clockwise direction. Then, from the fifth group it moves to the fourth group, and so on, also going in a clockwise direction from one group to the next. Each of the five circles recites the following poem,

> Oh Prophet, peace on you. Peace on you, the crown of prophets. Peace on you, the purest. Peace on you, the sinless. Peace on you from God. Peace on you, Ahmed. I love you. Peace on you, Taha. You are the only one who can cure me. Peace on you

6. The names mentioned here are the ninety-nine names of God, which are considered very effective in protection.

Mohammed, you are made of musk and ambergris . . . .

After reciting this poem, all sit down once more and the khatib asks them to

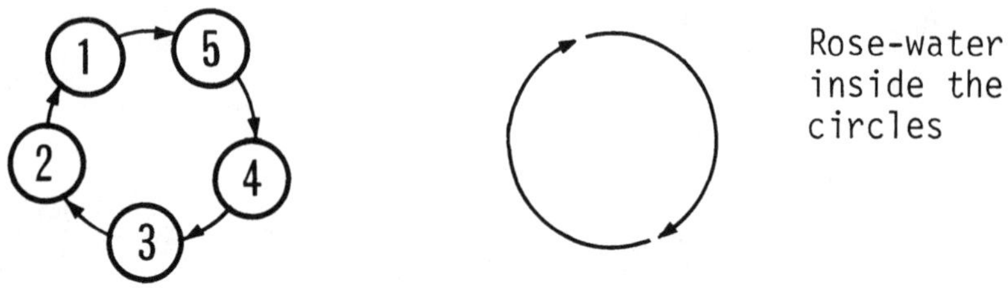

Fig. 45. Rose-water Movement Between the Groups

read the Fatiḥa together, which they do, sending it as a gift to the Holy Prophet. This marks the end of the ritual inside the mosque and all the wangwana depart through the west door.

After the bull is unfastened and trusted to an adult slave, the march begins. The marchers are arranged in the order indicated in Figure 47.

It is a rule that the bull has to be at least twenty yards in front of the flag and the flag has to be on the right side of the khatib, who is the leader of the ritual. The people who walk on the right side of the khatib are the oldest wangwana, while those who are middle-aged walk to his left. The children of the different social groups are mixed together, and all are led by a teacher of the Qur'ān school, who is himself a wangwana. The last group, which consists of male slaves, is led by another wangwana teacher.

The procession moves first around to the west of the town and then angles south, then to the northeast, and finally toward the north until it reaches the hill outside the Mkomani half of Lamu (see Fig. 47). The wangwana, led by the khatib, read the Qur'ān. The slaves also read the Qur'ān under the khatib's direction, but, instead of reading the long verses, they read the concluding short verses, 110–14, and repeat them time after time. At one point, the children recite the prayer on the Prophet, "Oh God, bless and greet Mohammed. Oh God, You have blessed him." This they repeat until they arrive at the Pwani Mosque, when they change to, "There is no God but Allah [repeated three times]. Mohammed, you are the victorious." ("*La Ilaha illa Allah, Mohammed*

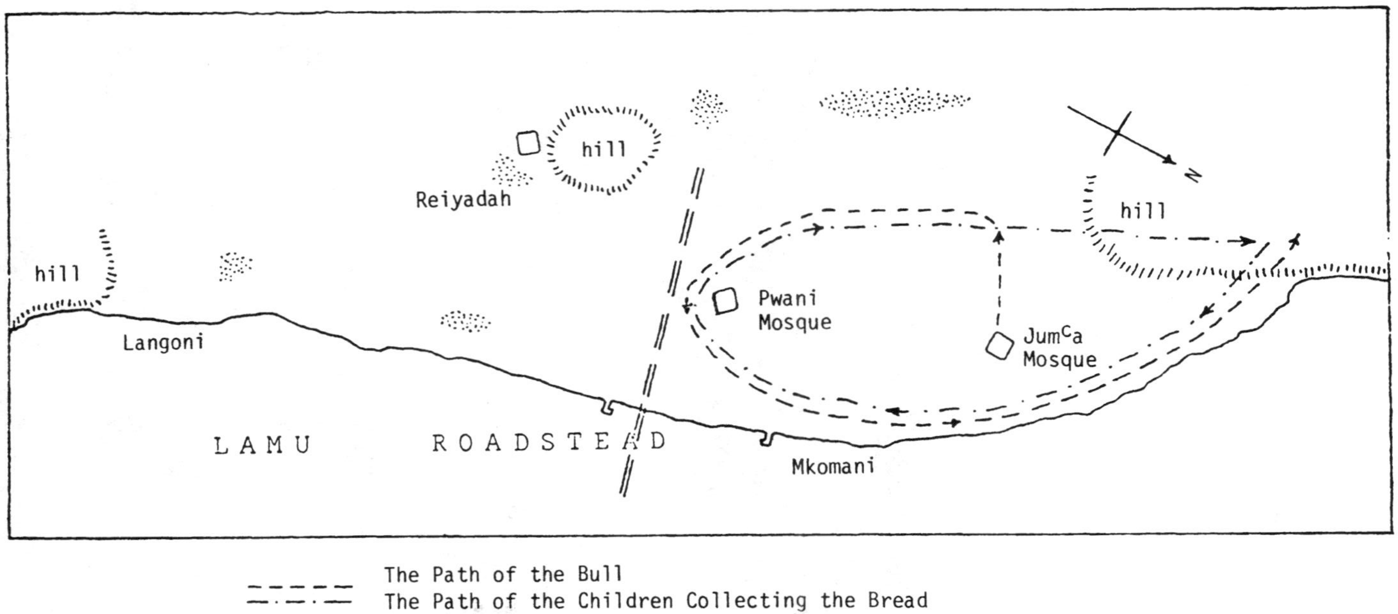

Fig. 46. Movements in the Ritual of the Circulation of the Bull

ya mansour.") When the children turn eastward toward the sea, they say, "Oh God, You are the most merciful, please release the Muslims from their sufferings." When they reach the seashore, they sing, "Oh God, by them [the

```
        West

           X  Bull led by a male slave

           X  Flag carried by a wangwana male child

    XXXXXX ⓧ XXXXXX
    XXXXXX X XXXXXX  Grown-up wangwana males
    XXXXXX X XXXXXX
    XXXXXX X XXXXXX        ⓧ Preacher
           ⊙.
    XXXXXX X XXXXXX  Wangwana male children
    XXXXXX X XXXXXX  and children of the slaves
    XXXXXX X XXXXXX  who live in Mkomani
    XXXXXX X XXXXXX
    XXXXXX X XXXXXX       ⊙ Teacher
           ⊙
    XXXXXX X XXXXXX
    XXXXXX X XXXXXX  Male slaves
    XXXXXX X XXXXXX
    XXXXXX X XXXXXX       ⊙ Teacher

        East
```

Fig. 47. The Procession

sharifs] and their ancestors, send quickly your victory and release us." The procession continues in this manner until it reaches the northern hill outside of town, where everything suddenly stops. At this point the bull is handed over to the khatib.

The children of the wangwana are separated from the children of the slaves. The wangwana children stand beside the khatib, while the children of the slaves go to join their fathers. Then the adult wangwana return to the town with their children, leaving the slaves and slave children alone with the bull. The slaves are busy preparing for a meal. They have to cut wood for a fire, make the stand for the large pot in which the meat is to be cooked, and also fetch the water needed for boiling the meat.

The khatib, the wangwana, and their children return to the town and take a ritual bath before going to the Jum'a Mosque to perform the Friday prayers. As soon as the Jum'a ritual is over, the wangwana adults return to their houses, but once there they have to avoid any kind of contact with their wives. The wangwana women also bathe and for their own part avoid contact with their husbands. The male mngwana usually goes to his own room and sits alone reading religious literature.

In the meantime, the khatib and the wangwana children return to the place where they left the bull and the slaves. The wangwana children stay with the khatib, separate from the slaves. Then the khatib orders them to return once more to the town from the seaside direction, collecting bread from each house inside the circle described by the movement of the bull during the procession around the town, and also borrowing some trays from wangwana women. They carry the bread and trays to the khatib (see the bread route, Fig. 47).

By the time the wangwana children arrive, the bull has already been slaughtered and skinned by the khatib. He cuts it into pieces and boils it. The wangwana children sit and cut up the bread and put it on the trays. The meat of the bull is boiled without any salt or spices. This is a hard and fast rule for this particular ritual: no spices or salt are to be used, none of the usual onion, pepper, cinnamon, or cardamom. Before offering the food, the liver of the bull is taken by the khatib and cut into small pieces. Half of it is mixed with some bread and soup, which the khatib carries on a plate in his right hand, while with his left, he throws some of the food on the trees around the area. This mixture is called *kutassa.* The other half of the liver is given to the slaves to eat.

After that, soup is poured over the bread, and the trays are distributed to all the people present. The slaves and their children eat together. The wangwana children eat in the place where they cut the bread, inside the circle made by the movement of the bull around the town. Interestingly enough, the wangwana children are told not to eat too much. They are told that they must not fill their stomachs. And, the khatib does not eat at all; he is busy all the time, taking care of the food distribution and looking after the remainder of the food.

After everyone finishes his meal, the wangwana children take the leftover food and throw it around on the ground. Then, they take the trays and go to the seashore, where they take a bath and wash the trays at the same time.

The trays must be cleaned before they can be taken back into the town. The remaining food–meat, soup, and bread–has to be left outside the town and the utensils must be thoroughly washed. No food at all is to return to the town; and this rule is strictly followed. Everyone knows that it is a bad omen if any of the food is taken back into the town. The khatib and the wangwana children return to the town first, and then, after a while, the slaves come back also. When the slaves enter the town, they do not do so in a large group, but scatter in twos and and threes. Everyone goes to his own home. However, before returning to their homes, the wangwana children return the trays they have borrowed. The entire ceremony of the cirulation of the bull around the town is completed before the 'Asr prayer.

ANALYSIS

Before analyzing the ritual of the circulation of the bull around the town it is necessary to clarify some points. First, let us consider the wangwana view of offerings and sacrifices. The wangwana differentiate between two kinds of religious offerings: the *kaffara,* and the *sadaqa.* The kaffara is a food offering upon which certain rituals have been performed, and which is intended to remove something bad from a person. It is passed out to many persons, thus diluting and dissipating the undesired element. For instance, if a person is sick, bread might be put under his bed for a period of time and then carried out into the town and distributed among the people. By contrast, the sadaqa is an offering that carries no taint and requires no preliminary rituals. In other words, the intention behind sadaqa is purely and simply to gain blessings. For instance, if someone is especially successful in a business venture, he might offer a sadaqa; he would slaughter a cow and hold a big feast. The point is to invite not only the rich but, more importantly, the poor. The poor are those, who, having eaten, would thank God or praise the Prophet for the good meal which has been given them. In turn, God and the Prophet extend their blessings to the one who has given the feast. However, for the sadaqa to be a true one, it has to be offered by a person who is not in a state of suffering. Thus, according to the wangwana, if a Muslim, well-known for his bad deeds, offered a sadaqa, the wangwana would strongly suspect it of really being a kaffara, and so they would not attend. In the sadaqa the state of the donor, like that of the recipient, is clearly defined: the donor has to be in a higher position than the recipient. In the kaffara, the relationship is reversed. By offering a kaffara the donor tries to rid himself of a bad element by distrubuting it among a number of others so that finally he could be equal to them. The kaffara takes something undesirable from the donor and passes it on to the recipients so all will be equal, while in the sadaqa, the recipients ask God and the Prophet to bless the donor, thus raising him even higher than he already is and making the distance between donor and receiver even greater.

Certain conditions have to be met for an effective kaffara. It has to be kept in close proximity to the sick person for three nights, during which time he is strictly forbidden to eat any of it. Since the kaffara carries the sickness or the bad luck within it, the sick person would only tie himself closer to his sickness if he eats from it. The kaffara meal cannot be sent to the mosque, for once inside the mosque it is automatically transformed into a *karama*[7] or ordinary meal. The transformation is explained by the people in this way: kaffara is defiled and therefore impure, but the mosque is undefiled and pure; so when the kaffara is sent to the mosque, the purity of the mosque overcomes the defilement and impurity of the kaffara and turns it into a karama, i.e., a good meal without religious value one way or the other.

In Lamu a sadaqa meal can be eaten by anyone. In many cases, the sharifs are the first to attend and eat. They participate in every communal meal except the kaffara. Since a kaffara carries sickness, defilement, perhaps even death, everyone in Lamu does his best to keep from eating any of it. People are naturally secretive about a kaffara and do not acknowledge it when they hand it out. Thus children are warned that if anyone tells them to eat something, they are to refuse, for fear it might be a kaffara. Although the people of Lamu think that kaffara hurts everyone, they also hold that it hurts the old more than the young. If a young man eats a kaffara he might be able to endure its effects better than an old man.

With this difference between sadaqa and kaffara in mind, we have to ask whether the ritual of the circulation of the bull is a kaffara or a sadaqa. Looking at it from the outside, it might be easily classified as a kaffara. However, whenever the people are asked, they say it is a sadaqa. This causes a good deal of confusion, especially for the anthropologist. Even though the form of the ritual makes it easily and clearly classified as a kaffara, the people insist it is a sadaqa. We have to look more closely at the ritual in the hope of discovering the people's reason for labeling it a sadaqa.

The Ritual as Sadaqa

Let us look at three aspects of the ritual. First, we see that the bull is kept

7. The word is an Arabic word, which means generosity, hospitality, honor. The word *karamat* is a derivation from the same Arabic stem.

outside the mosque the night before it is slaughtered. Second, it is noteworthy that the bull never enters the mosque. Third, it is clear from the invocations made inside the mosque that the intention of the ritual is to rid the town of the cause for its suffering. It is true that all these things point to the ritual as kaffara. Nevertheless, I think if we probe a little deeper we will also come to see the reason the people call it sadaqa. The wangwana consider themselves inherently pure and the slaves inherently impure. Historically, they have struggled hard to keep the slaves in the bush. But finally the slaves did succeed in invading the town and in maintaining a more or less continuous contact with it. I think it can be shown that the ritual of the circulation of the bull deals with this very problem of slave contact with the town. If the wangwana are pure, and the Wa Shenzi impure, how can the wangwana maintain continuous contact with the slaves without losing their purity? They have to create a medium that will act simultaneously as a buffer and a channel of communication between themselves (pure) and the Wa Shenzi (impure). In fact, if the ritual is intended as a simple kaffara, there is no way it can be effective. Since the slaves are already impure and lower than the wangwana (who would be the donors in this case), they are immune to any kaffara. Yet if it were a sadaqa it would appear that the performance is equally pointless. The slaves, being inherently impure, cannot receive any blessing or ask for blessing for anyone else, and that, of course, is the whole *raison d'être* for a sadaqa. In this case, with the wangwana on one side as donors and the slaves on the other side as receivers, with all purity in one place and all impurity in another place, it is impossible to have either sadaqa or kaffara. In other words, no communication is possible. In order for either sadaqa or kaffara to be performed, a medium for communication has to be established first.

If we look to the arrangement of the different groups of people during the ritual that precedes the actual circulation of the bull, we find that all the wangwana are inside the mosque. In the performance of this ritual they use ubani incense, which, as we have seen, works to provoke the angels to come down to earth and carry their invocations back up to God. Meanwhile, they burn aloe wood and recite the Maulidi. These last two ritual ingredients indicate that they are asking for the Prophet's blessings. Thus, inside the mosque, in addition to the wangwana, we find a clustering of highly pure elements. At the same time, some pure elements are not present: for example, the flag and the wangwana children. During this ritual they remain outside the mosque. Nevertheless, there is not a single element in the mosque that could be considered impure. In this elevated state, the mosque symbolizes the ideal state in which the town ought to live. It is a recreation of that state of affairs that existed when the town was completely separated from the bush. The rituals inside the mosque elevate the wangwana to the highest degree of purity they can obtain. At the same time, outside the mosque, the wangwana children who are considered pure mix with the slave children who are impure. The flag, one of the purest elements in the ritual, is also outside the mosque, in a position in front of the bull.

It appears that the medium of communication is established by placing the flag outside the mosque, and by mixing the wangwana children with the slave children. If the wangwana kept the flag and their children inside the mosque, they would have completely separated the pure and the impure, and it would have been impossible to establish communication between themselves and the Wa Shenzi. Communication is only possible when there is a degree of admixture of pure and impure elements, such as exists in the group outside the mosque. This is what actually makes the ritual possible. Since the group outside is not entirely impure, they can ask God and the Prophet to bless those who give them the meal. For this reason, the wangwana regard the ritual as a sadaqa.

As donors, the wangwana are higher than those who stand outside the mosque, yet there is a relation between them and those outside. The donors offer the bull to a group which is lower and yet not completely different from them. When the wangwana give the bull to the outside group, they themselves are in the highest state of purity, and so the food does not transfer any contamination to those who eat it; and for all these reasons it is not a kaffara.

However, there are still many questions to be raised. For example, if the ritual is defined as a sadaqa, how can we explain the fact that the wangwana abstain from eating it? When I asked them, they offered many different excuses for this. They told me that after the procession around the town they are tired and prefer to rest. This reply cannot be accepted, since their supposed fatigue fails to prevent them from performing Friday prayers as usual. Other wangwana said that the meat is left for the poor. Yet in all the other sadaqa rituals I attended in Lamu, the richest people were invited as well as the poor, and everyone ate. And besides, we have seen that the food is so plentiful on this particular occasion that some has to be thrown away.

Another question is why the sharifs, particularly the Ḥusseini and al Mahdali, who have long been associated with the wangwana, are absent from this feast. Even their children do not join the ritual, and their wives do not contribute bread. There are two elements, however, which can be said to represent the sharifs in the ritual: the flag, which was sent to Lamu by a sharif, and the songs which the children sing during the march. In these songs, the children call on the sharifs' ancestors to come to aid the town and to bring it victory and relief. Yet, in both cases the sharifs are treated as if they do not live in Lamu. On the day of the ritual of the circulation of the bull, the Reiyadah sharifs do not go to perform Friday prayers in the Jum'a Mosque.[8] On that day, they do not cross the lines described by the circulation of the bull and the collection of the bread. The Reiyadah sharifs carry on as if it were an ordinary day. They go to the market; they visit people outside the bull and bread lines; but they do not cross them. This, in fact, contradicts what I was told about the ritual before I observed it. All those whom I questioned beforehand had said that *everyone* in the town had to participate in the ritual. Yet, I discovered that not only the sharifs, but some other groups failed to participate. When I asked the Reiyadah sharifs about their failure to take part in the ritual, their excuse was, "We are strangers, Wa Geni. We are not the owners of the town, that is, we are not wangwana and therefore, we cannot participate."

This position is questionable for two obvious reasons. As I said before, even those sharif families that are for all other purposes considered owners of the town do not participate or contribute to the ritual. The heads of these families and all the members of their households stay secluded all day. While the Reiyadah sharifs perform the Friday prayers in their mosque, these sharif families do not even go out for prayers. The second objection to this excuse is even more obvious, for, while the slaves are certainly not owners of the town, they participate in the ritual.

Both the sharifs' failure to attend and the wangwana's reluctance to eat make the ritual look more and more like a kaffara. This conclusion can also be supported by other data. For example, in a kaffara, the animal or other food to be sacrificed has to be left under the bed of the sick person for three nights. After that, parts of the Qur'ān are read over the sacrificial material by the mwalim, who also has to pass it counterclockwise three times around the head of the sick person. Then, the animal is slaughtered by the mwalim, cooked by a relative of the sick person, and sent outside the house to be eaten by others. No member of the household is to eat any of it. In many ways, this personal kaffara resembles the ritual circulation of the bull around the town, in which the animal is left one night beside the Jum'a Mosque, and a counterclockwise circle is then made with it around the town. In the Kuzingu Kuzinguka Ngombe, it will be

8. To go to the Jum'a Mosque they have to cross the lines.

recalled, the Qur'ān is read, and finally the animal is sent outside the town. The wangwana and wangwana sharifs avoid eating any of the meat. The ritual, then, clearly looks like a kaffara. But if that is so, why do the wangwana allow their children to eat the food? Can we conclude that the wangwana intend to harm their children? This might be an easy explanation, yet surely it is the hardest to accept.

Furthermore, there are some clear differences between the personal kaffara and the town's ritual. First, the animal stays only one night in the town. Second, the animal is led in the counterclockwise procession not by a religious official but by a slave. Third, in the personal kaffara the food is eaten inside the town, not out in the bush.

Still, in the personal kaffara, the animal is sacrificed only after it has stayed three nights with the sick person; and the people say that during these nights the sick person and the animal have to be alone. No one is allowed to sleep with the sick person, and if someone should come to visit the animal has to be removed. During the day the animal is also kept elsewhere, out of sight. No casual visitor must see the animal. This is rule number one. In fact, I have been told that the *only* reason the animal is kept in contact with the sick person at night is because that is the time he is most likely to be alone. In other words, if it could be assured that the sick person would be alone during the day, then the animal could just as well be left with him then. The bull in the town ritual is left "alone" with only one group, the slaves and their children.

After taking the bull out, the wangwana and their children return to town, and the slaves are left alone with the bull. At this point, all the pure people are inside the town and the impure outside. Here we see for the first time an absolute separation between purity and impurity. So we can say that during this time of separation the animal is identified with the Wa Shenzi. It is contained and enveloped by them. At this point, the offering is transformed into a kaffara. Yet it carries not the sufferings of the town, but rather the impurity of the slaves. As I have already said, if a kaffara is taken into the mosque, it becomes a karama, a meal without any ritual value attached to it. The mosque is pure, and its purity neutralizes the impurity of the kaffara. And so now the animal that was given as a sadaqa (pure) is taken outside the town into the bush (impure), and thus in reverse fashion is also neutralized. This neutral animal is then left alone with the impure group and comes to share in the impurity of that group. This is the same transfer process that the animal undergoes with a sick person in the personal kaffara. Sickness in Lamu is thought to be caused by the bad jin or the impure elements; and, it will be remembered, it is also the bad jin that are associated with the slaves.

The personal kaffara has to be slaughtered by a mwalim; the bull in this ritual is slaughtered and skinned by the khatib. The sick person in the personal kaffara is not allowed to cook the animal; someone else has to do it for him. In the circulation of the bull ritual, the khatib does the cooking. In both the town's ritual and the personal kaffara the animal is transformed into kaffara after coming in contact with impurity associated with the bad jin. After being left alone with the slaves, the bull partakes of their impurity.

At this point within the town, conditions of absolute purity prevail. In fact, the whole town is elevated to the purity previously achieved in the Jum'a Mosque. And if this is so, when the khatib and the wangwana children go to cook for the slaves, the same arrangement exists as during the Jum'a Mosque ritual. The town equals the mosque, which in turn equals purity, while in the bush we have both purity and impurity, just as we did earlier in the group standing outside the mosque. However, in the bush the wangwana children and the khatib keep themselves separated from the slaves. In other words, they are no longer acting as a medium of communication.

The bread is collected from the town by the wangwana children in a clockwise movement. The other clockwise movement is that of the rose water inside the Jum'a Mosque. This movement is performed when the blessings of the Prophet are received, in other words, when the mosque is at its height of blessedness. As I have said, the ubani incense that is used provokes the angels to come down and carry up their invocations, while the aloe wood and the rose water indicate that the Prophet is giving his blessings. Thus it seems that the clockwise movement of the bread indicates that the town is, at that point, also receiving blessings. The town is pure and is being blessed as a result of that purity. It is the city of God, where the wangwana are completely separated from the slaves.

When the women of the town send the bread, it is in the state of highest purity; thus it is intended as a sadaqa. It is important here to note that the wangwana children's circle around the town is the only complete circle. The line of the bull does not constitute a complete circle around the town, but that of the children collecting bread does. This is very important, because the bread circle is the one that goes along the town's boundaries as conceived by the wangwana. Outside these boundaries the slaves and slave children sit waiting for the food, while inside the bread is cut into pieces by the wangwana children. The fact that the bread is kept inside the boundaries of the town means that the wangwana do not want it to be touched by the slaves or even to come in proximity to them. In other words, they do not want the bread to become kaffara. Meanwhile, the bull is cooked outside the wangwana children's circle, in the true bush, with the slaves. And so the preparation of the meal is another instance of a real separation between the realm of purity, or the town, and the realm of impurity, or the bush—the town in its blessed state and the slaves in their original condition. This is all symbolized by the separation of the bread (pure) from the soup and meat (impure).

The khatib is the only adult who is allowed to cook the meat and prepare the bread along with the wangwana children. He is allowed to go outside the children's line and come back inside it. Now, we have to see what the effect is of the khatib's switching back and forth between the bush and the town. To do this, we have to go back and consider what happens to the wangwana when they go into the bush with the bull. As we have said, all those who go into the bush have to take a ritual bath after they return to the town and before they go to the mosque to pray. This would seem to indicate that they are defiled, but earlier in the ceremony the wangwana read from the Qur'ān, something which is never done when the readers are polluted or defiled. This can be explained if we look closely at the format of the ritual; we will see that the wangwana stop reading the Qur'ān when they enter the bush and do not resume until they have taken a bath. Yet the wangwana take a ritual bath, as opposed to merely performing ablutions, only after being completely defiled, as they would be, for instance, after having sexual intercourse. Such activity produces "great defilement," whereas breaking wind, for example, constitutes only "minor defilement" and only requires ablutions. Thus the ritual bath after returning from the bush indicates that they are at this time suffering from great defilement, though they are still pure.

Again, we find that the wangwana children, after leaving the bull with the slaves outside the town, also take a bath before going to pray. This indicates that they too are in a state of great defilement. Nevertheless, they go to the bush and then return to the town to collect the bread, indicating that when they collect the bread they are defiled. The khatib is also defiled when he does the cooking.

From all of this we conclude that during the ritual meal the town line, that is the line described by the children collecting bread, divides the highest purity from the greatest defilement. This intensifies the ritual status which the wangwana have to maintain on this earth. Extreme purity without defilement is dangerous, because it is a state to be achieved only after death. As living human beings, the wangwana know that they have to be defiled in order to go on living. This is why they defile the newborn child. This is also the reason why, in every pure aspect of their life, they have to impose some kind of defilement. Even in the Kuzinguka, when the sharif spits on the person, it has to be followed by the spittle of ordinary men, lest that of the sharif prove too potent. Even the Prophet, who is pure light, was defiled when he lived on this earth.

Thus, viewing the situation as a whole, we see that inside the town wangwana adult males are separated from their wives and are reading the Qur'ān. In fact, the whole group living within the bread circle is in the highest state of purity, and acts likewise, while the wangwana children who are on the edge of the circle act as mediators. They are pure but defiled, as is the bread. Outside the bread circle, where the slaves and the bull are found, everything is impure and defiled. Considering only the food, we find that the bread is inside the circle while the meat is in the bush with the slaves. In other words, the bread symbolically expresses the wangwana view of their life on this earth (it is pure but necessarily defiled), while the meat is the symbolic expression of the slaves' impurity.

When the food is served, the khatib takes some of the meat to the trays of the wangwana children, and then carries some trays to the slaves and puts soup and meat on them. The wangwana children eat a little and then scatter the rest of the food around them. The slaves, in turn, eat some of their food and then they too scatter the rest. Now, if the bull really has been transformed into a state of impurity, then by eating it the wangwana children are eating the "sickness" of the slaves. In the final analysis this would mean that the wangwana allow their children to eat a kaffara which theoretically at least might cause them to die. Can we say then that the wangwana offer their children as a sacrifice in order to protect themselves? This explanation might be the simplest one, yet it is not the real one.

The wangwana consistently assert that if a kaffara entered a mosque, then the purity of the mosque would overcome the impurity of the kaffara and turn it into an ordinary meal, a meal which is called a karama. A karama is a meal given to friends or to people who respect each other and maintain hishima and kutunga. If we examine the state of the town during the time when the meat is offered, we find that the town—as demarcated by the bread circle—is in the highest state of purity. The town at this time is as pure as the inside of the Jum'a Mosque. During such a time the meat, like a kaffara taken into a mosque, would lose its impurity simply by being taken across the bread line. Thus, the meat which the wangwana children eat is a harmless karama. It carries no impurity.

The wangwana children eat very little of the meal, throwing most of it around them inside the bread circle. At this point, we should take note of their explanation for this behavior.

> When we have a benevolent jin who is the son of a wangwana, this jin likes to eat from our food. In many cases we put some of the food under the place where we eat so this jin can share our food. The jin who were born to wangwana respect and care for us. They will never sit beside us. They always sit down and eat by themselves. The wangwana jin are usually hungry, because people now do not leave food for them. They will eat and thank God for that meal.

Thus when the wangwana children offer the wangwana jin some of their food, the wangwana jin receive a sadaqa, and they thank God for it. So the wangwana who originally offer the bull and the bread obtain blessings for their offerings.

If we now turn to the slaves, we will find that they eat defiled bread and impure meat. In other words, they eat something which is equally as impure and defiled as they are. Yet, after they eat a little they too throw the food around. If we accept the wangwana ideology that there is a pact between the slaves and the malevolent jin, then it would appear that the meal is intended to strengthen this pact. However, it should be remembered that the bread, which is given to the slaves, is both pure and defiled. So here we have pure bread and impure meat mixed together, and then given to those who are impure. This mixture of pure bread is given first to the slaves by the khatib, who is himself pure and defiled. The preacher who is higher than the slaves, gives them food; thus this food forms a sadaqa, but one without blessing. The slaves, after eating some of the pure bread, throw it to the impure jin. The bread then serves as a medium through which the wangwana and their wangwana jin children establish a relation with the malevolent jin.

Through the bread circle and through the act of transforming the impure meal into a karama, the children are, in fact, informing the slaves and the malevolent jin that their own purity is able to overcome the impurity of the bush and of both the bad jin and the slaves. This message is also stressed by the khatib, who throws the rest of the meat into the bush. By that action he emphasizes for the bad jin that the appropriate place for impurity is in the bush, not in the town.

These messages are given out more than once. For example, when the slaves finish the meal and return to the town, they have to cross the bread line. They act as if they are entering a mosque; they take a bath in the sea and perform ablution. But here the message is that the impurity of the slaves is neutralized by the act of entering the town. Thus, if the bad jin try to enter the town, they too will lose their impurity; they too will be neutralized. In other words, this ritual succinctly expresses the wangwana ideology concerning purity and impurity: through ritual, purity overcomes impurity.

There is, however, one other interesting detail of the ritual meal that should be considered: the disposition of the liver of the bull. As we have seen, the liver is cut in two, and half is thrown on the trees by the khatib while the other half is eaten by the slaves. The act of throwing the liver on the trees is called kutassa. There is a wangwana custom that before any tree can be cut from the bush the kutassa has to be performed. Yet in the ritual of the circulation of the bull no tree is cut. The only thing which is in complete separation from the bush is the town. Can we say then that the kutassa is done to mark the separation of the town from the bush? The wangwana would not accept that because, for them, the town is never part of the bush. Moreover, the kutassa has to be done before cutting, not after. The only element that is separated after the meal is the group of slaves. In other words the offering of the kutassa can be seen as an emphasis on the idea of the separation of the slaves not only from the town but also from their allies, the bad jin. The impurity of the slaves is neutralized if they enter the town and therefore the bad jin cannot have the usual powerful effect on them.

The liver is thought of as that part of the animal that carries the intentions of the wangwana in a particularly condensed form. In other words, the liver works like an amplifier. In Lamu if a sadaqa is held the sharifs are always given the liver of the animal that was sacrificed. If the meal is a karama, the liver is given to the guests of honor. In both cases the liver serves an important function as the means for conveying the message and overall intentions of the feast. Thus, in the bull ritual the liver is put to similar use; it carries to the bad jin the message that a separation between them and the slaves is going to take place. The liver is given only to the bad jin and the slaves, which means that the wangwana know of the relation existing between these two groups; furthermore, it is given with the left hand, which means that both groups are defiled and bad.

The above theme is also expressed by the absence of spices from the meal. At first thought it seems strange that the meat is cooked without any spices, since, in Lamu, food is defined by its taste. Spices give the food taste (*tamu*); food without spices is tasteless (*passapo ladha*). Spices also provide the basis on which one kind of food is differentiated from another, even though the quantity and proportion of spices added to any particular dish depends mainly on the personal preference of the cook. Spices are what transform food from tasteless material to something enjoyable. Certainly, spices are not added to bread, but usually they are added to soup and meat. Why are they not? The meat is defiled and impure and is eaten in the bush. So at least one purpose of the exclusion of spices is to indicate that the bush is different from the town. Spices are added to all food prepared and eaten inside the town, regardless of whether it is kaffara or sadaqa.

The whole ritual is geared toward separating the town from the bush, or culture from nature. The wangwana use it to stress their claim that they are pure while the slaves are impure, that the town is their own appropriate place, while the bush is the true home of the slave. There is no place for the wangwana inside the bush. The impure cannot be pure and the pure cannot be impure. The separation between the two groups is a chasm so deep that no one can cross it.

Through the ritual, the wangwana are able to elevate the town to the highest level of purity; they turn the town into a sacred place. The whole ritual stresses the idea of space and its meaning. After the impure (Iblisi) is expelled and Adam remains, the town becomes paradise on earth. Yet, in order to create that paradise, the wangwana emulate Adam, except in one aspect—their defilement. The wangwana know that on earth they have to be defiled, and through that defilement they are able to sever their relationship with the bush (Iblisi). Iblisi is to be forced to stay outside the town; and while his agents (slaves) live inside, their power is neutralized—it can never be eliminated. The town is thus sacred and elevated space and, at the same time, defiled. In this ritual, light and purity are able finally to overcome impurity and darkness. Culture is able to defeat nature, and the town is made pure.

Such meaning, in fact, is the reverse of the symbolism evident in Ramadan rituals. The sharifs stress the idea that time is sacred during Ramadan, and they claim that, because of the sanctity of time, they are able to elevate the town to a higher degree of purity than usual, one that eliminates the impurity of the jin and drives them to their hiding places. According to the sharifs, the experience of sacred time (*durée*) is enough to elevate everyone—slaves and wangwana alike—to the highest degree of purity. Before Ramadan the sharifs go outside the town and eat with all the children of the town, regardless of their origin, and through that meal the children and sharifs are differentiated from all other people of Lamu. Here the sharifs and children are together as a group, while the slaves and adult wangwana constitute the opposing group. Yet the groups are able to interact through the medium of sacred time. All the people who live in Lamu carry a certain amount of purity due to the sacred time of Ramadan. These various degrees of purity are absent from the wangwana bull ritual. The only media of interaction left are defilement (shared through the bread) and space (the town as a mosque).

The sharifs define the slave not as inherently impure but as a Muslim who, like any other Muslim, might gain or lose purity. In this respect the sharifs are similar to the wangwana, who say that, even though a son of Sam might lose some of his purity, he would always possess a basic amount which he could never lose. For example, the child is viewed by the wangwana as higher in purity than the adult. Yet, the child is bound to lose a part of this purity through aging, and he must work hard if he is to gain it back. While the wangwana keep this privilege of purity exclusively for themselves, the Jamalilil sharifs open it up to any Muslim. Any Muslim can gain (or lose) purity (or impurity), regardless of his origin. The sharifs make one stipulation, however: they say that sharifs alone have an inherent degree of purity which they can never lose and which they have because they are related to the Prophet. Thus, although the sharifs might differ among themselves in the degree of purity they acquire during life, they all possess the basic amount which is stable. Here, we can see clearly that the sharifs have adopted the same concepts as the wangwana; however, the Jamalilil sharifs have resolved the paradox which the wangwana have created and which they cannot handle. The paradox is that of the difference between the mwana wa haramu (the children of questionable origin) and the wangwana jin. If both the mwana wa haramu and the wangwana jin are the offspring of wangwana fathers, and if in both cases the mothers are not equal to the fathers, then how could the same man get a child whom he would regard as impure from one, and a child whom he would regard as pure from the other? If the wangwana accept their souriya children as equal in purity to their half brothers from equal marriages, then the rule of mkufu marriage has to be discarded. If, however, the wangwana accept the fact that their jin children are impure, then they are unable to explain the hishima and kutunga exhibited by them. And yet, if in an effort to resolve the muddle they suggest that hishima and kutunga have nothing to do with descent and mkufu marriage, then it follows that anyone can possess such attributes regardless of whether or not he is a wangwana.

The sharifs stress the idea that all people, regardless of their origin, can achieve purity and/or impurity, inside or outside the town. They do not differentiate between the bush and the town at all. Any person, in any place, from any origin group can be impure and can do harm. In this context the ritual of Kuzingu Kuzinguka Ngombe is not important to the sharifs. And in fact this ritual is not practiced in the southern part of the town, where the Jamalilil sharifs, the Ḥadramis, and the slaves live together.

HIJABU YA MTAA: A RITUAL OF THE SHARIFS

The Hijabu ya Mtaa is performed when the inhabitants of one of the southern quarters feel that there is something wrong within their mtaa. The cause of unrest may be an especially high death rate, the frequent occurrence of theft, or an increase in sickness. All such things are taken to indicate that the mtaa has lost its protection. The people in the southern part of the town attribute such misfortunes to bad jin. The particular persons who are suffering may complain to each other or may go to consult the diviner, who will most likely prescribe some Qur'ānic amulets to protect their houses: but, when the misfortunes continue to multiply in a particular mtaa, the people realize that there is a more serious cause, something that involves the whole mtaa. At this stage, someone usually suggests that the Hijabu ya Mtaa be performed. If all the mtaa residents agree, then they must choose between two kinds of hijabu. The diviner is not involved in either kind of ritual; he is not consulted by anyone on behalf of the mtaa as a whole.

The First Kind

On the day chosen by the residents of the mtaa, one of them approaches a young Jamalilil sharif and asks him to come after midday prayer to perform the ritual for them. At the fixed time the young sharif comes with the Qur'ānic school children whom he teaches. The sharif, followed by his pupils, goes around the mtaa from the west to the north, i.e., counterclockwise, reading "The People of Badr" (*Ahl Badr*):

> In the name of God, Most Gracious, Most Merciful. We thank You our God, You made the people of Badr the full moons among the Prophet's companions. You God, made Your Prophet victorious by the help of his Medinan followers and those who migrated with him from Mecca. You helped him in defeating those who insulted him and his religion. After that, I have to pray and greet our master Mohammed, who defeated the infidel, the hypocrites, our Prophet who asked us to follow the right path. The Prophet who was sent by God to complete the morality of man . . . .
>
> In the name of God, Most Gracious, Most Merciful: Oh God, I ask You by our master Mohammed, Your immigrant messenger.
>
> Oh God, pray on him, and greet him.
>
> I ask You by the right of our master Abu Bakr, who was called the faithful and who was an immigrant also.
>
> Oh God bless him.

In this fashion the reading proceeds: it first mentions the names of the ten persons whom the Prophet has promised will go directly to paradise. Second, the reader begins calling the names of those who participated in the battle of Badr, but were not promised paradise. The readers first call out the names of those persons beginning with *A*, then *B*, and so on, to the end of the Arabic alphabet. Next the invocation is made. This is the most important part of the ritual from the people's point of view. An incense container (*chetezo*) is produced, and the incense which is to be burned is strictly ubani or frankincense from India. The young sharif sits facing the qibla with the children seated in front of him.

The sharif takes some ubani and puts it in the incense container. Then he begins the following invocation:

> Oh God, for the sake of the names which I have mentioned, please put me under Your protection, that protection which no one can attack . . . . Please God, protect us from all the evil doers. God protect me from the darkness, by leading me by Your sublime light . . . . I ask You God, You the One who has the real light, to send me, my parents, and those who taught me the blessings of the masters of Badr. You, Masters of Badr, send me your blessings, make me happy by seeing you. Give me power, help me . . . even if I do not deserve that, because of my deeds, yet I know your generosity; you protect everyone who asks you . . . .

The ritual ends with the sharif asking God to bless and greet the Prophet. When the young sharif teacher finishes, he is paid four shillings; no food is served at this Hijabu ya Mtaa.

The Second Kind

The second sort of Hijabu ya Mtaa differs from the first in three main respects. First, a bull has to be slaughtered; second, the head of the Reiyadah sharifs conducts the ritual; and third, some people from the other mtaas are invited.

In this ritual the diviner is not consulted and the bull may be purchased from any place. The residents of the mtaa collect money from each other for that purpose. The night before the ritual is to be performed, the bull is brought to the mtaa by one of the residents. It is then tied to a pole erected on the west side of the mtaa. From the time the bull is tethered to the pole, women are secluded; they are not allowed to pay visits to each other or even to go out of their houses. Meanwhile, the adults of the mtaa have to refrain from sexual relations. This night, both the women and the men have to be undefiled. Also, the children are washed and dressed in white.

Early in the morning, the adult males living in the mtaa, accompanied by their children, lead the bull inside the mtaa. Their procession moves in a counterclockwise direction from west to south, then east to north. The oldest man conducts the bull, with the adults and the children following him. When they reach the northern part of the mtaa, the old man turns the bull over to be slaughtered by any of the middle-aged men. The man who does the slaughtering has to face the qibla, i.e., north, and invoke the name of God just as he kills the animal. Other men around him help in skinning and cutting up the carcass.

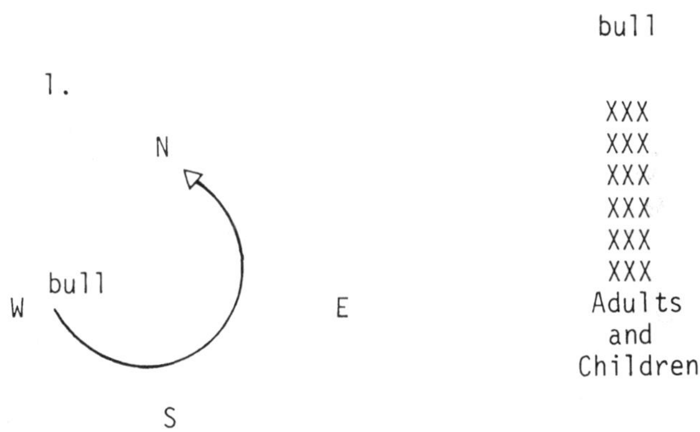

Fig. 48. The Procession with the Bull in the Hijabu ya Mtaa

The food is prepared at the same place the bull is slaughtered. In this instance, the meat is boiled with salt and other spices, *kitu kutamu cha kukdezea chakula*, things which make the food tasty. The women each separately prepare bread, and the liver of the bull is boiled with the rest of the meat.

Those people who have been invited from outside the mtaa come after midday prayer; they come directly from the mosque. By this time, mats are spread in front of the houses. When the leader of the Reiyadah sharifs arrives, accompanied by his relatives, they all sit facing north, that is, facing the qibla. The children from the mtaa sit in front of them, while the people form a big circle, always keeping inside the mtaa. The incense container is brought from one of the houses, and the sharif begins by asking all participants to read the

Fatiḥa. After this, the sharif begins a reading of the Ahl Badr. The head of the Reiyadah reads only the first part of the book; then he makes the invocation and concludes with a recitation of the Fatiḥa, which is sent as a gift to "our beloved Prophet." During the reading of Ahl Badr and the invocation, ubani is burned, but when the sharif finishes the incense container is removed.

Finally, some of the adult males from the mtaa prepare the trays for food. However, before any food is served, the children have to return to their houses, where they eat their portion of the meal. On this occasion, the first food to be served is the liver, and it is first given to the head of the Reiyadah sharifs, who is seated facing north. It is then passed in a clockwise direction to all the others around him. After this the trays are brought, one for every five persons. The sharifs do *not* eat together but rather move among the people and take their meal with them. Two or three of the oldest and most important persons of the mtaa staging the feast eat with the head of the Reiyadah sharifs. When the meal is over, someone from the mtaa stands and says "*ahsantum*" i.e., thank you. This is the sign that the ritual is over and anyone who wants to leave may do so. The Jamalilil sharifs are present at both kinds of Hijabu ya Mtaa that are performed in the southern, or Langoni, part of the town.

A COMPARISON OF THE RITUALS

At this point, I would like to compare the Hijabu ya Mtaa with the ritual Kuzingu Kuzinguka Ngombe, which is performed by the wangwana.

As we can see from Table 3, the sharifs have no part to play in the Kuzingu Kuzinguka Ngombe, while they do share the meal in the Hijabu ya Mtaa. The Jamalilil sharifs share the Hijabu meal with the Ḥadramis and their children, and with the slaves and their children, while the adult wangwana refuse to eat from the Kuzingu Kuzinguka Ngombe, and leave it to their children.

As we saw in the last chapter, counterclockwise movement may be initiated by non-sharifs, and this movement is one of separation. In the two types of hijabu described above, the initiators are different. In the first type, the initiator is a junior sharif, who moves around the mtaa in a counterclockwise direction. The second type begins before the sharifs arrive, and it too moves counterclockwise. The first type especially can be seen as a variation of the kuzinguka ritual.

The presence and absence of children in these rituals now has to be explained. The vijana, as was said before, have an especially high degree of impermanent or unstable purity. The sharif, by contrast, has stable purity, while the people of the mtaa are much lower in purity, even impure, since they are

TABLE 3. A COMPARISON OF TWO RITUALS

	Southern Part of the Town: Hijabu ya Myaa				Northern Part of the Town: Kuzingu Kuzinquka Ngombe			
	Sharing the Bull Price	Contributing Bread	Sharing the March	Sharing the Meal	Sharing the Bull Price	Contributing Bread	Sharing the March	Sharing the Meal
Sharifs:								
Adult Males	-	-	-	+	-	-	-	-
Women	-	-	-	-	-	-	-	-
Children	-	-	-	-	-	-	-	-
Wangwana:								
Adult Males	No wangwana live in this part of the town.				+	-	+	-
Women					-	+	-	-
Children					-	-	+	+
Hadramis:								
Males	+	+	+	+	-	-	-	-
Women	-	+	-	-	-	-	-	-
Children	-	-	+	+	-	-	-	-
Slaves:								
Males	+	-	+	+	-	-	+	+
Women	-	+	-	-	-	-	-	-
Children	-	-	+	+	-	-	+	+

in constant touch with impurity. The failure of the children to participate in this ritual appears to make them, along with the mtaa, the receivers of the ritual. Thus they have to be separated. However, at no point in the ritual do the children make a clockwise movement, such as the one made by the non-sharifs in the kuzinguka ritual, a movement which is considered an indicator that the receiver will be reinstated to his original position after the ritual is completed.

In the first type of Hijabu ya Mtaa, no one makes a clockwise movement. For that reason it is clear that the sharifs and children are only separating something, or discharaging something into the mtaa. If we associate this "something" with the recitation of Ahl Badr (commemorating the people who helped the Prophet to defeat the unbelievers), we are led to the conclusion that the sharifs discharge these fighters into the mtaa so they can drive away the impure, just as they did before. The Ahl Badr are able to protect and restore the mtaa to its old position, because as human beings they are similar to the people of the mtaa. Both groups have unstable purity, and so the corrective purity of the Ahl Badr will not destroy the people in the mtaa.

In the second type of Hijabu ya Mtaa, we have two movements, of which one is counterclockwise, and this is carried out by non-sharifs. It is also a movement of separation. As initiators, the people separate something from themselves. It will be remembered that the night before the ritual adults have to sleep in a state of non-defilement. And at this time the children also are ritually washed. Women, children, and men alike are secluded; no one goes outside the mtaa. And only in the morning do they emerge from their seclusion. These two states—before and after seclusion—are important.

In seclusion people do nothing; after seclusion they perform the ritual. Here we find that the initiators of the ritual and the recipients of the ritual action are one and the same. The people of the mtaa perform the ritual in order to separate something from themselves, or to be themselves separated from something. The something which they want to be separated from is bad or negative, and thus the whole ritual is performed in order to overcome the state of impurity resulting from contact with it. Thus, we can say that the first ritual is performed by the people of a certain mtaa in order to rid themselves of an impurity. However, the people realize that they cannot overcome that impurity with their own unstable purity. A sharif has to be invited into the mtaa to accomplish that. The sharif begins by calling down the angels and Ahl Badr; this is the reason for the use of the ubani incense. Then he sends the children away to their houses loaded with that purity. The whole atmosphere is then prepared for the meal.

The liver, the central and most significant part of any animal, is given first to the sharif, who then passes it to the man who sits to his left; and in this manner it moves all around the group until it returns to the sharif. The clockwise direction of the movement of the liver indicates that the initiators of the ritual, that is, those who have made the counterclockwise movement with the bull earlier that same day, have been restored to their normal position, that position which they had occupied before the impure jin attacked them. The sharif was able to reinstate the mtaa residents to this position. Both the movement of the bull and the movement of the liver correspond to the rules of ritual movement which were laid out in a previous chapter: the non-sharif can initiate a ritual with a counterclockwise movement, but he cannot initiate a ritual with a clockwise movement. The people of the mtaa initiate the ritual with a counterclockwise movement, and the sharif ends the same ritual with a clockwise movement, thus restoring the people to their original position.

If we now compare the movements in the three types of rituals—ku zinguka, or the curing ritual,[9] the first kind of hijabu, and the second kind of hijabu—we find that: (1) all of them are initiated by a counterclockwise movement; (2) in the ku zinguka the clockwise movement is performed by a non-sharif; (3) in the second kind of Hijabu ya Mtaa the clockwise movement is performed by the head of the sharifs. (Remember that sharif also makes a clockwise movement in the sama‘ ritual when he eats the ḥalwa.)

In the sama‘ we find that the clockwise movement indicates that the sharifs are restored to their old position with the Prophet, and also to their old position in society. After the third day of the sama‘, people have to depend on the sharifs, because they have established their position with the "Light," who will intervene with God to save them. Yet in the sama‘, the sharifs are the ones to offer the ḥalwa, while in the second kind of Hijabu ya Mtaa the people offer the meal. In the sama‘ the sharif offers the ḥalwa after the sharifs as a group are restored to their former position, and, similarly, in the second kind of hijabu the people of the mtaa offer the meal only after the sharif has restored them to their original position. In the rituals of the sama‘, the second hijabu, and the ku zinguka we find either rose water, a well-prepared meal, or ḥalwa.

In the Kuzingu Kuzinguka Ngombe, the wangwana—at one point— consider the meat from the bull to be impure and defiled, and in order to indicate that, they cook it in an "uncivilized" way—without spices. No one who shares in Astarabu would either cook or eat such food. And so the food is a sort of language through which the wangwana express their superiority. Through that

9. See above, pp. 267–68.

food they tell both the slaves and the malevolent jin, and even their own children, "this food is the food of the 'bush', it is the food of the Wa Shenzi."

In the sharifs' ritual the food offered to the participants expresses another set of concepts. The sweetmeat and the spicy food are filled with flavor. In their ritual the sharifs eat the things which their father Mohammed liked. Similarly, they beat the drums because Mohammed liked them. In every facet of their behavior they try to express their personal ties with the Prophet. In the same vein, other people cannot offer the sharifs something which their father Mohammed, the owner of the right of intervention and their *shafi'*, or intercessor, would not eat. Honoring the sharifs is an honor given to the Prophet himself.

Because the wangwana assume that purity and impurity are inherited properties, and that civilization and Islam are linked to the pure and denied to the impure, they are unable to create an effective relationship with the slaves or the uncivilized. By contrast, the sharifs are able to create ties with the ex-slaves by differentiating between stable purity, which they link with descent, and unstable purity, which, in contrast, can either be built up or lost all together. Through their unstable purity, all the Muslims, regardless of color or race, are linked together in one Islamic community. Within that community individuals can achieve different degrees of this unstable purity. The Islamic community is like a pyramid, and on its apex sit the sharifs with their stable purity. Above them, one finds only the Prophet and other stable lights. The ordinary people cannot share in this light except through those who sit at the top of the pyramid. Thus no ritual can ever be complete without the sharifs.

This difference in concept accounts for the fact that the wangwana ritual of Kuzinga Kuzinguka Ngombe is rapidly dying out in Lamu. Although the wangwana recognize their sharifs as equals, they do not consider them purer or in possession of anything like stable purity. From the wangwana point of view, all Arabs share in Sam's light, and for them the Prophet was an Arab first and a prophet second. Thus he must be respected primarily for being an Arab and only secondarily for being chosen as a prophet. The wangwana think that the Prophet could have been chosen from any other Arab tribe and could have come forth from another womb. If God had wanted to have another woman carry the light, this would not have been impossible for Him. In line with this reasoning the wangwana conclude that all Arabs are essentially equal, though some of them, the Ḥadramis for instance, are lower than others.

The exclusion of the sharifs from the wangwana ritual expresses this ideology. From the wangwana perspective, the presence or absence of the sharifs is not essential for the ritual to be effective. Some of the sharifs, for example Abu Bakr ibn Salim, whose flag is carried in the ritual, might have supernatural power, and he has to be respected for that. But there are many non-sharifs who also have that power, Al Ghazali being the best example. Al Ghazali died not because he carried the light—every Arab is said to carry that—but because God wanted him to die.

The battle waged in Lamu between these two ideologies of purity is well illustrated by the following story:

> In Lamu, a certain wangwana began to hold the darassa in one of the mosques. He attacked the sharifs, claiming that they have no stable purity. On the first day some wangwana attended his darassa, but on the second day the whole thing came to an end, because no one showed up to listen. When I asked him why the wangwana abandoned his darassa, he looked at me and said, "If you live in someone's house, then you have to hide the things which might give him reason to drive you out." When I asked who the owners of this house were, he laughed and said, "A year in Lamu and you want to tell me that you do not know them! They live under the green dome there, in the gardens of Eden, in Reiyadah." This learned man lost respect after making such an attack, and now the people call him *Shiki Kiemba,* or the sheikh of the turban, and they mean by that that while he has a turban, that is all he has, there is nothing under it.

The wangwana have in fact lost their traditional rights—their claim of superior descent and with it their claims of superiority. Some of them might still think they are the owners of the town, yet no one really pays attention to them. And even if it could be proven that they are the rightful owners, they lack the means to act like owners. The new tenants have new owners; the new owners make new claims which are more appealing to the people of Lamu. The new owners can provide the tenants with things that the old owners cannot. The new owners are directly related to the Prophet, and through him they can forgive and accept the sinners' repentance.

8

The Ideology of the New Owners

> Oh, descendants of Ba 'Alwi
> plead for us
> By your power all our mis-
> fortunes will vanish
> You are the closest people
> to God
> By your help everything can
> be achieved.
> —Song from the Mandari

In this chapter, I will deal with the Maulidi introduced into Lamu by Ḥabib Saleḥ, the founder of the Reiyadah Mosque and the original leader of the group of sharifs associated with it. The ideology of the Reiyadah sharifs, the new "owners" of Lamu, is nowhere better illustrated than in this Maulidi celebration. Yet there is a tension, almost a contradiction, present in their view of purity, just as we found there was in the ideology of the wangwana. This tension emerges clearly when the Reiyadah sharifs' Maulidi celebration is compared with their observance of the month of Ramadan, and this comparison will also constitute part of my final chapter.

THE MAULIDI OF THE REIYADAH SHARIFS

The Maulidi read by the Reiyadah sharifs was written by the qutb, 'Ali ibn Mohammed al Ḥabashy; and Ḥabib Saleḥ, as a follower of that qutb, made this

Maulidi the official one for all the Reiyadah sharifs. Ḥabib Saleḥ was licensed by Ḥabib 'Ali ibn Mohammed al Ḥabashy, and therefore he and his descendants had the authority to license others to perform the Maulidi. Strangely enough, Ḥabib Saleḥ licensed only one sharif, who was to lead the Maulidi in Mambrui, a small town fifteen miles north of Malindi. This sharif was called Sa'id al Beidh, and he was married to Ḥabib Saleḥ's daughter. At the present time, the descendants of that same sharif still control the Maulidi in Mambrui, and those people from Mombasa and Malindi who cannot travel to Lamu can at least attend the Maulidi in Mambrui.

Ḥabib Saleḥ and his descendants did not license anyone else in the Bajuni Islands, or in any other place for that matter, to read the Maulidi, and for that reason they were usually invited to travel to these places in order to conduct the ritual celebrating the Prophet's birth. The Maulidis of Lamu and Mambrui were set on the same day and at the same time, but in the Bajuni Islands the Maulidi was recited only after the Maulidi in Lamu had been completed.

The Reiyadah Maulidi is read in Lamu in the month of Rabi' al Awwal, which is called *Mfungu Sitta,* the sixth month of the Swahili Islamic calendar. This month is very important both ideologically and socially. In fact, we can immediately see the importance of it if we compare it with the month of the Qur'ān, or Ramadan. In contrast to Ramadan, the month of Rabi' al Awwal is the month of the Prophet, the month when it is said that the light is manifested and personified on earth. Mohammed, the bearer of the light, lived on earth, and, like anyone else, he functioned as a human being. Mohammed was a human being who carried the light, and in this respect he was like Adam; yet he differed from Adam in that he never lost his connection with that light. In other words, while Adam sinned, Mohammed never did. Mohammed, then, appears to have been the the perfect solution to the conflict of "culture" and "nature." He was dust and yet at the same time, light. He lived on earth, but he was never dominated by it. Mohammed was thus more than a prophet; he was, in himself, the logical solution to an existential contradiction. He was born without his father having had biological contact with his mother. He is dead now and yet also alive. In the future, he will attend the day of judgment, but he himself will never be judged. He was not God, but he could intervene for the Muslims with God, and because God loved him, the Muslims would be saved. For all of these reasons, the external expressions of the month of Rabi' al Awwal, the month of the Prophet, are different from those of Ramadan.

During Ramadan, as we saw, life is quiet, and involvement in everyday affairs is reduced to a minimum. The people suspend their interest in the world (nature), and try hard to elevate themselves to the realm of absolute obedience (culture). At these times the sharifs are separated from the people on all occasions except when they deliver a darassa. The Maulidi celebration, which is usually conducted every Thursday night in Reiyadah, is also abandoned for the month of Ramadan. Everyone worries about their behavior during this sacred month. Control and conservatism are the supreme rules regulating behavior. Even one's thinking has to be regulated and controlled; for instance, people are to refrain from thinking of sexual affairs. They are not to daydream about good meals. They are to concentrate on God and the Qur'ān; and any deviation would lead to breaking the fast.

By contrast, during the month of the Prophet, the days go very fast, everyone is happy, and the atmosphere is truly joyful. Drums and singing are heard all over Lamu. Life is easygoing, with behavior fluctuating between purity and impurity. Everything is tolerated; people accept the realities of this world (nature). Different groups compete with each other in celebrating the Maulidi, and while the competition is spirited both defeat and victory are acceptable. During this time, the social categories are recognized, and differentiation is expressed and intensified. In short, if Ramadan can be said to stress the separation of man from nature (and this resembles the goals of the wangwana ritual Kuzingu Kuzinguka Ngombe), the month of the Prophet stresses life as lived here and now. This is a life which human beings have to pass through; in the end, even if they sin, the Prophet will intervene to save them. In other words, the idea of shafa'ah, or the right of intervention, is stressed and developed during Rabi' al Awwal.

The Prophet will intervene for those people who love his descendants, and who care for them and respect them. For this reason, in this month the slaves, the Ḥadramis, and the Bajuni are always eager to express their love and their care for the sharifs. During the month of the Prophet, the sharifs are not separated from their followers. They carry on a normal life, going to the market and joking with the people, yet they are still looked upon as the center of light and as the manifestation of Mohammed's light on earth. Interestingly enough, during this month, the sharifs trace their relationship to Mohammed not through the normal genealogical lines, but through the particularly intense manifestation of this light at certain points in history. In reciting their genealogy they do not mention the names of *all* their ancestors; those are left out who did not go beyond the amount of stable light they possessed by virtues of birth. The only ancestors mentioned at this time are those who exceeded that original amount. In other words, during Rabi' al Awwal the Jamalilil sharifs do not follow their usual genealogy as we saw it earlier; instead, they move through it vertically and horizontally in a zigzag movement, lighting on those ancestors who were qutbs and ignoring those ancestors who failed to achieve such status. Thus, during the month of the Prophet the sharifs do not stress their equality or the basic and unalterable amount of light that distinguishes them from other Muslims; instead, they choose to differentiate among themselves, separating those who have had an intensified light from those who have not achieved anything beyond what they were given by birth. In this special genealogy Ḥabib Saleḥ is the link that ties the Jamalilil sharifs with their light centers.

Despite the fact that those who had received this intensified degree of light were not necessarily related directly to the Jamalilil sharifs, and that many were from completely different lineages, in that month the sharifs recognize them as their only true ancestors. Even the very basic notion of order of succession becomes unimportant at this time. And so one ancestor, a grandfather for instance, might be mentioned after his grandson. In other words, the grandson would come first and only then would his grandfather appear, thus indicating that the grandson is somehow more relevant than the grandfather. However, there is one consistent theme in all the alterations in traditional genealogies: neglect of 'Ali and stress instead on Mohammed and Fatima. Furthermore, only the names of the descendants of Ḥussein are brought into play in the special genealogies; the names of the descendants of his brother Ḥassan are never mentioned. Neither are the sons of Mousa al Kadhim ever mentioned, which means that the Mahdali sharifs in Lamu are excluded. During Rabi' al Awwal the ordinary ordering of genealogies is suspended; it becomes unimportant. At that time the sharifs are interested not in biological relations but in connecting themselves to the ancestors on the basis of the degree of importance possessed by the persons involved.

In some cases those sharifs who are local saints in certain areas are not included in the genealogy. They are not considered to have acquired the degree of a qutb. Their role is only provisional; they themselves depend on the qutb. While it is true that a local saint might be able to bless the local community, in order to do that he has to be assisted by the qutb. In other words, no one denies the religious power of these sharifs as local saints, but they are denied the power of connecting and transferring the highest degree of light, that which connects the qutb with the Prophet. Thus these local sharifs are no longer seen as links between the larger world and the qutb, who in turn links them with the Prophet. On the other hand, even the new genealogy recognizes that all the sharifs are linked intimately to the Prophet; he is their ancestor, and they inherit from him the stable degree of light, or purity, which is the very definition of what it is to be a sharif. Therefore, in the rituals of Rabiʿ al Awwal, the local saints are neglected, and the only sharifs mentioned are those who have achieved the degree of qutb—these are the ones who have kept the world in existence. Through the Maulidi, then, the sharifs overthrow the ordinary laws of descent and link themselves directly with the qutbs and then with the Prophet. With the new sacred genealogy, the intermediate links in that descent chain are neglected by the sharifs; in this month they call themselves the sons of Mohammed, or *Taha*. The unity of the world, then, is not achieved through local saints, but through the qutb and ultimately through the Prophet of God. During Rabiʿ al Awwal the sharifs acknowledge the multiplicity of the world, which is symbolically expressed by the various local saints; yet, at the very same time, they make a point of subjecting this multiplicity to unification through the figure of the qutb. This is the reason why the Jamalilil sharifs visit the local saints of the Bajuni before they conduct the Maulidi in these islands.

When the sharifs go to the Bajuni Islands, they visit the local saints one by one. At each visit they sit down and read the Fatiḥa for the local saint. After this they ignore him completely and begin chanting the sacred lineage, in which only the names of the qutbs are mentioned and those of the local saints are totally neglected. Through this mechanism, the sharifs intend to express the unity which lies behind multiplicity. Yet their visit to the local saints seems to indicate that they realize the existence of multiplicity as a part of the world of "nature." In other words, in the Maulidi their goal is not to neglect the world as nature and relativity, but to show that behind this there is a light who lives here and now while yet transcending the here and now. The Prophet, as light while in the world, is able to overcome the contradiction; he is able to remain alive in the world even though, as light, he is not part of nature and relativity.

In this respect, the month of Rabiʿ al Awwal differs from the month of Ramadan. During Rabiʿ al Awwal, *both* multiplicity and unity are stressed. The social distinctions between the non-sharif categories in Lamu, which are discarded in Ramadan, remain in force in the month of the Prophet. Similarly, the distinctions between Langoni and Mkomani, the slaves and the wangwana are not discarded in Rabiʿ al Awwal. Furthermore, the ex-slaves compete with the wangwana in celebrating the Maulidi during this month. The sharifs are invited by both groups to recite the holy text in the houses, and during the celebration each category tries hard to express both earthly wealth and sacred love. However, all the categories show love and respect for the sharifs, and thus are eligible for the blessings of the Prophet and the promise that he will intervene on their own behalf on the day of judgment.

The sharifs occupy this lofty and special place because of their relation to the holy ancestors, especially the Prophet, and, in turn, the Prophet, as the center of light (culture), is indissolubly linked to the Jamalilil sharifs through Ḥabib Saleḥ. With this Maulidi the relation between those Jamalilil sharifs who still live in the world of "nature," and those qutbs who live in the world of "culture," is symbolically reinforced. The sharifs are not separated from the town; on the contrary, their existence as part of the town is stressed. They are invited into most of the houses; they are touched and kissed. At this time also, girls offer themselves as wives or even mistresses for the sharifs. In short, while the sharifs are in contact with the light and are able to bring that light down into the town, they are not set apart from the world of relative knowledge, the world where sins and disobedience are possible. Though the sharifs possess the light of Mohammed, they do not thereby negate their existence in the real and present world. In other words, Mohammed's light is brought down to live in the town as it is and not as it ideally should be. In this the sharifs face reality: people live as bastards and adulterers.

During Rabiʿ al Awwal the focus of the town's life is not on achieving the highest degree of purity possible through separation from this world, but rather on finding the highest purity as it is in this world. The town during the month of the Maulidi is not at all like the town during the month of Ramadan. During the month of the Qur'ān, people stay in constant fear of becoming defiled. The people struggle to maintain a high degree of purity, in order that they will be suitable possessors of the Qur'ān. They must elevate themselves to the degree of purity that is in the Qur'ān itself, and this is done by discarding and neglecting this world. During Ramadan life is dominated by this intense struggle to elevate earthly life to heavenly life. In other words, people try to discard earthly life (nature); they struggle against it, forcing themselves away from all earthly connections. To the extent that they succeed, the time experienced in Ramadan is not the usual earthly time. During Ramadan earthly beings have to struggle very hard to separate "nature" from "culture" and to raise themselves to the level of "culture."

In Rabiʿ al Awwal, the month of the Maulidi, the Prophet is brought down by the sharifs as a personalized light. And during that time it is said he lives on earth and speaks to the people and loves and hates; he is pure and defiled; in short, he is a living human being. In the wall at the entrance of the Reiyadah Mosque, we find this theme expressed clearly: "As far as our knowledge can tell us, he [Mohammed] was a human being, but he was the best and the highest human being created by God." Mohammed was a human being, and no Muslim could deny that; yet he was the best of all human beings, and during the month of the Maulidi no one in Lamu could publicly deny that either. His was the only light that could live in "nature" without losing its brightness. He did not suffer diminution from life's multiplicity because he was loved by God; and he maintained that love and intensified it. Love was Mohammed's greatest attribute, and it kept him in continuous relation with God.

In the month that celebrates the Prophet's birth, love has to be intensified and expressed on all fronts. The people are free to live the life they choose and do the things they prefer, as long as they show and express love in what they do. If they love Mohammed, then they love God, and God will, in turn, love them. During this month, people can sin and commit adultery, and as long as they do not forget their love for Mohammed they will be saved. After all, Mohammed lived in the world of nature as all of them did, and through love he maintained and intensified his relation with God. This ideology of love is manifested in all aspects of life in Lamu during the month of the Prophet.

During Rabi' al Awwal, Lamu is not only full of pilgrims, who come from all directions—Somalia, Zanzibar, Zambia, Uganda, and even South Africa—but it is also full of prostitutes and thieves. After all, the Prophet's love is not only the possession of the 'ulama and those who behave well; his love is open wide for each and every person who would love him in return. And, if we look around in Lamu, we might find that sinners and deviants are among those who love Mohammed best.

The beginning of the month of the Maulidi is strikingly different from that of the month of Ramadan. As we have seen, there is always a conflict about the exact date of the beginning of Ramadan. People differ and quarrel with each other concerning that date. Those who delay their fasting are considered disbelievers by those who start earlier and vice versa. While those who start their fasting later do so because they want to see the crescent first with their own eyes in order to know Ramadan has actually begun, those who begin earlier feel that as long as the moon has been seen by any Muslim in any place, all Muslims should fast. In Lamu, this particular issue causes a lot of trouble and creates divisions and factions among the people. However, in the month of Rabi' al Awwal, it is simply not important to be so exact. The idea stressed in the latter case is that, since we are all human beings, we are allowed to make mistakes. People are not frustrated by trying to establish the exact date for the beginning of Rabi' al Awwal—one day in advance, or one day late, is not crucial.

This particular issue, like others, is related to the blessings of the Prophet. The Prophet, who was once "here" in the world, living like any other human being, knows that people differ and that they depend on their relative knowledge—since that is all they have. This easy attitude is in sharp contrast with the strictness of the decision about the first day of Ramadan. No one in Lamu is afraid of confessing that he might be wrong in deciding the beginning of the month of Rabi', but all are afraid to confess that they might make a mistake concerning the month of the Qur'ān. People have to make extensive preparations for the month of the Qur'ān, while this is not necessary for the month of Rabi'. In fact, during Rabi', people live an ordinary life, only in an intensified form. They do just what they are accustomed to doing but in a more concentrated way. This is not a fearful or awesome time; the Prophet understands human beings and their fraility.

Most mosques in Lamu invite the sharifs to read the Maulidi. The sharifs hold this celebration of the Prophet's birthday in sixteen mosques out of the nineteen mosques in Lamu. The two mosques which do not invite the sharifs to read the Maulidi are the Mwana Lalo Mosque, the mosque of the Wa Yumbili Pembe, and the Rhoda Mosque, which is headed by a Mahdali sharif who prefers to follow the Mwana Lalo Mosque in reciting the Maulidi Barzanji. The third mosque is not in use. The rest of the mosques arrange for the sharifs to come, although the sharifs themselves decide which of the mosques will hold the celebration on which day.

When Ḥabib Saleḥ adopted the Maulidi, he celebrated it on the same day as it was celebrated in Ḥadramaut. In other words, he read the Maulidi in his mosque on the same day and at the same time as Ḥabib Ali ibn Mohammed al Ḥabashy read his Maulidi. This happened to be the last Thursday of the month of Rabi', and to this day the Reiyadah sharifs celebrate their Maulidi after the last prayer on the last Thursday of Rabi' al Awwal. When one of the first slave students of Ḥabib Saleḥ built Anisa Mosque on the fringes of Mkomani, he asked Ḥabib Saleḥ to read the Maulidi there. Ḥabib Saleḥ accepted and set the day as the last Monday of the month of Rabi' al Awwal. Ḥabib Saleḥ also arranged to read the Maulidi in the Ḥadrami Mosque called Ba Wazir on the first Friday of the month. These were the first three mosques to recite the Maulidi, and when the others began to ask the sharifs to read it in their mosque, the sharifs assigned specific days to each: the second Wednesday, or the third Saturday, and so forth.

If we examine the above arrangement, we find that it insures a kind of rotation among the various mosques. At times the last Monday of the month comes after the last Thursday, and so the Maulidi in Anisa Mosque would be held after the Maulidi of Reiyadah. At other times the Maulidi of Reiyadah would be the final one. Sometimes, the Ba Wazir Mosque would be the first to read the Maulidi during the month of the Prophet, and sometimes it would be the second, or even the third. Through such a mechanism, Ḥabib Saleḥ was able to equalize the opportunities of the various supporters of the Maulidi. While the days assigned each mosque were fixed, the order of precedence was not.

The success of the Maulidi depends at least partially on the people of the mosque in which it is read. If they decorate, clean, and cook enough coffee and sweetmeat, then many will attend, and this will oblige the sharifs to be more enthusiastic in singing the poems and beating the drums. In other words, if the people show enough interest, the sharifs will put all their effort into making the Maulidi a successful one. On the other hand, if the people of a particular mosque fail to please the sharifs for some reason, the sharifs may take revenge by being careless and unenthusiastic in their recitation. By way of contrast this kind of "bargaining" between the sharifs and the people of the different mosques is almost absent from Ramadan rituals. Only in the month of Rabiʿ can the sharifs silently bargain with the people.

In the Rabiʿ celebrations, if the people displease them, then the sharifs can retaliate by reading the Maulidi very fast, or by beating the tambourines more slowly than they should be beaten to elicit a lively response. If the tempo drags, there will be no real participation; the chorus will be sluggish and, therefore, the Maulidi could be a real failure. The sharifs would never be blamed for such a failure because they are responsible only for the form of the Maulidi. The degree and quality of the people's participation is said to depend solely on the people of the mosques themselves.

Nevertheless, the failure of the participants to make the Maulidi a successful one has far-reaching consequences. It indicates that their amount of love and enthusiasm for the Prophet is not sufficient. In other words, a successful Maulidi indicates that those who sponsor it truly love the Prophet and, therefore, that the Prophet will love them. The success of their Maulidi is an expression of their love. Yet, achieving that success also involves showing love for the sharifs, who will transfer that love to the Prophet, who will only then reciprocate and show his love by guaranteeing success to the Maulidi.

As we have already seen, the ex-slaves and the Ḥadramis, each for their own reasons, stress this idea of the Prophet's free love. For them it is the core of their everyday life. The world of nature and the world of culture meet in the Prophet, who mediates between these two worlds. Through love of the sharifs—

especially the Jamalilil sharifs, the group of Ḥabib Saleḥ, the qutb—the Prophet can be brought down to bless them. It is interesting to find here that the only two mosques which do not read the Maulidi are dominated by wangwana groups who still insist on making an absolute separation between purity and impurity. They think that by attaching themselves to the Arabs, they share in the world of culture and therefore do not need the Prophet to come down on their behalf, or to mediate between them and the world of culture.

At the present time this ideology is losing ground in Lamu, a change which is evident in the move of the khatibs of the Jum'a Mosque toward the sharifs. Ten years ago, the khatibs contacted the sharifs and asked them to read the Maulidi in their mosque. The sharifs accepted on one condition—that the recitation would be placed in the middle of the month. In other words, they did not want their Maulidi to be privileged by coming in the beginning or at the end of the month.

If we study the mosques that hold these privileged positions at the beginning and at the end of the month of Rabi' al Awwal, we find that they are all located in the southern half of the town—all but one, and that is the Anisa Mosque in Mkomani. However, the great majority of people who pray in these mosques are Ḥadramis or ex-slaves. Thus all the mosques that hold prestigious Maulidi celebrations coming either at the beginning or end of Rabi' al Awwal are dominated by the ex-slaves or Ḥadramis, who have strong attachments to the Prophet, and who think that by gaining the sharifs' love, they will be able to bring the Prophet down into their midst. In other words, the Maulidi celebrations in these mosques have to be successful—by definition. In these privileged mosques the head of the Reiyadah conducts the ritual himself, while in the other mosques, a younger sharif is the leader.

However, regardless of order, the most important Maulidi is the one held in Reiyadah. People from a wide area come to the Reiyadah for that celebration, and they value this visit so much that they call it *hija mtoto* or "the little pilgrimage." The big pilgrimage is, of course, the one which is made to Mecca. The sharifs of Reiyadah begin to prepare for their Maulidi from the beginning of Rabi' al Awwal. One week before the celebration, the mosque is closed and painted; decorations and flags are hung, and loud-speakers are installed. The door outside the mosque is painted and decorated with lights. At the same time, the house of Ḥabib Saleḥ is opened to strangers, and the head of the Reiyadah sharifs establishes his headquarters there.

On Tuesday, just two days before the Maulidi, a cow is slaughtered early in the morning. It is cooked by a Hadrami, and during the cooking process the head of the sharifs comes in and reads parts of the Qur'ān, and then spits on the food. When the food is ready, the Ḥadrami portions it out onto trays to be distributed among all the strangers who come to attend the Maulidi. No one from Lamu itself is invited to share this food; it is only for the strangers. The food is called *harisa,* and it is made of wheat and beef with butter and sugar in the middle of each tray. When the trays are distributed, the head of the Reiyadah sharifs sits down to eat with the people. In the meantime, the liver of the cow is sent to the house of the eldest sharif woman to be cooked. The head of the Reiyadah sharifs has told me that this is eaten only by the sharifs. They share it with no one.

The First Ziyara

After the 'Asr prayer, the people begin to move toward the graveyard, to make a visit, or ziyara. This ziyara is different from any others I have attended, since people go without music; there are no drums and no singing. In fact, people go one by one, and not even in groups. Also, the movement within the graveyard is not first toward the place of the Ḥusseini sharifs, as is customary. On this occasion, people go directly to the Jamalilil shed. After everyone is seated, the head of the Reiyadah sharifs reads the Fatiḥa and asks all who are present to read Yasin in one voice (*soti moja*). When this is done, the head of the Reiyadah sharifs asks the people to read certain small verses of the Qur'ān, after which he begins to recite: "Oh God, please bless and greet Mohammed." Then, the tambourines are beaten by two younger sharifs, and the recitation of a poem is begun.

After the poem, the first part of the Maulidi is read by the head of the sharifs. This recitation is quite rapid, and the speed continues as the second part is read by another sharif. When the point is reached where everyone is to stand up (*qiyam*), rose water is distributed. The rose water moves in a clockwise direction, as do the tambourines when they change hands.

With the end of the poem, the people sit down once again, and the head of the sharifs begins to read a certain poem in which he refers to himself as Ḥabib Saleḥ, linking himself first to Ḥabib 'Ali ibn Mohammed al Ḥabashy, then to the other Ba 'Alwi sharifs who have achieved the degree of qutb, and lastly to the Prophet himself. When he finishes this recitation, the invocations are made. These ask God to bring them success in their Maulidi and accept their good deeds. Finally, the Fatiḥa is recited, and the head of the sharifs stands up, and everyone else follows.

The head of the sharifs is approached by different groups, who take his hand

and smell it. On the way back to Reiyadah, there is a big procession with tambourines and drums and sacred poems. Instead of having the head of the sharifs walking in the front, he walks, quite uncharacteristically, alone in the back. When the head of the sharifs arrives at the Reiyadah area, he goes directly to Ḥabib Saleḥ's house, where a chair is ready for him the middle of the doorway. He sits down there, and the different groups in the procession come before him one by one and play their music. After watching each group for a while, the sharif stands and blesses them and reads the Fatiḥa for them. Then as each group leaves, another takes its place. When the head of the sharifs finishes viewing all the different groups, he orders the drums to begin.

The first group of drums which plays in front of Ḥabib Saleḥ's house is called *uta*, and these are played by the Wa Gema, or the coconut cutters. These people were the first people to express their love for Ḥabib Saleḥ, and it was for their sake that he left the main part of the town and came and settled in Dari ya Mtanga, now called *Reiyadah.* Even though they are slaves, the coconut cutters still have the privilege of playing in front of the house of Ḥabib Saleḥ. What is more, they are the only group allowed to enter the house and play in front of Ḥabib Saleḥ's bed, now the bed of his grandson.

Other drums are played in different places. For instance, the *ngoma ya panga*, or the drum of the sword, is played in front of the house of the present head of the Reiyadah sharifs. Each village around Lamu sends a group of drummers, so we find players from the Bajuni Islands–Endao, Kizingitini, Siou, and so forth. There is even a group from Somalia and another from Tanzania. Lights are to be seen everywhere amidst the crowds of women and children, young men and old men who have come to the drum playing. The head of the Reiyadah sharifs sits, surrounded with the strangers who have come to Lamu especially for this ritual.

The drum playing continues in the same manner on Wednesday. On this day another cow is slaughtered for breakfast, and again the food is distributed only to the strangers. However, three other cows are slaughtered for lunch, and about four hundred pounds of rice are cooked along with the meat. The Reiyadah sharifs prepare what is called *pilow*, a very spicy rice. This meal is open to all the people of Lamu. Everyone can go and eat at this feast held in the hospice of the mosque. In addition, most of the houses around Reiyadah are also opened. Before being served, the food is blessed by the head of the Reiyadah, who reads part of the Qur'ān over it and then spits on it.

Old women, children, and old men wait long periods of time just to get a taste of this food, and sometimes they even fight over it. The food at this feast is reputed to have the power to cure sickness. Some people even keep it and send it to their relatives in Mombasa. Others take it with them to Somalia and Zanzibar. Once, when I was eating some of this rice, a Ḥadrami looked at me and said, "Now nothing can hurt you; this food is blessed. . . . it has the Prophet's birthday joy and happiness (*furaha ya Maulidi*). You will never suffer from hunger."

No food is prepared for Thursday; however, the drums are played in the afternoon. A short while before the maghrib, or sunset prayer, the playing stops, and the people begin to gather around the mosque. The door of the mosque is opened, and people fight and push to get inside. The prayer is led by the head of the sharifs, who is dressed in his best clothes. He wears a green turban and an overgarment which had been sent to Ḥabib Saleḥ as a gift from Ḥabib 'Ali al Ḥabashy. Above the niche there is a flag which was made by a Ḥusseini sharif. The mosque is decorated in every way possible and is full of enticing fragrances.

After the prayers, the head of the Reiyadah sharifs goes toward the niche and sits down.

The first part of the ritual begins with invocations: "Oh God, bless our Master Mohammed, who uncovered the truth, and who was the seal for the other prophets, and who was defending Truth by Truth." This is repeated three times and followed by, "There is no God but Allah. He has no partner. He owns the world. He can give or take life. He is able to do anything." This also is repeated three times. The last part of the invocation goes as follows: "I ask God to forgive me and drop all my bad deeds." This last section is repeated seven times by everyone in the mosque. Then the call for prayer is heard, and people end the invocation and begin the 'Isha' prayer.

The head of the sharifs leads the prayer, which ends with a short prayer for the Prophet. After the prayers, the previous seating pattern is resumed.

The Recitation of the Maulidi

The sharifs sit with their backs to the niche. The head of the Reiyadah sharifs sits on the left side of the niche with other sharifs beside him, the younger sharifs to his left, and the older to his right. In the first row, facing the sharifs, the Ḥadrami and some of the ex-slaves sit. The children are mixed throughout the group, and there are no definite places for the wangwana who attend.

Outside the mosque, women and children gather in large numbers. In fact, the whole town gathers in the Reiyadah area at the time of this Maulidi. It is interesting to note the direction in which the people standing outside are looking. If we imagine ourselves peering down on the mosque from above, we find different groups oriented in different directions. It is clear that all male non-sharifs are looking to the north, that is toward Mecca; while the sharifs and

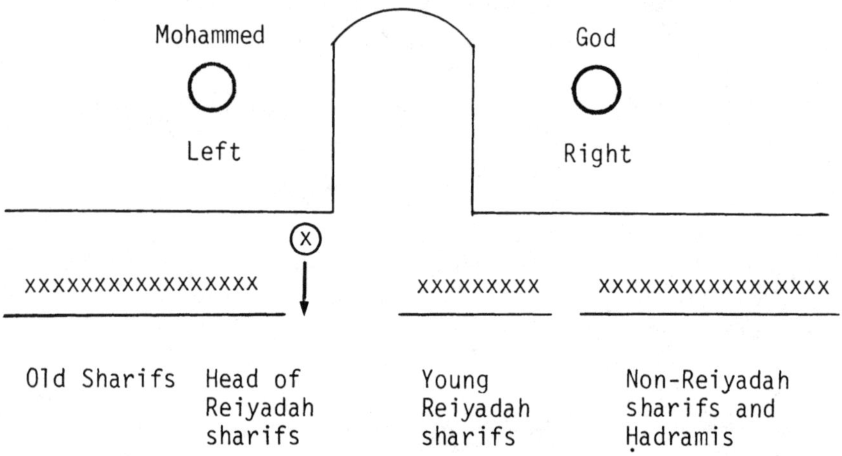

Fig. 49. The Seating of the Sharifs in the Most Important Maulidi of Reiyadha

the women are the only ones who are looking south. The sharifs separate the women from the males inside the mosque and from the males outside the mosque. Women and sharifs look in one direction toward the south, and the relation between these two groups is symbolically important. I will not attempt to deal with it in detail here.[1] Let it suffice to say that if we examine the arrangement, we will find that in simple form the sharifs are contained in a circle, half of which is made up of men looking north, while the other half consists of women looking south.

During the Maulidi the Reiyadah myth symbolizes the myth of creation in a

1. As we saw in the myth, Eve = life, Mohammed = Light, Adam = earth, and so darkness and death. However, life and light have a certain relation with each other. Light is always alive, and Eve is becoming (after being separated from the "before–" and the "after–" life). Eve mediated between life and death, while Mohammed mediated between light and darkness. So actually both Eve and Mohammed mediated between life and death. The sharifs are also mediators, following Mohammed, between life and death, just as Eve was. Thus there is a structural relation between Eve and Mohammed.

lively and exciting way. In the myth Adam was earth, dust, and death, and Eve was life, while the Prophet was light, earth as moistened and alive. The Prophet and the sharifs are the intermediating light that keeps life on earth.

Now, if we return to the recitation of the Maulidi, we find that as soon as everyone sits down, a decorated figure of the Ka'ba, the sacred Islamic shrine, is carried into the mosque and put in front of the head of the sharifs. The figure of the Ka'ba is covered with fresh flowers and with lights. On one of its sides is written, "As far as our knowledge can reach, He [Mohammed] was a human being, yet he was the best of God's creatures." And, on the opposite side, "And thou [standest] on an exalted standard of character."[2] On the other side are the words "Oh, Ḥabib 'Ali al Ḥabashy" and "Help us, Ḥabib Saleḥ." Jasmine flowers are thrown on the floor in front of the sharifs, and then the figure of the Ka'ba, placed on a tray covered with white cloth which is called *kinara*, is set on them. In addition to the kinara, rose water, aloe wood, and ambergris are also brought in. Lastly, the incense burner is set in front of the head of the Reiyadah.

For some time everything is quiet. Nothing can be heard. Everyone is silent and motionless, a vivid contrast to the noisy drums of the previous two days. Suddenly, after making the invocations asking God to accept this good deed and bless the Maulidi, the head of the sharifs asks the people to read Yasin together, and he puts some aloe wood in the burner. People begin to read Yasin together. When the people have finished reading, there is no invocation made, nor is the Fatiḥa read. The head of the sharifs immediately begins singing the first poem:

> Oh God, bless and greet Mohammed
> God bless and greet Mohammed
> He was the brightest moon rising on the universe.
>   [people repeat]
> He was the strongest defender and leader of the Truth.
>   [people repeat]
> He was the chosen and the one who was sincere and trust-
>   worthy.
>   [people repeat]
> His speech was the sweetest and the sincerest to hear.
>   [people repeat]
> He was the best human being who was realized on earth. . . .

The poem is long, taking about fifteen minutes to sing all the way through.

2. Qur'ān, Sura 68:4.

The voices are accompanied by the beating of the tambourines and two small drums. When this first poem ends, another is begun. The second poem is highly melodious, and the people participate exuberantly in reciting it:

> Greetings to you — The best of the prophets
> The more pious
> The beloved
> The purest
> From God of Heaven
> Ahmed my beloved
> Taha, you are my curer
> You are my perfume
> Ahmed, oh Mohammed
> Taha, you are glorified
> The light of darkness
> My hope and savior.

The tune changes very rapidly, while the tambourines are beaten quite softly. The melody goes from high to low and back like a spiral.[3]

A third poem, accompanied with different music, is read next. This poem is never read any place other than in Reiyadah; and even in Reiyadah, it is read only during this annual Maulidi. It is considered very sacred and very effective. It begins:

> Oh God, we ask you for the sake of the sacred and holy name.
> For the sake and for the honor of the chosen
> Your beloved prophet Mohammed
> To make it easy for us.

This poem is also lengthy, and in it we find a recitation of the sharifs' sacred genealogy (not the biological one) (see the Genealogical Chart). However, instead of mentioning the proper name of someone such as Mohammed al Faqih al Moqadim [9], we find him appearing under the title "the crown of those who know" (*Taj al 'arifina*). Similarly, Abu Bakr ibn Salim [14] is called the "one who is religiously distinguished" (*Wajihu al Dini*). These are the ancestors of Ba 'Alwi, and all of them are called on to intervene in order to make the Maulidi

3. In speaking about meolody, I have to admit that I am not well acquainted with musical theory. However, here I claim only to be speaking about the music and the melody as I "felt" it. All the rituals in Lamu are accompanied with music, and they certainly need to be studied from that aspect. I recorded most of their religious music, and I hope to be able to analyze it in the future.

praiseworthy. The poem ends with the name of the Ḥadrami Ḥabib 'Ali al Ḥabashy, the great qutb.

With each of these poems, reading begins with the head of the sharifs. In each case he is the one who initiates the recitation, while the tambourines are beaten by the sharifs sitting to his left, i.e., the younger sharifs. The drums are beaten either by the Ḥadramis or the ex-slaves, who sit in the first row. The head of the Reiyadah sits with his legs crossed, while the other sharifs sit on their knees. The slaves and the Ḥadramis sit in the same position as the young sharifs. The young sharifs, while beating the drums, sway backward and forward, and the Ḥadramis and ex-slaves repeat these motions as they sing. However, the slaves and the Ḥadramis are never to meet with the sharifs; when one goes forward the other moves back, and vice versa. And while the young sharifs, the slaves, and the Ḥadramis move to the music, the old sharif sits placid and motionless. He is a point of calm in a sea of movement.[4]

After these three poems are spoken, the music stops, and there is a moment of quiet before the head of the Reiyadah sharifs begins reciting the Maulidi. His voice in this ritual is modified from his regular speaking voice; his pronunciation is different. He starts by saying:

> In the name of God, Most Gracious, Most Merciful
>
> Verily we have granted
> Thee a manifest victory
> That God may forgive thee
> Thy faults of the past
> And those to follow;
> Fulfill his favor to thee;
> And guide thee
> On the *Straight Way*;
> And that God may help[5]
> Thee with powerful help.
> Now hath come unto you
> An apostle from amongst

4. When I attended the Maulidi, I was invited to sit in the row beside the head of the Reiyadah sharifs. However, I was told that I had to move like the others. However, since tape recording was not allowed at all (the police arrest anyone who tapes or takes photographs of the Maulidi), I preferred to sit at the end of one of the rows taking my notes. I felt that this was my only chance to record the Maulidi as accurately as I could. In fact, I was afraid to trust my memory. The only thing that I found I could not write down fast enough was the "sacred poem," and at first the sharifs would not give me the text. Finally, I was able to get it from one of them after promising not to publish it as a whole.

5. Qur'ān, 48:1–3.

Yourselves; it grieves him
That ye should perish:
Ardently anxious is he
Over you: to the believers
Is he most *Kind and Merciful.*
But if they turn away
Say: "God sufficeth me:
There is no God but He:
On Him is my trust,
He the Lord of the Throne
[of glory] supreme.[6]

When the sharif reaches the words "Straight Way," all repeat them after him, and then they add, "God bless him." When the sharif reaches "Kind and Merciful," the people repeat that, and again add "God bless him." When the sharif reaches the end of the poem, "On Him is my trust,. . ." the people repeat these last three lines and add, "God bless him" Finally, the sharif reads:

God and his angels
Send blessing on the Prophet:
O Ye that believe
Send ye blessings on him,
And Salute him
With all respect[7]

When the sharif comes to the line "Send blessing on the Prophet," everyone says "God bless him, our Prophet." The people also repeat the last part after the sharif, adding "God bless him, the best blessing of God is sent to our beloved, benevolent, and merciful Mohammed."

Then the sharif reads again, "In the name of God, Most Gracious, Most Merciful," and from here on the text of the Maulidi is read.

Thanks to God the Powerful who has given us the clearest proof* His generosity and kindness are extended over this world* His glory is elevated, and His power is great* He created the human beings for wisdom* He concealed that knowledge* He extended His mercy on them* Then He sent to them His most honorable creature* That slave, who is full of mercy* God from eternity decided to create that beloved creature and for that reason, the traces of the honor of that creature spread all over the worlds* We thank the Munificent for His blessing* The gift

6. Qur'ān, 9:128–30.
7. Qur'ān, 33:56.

is actualized as a complete perfection in a merciful body which perfumed all the world.

The above is the first section of the Maulidi and it is written in classical Arabic. When the sharif reaches the asterisk (*) he pauses, and in the first part of the poem the people say, "God be praised." However, after the line "Then He sent to them His most honorable creature," the refrain changes to, "God bless the Prophet."

When this first section is finished, a poem accompanied by music is read, and then another part of the Maulidi followed by another poem, and so on. All the sections except one are read by the head of the sharifs. This is the case only in Reiyadah, since in the other mosques the head of the sharifs reads only the first section, and other sharifs take over from there.

Just before the section where the Prophet's birth is declared, the head of the Reiyadah sharifs moves slowly into the niche, keeping to the left side. At that time, a poem is read. The poem is in praise of Ḥabib 'Ali al Ḥabashy, and it goes as follows:

> Oh God, Oh God, Oh God,
> God please make us good people
> I asked God our Creator* to help us reach our hopes*
> And send away our sorrow.
> And 'Ali al Ḥabashy contained all the secrets.
> Oh God, please make us pious* Send away all the
> misfortunes* For the sake of the chosen
> Oh God, Oh God, Oh God
> And 'Ali al Ḥabashy contained all the secrets.

The poem is highly mystical; it was written by 'Ali al Ḥabashy when he "passed away from self" (*fana'*), and "survived only in God" (*baqa'*). In the poem, he speaks about the wine he drank, and the lovely girl friend he had. During the recitation of the poem, the slaves and the Ḥadramis, who are beating the two drums, stop their swaying movement, raise their drums higher, and begin to beat them over the heads of the moving sharifs. They begin to move slowly toward the niche. Emotions and involvement become very strong. Finally, when the poem ends, the sharif who is second in rank and age begins to read the Maulidi. The head of the Reiyadah sharifs is still inside the niche. When that section comes to an end, the young sharif says, "God's will ordered that creature to come out, and here the peak of perfection came out as complete light." At this point, everyone has to stand up, and the head of the sharifs comes out of the niche. Rose water is distributed to everyone in a clockwise movement. Even the women outside the mosque receive some of it.

A long poem is then chanted, praising the Holy Prophet. Then, everyone sits down. The head of the Reiyadah sharifs begins to read the conclusion of the Maulidi in the same way. During this time people shout "*Nuri ya Mtumi,*" "*Nuri ya Mtumi,*" "the light of the Prophet," "the light of the Prophet," and others answer them saying, "God bless him, God bless him." When the Maulidi is finished, the head of the Reiyadah sharifs stands and goes to the top of the mosque and enters the green dome. He begins to speak through a loudspeaker:

> There is no God but Allah. Allah is praised in every place. Allah is eternal. Allah is mentioned every place by every human being. Allah is known through His mercy and generosity and kindness. Allah is the provider. Allah will protect us from the malevolent human beings and jin. There is no God but Allah, and Mohammed is His messenger. Mohammed is our light, our moon, and our leader. He is our protector, and he is the one who will intervene for us. God bless him and his relatives. God ordered us to salute and bless the Prophet. The Muslim cannot be a Muslim without believing and blessing the Prophet. The Prophet told us, "No one will be a real believer, except when he loves me more than himself." Love is the core of Islam, and without loving the Prophet and his relatives, there is no Islam. If you lose your Islam, then you will be no different from the animals. You have to obey the Prophet, who brought us light; he brought us the light of God. Look around you, and you will find that without his light, the world cannot exist.
>
> The Prophet ordered us to love each other, and to be kind to each other. You must not attack each other, or insult each other. Many of us are committing sins, but you must not despair. God's Mercy will come. The Prophet will help us. Finally, I ask God for the sake of the Prophet to forgive all of you, and to make it easy for you, so you can begin a new year as pure as a newborn child. Oh God, please grant us our wishes. Please God, do not treat us as sinners; help us to follow your beloved Prophet. God, for the sake of the Prophet, will accept our invocations.

Then other vows are made, and the Maulidi is over. Everyone comes to kiss the sharif's hand.

The Second Ziyara

Friday, after 'Asr prayer, a procession goes to the graveyard; however, the head of the Reiyadah sharifs does not join in the actual procession. This time tambourines are beaten and poems are read. This is the ziyara, or visit, made in order to thank the "dead" sharifs who have helped to make the Maulidi successful. In the procession, there are two main sections, and they take up the singing alternately. One group says:

> By the name of God our Master we begin
> We thank Him for His blessings.

The second group answers:

> Your requests have been accepted by God, for the sake of the Prophet, who will carry God's blessings to you.

The first group then says:

> We asked the Prophet to intervene on our behalf.
> The Prophet contacts God the Provider and the Master.

And to this the second group answers:

> The Prophet, the merciful Prophet, made the request
> And God sent His generous gifts to us,
> For the sake of the descendants of Taha [Mohammed]
> and the virgin [Fatima].

This visit to the graveyard is not like the one made on the previous Tuesday. This time, the sharifs do not go directly to the Jamalilil shed. Instead, they go first to the Ḥusseini and read the Fatiḥa for them; only at the end of this reading do they approach the Jamalilil shed. On their way to the Jamalilil shed, they begin singing their sacred genealogy; they say that everything is going nicely and smoothly in this world. However, all the singing is done by a young sharif, while the head, who has joined the group at this point, does no more than move around among the people, allowing everyone to kiss or smell his hand.

Inside the Jamalilil shed, the sharifs sit as they sat on Tuesday. The head of the sharifs arrives and makes the invocations; then all read Yasin together. Immediately after that, the head of the sharifs begins reciting the Maulidi. The second section is read by a younger sharif, who begins the singing:

The younger sharif:	We ask the Prophet to intervene so God will accept our deeds.
The head of Reiyadah:	The good news came that God accepted your request for the sake of the Prophet.
The younger sharif:	We thank the Prophet for his help and his blessing.

The head of Reiyadah:	Your request has been granted because you deserve it. When you stay in any place, you call the people to love the Prophet and God.
The younger sharif:	We tried to reach you, and thanks to God, we reached you and you came to us.
The head of Reiyadah:	The possibility of reaching me [the Prophet] is the fruit of your descent [Asoul].
The younger sharif:	Welcome, welcome amongst us. We love to have the Prophet and all the descendants of Taha and Batoul [Fatima, i.e., the virgin].
The head of Reiyadah:	I asked God to bless all of you and all those who love the Prophet. I asked God to show you the secrets of descent [the Prophet's descent].

At the end, the head of Reiyadah reads the first part, and then adds "God forgave all the sins for the sake of the Prophet. The Prophet for whom you came to attend his birth." Then he mentions the Prophet, Fatima, and their descendants again. When he reaches the point where everyone stands, the head of the Reiyadah reads the poem welcoming the Prophet. This poem is centered on forgiveness and mercy. At the end of the poem, the sharif says:

Oh God, forgive me, and clean my sins
Oh Prophet of God, welcome amongst us.
Because of you we are happy.
For your sake our sins have been forgiven.
For the Prophet's sake God forgive us
Oh God, for his sake lead us to paradise
God blesses and salutes His Prophet.

The tambourines are beaten quite fast, and the invocations are made in a quick high voice. When the people sit down, and after the head of the sharifs makes the invocations, he reads the whole list of the sharif qutbs. Then, he asks all to read the Fatiḥa. Following this he says:

God and His angels
Send blessing on the Prophet:
O ye that believe
Send ye blessing on him.

People wait outside the shed for the head of the sharifs to emerge, and when he does they begin to touch him and kiss his hand. The sharif walks at the head of the procession going to Reiyadah. The sharifs, the slaves, and the Ḥadramis, hand in hand, dance their way to the mosque. The people who customarily celebrate the shaking Maulidi walk at the end of the procession singing their Swahili songs. The procession reflects clearly the changes that have taken place in Lamu over the last one hundred years. The slaves have been freed; they walk hand in hand with the sharifs. The Ḥadramis are prosperous merchants and loyal followers. The waṇgwana join in the procession, but they have nothing to offer. The old Maulidis no longer have their original prestige and those who used to celebrate them are driven to the back. The sharifs of Reiyadah are the undisputed leaders in Lamu. The old wangwana have clearly lost their power, and now are even unable to stop the strangers—mostly Africans and Wa Shenzi—from living inside the town.

ANALYSIS OF THE MAULIDI RITUAL

If we look to the Maulidi itself, we find that the sharifs stress the idea that forgiveness is possible, that love is the real means to obtain that forgiveness, and that the Prophet is the only person who, as light, has lived in the world of nature, and, therefore, that he alone knows the pressures of that world on the human beings who still live within it. The only way for these people to be saved is through his *shafa'a*, or intervention. Since no one, except the sharifs, has stable purity, if all other humans love the Prophet, the Prophet will intervene on their behalf even after they have lost their purity. The Prophet is not only full of mercy, but he can also bestow purity and stabilize it.

Nevertheless, human beings cannot reach the Prophet directly; they have to reach him through his living children. If the people love his children, then through them they can get in touch with the Prophet, who alone has the right to intervene with God on their behalf and hence change impurity into purity. The sharifs are, then, the sole means by which the people can come in contact with the Prophet. If the people were to lose the good will of the sharifs, they would be unable to reach the Prophet and obtain his intervention, and God would not forgive them. The people need to be forgiven because they are living in this world of "nature." Thus the Prophet is needed not to help them separate themselves from the world of nature, but to enable them to stay in that world as it is without worrying about their resulting loss of purity. The sharifs not only have stable purity; they are also able to contact the Prophet and ask him to stabilize the purity of the non-sharifs, if those non-sharifs are able to show their love and respect for the Prophet and his living descendants.

The Prophet is said to give the people an amount of purity equal to that of the newborn child. Both the newborn child and the adult who has been to the

Maulidi will lose their purity through time. However, if they want to be saved, then they have to depend on the Prophet who can give them the purity they need. There is no doubt that the Prophet will give this purity, since before the Maulidi the qutb is contacted and asked to reach the Prophet and ask him for this favor. This is the reason why the Maulidi begins with a visit, or ziyara, to the qutb. The sharifs and others do not, as is customary at other times, visit the qutb only after visiting the sharifs who are buried behind him. They visit the qutb directly, in a way that would not be proper at any other time. This approach is very interesting symbolically. The Ḥusseini sharifs who are buried behind the qutb are completely neglected in the first ziyara, when the success of the Maulidi is still at stake. However, these same sharifs are not neglected after the Maulidi has proven to be a success. The people visit the Ḥusseini sharifs after the ceremonies and declare that they were happy in this world. In the second ziyara the head of the Reiyadah sharifs is absent, so he does not visit the Ḥusseini sharifs. But he is the one who asked the qutb to intervene in the first place.

As we have seen, the qutb has no power in himself. His power depends on the reciprocal love between himself and the Prophet. If the qutb asks the Prophet for something, then the Prophet and God will almost always give him what he requests. If God and the Prophet refuse, then the qutb will lose his position as a qutb; he will be neglected. So, by ignoring the other sharifs on the first ziyara, the people indicate what will happen to the qutb if the Maulidi is unsuccessful. The qutb will be neglected as the sharifs are; no one will visit him. It seems that the first ziyara expresses a kind of threat to the qutb. But, on the second ziyara, after a successful Maulidi, the people visit the other sharifs. Now they are visited not because they are powerful, but because the qutb has shown that he is still powerful. It is for his sake that visits are paid to the other sharifs.

We still have to explain why the head of the Reiyadah sharifs does not go to visit his Ḥusseini ancestors on this second ziyara. Even during the time of threat, he is treated with love and respect. Here it seems that the people unconsciously realize that if they carry their threat to the extreme, they will jeopardize the Prophet's love. The head of the Reiyadah sharifs is a symbol and as such he has to be shown that love. He is the person who will carry their petition to the qutb. If he himself pays the second visit to the Ḥusseini sharifs, it indicates that he, too, has doubted the qutb's power. Since he could never doubt this power, he abstains from making the second visit. However, his brothers and relatives go along on this visit, which means that they have doubted the power of the qutb; they are just like the ordinary people. We can say then that when the head of the Reiyadah sharifs goes inside the niche and makes a counterclockwise movement, he is in fact separating himself from all those who doubt the power of the qutb.

However, in the counterclockwise movement, he moves in the direction of the women, who are in complete obedience and submission. They, like Eve, have lost all their doubts. In fact, the head of the sharifs, whom the women are looking at, has never been doubted by the women. When the women face the sharif, they face south, yet as we have seen south is considered a bad direction. The only time people face that direction is when a sharif sits with his back to it. This is clear in the sama', and now, in the case of the women in the Maulidi, it is also the case. They face him and do not doubt him.

The success of the Maulidi is expressed by the amount of energy and involvement the people exhibit. The way the poems are read is also an index of the people's degree of involvement. The power, force, and strength of voice that the people use in repeating the poems after the head of the Reiyadah sharifs indicates whether or not they are caught up in the service. When the head of the Reiyadah sharifs shows the people that the Maulidi is successful, then he withdraws from them, indicating to them that he has known about their doubts. The young sharifs and the ordinary people are alike in this respect. This is expressed in their movement, especially at the point where the drums are beaten over the heads of the younger sharifs. As I have said, the drums are usually beaten by those who have no stable purity. These musicians seat themselves in the row facing the sharifs. In the Maulidi, after the head of the sharifs withdraws to the niche, the drums do not remain in front of the sharifs but are held over their heads. In other words, the order is reversed. The younger sharifs contribute to that reversal by doubting the power of their qutb. They act in a way that would ordinarily be expected only from the non-sharifs. For that reason they are punished, and the head sharif withdraws from them and leaves them alone. The language is clear; the younger sharifs, like all the other people of Lamu, need to be purified; they need to make an apology to all the sharifs' ancestors—even those who did not reach the degree of qutb. The younger sharifs have to reestablish their relationships, and not directly with the qutb, but through those who are far lower.

The head of the sharifs also expresses the idea of annual rebirth by moving inside the niche. After attending the Maulidi, the people are like newborn children; they have purity, but it is unstable purity. The people, like the children, gradually lose their purity during the year, and the head of the sharifs is then the only one who is able to maintain his purity and so promise them new life.

The head of the Reiyadah sharifs goes inside the niche, and he does not emerge until the Prophet's birth is proclaimed. This would seem to indicate an elevated position for him; yet on Tuesday, when he went to visit the graveyard, he sat at his ancestor's feet, a place of modesty and obedience. This ambiguity is illustrated again in the two movements the head of the Reiyadah sharifs initiates in the Maulidi. When he enters the niche he makes a counterclockwise movement, but he also starts the distribution of the rose water in a clockwise direction. As we have seen, counterclockwise movements are intended to either separate the initiator from the recipient, or separate something from the initiator and give it to the recipient. At first this does not seem a likely reading here, since during the month of the Maulidi the sharifs are not separated from the people. Yet it still may be a separating gesture, since, during the celebration, the head of the sharifs also physically separates himself from the people sitting beside him, i.e., from his own relatives. He is no longer their brother, because they doubt him and his ability to assure a successful Maulidi. Yet, when he comes out of the niche, he comes out as Mohammed, and so all the people's doubts vanish. When he emerges, the other sharifs sing to him the poem that welcomes the birth of the Prophet. The sharif emerges from the niche, leaving the women behind. Out of the niche, the purest point in the mosque, comes the sharif, just as the Prophet had come out of the womb of the purest woman—in neither case has there been biological contact with the father. In the meantime, the women and men of Lamu stand outside the mosque facing each other but completely without physical contact. It is a true virgin birth.

In his capacity as the Prophet, the head of the sharifs is able to forgive the people. He is able to cleanse them of their sins. When he climbs to the top of the mosque under the green dome, the resemblance with Mohammed is strengthened; he takes the position of intervention. Mohammed is the only one with the right to intervene; the head of the Reiyadah sharifs now possesses that power, which explains the clockwise distribution of the rose water before the sharif climbs to the top of the mosque. As a clockwise movement, it is intended to unify and cleanse the people. The head of the sharifs, acting as the Prophet, has the power to wash away sins.

The idea that the head of the sharifs is playing the role of the Prophet emerges even more clearly in the poems and answers recited on the way to the second graveyard ziyara. In fact, in that ziyara, which takes place on Friday, the head of the sharifs leaves no doubt that he is acting as if he were the Prophet.

Lamu is to enjoy the Prophet's presence, a presence which is made possible through the sharifs. The sharifs are the only human beings who are able to participate in both "nature" and "culture" without being subsumed under either; as such they are what make life possible.

Now, if we look to the Maulidi and compare it with the wangwana Kuzingu Kuzinguka Ngombe ritual, we find that the wangwana's rigid separation of the realm of purity from the realm of impurity makes it impossible for them to accept the slaves in any way. The slaves have to be expelled from the northern half of the town (Mkomani) in order for the town (as they define it) to be pure and safe. For them, culture has to be absolutely separated from nature. They see themselves as the only group that possesses culture. Non-Arabs, cannot, by definition, have culture. From the sharifs' point of view, the town of Lamu extends from Tundani to Langoni. It is a unified town, which, like anything else, shares in both culture and nature. For the sharifs, purity and impurity are poles of a continuum; they are not separate and mutually exclusive. It is possible in their way of thinking that even slaves can achieve a degree of purity higher than that of any of those who claim that they are Arabs. However, there is one qualification: the sharifs say no one can achieve the sharifs' degree of purity, since they are the descendants of that very light which gives the world of Lamu its meaning and makes the life of the people of Lamu worthwhile. Under the green dome not only the slaves stand waiting for forgiveness; even the wives of those Lamuans who oppose the sharifs are there. After all, no husband can stop his wife from attending the Maulidi. During that night Lamu gains a kind of purity which is not in conflict with nature. Through the sharifs, acting as symbols of light, the people in Lamu are able to overcome the most basic contradiction between culture and nature. It would, however, be a great mistake to think that the dialectic of life in Lamu stops here; in fact, other problems are already beginning to appear. I have no reason to think the dialectic will ever stop.

Glossary

abdal	substitutes
adabu	manners
'ālim (plural: *'ulama'*)	learned man, teacher
'ambari	ambergris
'aql	mind
Astarabu	civilization, referring to Arab or Islamic civilization
barzakh	world of spirits existing between paradise and earth
da'if	weak
darassa	lessons
Du'a	invocation or supplication
Fatiḥa	opening verses of the Qur'ān
Fatwa	formal legal opinion
fundi	leader of the Maulidi, skilled person
ganga	magic
hadimu	most-liked slave
Ḥadith	sayings and actions of the Prophet
ḥalwa	sweet meat
Hawia	Eve
hishima	respect and honor; the maintenance of the position in which respect and honor is due
ḥumaini	Ḥadrami colloquial poetry
hurulaini	paradise nymph
iḥya'	revival ceremony
ijaza	license
'ilm	religious knowledge
imam	religious leader
Jemadar	head of the sultan's garrison
kaffara	food offering which takes something bad out of a person
kafiri	unbeliever
karama	honor and generosity; also a meal in which honor and respect constitute important elements in the relationship between host and guest
khumoul	indifference and obscurity
kigoma	small drum
kijana (plural: *vijana*)	child
kinara	tray covered with a clean cloth on which are put the rose water and the incense

kutashi mtanga	reciprocal mourning arrangement
kutassa	throwing the bull's liver on the tree
kutunga	care
liwali	governor
madrassa	main Islamic school
maiti	corpse of a free man
mansib	person both of whose parents are sharifs
marashi	rose water
mashaikh (singular: *shaikh*)	traditional religious people
matari	tambourine
mawana wa haramu	bastards
mchafu	impurity
mfu	dead animal, or decaying cadaver
mganga	diviner/magician
mkufu	equal for the purpose of marriage
mlanti	month of the year
mngwana (plural: *wangwana*)	free man
mngwana swa swa	real free man
mtaa	locations, or quarters
mtanga moja	observing the mourning period together
mwalim (fundi)	leader of the Maulidi
mziwi wa tumu	month of commandment
na'ma	blessing
najisi	polluted, or defiled
naqib (plural: *nuqaba'*)	director
ngoma	drum
ngoma ya pepo	ceremony for appeasing the jin
numba serkali	government house
nyoke	serpent
pepo (sheitan)	devil
qaba'il	tribes
qutb	axis, head sharif
rak'a	prayer
Reiyadah	sacred meadows
ribat	hospice
ruhani	diviner/magician's jin
sadaqa	offering which carries no taint and is made to gain blessings
safi	purity
sama'	religious songs performed on Islamic occasions
shafa'ah	right to ask the intervention of the Prophet with God on behalf of the Muslims
sharifs	those who claim to be descendants of the Prophet
shoga	friend; carries the connotation of transvestism
Silwa	book containing the names of the various groups that live in Lamu and the rules of marriage
siwa	Lamu's brass horn, blown in marriage ceremonies of the wangwana
souriya	pastime girl
sufuria	vessel
tabia mbaya	earthly nature
tahara	unpolluted

tarawiḥ	Ramadan night prayers
tawasul	request to the sharif to intervene with the spirits
ubani	frankincense
'udi	aloe wood
wa geni	strangers
walis (nuqaba')	local saints
Wa Shenzi	uncivilized people of the bush, low-status people
watani	native country
Wa Zaliya	half slaves
zahid	ascetic
ziyara	visit to the graves of the sharifs

Bibliography

'Alawi, Saleḥ al Ḥamid al. *Tarikh Ḥadramaut.* [The history of Ḥadramaut]. 2 vols. Jaddah: Irshad Bookshop, 1968.

'Alwi, Ahmed ibn Abi Bakr al. *Tuḥfat al Labib fi Sharḥi Lameyat al Ḥabib.* Cairo: The Great Arabic Printing House, 1912.

'Attar, Farid Ud-Din. *The Conference of the Birds.* London: Routledge & Kegan Paul, 1954.

Badawi, Ḥassan ibn Saiyid Ahmad al. *Al Ta'asur wal Ibtida': Khata' al Muslimin al Akbar* [Modernization and innovation : the major Muslim error]. Unpublished manuscript, n. d.

Bakathir, Abdallahi ibn Mohammed. *Riḥlat al Ashwaq al Qawiya ila Mawatin al Sādah al 'Alwiya* [The journey of the strong desires to the homeland of the Alwy saiyids]. Cairo: Scientific Press, 1939.

Bergson, Henri. *Time and Free Will.* New York: Macmillan, 1910.

Buchler, Ira R., and Selby, Henry A. *A Formal Study of Myth.* Austin: The University of Texas Press, 1968.

Bujra, Abdallah S. *The Politics of Stratification: A Study of Political Change in a South Arabian Town.* London: Clarendon Press, 1971.

Bujra, Janet A. *Political Action in a Bajuni Village in Kenya.* Ph. D. dissertation, University of London, 1968.

Burridge, Kenelm. "Lévi-Strauss and Myth." In *The Structural Study of Myth and Totemism,* ed. E. Leach. Association of Social Anthropologists, Monograph no. 5. London: Tavistock Publications, 1967.

Cassirer, Ernst. *An Essay on Man.* New Haven, Conn.: Yale University Press, 1944.

____. *The Philosophy of Symbolic Forms.* Vol. I. New Haven, Conn.: Yale University Press, 1953.

Chittick, Neville. "East African Trade with the Orient." In *Islam and the Trade of Asia.* ed. D. Richards. Philadelphia: University of Pennsylvania Press, 1971.

Chomsky, Noam. "Language and the Mind." In *Changing Perspectives on Man,* ed. B. Rothblatt. Chicago: University of Chicago Press, 1968.

Clive, J. H. *The Political and Historical Records: A Brief History of Tanaland.* Unpublished manuscript.

Deb'i, 'Abdel Raḥman ibn 'Ali al. *Maulidi al Deb'i.* Bombay: Islamic Press, 1912.

de Planhol, Xavier. *The World of Islam.* Ithaca, N. Y.: Cornell University Press, 1959.

BIBLIOGRAPHY

Durkheim, Emile. *The Elementary Forms of Religious Life.* New York: Free Press, 1965.

Emmett, D. *The Nature of Metaphysical Thinking.* London: Macmillan, 1945.

Firth, Raymond. "Ethnographic Analysis and Language with Reference to Malinowski's Views." In *Man and Culture,* ed. R. Firth. London: Routledge & Kegan Paul, 1957.

Geertz, Clifford. "Religion as a Cultural System." In *Anthropological Approaches to the Study of Religion,* ed. Michael Banton. Association of Social Anthropologists, Monograph no. 3. London: Tavistock Publications, 1966.

Harries, Lyndon. *Swahili Poetry.* Oxford: Clarendon Press, 1968.

Holy Qur'ān, The. Translation and commentary by A. Yusuf Ali. 3d ed. 2 vols. Beirut: Printing Production, 1965.

Ḥusseiny, Ahmed Badawy ibn Mohammed al. *Ahlul Kissa': Makisa na ya sifa na tareikh ya sayyidna Ali, Fatima, Hassan na Hussein.* Mombasa: Rodwell Press, 1964.

Ingrams, W. H. *A Survey of Social and Economic Conditions in the Aden Protectorate.* Asmara, 1949.

____. *Zanzibar: Its History and Its People.* London: Frank Cass, 1967.

Jakobson, R., and Halle, M. *Fundamentals of Language.* The Hague: Mouton, 1956.

Kirkman, James S. *Men and Monuments on the East African Coast.* London: Lutterworth Press, 1964.

Knappert, Jan. *Traditional Swahili Poetry: An investigation into the Concepts of East African Islam as Reflected in the Utenzi Literature.* Leiden: E. J. Brill, 1967.

____. *Myths and Legends of the Swahili.* London: Heinemann Educational Books, 1970.

Kroef, Justus M. van der. "The Arabs in Indonesia." *The Middle Eastern Journal,* VII (1953), 300–23.

Lane, Michael. *Structuralism.* London: Jonathan Cape, 1970.

Langer, Susanne. *Philosophy in a New Key.* Cambridge, Mass.: Harvard University Press, 1942.

Leach, Edmund. *Political Systems of Highland Burma.* Boston: Beacon Press, 1954.

____. "The Epistemological Background to Malinowski's Empiricism." In *Man and Culture,* ed. R. Firth. London: Routledge & Kegan Paul, 1957.

____. "Claude Lévi-Strauss: Anthropologist and Philosopher." *New Left Review,* XXXIV (1965), 12–27.

____, ed. *The Structural Study of Myth and Totemism.* London: Tavistock Publications, 1967.

Lévi-Strauss, Claude. "*Le Structure et la forme: Reflexions sur un ouvrage de Vladimar Propp.*" *Cahiers de l'I.S.E.A.* XCIX, série M, no. 7 (1960), 3–36.

____. *Totemism.* Boston: Beacon Press, 1963.

____. *The Savage Mind.* Chicago: University of Chicago Press, 1966.

____. *Structural Anthropology.* New York: Anchor Books, 1969.

____. *L'Homme nu.* Paris: Librairie Plon, 1971.

Lienhardt, Peter. "The Mosque College of Lamu and Its Social Background." *Tanganyika Notes and Records,* LIII (1959), 228–42.

Malinowski, Bronislaw. *A Scientific Theory of Culture.* Durham: The University of North Carolina Press, 1944.

____. *Magic, Science and Religion.* New York: Anchor Books, 1954.

Mughere, 'Abdel Raḥman ibn Hāmād al. *Al Muntakhab fi Nasab Qaba'il al 'Arab* [The chosen description of Arab tribal genealogies]. Damascus: Islamic Office of Printing and

Publishing, 1965.
Pierce, F. B. *Zanzibar: The Island Metropolis of Eastern Africa.* London: T. Fisher Unwin, 1920.
Prins, A. H. J. *Sailing from Lamu.* Assen: Van Gorcum, 1965.
Ricoeur, Paul. "Structure et herméneutique." *Esprit,* XXXI (1963), 596–627. English translation by Kathleen McLaughlin. In *The Conflict of Interpretations,* ed. Don Ihde, trans. Kathleen McLaughlin et al., pp. 27–61, Evanston, Ill.: Northwestern University Press, 1974.
____. *The Symbolism of Evil.* New York: Harper & Row, 1967.
Saqaf, Abdullah ibn Mohammed al. *Tarikh al Shu'ara al Hadramien.* Vol. III. Cairo: Scientific Press, 1939.
Stigand, C. H. *The Land of Zinj.* New York: Barnes & Noble, 1966.
Turner, Victor. "Myth and Symbols." *International Encyclopedia of the Social Sciences. X (1968), 576.*
Yalman, Nur. "The Structure of Sinhalese Healing Rituals," In *Religion in South Asia,* ed. E. B. Harper. Seattle, Wash.: Asia Society, 1964.

Index